# PRAISE FOR THE CHINA BAYLES MYSTERIES

"Mystery lovers who also garden will be captivated by this uni... ries."
—*Seattle Post-Intelligencer*

"One of the best-written and well-plotted mysteries I've read in a long time."
—*Los Angeles Times*

"An entertaining detective writer."
—*The Dallas Morning News*

"A nice book to curl up with on a blustery day."
—*Chicago Tribune*

"Albert has created captivating new characters and a setting dripping with atmosphere."
—*Publishers Weekly*

"[China Bayles is] such a joy . . . an instant friend."
—*Carolyn G. Hart*

"A treat for gardeners who like to relax with an absorbing mystery."
—*North American Gardener*

"An appealing series."
—*Booklist*

"A wonderful reading experience."
—*Midwest Book Review*

"Gripping."
—*Library Journal*

"Cause for celebration."
—*Rocky Mount (NC) Telegram*

# CHINA BAYLES'
# Book of Days

# CHINA BAYLES'
# Book of Days

*365 Celebrations of the Mystery,*
*Myth, and Magic of Herbs from the*
*World of Pecan Springs*

## SUSAN WITTIG ALBERT

BERKLEY PRIME CRIME, NEW YORK

THE BERKLEY PUBLISHING GROUP
Published by the Penguin Group
Penguin Group (USA) Inc.
375 Hudson Street, New York, New York 10014, USA

Penguin Group (Canada), 90 Eglinton Avenue East, Suite 700, Toronto, Ontario M4P 2Y3, Canada
(a division of Pearson Penguin Canada Inc.)
Penguin Books Ltd., 80 Strand, London WC2R 0RL, England
Penguin Group Ireland, 25 St. Stephen's Green, Dublin 2, Ireland (a division of Penguin Books Ltd.)
Penguin Group (Australia), 250 Camberwell Road, Camberwell, Victoria 3124, Australia
(a division of Pearson Australia Group Pty. Ltd.)
Penguin Books India Pvt. Ltd., 11 Community Centre, Panchsheel Park, New Delhi—110 017, India
Penguin Group (NZ), Cnr. Airborne and Rosedale Roads, Albany, Auckland 1310, New Zealand
(a division of Pearson New Zealand Ltd.)
Penguin Books (South Africa) (Pty.) Ltd., 24 Sturdee Avenue, Rosebank, Johannesburg 2196,
South Africa

Penguin Books Ltd., Registered Offices: 80 Strand, London WC2R 0RL, England

This is an original publication of The Berkley Publishing Group.

A nonfiction work inspired by the author's favorite fictional characters.

Every effort has been made to ensure that the information contained in this book is complete and accurate. However, neither the publisher nor the author is engaged in rendering professional advice or services to the individual reader, and therefore neither is responsible for your specific health or allergy needs that may require medical supervision. The ideas, procedures, and suggestions contained in this book are not intended as a substitute for consulting with your physician. All matters regarding your health or dietary needs require medical supervision. Neither the author nor the publisher shall be liable or responsible for any loss or damage allegedly arising from any information or suggestion in this book.

PUBLISHER'S NOTE: While the author has made every effort to provide accurate Internet addresses at the time of publication, neither the publisher nor the author assumes any responsibility for errors, or for changes that occur after publication. Further, publisher does not have any control over and does not assume any responsibility for the web site or its content.

PRINTING HISTORY
Berkley Prime Crime trade paperback edition / October 2006

Library of Congress Cataloging-in-Publication Data

Albert, Susan Wittig.
    China Bayles' book of days : celebrating the mystery, myth, and magic of herbs : a treasury of
herbal lore, recipes, and crafts from the world of pecan springs / by Susan Wittig Albert.
        p.  cm.
    Includes bibliographical references and index.
    ISBN 0-425-20653-X (alk. paper)
    1. Cookery (Herbs)  2. Herbs.  I. Title.

TX819.H4A43  2006
641.6'57—dc22                                                    2006008501

PRINTED IN THE UNITED STATES OF AMERICA

10  9  8  7

# A NOTE TO READERS

*I have herein communicated such Notions as I have gathered either from reading of several Authors, or by conferring sometimes with Scholars, and sometimes with Country people; To which I have added some Observations of mine own, never before published: Most of which I am confident are true, and if there be any that are not so, yet they are pleasant.*

—WILLIAM COLE, *THE ART OF SIMPLING*, 1656

For years now, China Bayles has been nagging me about writing a book primarily about herbs—no murder, mayhem, or other unsavory doings, just herbs and the ways they are used in people's lives. China isn't the only one, either. I regularly receive letters that ask for information about growing and using herbs and close with the plaintive question: "When are you and China going to write a book about herbs?"

This book is our answer. In it, China and I have adopted the traditional format of the *book of days*, or daybook: the personal calendar in which people over the centuries have recorded meaningful events, ideas, things to do and to celebrate, and odds and ends of interest. A person's daybook might record religious and national holidays, saints' feast days, the sun's passage through the zodiac and the phases of the moon, and information about planting and harvesting. For centuries, people have found such personal calendars indispensable, as a kind of collective memory of what was important in the past and what might be of importance in each day of the present year.

Because herbs play such an important part in China's life, and in mine (and we hope in yours, too) our *Book of Days* is all about herbs. What is an herb? For me, the best and most inclusive definition is the one adopted by the Herb Society of America: Herbs are plants that are grown or gathered "for use and delight." Herbs may grow tiny or tall, in the tropics or the deserts, in a wild meadow or in our gardens or on our windowsills. We may grow or gather these ourselves, or purchase the dried or processed plant material. Indeed, herbs are plants for use and delight.

In this book, China and I have gathered together tidbits and treasures about the plants we love to live with, as well as their many mysteries and myths and magical uses. There are quite a few practical items, too—recipes, crafts, gardening tips, and ideas for ways you can put more *green* into your daily life. The recipes are uncomplicated and designed for average cooks, but all feature the flavors of our favorite herbs. We've also featured a few people who know and grow herbs, and a few gardens and herb farms you might like to visit. And because China's mysteries are all about herbs, we've included tidbits from her books, as well as brief essays about the mysteries and some special contributions by the irrepressible members of the Myra Merryweather Herb Guild, Pecan Springs' oldest civic organization.

I became interested in herbs many years ago, as a doctoral candidate working with medieval English texts in which both medicinal and culinary herbs figured prominently. Among my efforts: the translation of the earliest English cookery text, *A Forme of Cury*, compiled in 1381 by Richard II's cook for the Royal kitchen. For the past twenty years, growing and using and learning and writing about herbs has been a way of finding my place in life, on this green earth, and in this amazing universe, so full of mystery and magic. I have learned that when I live in harmony with the plants around me, with the circling seasons, and with the earth itself, I live in greater contentment and peace. And when China Bayles brought her herb shop into my life in the early 1990s, my sense of possibilities for living a green life grew even stronger. Perhaps this book will help you see how this can be true for you, too.

Some of this material has appeared in other forms: in the China Bayles Mysteries (I've noted the titles where appropriate); in the Book of Days pieces written for the *Herb Companion* from 1998–2002; in *China's Garden* (the herbal newsletter that China and I published from 1994–1999); and in China's pages on my web site (www.mysterypartners.com) and in "Lifescapes," my Internet journal (www.susanalbert.blogspot.com). It has been revised and rewritten and assembled here in a format that China and I hope will please you. You will find reading suggestions throughout the book, a glossary, and an index of recipes, crafts, and medicinal preparations. (One word of caution: Herbs contain plant chemicals that can affect you in a variety of ways. Never take a therapeutic preparation of a plant until you have done your homework!)

China and I hope that you will keep this book where you can dip into it daily. We will be delighted if it sparks your own creative imagination and encourages you to create your own personal place in the green, growing world.

Susan Wittig Albert
Meadow Knoll, near Bertram, Texas

# ACKNOWLEDGMENTS

I have plenty of people to thank for the material in this compilation of herbal history, lore, recipes, craft ideas, gardening tips, and factual information. I did not invent this stuff, folks; I collected it from here, there, and yonder, as herbalists have done from the beginning. My sources are acknowledged throughout the book, and I am grateful to each one. Special thanks goes to the staff of the Herb Society of America for help in researching dates; to Carolee Schneider, Jim Long, Theresa Loe, and Kathleen Halloran for their special contributions; and to the many herb-lovers across the country who badgered me into sitting down to write. Peggy Turchette's artwork enlivens the book with humor and charm. Thank you, Peggy!

As someone else has famously remarked, it takes a village. I have been writing for the same publishing house, Berkley Books, for nearly fifteen years, and continue to be both enormously cheered and humbled by the constant support I have received there. I am especially grateful to Natalee Rosenstein, who recognized the merit in my first "garden cozy" and has encouraged my work ever since. And to copy editor Pamela Barricklow, my deepest thanks. This was not an easy manuscript, and I appreciate her careful attention.

And of course to Bill, ever and always, thanks and love.

January

February

March

# JANUARY 1

*Love and joy come to you*
*And to our wassail too*
*And God send you a Happy New Year*
—THE YORKSHIRE WASSAIL SONG

## Wassaill

Wassail—the Old English word *waes haeil* means "be ye well"—is the centuries-old tradition of welcoming in the New Year by offering a warming (often spirited) drink to the friends and neighbors who dropped in. Over time, the spiced drink itself, which was sometimes shared in a common cup or bowl, became known as the "wassail." Traditionally, it contained cinnamon, a spice that is native to Southeast Asia. Cinnamon traveled from the Orient to the West some seven centuries before Christ, and has always been enormously valuable. During the 1500s and 1600s, it lured Portuguese, Dutch, and English traders to the Far East, where the illegal sale of even a single stick of cinnamon was punished by death. Now, researchers tell us that as little as a half teaspoon of cinnamon a day may help diabetics reduce blood sugar levels.

Here is a Pecan Springs' favorite recipe for cinnamon-rich wassail. You'll always find it in a big glass bowl at Ruby Wilcox's New Year's Day open house.

**RUBY'S SPICED CIDER WASSAIL**

2 quarts apple cider
1 quart orange juice
1 quart apricot nectar
½ cup fresh lemon juice
6 broken pieces of cinnamon
1 tablespoon whole cloves
one orange, sliced thin
one lemon, sliced thin
whole cloves

In a nonreactive pan, bring to a boil the cider, juices, cinnamon, and cloves. Simmer over low heat for 20 minutes. Transfer to a heat-proof punch bowl. Stud the orange and lemon slices with whole cloves and float them in the wassail. Serve in heat-proof punch cups. Makes about 4 quarts.

**Learn the history of the spices we take for granted:**
*Dangerous Tastes: The Story of Spices*, by Andrew Dalby
*Spices and Herbs: Lore & Cookery*, by Elizabeth S. Hayes

*Our wassail cup is made of rosemary-tree,*
*So is your beer of the best barley.*
—TRADITIONAL SONG

# JANUARY 2

*January may be called the digging month, as almost the only gardening operation that can be performed in it is digging, or rather trenching the ground.*

—JANE LOUDON, *INSTRUCTIONS IN GARDENING FOR LADIES,*
1840

## Beginning of Work Day

In Japan, where the second day of January is known as the "Beginning of Work Day," it is said that any project begun on this day will be successful. Since I'm always looking for all the help I can get, this sounds like a good day to pull out the plant catalogs that have been arriving in the mail and start making lists of the new varieties I want to try out this year. The day may be dark and gloomy outdoors, but if I'm dreaming about butterfly gardens and fragrance gardens, maybe the rest of the winter will pass more quickly.

**GARDEN PROJECTS**
Some garden-related projects to start on this "beginning of work day":

- Start collecting plant catalogs (if you haven't already).
- Choose three annual herbs to grow that you've never grown before. A new variety of dill, maybe. Or anise hyssop, an herb with a delicious scent, or borage, which has an edible blue blossom and a cucumber taste. Read about them, and research seed sources.
- Choose three perennial herbs—native to your area—to add to your garden. Do some research to find out how they were used, for and by whom. Some ideas: echinacea, artemisia, lavender, witch hazel.
- Pick out three containers to fill with herbs for your patio or deck. Some possibilities: a half-barrel, a large terra-cotta pot, a planter box. What herbs will you grow in each?
- Start a garden journal. Aim to record your planting and harvesting, as well as the way you use your plants and the enjoyment they give you.

*In the yeare that Januarie shal enter on the Thursday the winter shalbe long and most part drie and the yeare shalbe very holesome.*

—ERRA PATER

*Here in this place I'll set a bank of rue,*
*sour herb of grace;*
*Rue, even for ruth, shall shortly here be seen . . .*

—WILLIAM SHAKESPEARE, *RICHARD II*

## The Language of Flowers

Using plants as symbols is a human habit that dates back to classical times. The term *poet laureate*, for example, comes from the Roman practice of awarding their favorite poets with a coronet of laurel leaves. Napoleon used the violet to represent his promise to return from exile, while his followers wore violets in their lapels to symbolize their faithfulness to him. And "there's pansies," Ophelia says, in Shakespeare's *Hamlet*, "that's for thoughts."

But it was in nineteenth-century England where the romantic, ingenious, and secret "language of flowers" became most popular, and "floral dictionaries" were all the rage. Women and men who wanted to be successful in society were expected to know that a sprig of balsam meant "I am impatient," while an ox-eye daisy blossom meant, "I'll wait forever." They also had to know that if a flower was presented upside-down, its original meaning was contradicted, and that "Yes"—ah, the mystery and promise of that word!—was implied by touching the flower to the lips.

Throughout the China Bayles Mysteries, I often use the language of flowers to add depth and significance to the story. In *Lavender Lies*, for instance, China comments that dyer's bugloss (*Anchusa tinctoria*) was used as a rouge, which (in a time when women did not "paint") gave the plant the meaning of untrustworthiness. In *Rueful Death*, the herb rue often stands (as it does in Shakespeare) for *ruth*: pity, compassion, mercy, as well as for repentance and remorse.

**SOME FLORAL MEANINGS**
- catnip: I am intoxicated with love.
- clover: You are lucky.
- dandelion: I find your presumptions laughable.
- honeysuckle: I would not answer hastily.
- Jacob's ladder: Come down off your pedestal!

**Learn about the language of flowers:**
*Flora's Dictionary*, by Kathleen Gips

Today is the tenth day of Christmas, and in Celtic tradition, the end of the solstice celebration. The twelve days of Christmas begin on Christmas Day and end on January 6, Epiphany.

*We had a great cake made, in which was put a bean for the King, a pease for the Queen, a clove for the Knave, a forked stick for the Cuckold, a rag for the Slut.*

—HENRY TEONGE, 1676

## Twelfth-Night Cake

In most English and European households, the Twelfth-Night Cake was baked a day or two ahead of the merry celebration that concluded the holiday season. This eighteenth-century recipe will give you an idea of the work involved. Cakes like these were mostly baked in the kitchens of the gentry. Villagers (most had no ovens) usually made their cakes as puddings, which were boiled in a pot hung over the fire.

### TO MAKE A TWELFTH-NIGHT CAKE

*Put two pounds of butter in a warm pan and work it to a cream with your hand; then put in two pounds of loaf sugar sifted; a large nutmeg grated; and of cinnamon ground, allspice ground, ginger, mace and coriander each a quarter ounce. Now break in eighteen eggs by one and one, meantime beating it for twenty minutes or above; stir in a gill of brandy; then add two pounds of sifted flour, and work it a little. Next put in currants four pounds, chopped almonds half a pound; citron the like; and orange and lemon peel cut small half a pound. Put in one bean and one pea in separate places, bake it in a slow oven for four hours, and ice it or decorate it as you will.*

—ELIZABETH RAFFALD, *THE EXPERIENCED ENGLISH HOUSEKEEPER*, 1769

### THE TWELFTH-NIGHT BEAN

The tradition of the bean and pea came from medieval France, where, if you got the bean, you were crowned King of the Bean and everyone had to do as you directed. It's said that Mary Queen of Scots brought the custom to England, and added the pea. Whoever got the pea shared the throne with the king. Other items might also be hidden in the cake: If you got a clove, you were a rogue; if a twig, you'd best look to your spouse's virtue; if a bit of rag, your morals might be in question.

### EASY TWELFTH-NIGHT CAKE

If you don't have time to bake a traditional Twelfth-Night cake with 18 eggs and a gill of brandy, buy a fruitcake, insert whatever items you choose, and frost it to conceal your skullduggery. Wreathe your cake with rosemary and bay, traditional decorations.

# JANUARY 5

Today is Twelfth Night Eve, when the last Yule fire was traditionally lit.

*Beware of an oak,*
*It draws the stroke,*
*Avoid an ash,*
*It courts a flash,*
*Creep under the thorn,*
*It will save you from harm.*
—TRADITIONAL ENGLISH FOLK SAYING

## The Mysterious Thorn of Glastonbury

The mystery began on Twelfth Night in 1535, when somebody noticed that the hawthorn tree (*Crataegus monogyna*) in front of St. John the Baptist Church was blooming—in the chilly depths of winter. Thomas Cromwell, adviser to Henry VIII, dispatched a sleuth to investigate this miraculous phenomenon. The physical evidence (two blossoms) was sent to London, beginning the custom of sending the January blooms of the Glastonbury hawthorn to the monarch. Charles I put a stop to the custom, but Queen Mary revived it in 1922, agreeing to accept a blossom whenever the Holy Thorn lived up to its reputation.

The hawthorn has long been a mysterious plant. The Greeks and Romans associated it with marriage, fertility, and protection from evil; Greek brides and grooms wore hawthorn blossoms; and Roman parents placed hawthorn leaves in cradles to ward off evil spirits. In Europe, it was believed that hawthorn would protect you from lightning. However, hawthorn's fortunes took a turn for the worse in early Christianity, for the crown of thorns was reputed to have been made of hawthorn. Carrying hawthorn blossoms into the house was said to bring bad luck, and the tree became associated with disease and death.

Hawthorn holds another intriguing mystery: its long-recognized value as a gentle, effective herbal protection for the heart. The ancient belief that hawthorn promotes cardiac health has been confirmed by researchers who tell us that hawthorn can help to normalize blood pressure, reduce the heart rate, and promote oxygen uptake.

**HAWTHORN TEA**
Use 2 teaspoons of dried, crushed fruits per cup of boiling water. Steep 20 minutes. Drink up to 2 cups a day. In this therapeutic dosage, hawthorn is said to be safe for long-term use, and no toxic effects have been noted. (Pregnant women should not use it, however.)

**Read more about hawthorn as a healing herb:**
*The Healing Herbs*, by Michael Castleman

*A Gard'ner's work is never at an end, It begins with the year, and continues to the next.*
—JOHN EVELYN, 1620–1706

# JANUARY 6

## Apple Howlings

If you have an apple tree, Twelfth Day is the day to celebrate it. In England, people went into the orchards on this day, to toast the trees and bless them with last year's cider. When the celebrations got a little rowdy (they usually did), they were known as apple howlings, or "youlings." If you plan a rowdy howling around your apple tree, you might want to invite the neighbors to join in. Serve apple cider and warm apple-spice nut bars with ice cream.

### APPLE-SPICE NUT BARS

3 eggs
1½ cups sugar
1 teaspoon vanilla
1½ cups flour
1 teaspoon cinnamon
½ teaspoon nutmeg
¼ teaspoon cloves
½ teaspoon salt
3 teaspoons baking powder
3 cups apples, unpeeled, cored, finely chopped
1½ cups walnuts, coarsely chopped

Beat eggs until foamy; add sugar, beat until mixture is thick and lemon colored. Add vanilla. In a separate bowl, mix flour, spices, salt, and baking powder. Blend into egg mixture. Fold in chopped apples and walnuts. Turn into greased and floured 13 × 9-inch pan. Bake 30–40 minutes at 350° or until tester inserted in center comes out clean. Cut into squares. Serve warm with ice cream.

Apples were believed to have powerful medicinal qualities. Some apple lore:

- To keep colds away for a year, eat an apple at midnight on Halloween.
- To keep up the strength, sniff an old sweet apple.
- To remove warts, rub the warts with an apple and bury it. When it rots, the warts will disappear.
- John Gerard, author of the famous *Herbal* of 1597, recommended a cosmetic salve to keep the skin soft and supple: apple pulp, lard, and rosewater. Known as pomatum, it was popular well into the nineteenth century.

Apples are high in antioxidants, flavonoids, phytonutrients, and fiber, a potent good-health package.

January's theme garden: a Petting Garden.

*Laurel's sister Willow and I put in many long hours this spring transforming the entire yard, from Crockett Street back to the alley, into a collection of theme gardens: a silver garden, a tea garden, a butterfly garden, a dyers' garden, a kitchen garden. The work won't be done for a few more months—probably never, actually, since herb gardens have a way of inviting you to do just a little more here and a little more there.*

—ROSEMARY REMEMBERED: A CHINA BAYLES MYSTERY

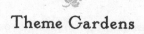

## Theme Gardens

China and her friends take great pleasure in the theme gardens she has planted around her shop. It's fun to define an area of the garden by dedicating it to a theme: to an historical period, for instance (a Civil War garden); to a literary figure (Shakespeare, Chaucer); to a craft (a garden of pressed plants); to the Bible; to butterflies; or to specific types and kinds of plants. January's theme garden is an indoor petting garden that's fun for both adults and children.

### A PETTING GARDEN—AND MORE

The sweet scents and pleasant breezes of summer are months away, but a wintertime windowsill collection of scented geraniums will buoy your spirits and keep your thumb green. These fragrant plants—strictly speaking, they are not geraniums but pelargoniums—come from South Africa, where a Dutch botanist found them in 1672. Their intriguing scents made them popular for Victorian potpourri.

Scented geraniums invite us to touch, sniff, and pet. They come in a variety of fruit and citrus scents—rose, lemon, apple, lime, apricot, strawberry, coconut, peppermint, cinnamon, ginger, nutmeg, pineapple, orange, rose mint, and citronella—and will thrive with a half-day's sunshine and regular watering. Move them outdoors for the summer, and back to your windowsill when frosts threaten.

### USING SCENTED GERANIUMS

- Freshen a closet or drawer with dried lemon geranium leaves tucked into a muslin bag.
- Scent a room with a potpourri of dried apple or lime geranium leaves.
- Use fresh or dried leaves to flavor tea, jelly (especially blackberry and apple), custard, sugar, sorbet, and vinegar.
- Toss the delicate edible flowers in a salad.
- Use rose geranium leaves to make a liqueur.
- Flavor cake by placing a leaf or two of rose geranium in the bottom of the pan and adding a teaspoon of rose water to the batter.

**Find out more about scented geraniums:**
*Scented Geraniums: Knowing, Growing, and Enjoying Scented Pelargoniums*, by Jim Becker

# JANUARY 8

Today is National Bubble Bath Day.

*Ruby wrapped her arms around herself, shivering. "Are we going to stake the place out and wait until she comes home?"*

*"On a night like this?" I put the key in the ignition and started the car. "Anyway, we were up at five this morning, and it's been a long, hard day. I'd rather go home and make myself a hot toddy and fall into a bubble bath."*

—*MISTLETOE MAN: A CHINA BAYLES MYSTERY*

## Bubble, Bubble

There's nothing nicer on a cold winter's night (especially if you've been with China and Ruby on a stakeout) than a long, luxurious bubble bath. And since today is National Bubble Bath Day, it's the perfect time to indulge.

Make your own unscented herbal bubble bath, using skin-softening, nondrying ingredients such as castile soap (made from pure olive oil), coconut oil, and glycerin, all of which can be purchased at most large drugstores. Then choose a scent to fit your mood—a combination of scents, if you choose.

### SPIRIT-SOOTHING LAVENDER BUBBLE BATH

In *Lavender Lies*, China includes these instructions for making a mild bubble bath. Grate one bar of castile soap into a quart of warm water. Mix well. To this liquid soap solution add 3 ounces of glycerin or coconut oil (either will make bubbles) and 2–4 drops lavender essential oil. Store in a glass or plastic container.

### OTHER HERBAL BUBBLE BATHS

Using the same basic recipe, try these essential oils, alone or in a fragrant combination:

- For a calming, soothing bath: lavender, rose, tangerine, sandalwood
- For a warming, relaxing bath: clary sage, ylang ylang
- For a refreshing, uplifting bath: rosemary, lemon, orange, bergamot

**Find out how to make many bodycare products:**
*Making Natural Liquid Soaps: Herbal Shower Gels / Conditioning Shampoos / Moisturizing Hand Soaps*, by Catherine Failor

*The garden is never dead; growth is always going on, and growth that can be seen, and seen with delight.*

—HENRY ELLACOMBE, *IN MY VICARAGE GARDEN*, 1902

*Love of gardening is a seed that once sown never dies.*

—GERTRUDE JEKYLL

## All About the Myra Merryweather Herb Guild

The herb guild, one of Pecan Springs' most energetic organizations, was established by Myra Merryweather during the Depression, when people gardened, not just to feed their families but to keep their minds off the sad fact that they didn't have a paying job. Myra was a woman of remarkable energies. She became interested in herbs on a visit to England, where she met the well-known herbalist Maud Grieve, the author of *A Modern Herbal*, and Gertrude Jekyll, who believed that the prettiest gardens were a medley of old-fashioned favorites, herbs, and native plants. Myra was so inspired that she came back to Pecan Springs, rolled up her sleeves, and started digging. Her neighbors, not to be outclassed, started digging, too. Before you could say *Salvia officinalis*, they had formed an herb guild. When Myra died, she left her historic house to the Guild.

Everybody in Pecan Springs would agree that the Merryweathers have contributed to the little town's unique charm. There's the Joe Pye Memorial Knot Garden, for instance, created in honor of the town's veterans, and the semi-annual Herb Bazaar and Pass-Along Plant Sale in the parking lot of the First Baptist Church, a slam-bang event whose proceeds recently furnished the Laverne Scurry Conversation Lounge at the Colonial Nursing Home. In appreciation, the Chamber of Commerce awarded the Merryweathers the Hilda Bonger Golden Trowel. Guild President Pansy Pride received loud applause when she said in her acceptance speech that the guild "stirs a pinch of savory, a potpourri of thymely delights, and a bushel of herbal joys into the melting pot of our fair city."

China Bayles, chair of the garden committee, extends an invitation to visit the Guild's gardens. While you're there, you can also admire the concrete armadillo recently donated by guild member Harold Thompson. Everyone who sees it is amazed. China reports that a subcommittee has been formed to investigate suitable locations for displaying Harold's generous gift. (Harold is now at work on a very large tumbleweed made of coat hangers.)

The guild is also at work. They are compiling a new book, *Happy Thymes: A Calendula of Herbal Dillies*. I am pleased to say that the guild has given their generous permission to print several items from this forthcoming publication in these pages. Thank you, Merryweathers!

**Read China's story about an unfortunate incident at the Merryweather Guild House:**

"The Rosemary Caper," in *An Unthymely Death and Other Garden Mysteries*, by Susan Wittig Albert

# JANUARY 10

## First Aid for Faces

Let's face it. January blasts can chap and crack your skin, and long days in overheated buildings can sap your spirits. But herbs can help to heal both body and spirit. And there's something especially healing in a soothing product you've made yourself, with all-natural ingredients. Almond meal (almond oil is used in many fine cosmetics) is used in both these recipes, which are favorites of Ruby Wilcox.

This soothing treatment for winter-worn faces is suitable for all skin types. The essential oils—you can choose from several, with different effects—provide a subtle aromatherapy, lifting and soothing your spirits, while the herbs and almond meal do their work.

### RUBY'S FACIAL MASK

2 tablespoons almond meal (almonds ground very fine)*

1 tablespoon powdered marigolds

1 tablespoon powdered chamomile

aloe gel, enough to make a paste (you can purchase this at the drugstore)

about half of a raw egg

2 drops chamomile essential oil, or oil of your choice

Mix the almond meal and herbs together. Add enough aloe gel and egg to make a paste. Add essential oil. If the paste is too thin, add more almond meal; if it's too thick, add a bit of aloe gel or egg. To use, wash your face. Pat dry, and apply the mask. Leave on for 10 minutes or so, while you're lying down, then wash off gently. Refrigerate for up to a week. (This will make 3–4 masks.)

*Almond meal and almond oil are recommended for cosmetics throughout this book, because both are superior moisturizing and softening agents. If you are allergic to nuts, or intend to make the cosmetic as a gift for a friend, you may substitute oatmeal (oat flakes ground fine) and a non-nut oil of your choice.

**Read more about home-crafted cosmetics:**

*Jeanne Rose's Kitchen Cosmetics: Using Herbs, Fruit, & Flowers for Natural Bodycare*, by Jeanne Rose

*Every gardener knows under the cloak of winter lies a miracle—a seed waiting to sprout, a bulb opening to light, a bud straining to unfurl. And the anticipation nurtures our dream.*

—BARBARA WINKLER

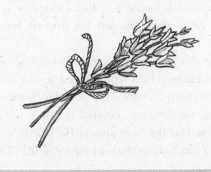

*"What's going on these days?" Amy's sharp-featured face was pale and set. "Well, for starters, I'm pregnant."*

*I said the only thing I could think of. "Let's have a cup of tea."*

—A DILLY OF A DEATH: A CHINA BAYLES MYSTERY

## Create an Herbal Tea Pantry

China often says that there's no puzzle that can't be solved over a cup of tea, and she may just be right! Throughout recorded history, herbs have been used to brew beverages that clear our minds, lift our spirits, and heal our bodies. With very little expenditure, you can create your own original blends and stock your herbal tea pantry with your personal favorites.

### GETTING STARTED

Set aside a cool, dark pantry or cupboard shelf, where you can keep your stash of teas and herbs. When you've created a favorite blend, put it into a lidded jar for storage. Keep notes on the blends you create, specifying the amount of herbs you use. Name your creations. (Chamomile Comfort? Lemony Luscious?) Nearby, cache your favorite teapot—or teapots, if you're a collector! You'll also want to have a tea ball (sometimes called an infuser) or tea strainer. For brewing tea from seeds, barks, or roots, a mortar and pestle are handy. And be sure to include a selection of pretty cups or mugs, so you can share your favorite teas with friends who drop in for a chat.

When it comes to brewing herbal tea, there are few rules. You'll have to decide how much to use and how long to let it steep. To intensify the flavor, use more herbs, rather than increase the steeping time. To sweeten or not to sweeten? That's another individual decision. In China's opinion, honey is always nice.

### Three of China's favorite herb combinations:

- Rosemary Renewal Blend: 2 parts dried rosemary leaves, 1 part dried juniper berries, crushed, 1 part dried mint, 1 part dried lemongrass
- Lavender Luscious Blend: 2 parts dried lavender buds, 2 parts dried chamomile flowers, 1 part dried elder flowers, 1/8 teaspoon powdered cloves
- Mint Magic Blend: 2 parts dried peppermint, 1 part China tea, 1 part lemongrass

### Read more about herbal tea-making:

*A Cozy Book of Herbal Teas: Recipes, Remedies, and Folk Wisdom*, by Mindy Toomay

*The path of the herbalist is to open ourselves to nature in an innocent and pure way. She in turn will open her bounty and reward us with her many valuable secrets.*

—MICHAEL TIERRA

*Good bread never loafs around.*

—CHINA BAYLES

## Quick and Easy Herb Breads

A loaf of hot bread is a welcome addition to the evening meal, especially in the winter. When you're tired from a day's work and in a hurry to get dinner on the table, preprepared products can make the task easier—and herbs make the bread special. Fannie Couch, the seventy-plus talk-show radio host at Station KPST-FM in Pecan Springs, has been collecting recipes from her Pecan Springs friends and listeners for years. Here are two of Fannie's fast, no-fuss favorites.

### BETSY BLUMEFIELD'S BEST HERB BISCUITS

2 cups baking mix
1 teaspoon dried parsley
½ teaspoon dried thyme
½ teaspoon dried basil
1 cup sour cream (low fat is fine)
½ cup melted butter or margarine
½ cup grated Parmesan cheese mixed with ¼ cup flour

Preheat oven to 400°. Lightly spray a mini-muffin pan. Mix baking mix, herbs, sour cream, and butter. Dough will be sticky. Scoop into 24 balls and roll in cheese/flour mixture. Place in mini-muffin pan and bake for 15–18 minutes, until brown.

### LILLIAN LIPPENCOTT'S SATURDAY NIGHT SPECIAL HERB BREAD

Lillian works at the dry cleaners in Pecan Springs and doesn't get home until four on Saturdays. She says that if she puts out frozen dough to thaw in the morning, and gets started on it when she gets home, she has hot bread on the table by 6.

1 1-pound loaf frozen white bread dough (follow package
    directions for thawing)
2 teaspoons dried basil, or 4 teaspoons fresh, minced
2 teaspoons minced dried rosemary leaves, or
    3 teaspoons fresh
1 tablespoon minced chives
flour for dusting

Briefly knead thawed dough on lightly floured board. Knead in minced herbs until evenly mixed. Add flour as needed to prevent sticking. Shape into a smooth ball and place in a loaf pan. Cover, let rise until doubled in size, about 40 minutes. Bake in 375° oven until golden, about 35–40 minutes.

**Learn how Fannie Couch catches a crook—on the radio:** "Fannie's Back Fence Caper," by Susan and Bill Albert, in *Malice Domestic 3: An Anthology of Original Traditional Mystery Stories*, edited by Nancy Pickard

# JANUARY 13

In pre-Christian Ireland, the Celts celebrated this day as the Feast of Brewing.

*A fine beer may be judged with only one sip, but it's better to be thoroughly sure.*

—CZECH PROVERB

## Beer: A Magical, Mysterious Brew

Brewing has been part of human history for more than six thousand years. It is thought that the Sumerians discovered the fermentation process by chance, perhaps when bread became wet. The earliest account of brewing pictures wheat or barley bread baked, crumbled into liquid, and fermented—a process involving natural yeasts—into a drink that is said to have made people feel exhilarated.

Beer (sometimes thought of as "liquid bread") has been an important foodstuff in many cultures, especially in places where the water was impure. People of all ages drank it throughout the day, and workers were often paid with jugs of beer. Some beers played an important part in worship, where they were considered to be the source of inspiration from the gods, and were ceremonially prepared and ritually drunk by priests, such as the Druids who celebrated the Celtic Feast of Brewing. Laws were frequently made to regulate the consumption of beer. For example, the Puritans were allowed to drink *only* two quarts of beer for breakfast.

Hops (which add bitterness and aroma) were not added to beer until the seventeenth century. Instead, other herbs provided a more subtle, complex flavor: bog myrtle, yarrow, rosemary, juniper berries, ginger, caraway seed, anise seed, nutmeg, cinnamon, wormwood, sage, broom. And rather than barley or malt, some herbs—such as ginger, nettles, Saint-John's-wort, and dandelions—were the primary ingredient of some delicious beers. Ginger beer was a much-loved nineteenth-century drink, in both England and America.

**MISS BEECHER'S FAMOUS GINGER BEER (1857)**

    3 pints yeast
    ½ pound honey
    1 egg white
    ½ ounce lemon essence (lemon zest)
    10 pounds sugar
    9 gallons water
    9 ounces lemon juice
    11 ounces gingerroot

Boil the ginger half an hour in a gallon of water, then add the rest of the water and the other ingredients, and strain it when cold, add the white of one egg beaten, and half an ounce essence of lemon. Let it stand four days then bottle it, and it will keep good many months. —*Miss Beecher's Domestic Receipt-Book*

**Read more about herbal beers:**
*Sacred and Herbal Healing Beers: The Secrets of Ancient Fermentation*, by Stephen Harrod Buhner

*When I was young, I said to God, "God, tell me the mystery of the universe." But God answered, "That knowledge is for me alone." So I said, "God, tell me the mystery of the peanut." Then God said, "Well, George, that's more nearly your size."*

—GEORGE WASHINGTON CARVER

## Herbs, Gardens, and Mysteries

If it's cold, gray, and dreary out-of-doors, it's a perfect day to settle down with a wooly afghan, a cup of hot herbal tea, a plate of cookies, and something interesting to read. Of course, China's herbal mysteries will be at the top of your reading list—right? But there are other herb and gardening mysteries you're sure to find delightfully deadly and chock-full of garden lore. China joins me in recommending these favorites:

**THE BROTHER CADFAEL MYSTERIES, BY ELLIS PETERS**
Brother Cadfael is a fictional twelfth-century Welsh monk and herbalist, a brother in the monastery of Saints Peter and Paul, in Shrewsbury, England. Cadfael's adventures are centered on life in the monastery, where he grows herbs and prepares them for their medicinal and culinary uses—as well as using his skills, knowledge, and sleuthing talents to solve murder mysteries. You might also be interested in *Brother Cadfael's Herb Garden: An Illustrated Companion to Medieval Plants and Their Uses*, compiled by Rob Talbot and Robin Whiteman.

**THE LOUISE ELDRIDGE GARDEN MYSTERIES, BY ANN RIPLEY**
Louise Eldridge is an amateur gardener, garden writer, and garden-show host with a penchant for digging up dead bodies. Ripley's fictions are filled with sophisticated, reliable gardening advice, arranged in separate essays throughout the novels. A few titles: *Death of a Garden Pest, The Perennial Killer, Death of a Political Plant*.

**THE CLAIRE SHARPLES BOTANICAL MYSTERIES, BY REBECCA ROTHENBERG**
Before her death in 1998, Rebecca Rothenberg wrote three mysteries featuring fictional microbiologist and plant pathologist Claire Sharples: *The Dandelion Murders, The Shy Tulip Murders*, and *The Bulrush Murders*. Lots of interesting botanical details are woven into the plots.

**THE CELIA GRANT MYSTERIES, BY JOHN SHERWOOD**
This ten-book series (which ended in the mid-1990s) featured fiftysomething British widow and horticulturist Celia Grant. A few titles: *Menacing Groves, Bouquet of Thorns, Sunflower Plot, Hanging Garden, Creeping Jenny, Bones Gather No Moss*.

# JANUARY 15

*Dreams are illustrations from the book your soul is writing about you.*

—MARSHA NORMAN

## The Magical New Moon of January

January's new moon—the first new moon of the first month of the new year—was thought to be full of magical powers. If you had lived in 1695, when people believed in such things, you might have followed these instructions:

*At the first appearance of the New Moon after New Year's Day, go out in the Evening and stand astride the Bars of a Gate, or Stile (in Yorkshire they kneel on a ground-fast Stone), looking at the Moon, and say:*

*All Hail to the Moon, all Hail to thee*
*I prithee good Moon reveal to me*
*This Night who my Husband (or Wife) must be.*

*You must presently after go to Bed. I knew two Gentlewomen that did thus when they were young Maids, and they had Dreams of those that afterwards Married them.*

—JOHN AUBREY, *MISCELLANIES*, 1695

### ENHANCE YOUR MAGICAL MOON DREAMS

Ruby Wilcox (who has cast a magical spell or two in her lifetime) suggests that you enhance your New Moon dreams with a romantic herb mixture. This ancient practice is a form of aromatherapy.

### RUBY'S MAGICAL NEW MOON DREAM PILLOW BLEND

½ cup dried rosemary
½ cup dried rose petals
¼ cup dried lavender flowers
½ cup dried lemon verbena
½ cup dried mint
4–5 whole cloves
1 cinnamon stick, broken

Mix all ingredients. Tuck into a muslin bag and place inside your pillowcase or under your pillow. If you want a stronger, dreamier scent, add a few drops of essential oil (rose, lavender, or verbena) to the mix.

**Learn about dreaming and dream pillows:**
*Making Herbal Dream Pillows—Secret Blends for Pleasant Dreams*, by Jim Long

*In winter, when the moon's horns are sharply defined, expect frost.*

—TRADITIONAL WEATHER LORE

# JANUARY 16

*Pleasure for one hour, a bottle of wine. Pleasure for one year, a marriage; but pleasure for a lifetime, a garden.*

—CHINESE PROVERB

## Fruit, Herb, and Spice Liqueurs

These wonderful drinks had their beginnings in medieval monastic gardens and stillrooms. Many are easy to make, but they do take time to age. If you start now, you'll be offering your liqueur to guests at your summer outdoor dinner parties, spooning it onto ice cream for a delightful hot-weather dessert, or adding it to the marinade for your holiday duck.

**ROSE GERANIUM BERRY LIQUEUR**

    2 pints blackberries or raspberries
    1 cup fresh rose geranium leaves
    4 cups vodka
    ½ cup white wine

*Syrup:*
    1 cup sugar
    ½ cup water

Combine the berries, geranium leaves, vodka, and wine in a wide-mouth jar with a tight-fitting lid. Steep for one month in a cool, dark place. Open and crush the berries slightly with a potato masher and steep for another 4–5 days. Strain, pressing the juice from the berries, then filter through a coffee filter or double layer of cheesecloth. To make the syrup, bring the water to a boil in a small saucepan, add sugar, and stir until dissolved. Cool. Add half the syrup to the liqueur; taste, then continue to add and taste until it is as sweet as you like. Pour into a bottle, cap it, and age for three weeks in a cool, dark place. Makes about 1 ½ quarts.

**SPICED PEAR LIQUEUR**

    8 ripe pears, juiced (about 4 cups juice)
    2-inch piece gingerroot, peeled, sliced
    1 whole nutmeg
    1 cinnamon stick
    4 cups vodka
    ½ cup white wine

*Syrup:*
    2 cups sugar
    1 cup water

Combine the pears, gingerroot, spices, vodka, and wine and proceed as above, steeping for 5 weeks. Strain, filter. Make the syrup and add as above. Bottle and age for about 4 weeks.

**Read more about making liqueurs:**
*Cordials from Your Kitchen: Easy, Elegant Liqueurs You Can Make & Give*, by Patti Vargas

# JANUARY 17

Today is Blessing of the Animals at the Cathedral Day.

*I value my garden more for being full of black-birds than of cherries, and very frankly give them fruit for their songs.*

—JOSEPH ADDISON, 1672–1719

## Just for the Birds: From Susan's Journal

One of my great delights in the winter is to watch the flocks that gather around the bird feeders that my husband, Bill, has built at Meadow Knoll, our 31-acre corner of the Texas Hill Country. Most days, I can look out my kitchen window and see a dozen different kinds of birds, all feasting together in harmony. (Well, relative harmony, that is, until one of the bird bullies—a jay, or a red-wing blackbird, or a big white-wing dove—shows up.) The bird seed is their staple diet, of course, but I always put out generous servings of my homemade bird pudding.

### JUST-FOR-BIRDS PUDDING
  ½ pound lard
  1 cup crunchy peanut butter
  ½ cup raisins
  ½ cup sunflower seeds
  ½ cup mixed bird seeds
  ¼ cup honey or molasses
  about 3–4 cups cornmeal

Soften the lard and peanut butter briefly in the microwave to make it easier to mix. Add raisins, seeds, honey or molasses, and as much cornmeal as the mixture will absorb. I keep this in the refrigerator and soften it in the microwave when I'm ready to put it out. I "butter" it directly onto tree branches and place big dollops of it on the tops of bird feeders; it will, however, stain tree bark. You can also freeze it, cut it into square blocks, and insert the blocks into suet feeders.

### OTHER WINTERTIME TREATS FOR BIRDS
- Hang strings of popcorn from tree branches, or scatter popped corn with the other seeds in the feeder.
- Many of summer's flowers will provide dried seeds for tasty winter treats for birds: sunflowers and coneflowers, especially. Store them in mouse-proof tins or in the freezer.
- Punch holes in a mostly-empty orange or grapefruit half (leave some for the birds!) and hang from a tree branch.
- Be sure your birds have plenty of fresh water—and keep the ice clear so they can get to it.

**Read more about being a bird's best friend:**
*The Backyard Bird Feeder's Bible: The A-to-Z Guide to Feeders, Seed Mixes, Projects and Treats*, by Sally Roth

*As the days lengthen,*
*So the cold strengthens.*

—WEATHER LORE

On this day in 1990, I began writing *Thyme of Death*, the first China Bayles mystery.

*If I'd known how the week was going to turn out I would have sent it back first thing Monday and asked for a refund.*

—THE OPENING LINES OF *THYME OF DEATH:*
*A CHINA BAYLES MYSTERY*

## Parsley, Sage, Rosemary, and Crime: About China's Books

I created China Bayles because I was interested in writing about herbs, gardening, and mysteries. I had lived in Texas since the 1970s, and I was already growing herbs in my garden at Meadow Knoll, the thirty-one acres where Bill and I live in the Hill Country. China abandons her career as a criminal defense attorney (much as I left my own university career) and buys Thyme and Seasons herb shop, in Pecan Springs, Texas, halfway between Austin and San Antonio. Her best friend is Ruby Wilcox, a six-foot-plus flamboyant redhead who owns the Crystal Cave, Pecan Springs' only New Age shop. China and Ruby would be good partners, I thought: China is the dry, sometimes cynical voice of reason and logic, while Ruby is a True Believer who always leads from the heart. I decided that every book would have a "signature herb" that would define the theme, and that I would include as much information about herbs as I could squeeze in without slowing the story. Here are descriptions of the first two books. You'll find others throughout this *Book of Days*.

### THYME OF DEATH

Life is good for China Bayles. She lives in a neat apartment behind Thyme and Seasons, she has some great gal pals, and she's in love with ex-cop Mike McQuaid. But things go awry when China's friend Jo Gilbert is found dead and China uncovers a stash of torrid love letters from someone who is now very much in the public eye.

Thyme has been used for centuries to preserve and season food and as a cough remedy, a digestive aid, and an antiseptic. In the Middle Ages, the herb was thought to be an antidote against fear and nightmares.

### WITCHES' BANE

Halloween is supposed to be scary—but the holiday hijinks in Pecan Springs are hardly your everyday kids' pranks. The all-around creepiness culminates in the Halloween-night murder of one of Ruby's tarot students. Ruby becomes a prime suspect when a mud-slinging minister accuses her of New-Age witchcraft.

Witches' bane, wolfsbane, and monkshood are all names for the deadly herb aconite, said to be the creation of Hecate, the goddess of the underworld. Through the centuries, the herb has been used to kill wolves, poison wells, execute criminals, and commit murders. Its root has occasionally (and fatally) been mistaken for horseradish.

Today is National Popcorn Day.

*[Peruvian Indians] toast a certain kind of corn until it bursts. They call it pisancalla, and they use it as a confection.*

—BERNABE COBO, SEVENTEENTH-CENTURY NATURALIST

## Popcorn

Popcorn has been around for a lot longer than Super Bowl Sunday, movies, or the popcorn man in the park. The oldest popcorn ever discovered (more than 5,000 years old) was found in a cave in central New Mexico. Grains of viable popcorn—so well preserved that they can still be popped—have been found in ancient tombs in Peru. Today, the average American eats seventy quarts of popcorn a year.

The menfolks at China Bayles' house—her husband, Mike McQuaid, and teenaged stepson, Brian—put away more than their share of popcorn, especially during the long winter evenings. To cut down on the salt, China makes herbal popcorn sprinkles. For your next movie night or TV football game, put out those super bowls of popcorn with a variety of sprinkles in labeled shaker-top bottles, and let everybody choose. Each recipe uses dried and finely powdered herbs and makes about one-half cup. A great kids' project—unique gifts, too!

**MIX-N-MATCH POPCORN SPRINKLES**
- Mama Mia Sprinkle: 2 tablespoons each of basil, thyme, marjoram, garlic powder. Serve with a shaker of Parmesan cheese.
- Creole Crazy Sprinkle: 2 tablespoons of paprika; 1 tablespoon each of onion powder, garlic powder, oregano, basil; 1½ teaspoons salt
- Mexi-Corny Sprinkle: 2 tablespoons each of chili powder (mild, medium, or hot), parsley flakes, cumin; 1 tablespoon each of onion powder and garlic powder; 1 teaspoon dried red pepper flakes, salt

*The Aztec Indians strung popped kernels of corn and made them into ceremonial headdresses, necklaces, and ornaments. These were worn in honor of their god, Tlaloc, the god of fertility and of rain.*

**To learn more about popcorn, read:**
*Popped Culture: A Social History of Popcorn in America*, by Andrew F. Smith

Zodiac: Today or tomorrow, the Sun enters the astrological sign of Aquarius.

> *The eleventh sign of the zodiac, Aquarius, an Air sign, is ruled by a pair of planets. Its first ruler was Mercury; its second, Uranus, discovered in 1781. A fixed sign (suggesting strength and resolve), Aquarius governs intellect and originality. Aquarians are intelligent, unorthodox, and inventive. They may also be detached and uninvolved.*
>
> —RUBY WILCOX, "ASTROLOGICAL SIGNS"

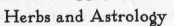

## Herbs and Astrology

Until a few hundred years ago, the idea of writing about astrology and herbs together would have seemed perfectly natural. In earlier times, people saw all things as parts of one coherent whole. They applied their understanding of one aspect of the cosmos—the planets, say—to all other parts: the plant and animal kings, for instance, or the human body. They called this the Law of Correspondences: As above, so below. As in the macrocosm, so in the microcosm.

In this scheme of things, certain plants were classified as "belonging" to certain planets, and were thought to be useful to people who were born under that planet's influence, or to people who suffered ailments related to that sign. In modern times, Aquarius is said to be ruled by the planet Uranus, but the ancients ascribed the rulership to Mercury, which also ruled the human nervous system, the respiratory system, and the shoulders, arms, and hands. The plants that belonged to Aquarius were those thought to be ruled by Mercury.

### SOME HERBS OF AQUARIUS

- Skullcap. Skullcap has a long history of use in the Orient as a sedative and a treatment for Mercury-ruled nervous disorders, such as convulsions. Modern herbalists suggest it for nervous tension and PMS.
- Lemon balm. Lemon balm makes a delicious tea that contains plant chemicals that gently relieve tension and stress and lighten depression. It is thought to lower blood pressure by causing a mild dilation of the blood vessels.
- Lavender. Lavender provides a gentle strengthening of the entire nervous system. It soothes the nerves, eases headache, promotes healthy sleep, and relieves depression.
- Other Aquarius herbs: hops, lady's slipper, valerian, and passionflower, all of which have been traditionally used as sedatives and nervines.

**Read more about astrological herbalism:**
*Culpeper's Complete Herbal*, by Nicholas Culpeper

# JANUARY 21

According to some sources, the Celtic Month of the Rowan (January 21–February 17) begins today.

*Rowan-tree and red thread*
*Hold the witches all in dread.*
—OLD ENGLISH SAYING

## The Magical Rowan

Each of the thirteen months in the Druids' lunar calendar was represented by a sacred tree with a traditional symbolic significance. This month, the tree is the rowan tree (*Sorbus aucuparia*), known as the European Mountain Ash. The gods were said to feed on its red berries, and it was thought to protect against enchantment. The name *rowan* is related to the Norse "runa," or charm, used for divination. Runes were inscribed on pieces of rowan, and the wood was used for magical wands.

Traditional uses of the rowan tree persist through Europe even into modern times. In England, as recently as fifty years ago, farmers hung rowan wreaths on their cattle sheds to protect the animals from harm. Sprigs were hung over the doors of houses and worn around the neck to protect against evil enchantments (the "evil eye"). In Wales and in Ireland, rowan trees were planted in graveyards. In Yorkshire and Lancashire, divining rods were made from rowan, and in Cornwall, people carried rowan in their pockets to ward off ill-luck. In Cumbria, butter was churned with a rowan staff.

The rowan's dense, hard wood is useful in crafts, as well, especially for fashioning bowls, platters, tool handles, and cart wheels. The orange berries are made into a tart, sweet jelly especially good with game, and into pies and wine. Medicinally, a decoction of the bark was considered a blood cleanser and was used to treat diarrhea, nausea, and upset stomach.

The rowan tree has been naturalized from Canada through the northern United States. In the language of flowers, it symbolizes beauty, hospitality, and protection.

**For more about the rowan and other magical trees:**
*Tree Wisdom: The Definitive Guidebook to the Myth, Folklore, and Healing Power of Trees*, by Jacqueline Memory Paterson

*Rowan in Ireland keeps the dead from rising. For the same good purpose it was planted in graveyards in Yorkshire and in Wales; and in the Highlands it was built into coffins and biers.*
—GEOFFREY GRIGSON, *THE ENGLISHMAN'S FLORA*

# JANUARY 22

St. Vincent's Day: St. Vincent is the patron of vintners.

*Come, come; good wine is a good familiar creature if it be well used.*

—WILLIAM SHAKESPEARE, *OTHELLO*

## Natural Partners

Wine and herbs have been paired since the beginning of human history. So on this day that celebrates the patron saint of vintners, let's try a bit of herbal magic: turning a bottle of ordinary wine into a savory herbal wine. It's as easy as making an herb vinegar! Here are three recipes to help you get started; after that, let your creative imagination play. Viva St. Vincent!

### CHARDONNAY WITH ROSEMARY, BASIL, AND GARLIC

    3 sprigs rosemary
    2 large basil leaves
    2 cloves garlic, peeled, quartered
    1½ cups Chardonnay

Wash herbs and place them into a clean pint jar. Add wine and cover. Store in a cool, dark place for at least a week, or until the flavor suits you. Remove herbs. Use to marinate fish or chicken, wine sauce, or as part of the cooking liquid for rice or beans.

### BURGUNDY WITH THYME, MARJORAM, AND PARSLEY

    4 sprigs thyme
    4 sprigs marjoram
    4 sprigs parsley
    1 ½ cups burgundy

Wash herbs and place them in a clean pint jar. Add wine and cover. Store in a cool, dark place for at least 2 weeks, or until the flavor is full and mellow. Use to marinate beef and ham, in making beef stew, vegetable soup, and tomato sauce.

**Read more about herbs and wine:**
*Herbed-Wine Cuisine: Creating & Cooking with Herb-Infused Wines*, by Janice Therese Mancuso

*Remember on St. Vincent's Day
If that the Sun his beams display
For 'tis a token, bright and clear
Of prosperous weather all the year.*

—TRADITIONAL WEATHER LORE

Today is National Handwriting Day.

## Think Herbal Inks

Did you ever wonder what people used for ink before the ballpoint pen was invented? You'd be correct if you suggested berry juice (blueberries, cherries, pokeberries, strawberries) or chimney soot—the sort of thing that would definitely intrigue a forensic analyst. But the most important ink in Western history was made from oak galls and iron. Leonardo da Vinci invented with it; Van Gogh and Rembrandt drew with it; Bach made music with it; and the framers of the Constitution of the United States made history with it. This famous seventeenth-century recipe certainly involves a great deal of preparation.

### OAK GALL-IRON INK

To make good ink. Take 5 ounces of the best Nuttgalls, break them in a mortar but not in small pieces, then put the galls into one quart of clear rain water or soft spring water, let them stand 4 or 5 days shaking them often, then take 2 ounces of white gum arabick, 1 ounce of double refined sugar, 1 piece of indigo and put in the same container and shake them well and let them stand 4 or 5 days more. Then take 2 ounces of good green copperis, the larger the better, and having first washed off the filth, put in to the rest and also a piece of clear gum, about as big as a walnut to set the colour and it will be fit for use.

### WALNUT HULL INK

Try this easier Colonial American ink with your children.

> 12 walnut hulls
> 1 cup water
> ¼ teaspoon vinegar

(This is smelly. Open your kitchen window before you begin!) Put the hulls into an old sock, tie securely, and hammer to break up the hulls. Empty into an old saucepan, add water and vinegar, and bring to a boil. Reduce heat, and simmer for 30 minutes. Pour into a small lidded jar and store in the refrigerator.

### LAVENDER INK

When Victorian ladies wrote to friends, they often used scented ink. Lavender was a favorite.

> ¼ cup lavender blossoms
> 1 bottle ink
> ⅓ cup water

Crush herbs and place with water in a nonreactive saucepan. Bring to a boil and simmer for 30 minutes, watching to be sure that the water does not completely boil away. The scent is ready when the liquid is brown. Strain, and discard the leaves. Add 4 teaspoons to a bottle of ink.

# JANUARY 24

January is National Soup Month.

> *My plate of flautas arrived, sizzling hot, with a pottery bowl of beans on the side, redolent with comino and the slightly resinous epazote, a traditional Mexican herb used to reduce flatulence. It makes the enthusiastic bean-eater more socially acceptable.*
>
> —*INDIGO DYING: A CHINA BAYLES MYSTERY*

## Black Bean Soup

There's nothing heartier and healthier than a hot soup for lunch or supper. This recipe for *Frijoles de Olla* (Beans in a Pot) comes from Carl, who owns the café in the small town of Indigo. You can meet him in *Indigo Dying*.

Carl's soup features black beans, garlic, and epazote (*Chenopodium ambrosioides*), a Mexican herb with carminative properties. (This is a polite way of saying that it reduces flatulence.) Epazote also has a resinous flavor, and can be omitted. You'll find the fresh herb in Mexican food stores, and the dried herb in large supermarkets, or you can easily grow your own. If you are lucky enough to have Mexican oregano (*Poliomintha longiflora*) in your garden, substitute it for regular oregano.

### *FRIJOLES DE OLLA* FROM THE INDIGO CAFÉ

4 quarts water

1 pound black beans, washed, picked, and soaked overnight

2 onions, sliced

12 whole cloves garlic

salt to taste

2 teaspoons fresh minced oregano, or 1 teaspoon dried

1 ½ teaspoons cumin

2 sprigs fresh epazote, minced, or 1 teaspoon dried

Garnish: chopped cilantro, chopped tomato, sliced green onion, chopped jalapeño pepper, sour cream, grated Monterey Jack cheese

In a large pot, bring the water to a boil. Add soaked beans, onion, and garlic. After an hour of cooking, add salt, oregano, cumin, and epazote. Cook for another half hour, or until beans are done. (Beans are cooked when you can easily mash one against the roof of your mouth with your tongue.) Puree about 1 cup of the beans (use your blender); return pureed beans to the beans in the pot. Serve in pottery bowls, garnished with sour cream and grated Monterey Jack cheese. Serve other garnishes in small bowls.

**Read more about soups, including bean soup:**

*Book of Soups: More Than 100 Recipes for Perfect Soups*, by Mary D. Donovan

# JANUARY 25

Today is the birthday of Robert Burns (1759–1796), Scotland's most loved poet.

*O, my luve is like a red, red rose,*
*That's newly sprung in June.*
*O, my luve is like a melodie,*
*That's sweetly play'd in tune.*

—ROBERT BURNS

## Celebrating Robert Burns

On Burns' birthday, of course, the most suitable dish is a haggis. This large, round sausage was traditionally made of deer heart and liver and sheep's blood, boiled in a sheep's stomach, and served in thick, hot slices. If your family would not appreciate this delicacy, you could honor this day with traditional Scottish oatmeal gingerbread, rich in spices. Oats were among the basic Scottish food staples; oat was used medicinally (as a nerve and uterine tonic) and as a softening poultice.

**OATMEAL GINGERBREAD**
½ cup butter or margarine
½ cup granulated sugar
2 tablespoons black treacle (molasses)
1½ cups flour
1 teaspoon baking soda
½ cup oatmeal (make this by whirring rolled oats in your blender)
½ cup brown sugar, packed

1 teaspoon powdered ginger
½ teaspoon cloves
½ teaspoon cinnamon
3 tablespoons milk
1 large egg, beaten

Preheat oven to 350°. Line a 7-inch baking pan with wax paper and spray with a nonstick spray or grease with margarine. Heat the butter, granulated sugar, and treacle together in a saucepan until the butter has melted. Sift the flour and baking soda into a bowl and add the oatmeal, brown sugar, and spice. Add the melted butter mixture and the milk, then stir in the egg. Stir until blended. Pour into the lined pan and bake for about 45 minutes. Cool in the pan for about 10 minutes then turn out onto a wire tray.

**Learn about Scottish herbs:**
*The Scots Herbal: Plant Lore of Scotland*, by Tess Darwin

*Ginger . . . is of an heating and digesting qualitie, and is profitable for the stomacke, and effectually opposeth it selfe against all darknesse of sight; answering the qualities and effects of pepper.*

—JOHN GERARD, *HERBAL*, 1597

# JANUARY 26

Today is National Australia Day, celebrating the rich cultural diversities of the entire continent.

❧

## A Quartet of Australian Herbs

A reader in Australia, Brother Jim Cronly, enjoys the Victorian-Edwardian mysteries that Bill and I write as Robin Paige. Not long ago, he sent us a sampler of Australian herbs, plants that add their unique flavors to Australian foods. I've enjoyed experimenting with and learning about these four interesting herbs.

- Wattleseed (*Acacia victoriae*), roasted and ground, has a complex flavor reminiscent of hazelnut, coffee, and chocolate. For centuries, indigenous peoples ground it into flour staple foodstuff. We combined it with cocoa to make a rich-tasting ice-cream sauce.
- Mountain Pepper (*Tasmannia lanceolata*) is a small tree found in New South Wales, Victoria, and Tasmania. The leaves have a smoked, chile-pepper taste, good with chicken and fish; the berries are more fruity and are a nice addition to marinades and soups.
- The bush tomato (*Solanum centrale*) is a perennial shrub, a relative of the tomato and potato, that grows in the deserts of Central and Eastern Australia. The nutritious dried fruit, which looks like a raisin, has the intense tang of a sun-dried tomato, but with a subtle caramelized taste. The aboriginal tribes of the region call it *kampurara*; for centuries, they gathered it as a staple food.
- Lemon myrtle (*Backhousia citriodora*) is a native of the coastal rainforest. The leaves have a strong lemon aroma and taste with eucalyptus overtones. They are often used to flavor poultry and seafood, and make excellent vinegar, mayonnaise, and vinaigrettes. Researchers have found that the oil has antibacterial and antifungal properties that make it more effective than the better known tea tree oil.

### WATTLESEED CHOCOLATE SAUCE

2 tablespoons roasted ground wattleseed
2 tablespoons cocoa
⅔ cup sugar
1 cup water
½ teaspoon vanilla

In a saucepan, combine the wattleseed, cocoa, and sugar. Add water gradually, stirring until smooth. Add vanilla. Bring to a boil, then reduce heat and simmer for 2–3 minutes. Strain if desired. May be refrigerated for up to a week; reheat in the microwave.

*More than anything, I must have flowers, always, always.*

—CLAUDE MONET

## A Floral Calendar

Medieval monks devised a catalogue of herbs and flowers in the form of a calendar, dedicating each day to a particular plant. This calendar was not generally available until William Hone reprinted it in his popular *Every Day Book*, which was published in weekly installments in 1826. Partly an almanac, the book, as the title page announces, offers a miscellaneous collection of "useful knowledge" for "daily use and diversion."

### COLTSFOOT: WHAT'S IN A NAME?
The herb chosen by the monks for this day is coltsfoot (*Tussilago farfara*). The common name referred to the shape of its leaves, which looked like the hoof of a horse. (Different people saw it differently and named it assfoot, foalfoot, and bull's-foot.) The plant flowers in the early spring before the leaves appear, leading some to call it *filius ante patrem*, or son-before-father.

Other names—coughwort and British tobacco—give a clue to the plant's traditional medicinal uses. Smoking coltsfoot for the relief of coughs and asthma was recommended by the Greek physician Dioscorides; later, it was mixed with yarrow and rose leaves, as an herbal remedy for asthma. Coltsfoot lozenges were used (like horehound lozenges) as cough drops. The fresh leaves were applied to boils, abscesses and ulcers, and coltsfoot compresses were used to relieve joint pain.

**Read more about the floral calendar:**

*Flora's Dictionary: The Victorian Language of Herbs and Flowers*, by Kathleen Gips (The monks' calendar is reprinted on pp. 170–177.)

*Excellent herbs had our fathers of old—*
*Excellent herbs to ease their pain—*
*Alexanders and Marigold,*
*Eyebright, Orris, and Elecampane.*
*Basil, Rocket, Valerian, Rue,*
*(Almost singing themselves they run)*
*Vervain, Dittany, Call-me-to-you—*
*Cowslip, Melilot, Rose of the Sun.*
*Anything green that grew out of the mould*
*Was an excellent herb to our fathers of old.*

—RUDYARD KIPLING, "OUR FATHERS OF OLD"

# JANUARY 28

*Bright flowers whose home is everywhere.*

—WILLIAM WORDSWORTH

## "Daisies Don't Tell"

In the monks' medieval calendar, today was the day to celebrate the daisy (*Bellis perennis*), which had a wide variety of uses. Daisies don't tell? The meaning of that phrase probably has something to do with the daisy's unreliability in forecasting future events.

### THE MEDICINAL DAISY

The daisy's genus name, *Bellis* (martial or warlike) refers to its use by Roman doctors as a common treatment for battlefield wounds. John Gerard, the sixteenth-century herbalist and author of the first important herbal in English, wrote: "The leaves stamped take away bruises and swellings . . . whereupon it was called in old time Bruisewort," adding, "The juice of the leaves and rootes snift up into nostrils purgeth the head mightilie, and helpeth the Megrim [migraine]." If daisy snuff didn't do the trick, one early herbalist advised simply chewing the fresh leaves.

### THE DIVINING DAISY

But daisies weren't just popular medicine. They were also popular for making prophesies. You've certainly learned the most famous one: "He loves me, he loves me not." The last petal decides the question—but its unreliability is unfortunately notorious. You can,

however, tell the seasons by the coming of daisies: It's spring in the English Midlands, people say, when you can put your foot on nine daisies. But be careful: Dreaming of daisies in spring or summer brings good luck; if you dream of them in fall or winter, however, bad luck is on the way.

**Read more about daisies:**
*A Modern Herbal*, by Mrs. Grieve (1931)

*Let the housewife be skilful in natural physick, for the benefit of her own folk and others: for to have a physician alwaies when there is not very urgent occasion and gret necessity, is not for the profite of the house.*

—GERVASE MARKHAM, *MAISON RUSTIQUE, OR A COUNTRY FARME*, 1616

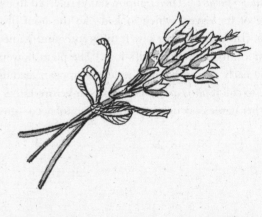

# JANUARY 29

*My usual hair-care regimen is homemade and simple. I concoct my own herbal castile shampoo with aloe, chamomile, and lemon juice, and occasionally I beat up an egg yolk and rub it in after a shampoo. When it gets really dry, almond oil is good. The almond oil treatment usually takes care of dandruff as well, but if it's a problem, I massage in mint vinegar three or four times a week until it clears up.*

—LAVENDER LIES: A CHINA BAYLES MYSTERY

## Herbal Hair Care

Herbal shampoos are easy to make, and you can choose the ingredients that are especially suited to your needs, whether your hair is light or dark, oily or dry. You can buy the inexpensive ingredients at a natural foods store. This basic recipe makes about two cups of a no-suds shampoo.

### HERBAL SHAMPOO

    16 ounces distilled water
    2 ounces herbs (see suggestions)
    6 ounces liquid castile soap
    2 tablespoons aloe
    ½ teaspoon jojoba oil
    ½ teaspoon pure essential oil (see suggestions)

Bring the water to a boil. Add herbs, cover, and reduce heat. Simmer 15–20 minutes. Strain and cool. Gradually add the castile soap, mixing gently, then the aloe, jojoba, and essential oil. For easy use, pour into a plastic squeeze bottle. Shake gently before using.

### SUGGESTED HERBS:

- For blond hair: 1 ounce calendula flowers; ½ ounce each of chamomile flowers and comfrey leaf (OR dried orange peel OR 1 tablespoon aloe gel).
- For dark hair: 1 ounce sage leaves; ½ ounce each comfrey leaf (OR rosemary, if your hair is oily) and Irish moss.
- For dry hair: ½ ounce each nettle leaf, marshmallow root, calendula flower (OR substitute elder flowers OR orange blossoms).
- For oily hair: ½ ounce each yarrow leaf and flower, witch hazel bark, rosemary.
- For dandruff: 1 ounce rosemary, 1 ounce thyme. Rinse with cider vinegar.

### SUGGESTED ESSENTIAL OILS:

- For normal hair: lavender, clary sage, chamomile
- For oily hair: basil, lemon, patchouli, rosemary, tea tree, witch hazel, ylang-ylang
- For dry hair: myrrh, peppermint, calendula
- For dandruff: clary sage, lavender, lemon, patchouli, rosemary, tea tree, ylang-ylang

**Read more about making your own bodycare products:**
*Earthly Bodies and Heavenly Hair: Natural and Healthy Personal Care for Every Body*, by Dina Falconi

# JANUARY 30

In the medieval floral calendar, today's herb is spleenwort.

✻

## Spleenwort and the Doctrine of Signatures

Spleenwort (*Asplenium scolopendrium*) isn't an herb you're likely to run into every day. But the monks who compiled the floral calendar thought that today was a good day to celebrate spleenwort (*wort* is the Anglo-Saxon word for "plant"). I thought I'd use the occasion to tell you about the Doctrine of Signatures, which explains how spleenwort (and other herbs) were named.

### THE DOCTRINE OF SIGNATURES
In earlier days, it was believed that plants were "signed" by the Creator with visible clues to the purpose for which they were designed. Red plants could treat the blood, yellow plants would be effective against jaundice, blue-flowered plants could treat a bruise; plants with bloom or fruit shaped like the genital organs promoted fertility. Plants with leaves shaped like the spleen, the liver, or the lungs were thought to be medicinally useful to treat these human organs. This theory, promulgated in Renaissance Europe by Paracelsus (1493–1541) and Jacob Boehme (1575–1624), is also found in Chinese philosophy, in the Qur'an, and in the plant lore of Native Americans. The theory fell into disrepute during the eighteenth century, but many of the plants retained the names they were given.

### SPLEENWORT
Spleenwort is a pretty fern that thrives in dry, shady areas. We no longer grow it as a treatment for diseases of the spleen, for which it has no proven efficacy. But we grow herbs for all sorts of reasons: because we like to use them in cooking, crafting, and healing; because they grow comfortably in our gardens; and because they are powerful symbols, conveying meanings through the rich associations of human history.

And sometimes (my personal philosophy here) we grow a plant because it teaches us something. Spleenwort teaches us that appearances can be deceiving and that we can be wrong (sometimes dead wrong) when we try to reconstruct the facts so that they fit our theories. If for that reason alone, I'm glad to grow spleenwort in my garden and to know how it got its curious name.

But please, don't use it to treat your spleen. It's not toxic, but it won't work, and it might keep you from searching for the treatment you need.

*Lerne the hygh and marvelous vertue of herbes. Know how inestimable a preservative to the helth of man God hath provyded growyng every day at our handes.*

—MASTER JHEROM BRUNSWYKE, 1527

January is National Candy Month. We can't let the month end without a few herbal candies!

## Herbal Candies

For centuries, herbal hard candies and similar confections had an important medicinal use: to make the herb palatable and to deliver it slowly to the area to be treated—especially important for the mouth and throat. Strong teas were brewed from the herbs, sugar was added to make a syrup, and the syrup was cooked into a candy that could be held in the mouth until it dissolved. Some herbs have a long tradition of this sort of use: horehound, as a treatment for coughs and sore throats; licorice, for mouth ulcers and sore throats; ginger, for upset stomachs; peppermint, for digestive difficulties.

### TRADITIONAL RECIPE

1½ cups strong herb tea

4 cups sugar

Mix sugar and tea in large saucepan. Without stirring, heat to 300°F on a candy thermometer or until a small amount of syrup dropped into cold water forms hard, brittle threads. Pour onto a greased cookie sheet and let cool. Cut into pieces before it completely hardens. Store in an airtight container.

### CONTEMPORARY RECIPE

3¾ cups white sugar

1½ cup light corn syrup

1 cup water (or herbal tea)

1 teaspoon flavored extract (peppermint, orange, etc.)

½ teaspoon food coloring (optional)

¼ cup confectioners' sugar for dusting

In a medium saucepan, stir together the white sugar, corn syrup, and water. Cook, stirring, over medium heat until sugar dissolves, then bring to a boil. Without stirring, heat to 300°F on a candy thermometer or until a small amount of syrup dropped into cold water forms hard, brittle threads. Remove from heat and stir in flavored extract and food coloring, if desired. Pour onto a greased cookie sheet, and dust the top with confectioners' sugar. Let cool, and break into pieces. Store in an airtight container.

*Candied horehound is made by boiling down the fresh leaves and adding sugar to the juice thus extracted, and then again boiling the juice till it has become thick enough to pour into little cases made of paper.*

—LADY ROSALIND NORTHCOTE, *THE BOOK OF HERBS*, 1903

# FEBRUARY 1

*Candlemas Eve.*
*End now the white-loafe and the pye,*
*And let all sports with Christmas dye.*

*Kindle the Christmas Brand, and then*
*Till sunne-set let it burne,*
*Which quencht, then lay it up agen,*
*Till Christmas next returne.*

—RICHARD HERRICK

The equinoxes and solstices divide the year into quarters, while other celebrations mark the "cross-quarters." Today is Imbolc, the first cross-quarter day of the Celtic year, celebrating the goddess Brighid. Other cross-quarter days: Beltane (May 1), Lughnasadh or Lammas (August 1), Samhain (November 1).

## Brighid's Day

Brighid (Bridget) is the Celtic goddess of poetry, healing, and metal crafting. Traditionally, hers was a feast of purification and new beginnings. Candles were lit on this night and on the following day, then saved to light the next year's Yule log.

Ruby Wilcox celebrates Brighid's Day by making a special herbal candle for this purpose, which she ceremoniously lights on Candlemas Eve. Here are the supplies you'll need to make your own.

**BRIGHID'S CANDLE**

- a pillar candle
- votive candles in the same color as the pillar candle
- empty, clean metal can
- pan
- small paintbrush
- several kinds of dried and fresh herbs and flowers:
    - leaves of bay, sage, fern, rue, thyme, germander, boxwood, costmary
    - blossoms of violets, lavender, pot marjoram, chive, hyssop, tansy, feverfew
- seeds of dill, coriander, fennel
- essential oil to scent the candle
- ice pick or similar sharp-pointed tool

Melt votive candles in the metal can, placed in the pan of water over low heat. Lay out the herbs and plant material you're going to use, either randomly or in a pattern. Use the paintbrush to dot melted wax onto the pillar candle where you want to apply an herb. Place the herb or flower on the wax and hold until fixed. Brush a thin layer of wax over the plant material. Continue this process until you like what you see. Brush a thin layer of wax over the pillar candle to cover and seal the herbal material. To scent your candle, heat the ice pick and drill five holes around the wick. Drop 2–3 drops of essential oil into each hole.

**Read more about making candles:**
*The Big Book of Candles: Over 40 Step-by-Step Candle-making Projects*, by Sue Heaser
*Creative Candles*, by Chantal Truber

# FEBRUARY 2

Today is Candlemas Day.

*If Candlemas day be fair and bright,*
*Winter will have another flight;*
*But if Candlemas day be clouds and rain,*
*Winter is gone, and will not come again.*

—TRADITIONAL ENGLISH WEATHER RHYME

## Blessed Beginnings

The Catholic Church assimilated the pagan purification festival by linking it to the purification of the Virgin after the birth of Christ, "the light that brightens the darkness." Worshippers brought their year's supply of candles to the church to be blessed by the priest in a special Candle-Mass.

Candlemas continues the celebration of new beginnings. It was a day to prepare the fields for new plantings and to bless the fields to ensure a good harvest. In England, the holiday greens were taken out of the house, and if even a leaf was left behind, it was unlucky. "Out with the old, in with the new" is the theme for Candlemas. It's a good day to make commitments, renew pledges, and plant seeds for new growth.

In your herb garden, celebrate this day of new beginnings by turning over a piece of earth and repeating this ancient Anglo-Saxon plowing charm:

*Whole be thou Earth*
*Mother of men.*
*In the lap of God,*
*Be thou growing.*
*Be filled full of fodder*
*For fare-needs of men.*

Or plant some seeds of annual herbs in pots on a sunny windowsill, for later transplanting into your garden or deck containers. Some good choices: chives, dill, basil, cilantro.

**Read more about the transition from Pagan to Christian cultures:**

*The Goddess Obscured: Transformation of the Grain Protectress from Goddess to Saint*, by Pamela Berger

*About Candlemas Day*
*Every good goose should lay.*

—TRADITIONAL LORE

*As long as the sunbeam comes in on Bridget's feast-day, the snow ends before May-day.*

—TRADITIONAL LORE

# FEBRUARY 3

St. Blaise is the patron saint of sore throat sufferers. Today is his feast day.

*Good for the throat: Honey, sugar, butter with a little salt, liquorice, to sup soft eggs, hyssop, a mean manner of eating and drinking, and sugar candy. Evil for the throat: Mustard, much lying on the breast, pepper, anger, things roasted, lechery, much working, too much rest, much drink, smoke of incense, old cheese and all sour things are naughty for the throat.*

—THE KALENDAR OF SHEPHEARDES, 1604

## Scratchy throat?

If you're bothered by a scratchy throat, gargle with a strong sage tea (*Salvia officinalis*). Studies have found that sage has antibacterial, antifungal, and antiviral properties. To make tea: pour two cups boiling water over 4 teaspoons dried sage. Steep 8–10 minutes. Gargle several times a day. Refrigerate the unused portion, and warm before gargling.

**HOW OUR FOREMOTHERS COPED WITH SORE THROATS**

- A poultice: The pulp of a roasted apple, mixed with an ounce of tobacco, the whole wet with spirits of wine, or any other high spirits, spread on a linen rag, and bound upon the throat at any period of the disorder. —*The American Frugal Housewife*, by Mrs. Child, 1833

- A syrup: Take of poplar bark and bethroot [lamb's quarters, *Trillium pendulum*], each 1 lb.; water, 9 quarters; boil gently in a covered vessel 15 or 20 minutes; strain through a coarse cloth; add 7 lbs. loaf sugar, and simmer till the scum ceases to rise. —*Family Hand Book*, c. 1855

- A candy. Horehound lozenges are good for a sore throat. —*A Dictionary of Every-Day Wants*, by A. E. Youman, M.D., 1878

- A bedtime snack: Water-gruel, with three or four onions simmered in it, prepared with a lump of butter, pepper, and salt, eaten just before one goes to bed, is said to be a cure for a hoarse cold. —*The American Frugal Housewife*, by Mrs. Child, 1833

- A hot toddy and a cuddle: Before retiring soak the feet in mustard water as hot as can be endured. . . . On getting into bed take a hot camphor sling. [A hot toddy made with brandy or rum, honey, and tincture of camphor, (*Cinnamonum camphora*)] Rub the bridge of the nose between the eyes with a little oil. Cuddle in bed and sleep it off. —*Healthy Living*, 1850–1870, compiled by Katie F. Hamilton

**Read more about early American medicine:**
*Early American Herb Recipes*, by Alice Cooke Brown

## Carnival!

The weeklong festival that takes place about now offers Christians a chance to enjoy themselves (*carne vale* means "farewell, meat") before the penitential season of Lent. The festival culminates on Shrove Tuesday, the famous Mardi Gras celebration. Pancakes are a traditional fare.

In Pecan Springs, Ruby always celebrates this ritual with a masquerade party (of course), and Sheila Dawson (who cooks as good as she looks) always brings Orange-Mint Crepes.

**SHEILA'S ORANGE-MINT MARDI GRAS CREPES**

*To make crepes:*

   2 cups all-purpose flour
   4 large eggs
   1 cup milk
   1 cup water
   1 teaspoon orange flavoring
   ¼ teaspoon mint flavoring
   1 tablespoon minced fresh orange mint
   ¼ cup salted butter, melted

*Garnish:*

   whipped cream
   8 sprigs of rosemary
   orange-peel curls

In a large mixing bowl, whisk together the flour and eggs. Gradually add milk, water, and flavorings, stirring to combine. Add the orange mint and butter; beat until smooth. Batter should be thin; if it thickens, add a few drops of milk. Heat a lightly oiled crepe pan or 7-inch frying pan over medium-high heat. Pour ¼ cup batter into the pan. Lift and tilt, using a circular motion, so that the batter coats the surface evenly. Cook the crepe for about 2 minutes, until the edges are firm and the bottom is light brown. Loosen with a spatula, turn and cook the other side. Stack, separated with cling-film or wax paper. May be frozen. Serve rolled, with orange-mint sauce, a dollop of whipped cream, and garnish of rosemary and orange-peel curls. Makes 16 crepes. (Sheila says to tell you that it's hard to work with this recipe when it's doubled. If you're serving a crowd, she suggests making the batter in several batches.)

*To make orange-mint sauce:*

   1 ⅓ cups sugar
   ⅔ cup unsalted butter
   ⅔ cup light corn syrup
   ¼ teaspoon mint flavoring
   ⅔ cup frozen orange juice concentrate, thawed
   1 tablespoon minced fresh mint

In a medium nonreactive saucepan over medium heat, combine sugar, butter, corn syrup, and concentrate. Bring to a boil. Add mint and mint flavoring, reduce heat and simmer 5 minutes. May be reheated to serve; may be doubled or tripled.

# FEBRUARY 5

*In the black seed is the medicine for every disease except death.*

## Love-in-a-Mist

February is the month for love, and love-in-a-mist is the romantic name for *Nigella*, or black cumin, an old-fashioned cottage garden flower and ancient medicinal herb. Its blossom resembles the bachelor button, and hybrid varieties come in a variety of colors, some with a double ruffle of petals. Its tiny black seeds are contained in a puffy, papery striped balloon. Both the flowers and the pods are attractive additions to dried flower arrangements. For centuries, this annual has been cultivated throughout the East, the Middle East, and the Mediterranean area for its many culinary and medicinal purposes.

### AS A SEASONING

*Nigella*'s black seeds have a fruity fragrance, rather like anise or fennel. Spicy and piquant, they have been used as a substitute for caraway and black pepper. *N. damascena* tastes like nutmeg and can be used to season cookies and fruit salad. The seeds are tiny, though. You'll need at least 3 teaspoons to flavor a large bowl of salad or a batch of cookies. Experiment for taste.

### AS A MEDICINE

*Nigella* has been used as a digestive aid, an appetite stimulant, and a cure-all remedy. A bottle of black cumin oil was discovered in the tomb of King Tutankhamun. Queen Nefertiti used the oil to keep her skin supple and to preserve her bronze complexion. To treat insect stings, the Romans applied a paste of crushed seeds mixed with vinegar and honey. Now, *Nigella* is found in cough syrups, wound salves, and topical preparations. Modern research has confirmed that the oil is antimicrobial and is an effective treatment for asthma and intestinal parasites. Some researchers suggest that it may be an immune-system booster.

### IN YOUR GARDEN

*Nigella* prefers to be sown in the ground, but you can start it indoors and transplant it outside after your last frost date. You'll have flowers in June or July. Make successive plantings in your garden for bloom until frost. Next year, don't bother, unless you're planting a hybrid. These plants self-seed readily. The fresh blossoms are lovely; the dried seed pods unusual.

**Read more about this ancient herb:**
*The Healing Power of Black Cumin*, by Sylvia Luetjohann

*Nigella serveth well among other sweets to put into sweet waters, bagges, and odoriferous pouders.*

—JOHN GERARD, *HERBAL*, 1597

# FEBRUARY 6

*Even a modest garden contains, for those who know how to look and to wait, more instruction than a library.*

—HENRI FRÉDÉRIC AMIEL

## Love-in-a-Puff

Another herb for the month of love is love-in-a-puff (*Cardiospermum halicacabum*), a fast-growing, woody vine (an annual in USDA zones 5–8, a perennial in zones 9–11). Plant it against a trellis to provide support for its tendrils, then stand back and watch it grow—up to 10 feet in a single season. China has planted it in the perfect place: the trellis that hides the garbage cans behind Thyme and Seasons.

### BALLOON VINE

The blooms of love-in-a-puff aren't much to brag about. It's the unique seed pods that will get your attention. Each pod is an inflated balloon that turns from green to brown as it ripens in the fall, hence the name balloon vine. Squeeze, and the pod pops, revealing three seeds, each bearing the white heart that gives the plant its Latin name, *Cardiospermum* (*cardio*: heart, *spermum*: seed). But do watch where you pop those seeds, for the plant can be invasive.

### MEDICINAL USES

In Chinese medicine, a tea brewed from the leaves is used to treat skin ailments and promote wound healing. In India, the leaves are mixed with castor oil and used to treat rheumatism and joint stiffness. The leaf juice soothes earaches.

### IN YOUR GARDEN

You can sow love-in-a-puff directly into the ground when the weather warms, or start the seeds indoors. When the plants have fruited, save the seeds and give them away (tied with a ribbon bow in a bit of tulle) for Valentine's Day next year. For an especially unique gift, string them as a necklace or a bracelet. They're said to bring good fortune and good health!

**Read more about herbal climbers and the trellises to support them:**
*Climbing Plants: Enhance Your Garden with Climbers*, by Barbara Abbs
*The Garden Trellis: Designs to Build and Vines to Cultivate*, by Ferris Cook

*In February the farmer shall make ready his garden grounds to sow and set therein all manner of herbs. He shall repair the hedges of his gardens. He shall buy Bees, he shall make clean their hives very carefully and kill their kings.*

—GERVASE MARKHAM, THE ENGLISH HOUSEWIFE, 1615

Today is the birthday of Laura Ingalls Wilder, the author (with her daughter, Rose Wilder Lane) of the beloved Little House books.

*It is still best to be honest and truthful; to make the most of what we have; to be happy with simple pleasures and to be cheerful and have courage when things go wrong.*

—LAURA INGALLS WILDER

## A Garden of Used-to-Be

Laura Ingalls was born in Pepin, Wisconsin, in 1867 and spent her girlhood moving with her family, to Kansas, Minnesota, and South Dakota. Her mother, Caroline, like so many other pioneer women, had the task of making a home wherever the family happened to settle. Pioneer women always took seeds and "starts" (plant divisions) from one home to another, for they could not expect to have what they needed where they settled. Gardens were vital to survival, producing not only vegetables for the table but also the medicinal herbs that women used to treat the family's common ailments and sweeten their lives with fragrance and flavor.

Planting a pioneer garden—a "Garden of Used-to-Be," as Laura called it—can be especially fun for chil-dren and will help them to learn something about the great variety of uses for important herbs. It also makes an interesting theme in an established garden. If you'd like to include a pioneer corner in your herb garden, consider these plants:

- Medicinal herbs: thyme, lavender, yarrow (also called woundwort), horehound, feverfew, echinacea (a favorite Indian remedy for colds)
- Tea herbs: mint, beebalm, lemon balm, catnip
- Culinary herbs: sage, thyme, dill, horseradish, mustard, rosemary
- Housekeeping herbs: southernwood, santolina, and lavender (repel moths), tansy and pennyroyal (repel fleas), mint (repel mice), bay (keep weevils out of flour and grains), soapwort (wash fabric), lemon balm (polish furniture), sorrel (polish copper)
- Insect repellent: catnip, pennyroyal, basil

**Read more about Laura's life:**
*Becoming Laura Ingalls Wilder*, by John E. Miller
*The Little House Books*, by Laura Ingalls Wilder

*Horseradish, grated and pounded, makes a warming poultice. Eaten, it is a spur to diges-tion.*

—A DICTIONARY OF EVERY-DAY WANTS, BY A. E. YOUMAN, M.D., 1878

*Auntie Hannah, who had got on to the parsnip wine, sang a song about Bleeding Hearts and Death, & then another in which she said her heart was like a Bird's Nest; & then everybody laughed again; & then I went to bed.*

—DYLAN THOMAS, *A CHILD'S CHRISTMAS IN WALES*

## Bleeding Hearts: About China's Books

Some of the China Bayles mysteries are related to seasonal events and holidays. *Bleeding Hearts*, the fourteenth novel in the series, is set in February, around Valentine's Day. For the signature herbs, I usually try to choose herbs that China can grow in her Texas garden, but the bleeding heart (*Dicentra sp.*), was such a natural for this book that I found ways to use it. The story is about romantic longing, romance gone wrong, and desire that ends in death—in other words, bleeding hearts.

Bleeding heart is a shade-loving perennial herb, native to the Orient and happiest in cool, moist woodlands (not many of those around Pecan Springs!). The plant was said to be related to the *Papaveraceae* family (which also includes the opium poppy, from which morphine is derived), and has several cousins with such descriptive names as Mary's heart, golden eardrops, and Dutchman's breeches. They share a unique blossom shaped like a dangling red, pink, or white heart; in some, the darker inner petals give the appearance of drops of blood.

In William Cook's *The Physiomedical Dispensatory* (1869), bleeding heart is described as a useful medicinal herb. Topically, it was employed in a poultice to treat toothache and other pain. Taken internally, it treated headache, menstrual disorders, Parkinson's disease, and rheumatism. In Chinese medicine, where it is called *yan hu suo*, it is prescribed as an antidepressant and sedative, and used to treat tremors and lower blood pressure. Dutchman's-breeches (*Dicentra cucullaria*), was used by Menominee Indians as a love charm. The blossom was thrown by a young man at the girl he fancied; if it hit her, she was bound to fall in love with him. If she hesitated, he chewed the plant's root and then breathed on her, which was bound to win her over. (The literature doesn't tell us whether this worked for women as well as men.)

Bleeding Hearts is also the name of a traditional quilt pattern, which is the theme of the first quilt show put on by the Pecan Springs Scrappers (Ruby's quilt guild). Ruby and I will let you guess how this figures in the plot.

**Read more about bleeding heart:**
*Hedgemaids and Fairy Candles: The Lives and Lore of North American Wildflowers*, by Jack Sanders
*Bleeding Hearts: A China Bayles Mystery*, by Susan Wittig Albert

Today is the feast day of St. Apollonia, the patron saint of dentists. It is also (somebody had a sense of humor here) National Toothache Day.

*Wash your Mouth every Morning with Juice of Limons, mix'd with a little Brandy; and afterwards rub your Teeth with a Sage-Leaf, and wash your Teeth after Meat with Rosemary Water mix'd with Brandy.*

—DR. WILLIAM SALMON, 1710

## Herbs for the Teeth?

You bet. Here's Hippocrates' recipe for good dental hygiene, written in the third century BCE: "Clean teeth with ball of wool dipped in honey and rinse with a teaspoon of dill seed boiled in one-half cup of white wine."

In the Middle Ages, people cleaned their teeth by chewing the roots of marshmallow, licorice, alfalfa, and horseradish. For infections, they chewed sage and thyme leaves, both of which have antibiotic properties. After the spice trade made it available, clove oil, a potent topical analgesic, became popular.

In America, the Plains Indians chewed the fresh leaves of echinacea to relieve toothache; the juice produced such a numbing effect that the herb was also called the toothache plant. The Comanches chewed the bark and roots of the prickly ash (*Zanthoxylum americanum*), and called it the toothache tree. To clean the teeth, Native Americans chewed twigs of bay, eucalyptus, oak, fir, and juniper. Dogwood was a favorite toothpick.

To brighten their smiles, American colonists rubbed on a mixture of ground charcoal, honey, rosemary, and oil of cloves. Burnt toast mixed with oil of cloves was another favorite. And strawberries (mildly acidic, with a variety of medicinal uses) were mashed and rubbed onto the teeth.

### HERBAL MOUTH RINSE

This rinse tastes good and contains several antiseptic compounds to help prevent infection and cleanse your mouth.

> 1 tablespoon each of dried sage, thyme, eucalyptus, rosemary, dried lemon zest
> 1 cup brandy or vodka
> 1 cup distilled water with ½ teaspoon vanilla

In a jar with a lid, place the dried herbs and pour the brandy over them. Cover and set aside for two weeks, shaking occasionally. Strain, add water and vanilla, and stir. To use, pour a few tablespoons into a glass, swish in the mouth, and spit.

**Read more about natural dental care, including the use of herbs:**
*Healthy Mouth, Healthy Body*, by Victor Zeines

# FEBRUARY 10

February is National Heart Month. February's Theme Garden: A Garden of the Heart.

*Let my beloved come into the garden, and eat the pleasant fruits. . . .*
—*THE SONG OF SOLOMON*

## A Garden of the Heart

Gardens have been a natural trysting place for lovers since the Garden of Eden. To capture this beautiful idea in a theme garden, you might construct something elaborate, with a shaded pavilion, an ornamental pool, bowers of graceful vines, banks of fragrant lilies, and beds of dreamy flowers.

But your garden of the heart doesn't need to be quite so ambitious. Imagine this: a quiet corner of your garden, perhaps against a wall, with a birdbath, a trellised vine, a garden-art heart on the wall, and a few pieces of heart-shaped yard art. Add several small heart-shaped beds, outlined with bricks, garden edging, perhaps even a low, clipped boxwood edging. Plant some love-in-a-mist and a love-in-a-puff vine against the fence, and paint a "Love Grows in My Garden" sign.

Thyme lends itself to a small, showy garden. You can make a very simple thyme garden by laying out the shape of a heart in a sunny spot. Then lift the sod and till, enrich the soil, and add a border. Fill your heart garden with fragrant creeping thyme transplants, which will mat together to completely fill the space. Keep the thyme weed-free (medieval monks set their novices to this task, as an exercise in humility), and snip it back occasionally.

Looking for a special Valentine's gift for a gardening friend? Find a pretty heart-shaped container with drainage holes, suitable for use as a planter. Add a small bag of potting soil, a bag of lightweight drainage medium (small pebbles, foam chips), and a packet of thyme seeds. Wrap, add a bow, and deliver with your heartfelt sentiments.

**Read more about designing and planting a theme garden:**
*Theme Gardens* (Sunset Series), by Hazel White

*Almost any garden, if you see it at just the right moment, can be confused with paradise.*
—HENRY MITCHELL

# FEBRUARY 11

*The Guarani Indians had known for centuries about the unique advantages of* **kaa he-he** *(a native term which translates as "sweet herb")— long before the invaders from the Old World were lured by the treasures of the New. These native people knew the leaves of the wild stevia shrub (a perennial indigenous to the Amambay Mountain region) to have a sweetening power unlike anything else; they commonly used the leaves to enhance the taste of bitter* maté *(a tealike beverage) and medicinal potions, or simply chewed them for their sweet taste.*

—DONNA GATES, *THE STEVIA STORY: A TALE OF INCREDIBLE SWEETNESS & INTRIGUE*

## A Sweet Secret

Stevia (*Stevia rebaudiana*) is a sweet-tasting calorie-free herb native to Paraguay, a small perennial shrub belonging to the *Chrysanthemum* family. It is said to be ten to fifteen times sweeter than granulated sugar, with several important plusses: It's nontoxic, does not affect blood sugar levels, and can be used in cooking, with a little experimentation. The "Honey Leaf plant" used to be a well-kept secret, but now the dried herb is available at large natural food stores and on-line. You can grow it in your garden, as well.

### GROWING STEVIA

Stevia is difficult to grow from seed, so start with plants, putting them out about the time you'd set out tomatoes. Stevia likes a rich, well-drained soil, so use organic compost generously, mulch to shade the shallow roots, and don't overwater. Pinch out the tips to produce a bushy plant, and harvest stevia before flowering, for flowering imparts a bitter taste to the leaves. Cut the plant at the base and hang in a warm, airy place. Remove the dry, crisp leaves and sift out stems and branches. Pulverize the leaves and store the powder in lidded jars or zip-top bags.

### USING STEVIA

Use stevia in most recipes in place of sugar: 1 teaspoon crushed/powdered leaves equals 1 cup of sugar. Don't use stevia in baking, because it does not supply the bulk of sugar. Dry stevia may produce an aftertaste, while liquid stevia does not. To make the liquid sweetener, pour one cup boiling water over 1 tablespoon of dried, powdered stevia. Steep for 3–4 minutes, then strain through a coffee filter. Refrigerate for up to 2 weeks.

**Read more about this interesting herb:**
*The Stevia Story: A Tale of Incredible Sweetness & Intrigue*, by Donna Gates
*Stevia-Sweet Recipes*, by Jerry Goettemoeller

Today is the feast of Artemis (Diana), the threefold goddess of the moon, the hunt, and chastity.

## Artemisia

The genus of gray and silvery plants named Artemisia were sacred to Artemis. There are some 180 species, all decorative, most medicinal, a few culinary.

### CULINARY ARTEMISIAS

- Tarragon: *A. dracunculus*. *Dracunculus* means "little dragon." Not very pretty to look at, but has a lovely anise flavor. Difficult to grow in Southern gardens.

### MEDICINAL ARTEMISIAS

Artemisias have been used medicinally around the world. All are decorative, in various shades of green, pale green, and gray, and make a pretty show in your garden. These are the two most often mentioned, although *A. tridentata* (sagebrush) is widely used by native peoples in the American Southwest.

- Mugwort: *Artemisia vulgaris*. Some say that the common name comes from its use as a flavoring for beer, the people's beverage. It was used chiefly as a vermifuge (to repel intestinal parasites, hence the name wormwood), but also to stimulate menstruation, as an abortifacient (to induce abortion), and to treat epilepsy, colds, fevers, bronchitis, colic, sciatica, kidney ailments, and indigestion. Also used in dream pillows, in purification smudging, and as an insect repellant. Medieval travelers put mugwort in their shoes.

- Wormwood: *A. absinthium*. A very bitter herb, it was used like mugwort. It was the chief ingredient in absinthe, the infamous emerald liqueur (which also contained the aromatic herbs melissa, anise, marjoram, and angelica). In concentrated form, a volatile poison. Best to use it as a natural pest control, to repel fleas and ants, and in companion plantings.

### DECORATIVE ARTEMISIAS

Their cool, crisp silver foliage makes these plants a delight in the garden and useful in wreaths and dried arrangements. A landscaping bonus: deer don't like the bitter taste!

- Silver King and Silver Queen: varieties of *A. ludoviciana*
- Powys Castle: *A. arborescens*, one of my favorite artemisias
- Dusty Miller: *A. stelleriana*, mostly grown as an annual
- Southernwood: *A. abrotanum*, green and ferny. Especially useful as a border or green groundcover. Also used as a moth repellant
- Desert sage: *A. palmeri*, used in purification smudging

**Learn how to grow and use artemisia:**
*The Rodale Herb Book*, edited by William H. Hylton

# FEBRUARY 13

*I am fully and intensely aware that plants are conscious of love and respond to it as they do to nothing else.*

—CELIA THAXTER (1835–1894)

## Love Charms

Tomorrow is Valentine's Day, so you might want to brush up on your herbal love lore. For centuries, plants have been important to lovers, for a whole bouquet of reasons! Here are a few you might not have thought of:

- Honeysuckle. The scent of honeysuckle was thought to induce erotic dreams; hence, many parents forbade their daughters to bring it into the house.
- Periwinkle. It was believed that people who ate periwinkle leaves together would fall in love. Another potion, less tasty: powdered periwinkle, houseleek, earthworms.
- Bay. If you want to dream of your future lover, pin five bay leaves to the four corners and the center of your pillow, before you go to bed tonight. Be sure to repeat the traditional charm (it won't work if you don't): St. Valentine, be kind to me, in dreams let me my true love see.
- Cornflower. A lover was advised to put a cornflower into his lapel. If the color stayed true-blue, the young lady would be his; if it faded, he'd lost her. Goethe's Faust illustrates:

*Now gentle flower, I pray thee tell*
*If my lover loves me, and loves me well,*
*So may the fall of the morning dew*
*Keep the sun from fading thy tender blue.*

- Yarrow. A lady hoping to attract a reluctant lover was advised to walk through a patch of yarrow, barefoot at midnight under a full moon. She was to pick some blossoms (with her eyes shut), then take them home and put them under her bed. If the flowers were still fresh, it was a sign that her lover would come around to the idea before long; if the flowers were dry, she should think about looking for another fellow.
- A two-leaf clover in your shoe could predict your mate:

*A clover of two, a clover of two,*
*Put it in your right shoe.*
*The first young man you meet,*
*In field or lane or street,*
*You'll have him or one of his name.*

**Learn how to use herbal love charms:**
*Love Potions: A Book of Charms and Omens,* by Josephine Addison

In the floral calendar, today's flower: yellow crocus.

# FEBRUARY 14

Today is Valentine's Day.

## Chocolate Is an Herb, Too!

We're not the first civilization to believe that chocolate is a gift of the gods. The Mayans worshipped the cacao plant (*Theobroma cacao*), used its beans as currency, and brewed them into a medicinal drink called *xocolatl*. The Aztecs believed that the god of agriculture carried the plant to earth. Clever folks: they mixed it with chile peppers and used it as an aphrodisiac.

The Spanish explorers knew a good thing when they saw it, and took the cacao beans home to make a drink for their wealthy patrons, who naturally added sugar to sweeten the bitter brew. Doctors prescribed the new drink for everything from tuberculosis to intestinal parasites and sexual dysfunction. The French feared that chocolate might raise passions to an uncontrollable frenzy (you know those French), but the Brits loved it enough to take the risk, and before long, London was chock-full of chocolate houses. Chocolate-loving English emigrants took the confection with them to North America, and before you knew it, we had Hershey's. More recently, scientists have learned that chocolate has twice as many antioxidants as red wine, that it relaxes blood vessels and reduces the risk of blood clotting—and that it triggers the same brain responses as falling in love. But you knew that already, didn't you?

## MCQUAID'S HOT 'N' SPICY CHOCOLATE

This wintertime drink, reminiscent of the Aztec's *xocolatl*, combines two of McQuaid's favorite herbs, chocolate and chile pepper—both reputed to have aphrodisiac properties, perfect for a Valentine's Day evening.

½ cup sugar

¼ cup cocoa

1 teaspoon fine-ground chile powder

1 teaspoon cinnamon

¾ teaspoon cloves

¼ teaspoon salt

2 cups water

6 cups milk

1 teaspoon vanilla

whipped cream

nutmeg

8 cinnamon sticks

Blend dry ingredients together in a large saucepan. Add water, stirring, and simmer for 4 minutes. Stir in milk and reheat. Whisk in vanilla and pour into warm mugs. Top with whipped cream and a sprinkle of nutmeg, and add a cinnamon stir stick. Makes 8 1-cup servings.

**Read more about the mysteries of chocolate:**

*Chocolate: A Bittersweet Saga of Dark and Light*, by Mort Rosenblum

# FEBRUARY 15

*The splendor of the rose and the whiteness of the lily do not rob the little violet of its scent . . . If every tiny flower wanted to be a rose, spring would lose its loveliness.*

—THERESE OF LISIEUX

## The Violet: "A Fine, Pleasing Plant of Venus"

According to Greek mythology, violets helped the god Zeus out of a bind. You see, he fell in love with a priestess named Io. When Zeus' long-suffering wife, Hera, found out about this illicit affair, she was understandably miffed. To keep Io out of his wife's way, Zeus turned the young lady into a white heifer. To give her something to eat, he created a field of violets for her—and while he was at it, he sent a bunch of violets to Hera, as an apology. The flowers soothed the jealous goddess, suggesting to the Greeks that these pretty blossoms might have a therapeutic, calming effect. It wasn't long before violets were being used everywhere as a fragrant sleep aid.

In the Middle Ages, Hildegard von Bingen used violet juice as the basis for a cancer salve, while physicians employed the herb to treat insomnia, epilepsy, pleurisy, and rheumatism. The plant was said to be ruled by the planet Venus (which ruled the throat), making it a natural as a treatment for throat ailments, too.

In fact, violet leaves and stems do contain a soothing mucilage, as well as salicylic acid, the precursor of aspirin—good for the throat. They're also rich in vitamins A and C, and for people who didn't have access to fresh veggies in the winter, an early spring salad of violet leaves was a very good idea. The flowers taste sweet and are often made into syrup or jelly, candied, and crystallized. Try violet syrup with your favorite pancakes—and a spoonful for that scratchy throat.

### SWEET VIOLET SYRUP

    2 cups boiling water
    6 cups freshly picked violet blossoms (unsprayed), washed thoroughly
    2 cups sugar
    2 tablespoons lemon juice

Place violets in a large bowl. Pour boiling water over them, then place a saucer on top to submerge the flowers. Let stand for 24 hours. Line a colander with cheesecloth and pour the violets and liquid through it, squeezing out the liquid. Discard the blossoms. Add sugar and lemon juice to the liquid and simmer in a nonreactive pan until the mixture is the consistency of syrup. Cover and refrigerate. Use within a week.

**Read more about violets:**
*Flowers in the Kitchen: A Bouquet of Tasty Recipes*, by Susan Belsinger
*Violets: The History & Cultivation of Scented Violets*, by Roy E. Coombs

# FEBRUARY 16

*Forget not that the earth delights to feel your bare feet and the winds long to play with your hair.*

—KAHLIL GIBRAN

## Wind-tossed?

If the winds have been playing havoc with your hair, you may need some extra hair care. Hair conditioners help keep hair soft, manageable, and healthy. Ruby Wilcox (who is always playing with hair color and style) has designed two simple home-crafted jojoba-based conditioners that help her get the upper hand over frizzes and tangles. Jojoba (pronounced "ho-ho-ba") oil is derived from the jojoba bean and especially valued for cosmetic uses. It is a liquid wax (rather than an oil) that helps tame roughness and flaking, and has healing properties. Many conditioning recipes also use eggs, for extra protein.

### ROSEMARY JOJOBA CONDITIONER

1 cup rose floral water (available in drugstores and on-line)
1 tablespoon jojoba oil
10 drops vitamin E oil
4–5 drops essential oil of rosemary

In a nonreactive pan, over low heat, warm the rose water. Add jojoba oil. Pour into a blender and add vitamin E oil and rosemary oil. Blend for 1–2 minutes.

To use: Before shampooing, wet your hair and pour the conditioner onto your hair and scalp. Massage it in. For extra conditioning, wrap your head in a warm, damp towel and leave it on for 20–30 minutes. Rinse thoroughly with warm water and shampoo.

### ROSEMARY AND EGG CONDITIONER

1 egg yolk
2 teaspoons jojoba or almond oil
4–5 drops essential oil of rosemary
1 cup water

Beat the egg yolk until frothy. Beat the jojoba oil and rosemary oil into the egg, thoroughly incorporating. Add this egg-oil mixture to the water, stirring to blend. Massage into scalp and hair. Rinse and shampoo gently.

**Read more about hair care and other herbal beauty treatments:**
*Natural Beauty from the Garden,* by Janice Cox

*Jojoba* (Simmondia chinensis) *is . . . a handsome, distinctive desert plant . . . The oil (actually a liquid wax) extracted from the seeds . . . is an excellent scalp treatment for either dry, flaky dandruff or brittle hair.*

—MICHAEL MOORE, *MEDICINAL PLANTS OF THE DESERT AND CANYON WEST*

*I whipped two eggs with feta cheese, added some basil and thyme, topped the cooked omelet with yogurt and chives, and sat down to eat and think.*

—*THYME OF DEATH: A CHINA BAYLES MYSTERY*

## Eggs and Herbs: A Perfectly Delicious Breakfast

There's nothing more perfectly natural than an egg, and eggs and herbs together are perfectly perfect. An omelet for one or two is easy, but omelets for a crowd are a different story. Here's an easy way to manage breakfast eggs for a large, hungry family—in your oven!

**BAKED EGGS WITH GARDEN HERBS**

4 tablespoons butter or margarine, softened

1 teaspoon chopped chives

1 teaspoon dried parsley flakes, or 2 teaspoons fresh minced parsley

dash crumbled dried tarragon

dash dried leaf thyme

½ teaspoon freshly ground black pepper

8 eggs

½ cup half-and-half or sour cream (low-fat is fine)

½ cup shredded Gruyère or Swiss cheese

Preheat oven to 350°. Combine butter with herbs; divide among 8 6-ounce ovenproof custard cups. Place cups in a large shallow baking pan and place in oven until butter has melted. Break an egg into each cup. Top with 1 tablespoon half-and-half or sour cream and 1 tablespoon shredded cheese. Bake for 12–15 minutes, or until eggs reach desired doneness. Serves 8.

**Read more about eggs and herbs:**

*Omelettes: Eggs at Their Best: Quick and Easy Recipes for 50 Sensational Omelettes*, by Laurence Sombke

*In February, in the New of the Moon, sow Borage, Coriander, Marjoram, Radish, Rosemary and Sorrel.*

—GERVASE MARKHAM, *THE ENGLISH HOUSEWIFE*, 1615

*At the waning of the February Moone, sow onions and leeks. Sow parsley at February full Moone.*

—*THE EXPERT GARDENER*, 1643

Today is the first day of the Celtic Month of the Ash (February 18–March 17 ), according to some calendars.

*Igdrasil, the Ash-tree of existence, has its roots deep-down in the kingdoms of Death: its trunk reaches up heaven-high, spreads its boughs over the whole Universe: it is the Tree of Existence. Is not every leaf of it a biography, every fiber there an act or word? Its boughs are the Histories of Nations. The rustle of it is the noise of Human Existence, onwards from of old. . . .*

—THOMAS CARLYLE (1795–1881)

## The Mythical, Magical Ash

This month is sacred to Yggdrasil, the ash tree (*Fraxinus excelsior*), one of the most powerful of all trees. In Viking mythology, it was known as the Tree of Life. Because the ash tree was revered for its powerful protection, healing wands and protective staffs were made from it. It was also used as a traditional Yule log, bringing the powerful, protective light of the sun into the hearth on the darkest day: the winter solstice.

In the English Midlands, the ash was used in many divinations, and had other magical uses. To cure warts, you obtained a new pin for each wart you wanted to get rid of. You pushed a pin into the tree, then into your wart, then back into the tree again, chanting this charm: *Ashen tree, ashen tree, Pray buy these warts of me.* (If it didn't work, you tried a different tree, or lived with your warts.)

### THE MEDICINAL ASH

The bark of the ash has been used as a substitute for quinine in the treatment of fevers, and was thought to clear obstructions from the spleen and liver. The leaves were used as a laxative, as a treatment for rheumatism, and—through diuretic action—as a weight-loss aid and treatment for congestive heart failure.

### THE USEFUL ASH

The crisp, green fruits of the ash tree (called "keys") were pickled for use in sauces and salads. The wood of the tree was both strong and flexible, and so was widely used to make wheels, skis, and agricultural implements. The attractive grain and flexibility made it a popular furniture wood.

**Read more about pickling ash keys and using the ash medicinally:**
*The Countryside Cookbook: Recipes and Remedies*, by
    Gail Duff

*Even ash, even ash,\* I pluck thee off the tree.*
*The first man I meet, my true love he be.*

—TRADITIONAL LOVE CHARM

\*Even ash: leaves with an even number of leaflets

*Only with winter-patience can we bring*
*The deep-desired, long-awaited spring.*
—ANNE MORROW LINDBERGH

❧

## Winter Patience

If you'd like to have early plants or special varieties for your herb garden, you'll probably want to grow them yourself. If you start them now, in a sunny window, your winter patience will be rewarded in the spring. Easiest annuals to try: basil, dill, chervil, summer savory, and sweet marjoram.

You'll need seed flats, peat pots, or recycled containers (mushroom boxes and egg cartons, with drainage holes). Fill with a purchased potting medium or use a mix of 2 parts sand and 1 part vermiculite. Moisten, sow the seeds, and barely cover with soil. (Read the seed packet to learn the germination requirements.) Cover the container with plastic and put in a well-lighted place, watering from the bottom, if possible, to keep the surface evenly moist. As soon as germination begins, move into full sun. When the herb seedlings are large enough to handle, transplant them into individual pots. In another week or so, begin hardening them off by moving the pots onto a protected porch or setting them into a ventilated cold frame (easily made with boards or bricks stacked 3–4 high, covered with an old window or sheet of plastic or fiberglass that allows the sunlight in). After a week, the seedlings will be sturdy enough to survive the shock of transplanting into the garden.

## STARTING TINY SEEDS IN A PLASTIC BOTTLE GREENHOUSE

Some herb seeds—artemisias, pennyroyal, ambrosia—are powder-fine. To start these, cut a 2- or 3-liter soft drink bottle in half. Using a heated ice pick (careful!) punch 5–6 holes in the bottom. Fill the bottom half to a depth of 4–5 inches with potting medium and cover with vermiculite or fine-sieved sphagnum moss. Moisten the medium, then sow the seeds as evenly and thinly as possible, pressing into the surface. (Don't cover with soil.) Put the top half onto the bottom half, so that you have a mini-greenhouse. Screw on the plastic bottle cap and put in a window with good indirect light. Water from the bottom, so as not to disturb the soil surface. As soon as the seeds are growing strongly, remove the bottle cap. A few days later, take the top off the bottle. Transplant into individual pots when large enough to handle. Harden off on a porch or outdoors.

**Read more about seeds and seedling care:**
*Growing Herbs from Seed, Cutting & Root: An Adventure in Small Miracles*, by Thomas Debaggio

*To make a hot Bed in February, for the raising of any tender Plants of Flowers, you must provide a warm place defended from all Winds by a Pale made of Reed or Straw, about six feet high: within which you must raise a Bed . . . of new horse-dung. . . .*
—WORLIDGE *SYSTEMA AGRICULTURAE*, 1697

# FEBRUARY 20

Zodiac: Today or yesterday, the Sun enters the astrological sign of Pisces.

*Like several other signs, Pisces is ruled by two planets: Venus (its early ruler) and Neptune (discovered in 1846). A mutable sign—changeable and communicative—dreamy Pisces is a water sign. Piscean people are creative, sensitive, and empathic, with strong desires. They can be emotionally vulnerable and rather melancholic.*

—RUBY WILCOX, "ASTROLOGICAL SIGNS"

## Pisces Herbs

For centuries, Pisces was said to be ruled by Venus, and many of its herbs are related to Venus. Ailments associated with Pisces have traditionally included insomnia (and its opposite, a tendency to sleep too much!), addictions, psychotic disorders, lung diseases, and afflictions of the foot. To this list, contemporary herbalists also add immune system disorders. Herbs associated with Pisces, Venus, and Neptune are said to improve the immune and lymphatic systems, assist in sleeping, and strengthen the feet. Many have an antibacterial effect. Here are some of the Pisces herbs:

- Mugwort is used in dream pillows to promote dreams; it has also been used traditionally as a nervine, to treat insomnia.
- Kava-kava is a Polynesian herb. Its root is used to make a decoction to treat insomnia and nervousness, and a diuretic to treat urinary tract infections.
- Echinacea root is one of the most widely used herbs for treating infections, teeth abscesses, lymph swelling, and insect bites, and to ease congestion in lungs and sinuses.
- Irish moss (*Chondrus crispus*) has been considered an excellent remedy for tuberculosis, coughs, and bronchitis. It is a seaweed found off the coast of France.

**Read more about herbs and astrology:**

*An Astrological Herbal for Women*, by Elizabeth Brooke

*Mugwort, eldest of worts,*
*Thou hast might for three*
*And against thirty*
*For venom availest*
*For flying vile things*
*That through the land rove.*
—SAXON CHARM

# FEBRUARY 21

Today is the feast day of St. Peter Damian, the patron saint of headache sufferers.

*The headache wasn't going to go away by itself. I got dressed and went out to the herb garden, where I picked a leaf off a feverfew plant and chewed it, making a face at its bitterness . . . By the time I'd gotten dressed, made the bed, and fixed breakfast, the headache was under control. I couldn't say the same for my melancholy and heaviness.*

—WITCHES' BANE: A CHINA BAYLES MYSTERY

## Headaches Happen

You're shopping, traveling, wrapping, cooking, and—whoomf!—a headache happens. For ordinary headaches caused by the stresses and strains of daily life, a calming cup of herbal tea may be all you need to get going again. Use these dried headache herbs, brewed with 1 cup of just-boiling water and sweetened with honey:

- Lavender, lemon balm, meadowsweet, ½ teaspoon each
- Sage, rosemary, mint, ½ teaspoon each
- Rosemary, marjoram, peppermint, ½ teaspoon each

## Herbs for Migraine Relief

Some migraine sufferers have reported relief with feverfew (*Tanacetum parthenium*), which contains an anti-inflammatory compound known as parthenolide. (Do not use feverfew if you are pregnant or using blood thinners.) Herbalist David Hoffmann recommends making a tea of equal parts of black willow, meadowsweet, passionflower, valerian, and wood betony. Herbalist Susun Weed suggests tincture of vervain (20–40 drops in water, at bedtime), or a mixture of skullcap tincture (3–5 drops) and Saint-John's-wort (25–30 drops), repeated every ten minutes for 3–5 doses.

**Read more about headache relief and other herbal remedies:**

*Healing Wise*, by Susun Weed

*Holistic Herbal: A Safe and Practical Guide to Making and Using Herbal Remedies*, by David Hoffmann

*Feverfew dried and made into pouder, and two drams of it taken with honey or sweet wine, purgeth by siege melancholy and flegme; where it is very good for them that are giddie in the head, or which have the turning called* Vertigo. . . .

—JOHN GERARD, HERBAL, 1597

# FEBRUARY 22

Today is George Washington's birthday . . . but I'll bet dollars to donuts that his wife had a great deal to do with his long and successful life. So today, let's celebrate Martha!

*I am still determined to be cheerful and happy, in whatever situation I may be; for I have also learned from experience that the greater part of our happiness or misery depends upon our dispositions, and not upon our circumstances.*

—MARTHA WASHINGTON (1732–1802)

## Martha Washington's Medicine Cabinet

These are some of the herbs that our first First Lady would likely have used to keep the Father of our Country in the best of health.

- Calendula — relieve muscle spasms, treat sores
- English ivy — ease colds, diarrhea, gastritis
- Horseradish — kill parasites, treat sciatica
- Lavender — ease headaches, encourage sleep
- Mint — soothe stomachaches, treat colic
- Nasturtium — treat respiratory and urinary tract infections
- Roses — improve digestion, ease headaches
- Wormwood — get rid of intestinal parasites

## AN HERBAL FIRST-AID KIT

You don't have to be a Martha Washington to assemble your own collection of naturally potent and effective remedies. Here are some herbal first-aid products you can purchase or make.

- For cuts, scrapes, and minor burns: A comfrey salve, which could also include aloe vera, plantain, Saint-John's-wort, calendula, and echinacea, will soothe and facilitate healing.
- For muscle aches: Tinctures of arnica, witch hazel, and Saint-John's-wort (combined) and essential oils of camphor, eucalyptus, rosemary, and clove bud are all excellent. Some people are sensitive to arnica; stop using it if you suffer an adverse reaction.
- For an upset stomach, motion and morning sickness, and gas: Ginger, peppermint, and fennel, usually brewed as a tea, all provide relief. (Do not use ginger during pregnancy or breastfeeding.)
- For a sore throat: 2 drops essential oil of thyme in 4 ounces water makes a healing gargle.
- For insect bites and itchy skin: Tinctures of witch hazel, plantain, comfrey, lavender, and Saint-John's-Wort help to stop the burning and itching.

**Read more about herbs for home remedies:**

*Herbs for the Home Medicine Chest*, by Rosemary Gladstar

*Natural First Aid: Herbal Treatments for Ailments & Injuries*, by Brigitte Mars

Today is International Dog Biscuit Appreciation Day (honestly!).

*Ruby took the lawn chair next to Sheila, kicked off her sandals, and propped her bare feet on Howard Cosell. He rolled over to expose his stomach, all four paws in the air, a foolish doggy grin on his face.*

—ROSEMARY REMEMBERED: A CHINA BAYLES MYSTERY

## Healthy Doggie Biscuits

Like most dogs, Howard Cosell (McQuaid's ancient basset hound) prefers people food to anything else. He is very partial, however, to the dog treats China bakes for him, which he gets when he's been a very good boy. They contain two natural flea-fighters (brewer's yeast and garlic) and tasty grated carrots.

**HOWARD'S GOOD BOY BISCUITS**

1 cup flour

¼ cup wheat germ

¼ cup brewer's yeast (available at health-food stores)

¼ cup finely grated carrots

2 teaspoons minced fresh parsley

1 clove garlic, minced

½ cup chicken stock

scant ¼ cup canola oil

3 tablespoons chicken stock for basting

Heat oven to 400°. Spray a cookie sheet with nonstick spray. Mix flour, wheat germ, brewer's yeast, carrots, parsley, and garlic. To this mixture, alternately add chicken stock and oil, in 3 parts. Mix until a sticky dough forms. Knead about 2 minutes by hand on floured surface. Roll dough out about ⅜-inch thick. Cut into squares, triangles, or other shapes. (Howard likes his shaped like bones.) Place on cookie sheet. Bake 10 minutes, turn the cookie sheet, and baste with 3 tablespoons chicken stock. Bake 10 minutes longer. Turn off heat, leave pan in closed oven for about 90 minutes.

**Read more about using herbs to make your animal companion happier:**
*The Complete Herbal Handbook for the Dog and Cat*, by Juliette de Bairacli Levy

*Sow cabbage when the February moon is old.*

—TRADITIONAL GARDEN LORE

# FEBRUARY 24

## Candytuft: An Old-fashioned Favorite

If you're looking for a colorful, fragrant edging for your herb garden, you don't have to look any further than a cottage garden favorite, candytuft, sometimes called hyacinth-flowered candytuft, globe candytuft, or rocket candytuft. Whatever name it's given, it's a perfect herb for borders and rock gardens. What's more, it comes in both an annual and a perennial form, and a variety of colors: white, pink, lavender, and crimson. Annual candytuft (*Iberis umbellata*) is a cool-season annual that blooms until the thermometer reaches 80°, while perennial candytuft (*Iberis sempervirens*) comes back, year after year.

You can start candytuft (both annual and perennial) from seed indoors, six to eight weeks before your last frost date. Since candytuft doesn't like to be transplanted, start the seeds in biodegradable peat pots. When the danger of frost has passed, transplant outdoors, 6–12 inches apart, in a well-drained area. If you'd like some color now and you live in a region where the weather is warm, look for flowering plants at your local nursery. If you shear the flowers off when they've faded, your plant may bloom again in the fall.

Candytuft is not named for a confection, as you might guess from the name, but for the place where it was found, on Candia, the ancient name for the Isle of Crete. The plant has been cultivated since 1596, and ever since has been a familiar cottage garden favorite.

It was included in early American herb gardens as a treatment for rheumatism, gout, asthma, bronchitis, and dropsy (congestive heart failure). Since the plant belongs to the *Brassica* family, its seeds have a peppery taste and have been used as a substitute for mustard seeds.

**Read more about old-fashioned plants:**
*Cottage Gardens*, by Philip Edinger
*Creating a Cottage Garden in North America*, by Stephen Westcott-Gratton

*Whortleberries, commonly called huckleberries, dried, are a useful medicine for children. Made into tea, and sweetened with molasses, they are very beneficial, when the system is in a restricted state, and the digestive powers out of order.*

—MRS. CHILD, *THE AMERICAN FRUGAL HOUSEWIFE*, 1833

# FEBRUARY 25

*Plants in pots are like animals in a zoo—they're totally dependent on their keepers.*

—JOHN VAN DE WATER

## Classy Clay Pots

Got pots? New clay pots that look so spanking clean that they might be mistaken for plastic? Want elegant, chic, antique clay pots, with a green, mossy patina? Here's an easy way to get that prized vintage look, complete with moss.

Brush a generous coating of yogurt, buttermilk, or beer onto your new, unglazed clay pots, then give them a good dusting with pulverized earth (the real thing, not sterile potting soil). Put them somewhere out of the sun and keep them damp. (Yes, you can keep them indoors, in a corner of the basement or garage. And you can certainly plant something in them!) In three or four months, you'll have those wonderfully romantic vintage pots you've been wanting. All your plant companions will be stylishly and happily housed and ready for your thoughtful attention.

HERE IS A LIST OF CLASSIC HERBS TO GROW IN YOUR CLASSY POTS:

| | |
|---|---|
| Sage | Calendula |
| Rosemary | Lavender |
| Chives | Catnip |
| Dill | Anise |
| Basil | Nasturtium |
| Thyme | French Tarragon |
| Cilantro (Coriander) | Fennel (Sweet Florence) |
| Chamomile | Summer Savory |
| Garlic | Sweet Marjoram |
| Mint | Scented Geraniums |
| Oregano | Sesame |
| Lemon Balm | Ginger |

**Read more about potted herbs:**

*Herbs in Pots: Artful and Practical Herbal Containers*, by Rob Proctor and David Macke

*Horehound and Rue may be coupled together as liking a shady border and a dry, calcareous soil, and I have always heard that the latter thrives best when the plant has been* stolen!

—LADY ROSALIND NORTHCOTE,
THE BOOK OF HERB LORE, 1912

# FEBRUARY 26

This day celebrates Hygeia, the Greek goddess of healing and disease prevention. She is honored as the wise goddess of women's health.

*I think the best teachers are the plants themselves. . . . They teach us about the magic and beauty of life, the life force inherent in the green world. When you sit with a plant, observing its color and scent, aware of the community of different plants it grows with, sensing its relationship to the world, you begin to develop a deep sense of peace, joy, and wisdom.*

—ROSEMARY GLADSTAR, *HERBAL HEALING FOR WOMEN*

## A Green Life: From Susan's Journal

When we start using herbs, growing them in our gardens, and learning about them, something magical happens. We begin to pay attention to the cycles and rhythms of nature, times of birth and growth, times of resting and waiting—and yes, times of dying. As we do this, we become more conscious of the way we live and the choices we make. How do we get to that place? Here's what I've noted in my journal.

• *I need to grow herbs.* I grow as many as I can, in the garden, in pots on the deck, on my windowsills, herbs that belong to the multicultural tradition and herbs that are native to my own place. I learn about the wild herbs that are all around me, about their seasons, their life cycles. Gardening (indoors and out) teaches me to pay attention and be patient.

• *I need to use herbs.* I began in the kitchen, adding them to different foods and tasting the difference, especially as I reduced salt, sugar, and fat in my diet. Then I thought of ways I could use herbs to make the house smell good, and to make me feel good: herbal baths, herbal creams and lotions, herbal scents. I learned how to craft with herbs, dye with them, use them to make paper. I began to use them to treat my minor ailments and prevent illness. It's all part of a healthy lifestyle.

• *I need to learn more about herbs.* There is an astonishing treasury of available information, in books, magazines, on the Internet, and from wise teachers everywhere. I try to learn something new every day.

• *I enjoy keeping an illustrated journal*, with sketches, clippings, pressed leaves, and flowers. Journaling makes me more aware of what I'm doing and, more important, why. My journal has been an invaluable source of information and pleasure.

**Read about journaling:**

*A Life in Hand: Creating the Illuminated Journal*, by Hannah Hinchman

# FEBRUARY 27

## An Excerpt from *Happy Thymes: A Calendula of Herbal Dillies*

China got a sneak peek at the Merryweathers' new book, and asked permission to share a few items with you. This excerpt comes from Nelda Narendorf, head librarian at the Myrtle Masters Free Library in Pecan Springs. If you enjoy the little herb garden behind the library, Nelda is the one you should thank. (You might also offer her a hand, the next time you see her out there pulling weeds.)

You can also thank Nelda for this formula for fizzing bath salts, which appears on page forty-six of *Happy Thymes*. She claims that taking a bath in her salts is just as good as a trip to the hot springs at Mineral Wells. "It makes a pretty gift, too," she says. "Last year at Christmas, the Merryweathers made up a washtub of it, poured it into jelly jars prettied up with ribbons and lace, and gave them to people at the nursing home. They all loved it, except old Mr. Boggings, who said it didn't taste too good when he tried it on his mashed potatoes."

**NELDA NARENDORF'S OLD-TIMEY FIZZY BATH SALTS**
- 1 cup Epsom salts
- 1 cup sea salt
- 1 cup baking soda
- food coloring: 4 drops blue, 6 drops green
- 8 drops lavender essential oil
- 6 drops orange essential oil
- 6 drops neroli essential oil
- 4 drops peppermint essential oil
- ½ cup citric acid

Mix salts first, then add baking soda, food coloring, and oils. Add the citric acid last, and mix thoroughly.

*Let's be grateful for those who give us happiness; they are the charming gardeners who make our souls bloom.*

—MARCEL PROUST

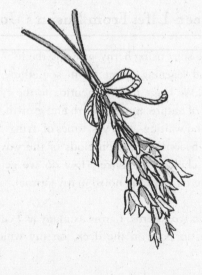

# FEBRUARY 28

*Love is the only flower that grows and blossoms
without the aid of the season.*

—KAHLIL GIBRAN

## A Splash of Spring Color

If you have forsythia (*Forsythia suspensa*) in your garden, you can have a splash of colorful springtime magic in your home. Look for branches that have plump buds on them; the closer they are to blooming, the sooner you'll have flowers. Snip in three-foot lengths and remove any buds or twigs that will be covered with water. Plunge the stems into a bucket of warm water, and (holding stems under the water so air doesn't get into them) cut off the bottom inch or so. Put them in a cool, dry corner and give them occasional sun. It may be snowing outside, but before long, you'll be rewarded with forsythia's bright yellow blossoms and green leaves.

First introduced into Europe from the Orient in the early 1800s, forsythia is a deciduous, early-blooming yellow-flowered shrub with graceful, arching branches. In China, the seeds are used medicinally, for their antiviral, antibacterial, antifungal, and laxative properties. Yes, forsythia is an herb, too!

## A Soft Touch of Spring

Another harbinger of warm days to come is the pussy willow, which I remember fondly as the surest celebration of spring on our Midwestern farm. These shrubby bushes grew beside the river, and when I found them on my Saturday hikes, I would carry home an armload, fill a vase with water, and marvel at their silvery gray, silky-soft catkins. In a week or two, the catkins would be replaced by little green leaves, and the cut branches would be sprouting roots.

In one of my childhood books, I read the story of the pussy willow. Early one spring, three kittens fell into a river. A compassionate willow, hearing their frantic cries, drooped graceful branches into the water to catch them as they swept past in the current. The kittens clung tightly to the branches and were saved. Each springtime since, the willows sprout furry buds at their tips where the kittens once clung. I still think of that lovely story when I see the soft catkins.

Our American pussy willow, *Salix discolor*, is a relative of the willow tree. Compassion is only one of its many virtues: see April 17 for others.

*If snails come out in February, they will stay at
home in March.*

—TRADITIONAL WEATHER LORE

Every four years, February 29 is celebrated as Leap Year Day.

> *There is a belief in Gloucestershire and other counties, that Rosemary will not grow well unless where the mistress is master; and so touchy are some of the lords of creation upon this point, that we have more than once had reason to suspect them of privately injuring a growing rosemary in order to destroy this evidence of their want of authority.*
>
> —THE TREASURY OF BOTANY, 1855

## Rosemary Remembered: About China's Books

Today—the day when ladies traditionally rule—is a good day to celebrate rosemary, the herb that is traditionally under the sweet sway of the mistress of the house. For readers who enjoy rosemary lore and a mystery that revolves around this beautiful plant, *Rosemary Remembered*, the fourth in the China Bayles series, might be a good choice. The story begins when China finds her look-alike accountant, Rosemary Robbins, dead in the front seat of Mike McQuaid's truck. What's going on here? A case of mistaken identity, or something even more sinister? With Rosemary's abusive ex-husband and plenty of former clients on the suspect list, China has lots of investigating to do, with the help of her new friend Sheila Dawson and a disembodied spirit who calls herself La Que Sabe.

But it is Ruby who comes up with the winning clue. Ruby has come up with a winning recipe for rosemary biscuits, as well: good for breakfast with strawberry jam, or as hot appetizers for a party.

**RUBY WILCOX'S ROSEMARY BISCUITS**

    2 cups flour
    ¼ teaspoon salt
    1 teaspoon baking powder
    1 teaspoon baking soda
    1½ teaspoons sugar
    2 tablespoons butter
    1 tablespoon minced fresh rosemary leaves or 1 teaspoon
        crumbled dried rosemary
    ¾ cup milk

Preheat oven to 400°. Grease and flour a baking sheet. Sift the flour, salt, baking powder, baking soda, and sugar together. Cut the butter into the dry ingredients. Add rosemary and milk and mix together into a soft dough. On a lightly floured board, roll out dough ½-inch thick. Cut into 1½-inch squares (¾-inch squares or rounds, for appetizers) and place close together on the baking sheet. Bake for 20 minutes. Cool on a rack, or serve hot. Makes about 15 biscuits or 30 appetizers.

**Read more about rosemary in:**

*Rosemary Remembered: A China Bayles Mystery*, by Susan Wittig Albert

The first of March is the feast day of St. David, the patron saint of Wales. It is a Welsh national holiday.

*The gardener's autumn begins in March, with the first faded snowdrop.*

—ANNE RAVER

## The Welsh Leek

The history of the leek (*Allium ampeloprasum*) as the emblem of Wales goes back to the battle of Heathfield in 633 CE, when the Welsh wore leeks in their caps to distinguish themselves from their Saxon foes. That's one story. Another variant: Welsh archers wore leeks in their caps at the Battle of Agincourt, fighting with Henry V against the French. Whatever the explanation, the Welsh now wear the leek on March 1, just as the Irish wear shamrocks on St. Patrick's Day. If you don't have a leek handy, wear a daffodil, also an emblem of Wales. And if March has come in like a lion in your neighborhood, it's undoubtedly a good day for a bowl of hot soup.

**POTATO LEEK SOUP**

- 3–4 leeks
- 2 tablespoons butter or olive oil
- 1 medium onion, finely chopped
- 3 cups chicken stock
- 4 large potatoes, peeled and cubed
- 1 tablespoon fresh minced thyme
- 1 cup half-and-half (you can substitute milk)
- Salt and pepper to taste
- Chopped parsley and chives for garnish

Slice the root ends from the leeks, and remove the fibrous dark green tops (save for vegetable stock). Slice lengthwise, wash, and chop the leeks. Heat the butter or olive oil in a medium-size stock pot. Add leeks and onion. Cover and cook over low heat until the onion is soft, about 5 minutes. Add the chicken stock and bring to a boil. Add potatoes. Reduce heat, cover, and simmer until the potatoes are thoroughly cooked, about 20 minutes. Add thyme in the last 10 minutes. Remove the pot from the heat. Lightly mash the potatoes in the stock, using a masher or spoon. Stir in milk, and add salt and pepper to taste. Reheat before serving. Garnish with chopped parsley and chives.

**Read about growing leeks and other alliums in your garden:**

*Onions, Leeks, and Garlic: A Handbook for Gardeners*, by Marian Coonse

*If they would eat leeks in March*
*and mugworts in May*
*so many young maidens wouldn't*
*go to the clay.*

—TRADITIONAL

About this time every year, the National Fiery-Foods Show is held, celebrating the authentic fire-power of the chile pepper.

> *It doesn't matter who you are, or what you've done, or what you think you can do. There's a confrontation with destiny awaiting you. Somewhere, there's a chile pepper you cannot eat.*
>
> —DANIEL PINKWATER, "A HOT TIME IN NAIROBI" (IN *CHILE DEATH: A CHINA BAYLES MYSTERY*)

## Fire Power

It's a mystery. How can an herb that causes an intense burning sensation, tears, and sweating be one of the most popular in America? And how can a plant that packs a painfully disabling wallop also lessen the disabling pain of arthritis, shingles, and herpes? Mystery or not, it's a fact. The popular, painful chile pepper can knock you down—and pick you right up again.

The most fascinating feature of the chile pepper is its ability to inflict pain and create pleasure at the same time. This personality quirk is caused by a plant alkaloid called *capsaicin* (cap-say-a-cin), unique to chiles, which causes the sensation of heat. How hot? The chile pepper's fire power is measured in "Scoville units," named for the courageous taste-tester Wilbur Scoville.

On the Scoville scale, a bell pepper clocks in at 0 units, a jalapeño at 5,000, and the fiery habanero at a blistering 300,000. Capsaicin itself is an inferno, measured at 15 million units. When you're in pain (a natural consequence of eating a jalapeño), the nerve endings release a neurotransmitter called Substance P, which travels to the brain with the message, "Hey, I'm hurting!" In response, the brain releases neurotransmitters called endorphins, which produce the pleasurable sense of well-being that chile-heads call "the hot sauce high."

Something similar happens when peppers are used medicinally. In an ointment, capsaicin has been shown to reduce arthritis pain and inflammation, ease cluster headaches, prevent herpes flare-ups, treat psoriasis, and alleviate surgical and burn pain. Dr. Roy Altman, of the University of Miami School for Medicine says: "The mystery is that it took us so long to figure out just how to use this stuff."

The next time you pick a pepper from your garden or bring one home from the market, think of all its mysterious properties and marvel. Nature definitely knew what she was doing when she gave us the chile.

**Read more about chiles:**
*The Chile Pepper Book: A Fiesta of Fiery, Flavorful Recipes*, by Carolyn Dille and Susan Belsinger
*The Healing Powers of Peppers*, by Dave DeWitt, Melissa T. Stock, and Kellye Hunter

*I have eaten nettles, I have slept in nettle sheets, and I have dined off a nettle tablecloth . . . I have heard my mother say that she thought nettle cloth more durable than any other.*

—THOMAS CAMPBELL, 1803

## The Notorious Nettle

If you've been stung by a nettle (*Urtica dioica*), you probably haven't forgotten the experience, and you may have avoided this notorious weed ever since. But over the centuries, the nettle has been a valuable wild herb.

### THE GARDEN NETTLE

As liquid compost, nettles make a great fertilizer. Pick them in spring and pack them into a bucket with a lid, adding one-half gallon of water to each pound of nettles. Let sit for 2–3 weeks, stirring occasionally. Strain out the nettles and put them on the compost heap. Use the liquid as a fertilizer (1 cup nettle liquid to 10 cups water), on container and garden plants. In a stronger mixture (1 cup to 5 cups water), you can use it to spray aphids and black fly. The nettle itself is a food plant for butterflies.

### THE MEDICINAL, COSMETIC NETTLE

Nettles have been used for centuries to treat osteoarthritis, eczema, prostate problems, and dandruff. The leaves contain a natural histamine that may be useful in treating allergies. And yes, it's true that the leaves of the dock, which often grows companionably with nettle, contain chemicals that neutralize nettle sting and cool the skin. "Nettle in, dock out," as the old saying goes! And nettle is said to make your hair shine and feel thicker and smoother. To make a hair rinse, collect 2–3 cups of nettle leaves (wear gloves!). Cover with water in a nonreactive saucepan and simmer for 15 minutes. Strain and cool for use as a rinse after washing your hair.

### THE EDIBLE NETTLE

The nettle is an excellent source of calcium, magnesium, iron, and vitamins. The young plants have been used in soups, stews, and as a spinachlike vegetable. In Scotland, oats and nettles were cooked as a porridge, and nettles were used to flavor and color cheese.

### THE FIBER NETTLE

The nettle contains long, pliable fibers that can be spun and woven to make smooth, supple nettle cloth, or cooked and processed as paper. The leaves are used to make a green dye; a yellow dye is made from the roots.

**Read more about this valuable herb:**
*Healing Wise*, by Susun S. Weed
*Nettles*, by Janice Schofield

*Cows fed on nettle give much milk and yellow butter. Makes horses smart and frisky. Stimulates fowls to lay many eggs . . .*

—CONSTANTINE RAFINESQUE (1830)

*I turned to Ruby. "I've got a couple of salmon steaks I was planning to bed down in lemon butter and dill. Want to stay for dinner?"*
*"Offer I can't refuse," Ruby said promptly.*
—THYME OF DEATH: A CHINA BAYLES MYSTERY

## Better Butters

China Bayles uses herbed butters to replace regular butter in soups and sauces, on vegetables, rice and pasta, and broiled fish and poultry. Herbed butters can be stored in the refrigerator for 2–3 weeks, or frozen. Use unsalted butter to permit the fullest herb flavor, adding salt and pepper later.

### CHINA'S LEMON DILL BUTTER
    1 cup unsalted butter
    2 tablespoons chopped fresh dill
    grated zest of 1 lemon

Melt butter in a small saucepan over low heat, without stirring. Skim off any foam. Pour clarified butter into a medium bowl, leaving sediment in the bottom of the pan. Stir in dill and lemon zest. Keep warm until ready to serve. Wonderful on fish.

### MARGE'S PARSLEY BUTTER
Indiana herbalist Marge Clark liked this butter because, she said, you can find fresh parsley in the supermarket, even in the dead of winter.

    1 cup unsalted butter, softened
    1 cup fresh parsley, minced
    freshly grated black pepper, to taste
    1 tablespoon fresh lemon juice
    1 or 2 cloves garlic, minced

Combine all thoroughly. Cover tightly and refrigerate up to 2 weeks. Good on any meat, fish, chicken, bread, or vegetable.

### DRIED IS FINE HERB BUTTER
It's March, and all you have are dried herbs. Don't fret—this blend is almost as tasty as if you'd used garden-fresh herbs.

    ½ teaspoon lemon powder
    1 teaspoon garlic powder (not salt)
    1 tablespoon dried oregano
    1 tablespoon dried basil
    1 tablespoon dried tarragon
    1 tablespoon dried rosemary
    1 tablespoon dried chives
    ¼ teaspoon freshly ground pepper

Mix thoroughly, grind fine using a mortar and pestle or a spice grinder, and store tightly lidded, away from the light. To make butter, add 2 ½ teaspoons to 1 cup of softened butter.

**Read more of Marge Clark's herbal recipes:**
*The Best of Thymes*, by Marge Clark

Today is the Egyptian festival honoring Isis, the Lady of Ten Thousand Names.

*Isis of the winged arms was first daughter of Nut, the overarching sky, and the little earth-god Geb . . . From the beginning, Isis turned a kind eye on the people of earth, teaching women to grind corn, spin flax, weave cloth, and tame men sufficiently to live with them.*

—PATRICIA MONAGHAN, *THE BOOK OF GODDESSES & HEROINES*

## Flax

Flax, like nettle, is an ancient fiber herb, its cultivation and use dating back to the beginnings of civilization. From flax (*Linum usitatissimum*) is spun linen, which is frequently mentioned in the Bible. In Egypt, coarse linen was the common domestic cloth, while "fine" linen was reserved for the wealthy. Mummies were wrapped in linen shrouds. Many tomb paintings of people cultivating and dressing flax and spinning and weaving linen thread have been found.

### FROM FLAX TO FIBER

Preparing flax for spinning was a laborious process, and most of the work was done by women. The 2–3 foot stalks of this annual plant were cut green and soaked for several days to remove the outer casing, laid out on the flat roofs of houses to "ret" (rot), and then beaten to soften the long fibers and separate them from the pith. The fibers were combed, spun on hand spindles (the spinning wheel didn't come along until the thirteenth century), and woven into cloth.

### FLAXSEED FOR HEART HEALTH

Flaxseed (or linseed, as it is also called) has been used in medicine since ancient times. It was valued as a poultice for pleurisy, skin eruptions, tumors, and burns, and was used in cough medicines. Flaxseed itself (ground or whole) contains the antioxidant lignan, which may help protect against certain cancers. Flaxseed oil, containing alpha-linolenic acid, is highly unsaturated and heart-healthy. (Do not ingest industrial linseed oil!)

The seeds themselves have a nutty taste and are highly nutritious. Grinding them just before using preserves flavor and nutrition, but preground seeds are more convenient. Keep them refrigerated. Combine flaxseed flour with wheat flour for breads, quick breads, and pancakes, and sprinkle the ground seeds on cereals for additional crunch. Isis would be pleased.

**Read more about flax:**
*Flax Your Way to Better Health*, by Jane Reinhardt-Martin

*Get thy distaff and spindle ready and God will send the flax.*

—TRADITIONAL SAYING

*There is a legend that bad fairies gave the blossoms of foxgloves to the fox that he might put them on his toes to soften his tread when he prowled among the roosts.*

—MRS. M. GRIEVE, *A MODERN HERBAL*

## The Mystery of Foxglove: A Love Story

It all started in the spring of 1768, in the English county of Shropshire, when Dr. William Withering rode out to make a house call on Miss Helena Cooke. Her illness confined the young lady to her home and required the good doctor to visit frequently. The two young people fell in love. He proposed marriage and she accepted.

Miss Cooke's favorite occupation was painting watercolors of plants and flowers. As a medical student, Dr. Withering had found botany exceedingly dull and disagreeable, but his fiancée's fascination with plants quite naturally charmed him. By the time they were married in 1774, Dr. Withering was as passionate about plants as was his new wife.

One subject of the doctor's passion was the poisonous foxglove, known by its Latin binomial as *Digitalis purpurea*. The year after his marriage, the doctor acquired an herbal recipe from Mrs. Sutton, a Shropshire herbalist. She had been using the recipe, which contained foxglove and other herbs, to treat dropsy—the disease we now know as congestive heart failure. Although none of the authoritative herbals recommended the use of foxglove, Dr. Withering began to experiment with this powerful herb, administering it in different forms and dosages and carefully observing its effect on his patients. He learned that the plant increased the strength and efficiency of the heart muscle without requiring more oxygen. He also learned that the most reliable effects were obtained from the leaves of a two-year-old plant, gathered just before it bloomed.

By 1780, the success of Dr. Withering's clinical trials encouraged him to recommend foxglove to his fellow practitioners. Five years later, he published his now-classical study, *Account of the Foxglove*. Eventually, the plant's compound was synthesized, and digitalis—as it was now called—came into common use.

If you use digitalis, you can thank Mrs. Sutton for making the recipe available to Dr. Withering. You can thank the good doctor for his careful trials, and his patients for their courage. And you can thank Mrs. Withering for inspiring the doctor's interest in plants. Yes, sometimes it does take a village.

**Read more about plant-based medicine:**

*Green Pharmacy: The History and Evolution of Western Herbal Medicine*, by Barbara Griggs

*The fascinating question thus presents itself: how many other country remedies—like the foxglove, unrecorded in the herbals—have never met their Withering, and have been lost for ever to orthodox medicine?*

—BARBARA GRIGGS, *GREEN PHARMACY*

# MARCH 7

*A Jesuit priest living among the Onondaga of New York—and probably taught by them—wrote the following about sassafras's healing powers: "But the most common and wonderful plant . . . is that which we call the 'Universal Plant,' because its leaves when powdered heal wounds of all kinds in a short time."*

—ALICE THOMS VITALE, *LEAVES: IN MYTH, MAGIC & MEDICINE*

## Sassafras, the "Universal Plant"

Tea made from sassafras twigs and leaves was my Missouri grandmother's favorite spring tonic, which she prescribed liberally for internal spring cleaning and as a cold and flu fighter. As a child growing up in Illinois, my favorite treat was a frosty mug of root beer—originally a product of the sassafras tree. When I lived in Louisiana, I learned that Creole filé gumbo just wasn't the same without filé powder, made from sassafras. And recently, I've seen fabric dyed a deep, pretty yellow from sassafras bark. No wonder it's been called the "universal plant"!

The sassafras tree (*Sassafras albidum*) is common throughout the eastern United States. It was the New World's first cash crop, and made quite a sensation in the early 1600s in Europe, where its health-giving roots and wood were more prized than chocolate and tobacco, two other wildly popular New World herbs. Its popularity declined sharply, however, when word got around that it was being used to treat syphilis. Its main constituent, safrole, is now considered carcinogenic.

Because of this concern for toxicity, root beer is now made from artificial flavors, and people have been warned to reduce their consumption of sassafras tea. (My grandmother would undoubtedly have gone right on drinking it.) Used in small quantities as a flavoring, the leaves are safe and are available, in the form of filé powder, from many supermarkets. If you want to make your own filé, dry the young sassafras leaves until they're crisp, then powder them. To flavor and thicken gumbo, add the powder at the very end of the cooking period, after you have taken the pot from the heat, and add it only to the portion you plan to serve. (Filé powder becomes stringy when it's heated or reheated.)

**Read more about sassafras:**

*Sacred and Herbal Healing Beers: The Secrets of Ancient Fermentation*, by Stephen Harrod Buhner
*Wild Roots: A Forager's Guide*, by Doug Elliott

*Fill me with sassafras, nurse*
*And juniper juice!*
*And see if I'm still any use!*
*For I want to be young again and to sing again,*
*Sing again, sing again.*

—DON MARQUIS, "SPRING ODE"

# MARCH 8

*In the early church, rue was dipped in holy water and shaken in front of the doors and in the aisles to repel demons and evil. By the sixteenth century, the plant had come to be associated with the idea of ruefulness and repentance, with sorrow for one's wrongdoing. Perhaps that was why the poison pen writer had put it into the envelopes. Rue, regret, repentance, grace. It was a powerful symbol.*

—RUEFUL DEATH: A CHINA BAYLES MYSTERY

## *Rueful Death*: About China's Books

When I chose rue as the signature herb for the fifth of China's herbal adventures, I didn't have a very clear idea of how I was going to use it. Once I began to work with the herb, however, I quickly turned up two interesting things. The first had to do with rue's symbolic association with ruefulness and repentance. The second was inspired by a remark in Steven Foster's book, *Herbal Renaissance*: the frequently reported "burns" caused by rue sap are the result of "photosensitization resulting from a reaction of the furocoumarins in the fresh leaves to sunlight." Putting these two things together, I came up with a plot in which a poison-pen writer includes a leaf of rue with her messages and is betrayed by the rue-burns—photodermatitis—on her arms.

I have to confess to being less interested in the mechanics of the plot, however, than in the herb itself, for rue's rich symbolism brought a special depth of significance to what was a fairly simple mystery novel. The plant gave me a way of seeing and understanding the events of the story: a special dimension, symbolic, allegorical even. And although readers don't have to perceive this dimension of the book in order to understand its plot, it can certainly enrich the reading experience.

When I was doing research for *Rueful Death*, I harvested many fascinating snippets about the plant. Here are some:

- Rue lends second sight. With it, you'll be able to see a person's heart and know whether she's a witch. —Medieval folklore
- If gun-flints are wiped with rue and vervain, the shot must surely reach the intended victim, regardless of the shooter's aim. —C. M. Skinner, *Myths and Legends of Flowers, Trees, Fruits, and Plants*
- Rue in Thyme should be a Maiden's Posie. —Scottish proverb
- What savor is better, if physicke be true
  For places infected than Wormwood and Rue?
  —Thomas Tusser, *Five Hundred Points of Good Husbandry*, 1580
- And from Shakespeare's *Hamlet*, famously and memorably: *I wear my rue with a difference.*

**Read more about rue:**
*Rueful Death: A China Bayles Mystery*, by Susan Wittig Albert

*I plant rosemary all over the garden, so pleasant is it to know that at every few steps one may draw the kindly branchlets through one's hand, and have the enjoyment of their incomparable incense; and I grow it against walls, so that the sun may draw out its inexhaustible sweetness to greet me as I pass.*

—GERTRUDE JEKYLL (1843–1932)

## It's Not Easy, But You Can Do It

Yes, you really can grow rosemary from seed. Rosemary (*Rosmarinus officinalis*) seeds have a fairly low germination rate (around 25 percent) and germination may take anywhere from a couple of weeks to two months. But if you plant 100, you'll have 25. It's certainly worth a try.

Sow the seeds on the surface of a small container of sterile potting medium (do not cover with soil). Moisten, and put the container into a plastic bag in a warm, light place—light helps them to germinate. As soon as you can handle the small green plants (some 10–12 weeks from now), transplant them to individual pots, using good soil, enriched with compost and plenty of sand for drainage. Keep them on a bright, cool windowsill, then move them outdoors in stages: from the windowsill to a protected porch, bringing them in on cold nights; from the porch to an outdoor spot with morning sun and plenty of moving air; then (still in the pot) to the bed where they're going to grow; and finally, into the ground.

Growing rosemary from seed is one of those things you just have to want to do. But think of your friends' surprised shock when you say, with a casual wave of the hand, "Oh, those rosemarys? I grew them myself, from seed."

**Read more about growing from seed:**
*Growing Herbs from Seed, Cutting & Root: An Adventure in Small Miracles*, by Thomas Debaggio

*To make Conserve of Rosemary Flowers.—Take two Pound of Rosemary-flowers, the same weight of fine Sugar, pownd them well in a Stone-Mortar; then put the Conserve into well-glaz'd Gallipots. It will keep a Year or Two.*

—SIR HUGH PLATT, *DELIGHTS FOR LADIES*, 1594

In the floral calendar, today's flower: daffodil.

# MARCH 10

Native Americans called the March Full Moon "The Sap Moon."

*Botanists say that trees need the powerful March winds to flex their trunks and main branches, so the sap is drawn up to nourish the budding leaves. Perhaps we need the gales of life in the same way, though we dislike enduring them.*

—JANE TRUAX

## Sap's Rising!

Throughout the Northeast, March is the month to tap the trees, an activity that was an important ritual in Native American Indian cultures, where all six maple species (especially *Acer saccharum*, sugar maple) would be tapped, as well as birch, butternut, box elder, and hickory trees.

For the Mohawks and other tribes, tree-tapping was preceded by a major religious ceremony. Before the sap—the tree's lifeblood—was collected, tobacco was thrown onto a fire of maple twigs in a ceremony of thanksgiving for what the tree was about to share. A community feast followed, and then bark sap baskets were attached to the trees to be tapped. The sap was boiled down into syrup and sugar. Maple bark was also used to prepare a blood purifier, eye medicine, and cough medicine.

**MAPLE AND BALSAMIC VINAIGRETTE**

Try this sweet-sour dressing on a hearty spinach salad, with sliced red onions, crimini mushrooms, cherry tomatoes, and feta cheese.

    1 teaspoon chopped cilantro
    3 tablespoons balsamic vinegar
    2 tablespoons maple syrup
    1 tablespoon lime juice
    1 clove garlic, minced
    1 cup extra-virgin olive oil
    ½ teaspoon salt
    ¼ teaspoon freshly ground black pepper

Mix together the first five ingredients. Whisk in oil. Salt and pepper to taste. Refrigerate.

• *Sap from a maple tree flows faster before a rain shower.*
• *You'll get more sap if you hang the buckets on the south side of the tree.*
• *Maple leaves curl up at the edges when it's going to rain.*

—MAPLE LORE

**Read more about maple lore and cookery:**

*Maple Syrup Cookbook: 100 Recipes for Breakfast, Lunch & Dinner,* by Ken Haedrich

*In March, the Moon being new, sow Onions, Garlic, Chervil, Marjoram, white Poppy, double Marigolds, Thyme and Violets. At the full Moon, Chicory, Fennel, and Apples of Love. At the wane, Artichokes, Basil, Cucumbers, Spinach, Gillyflowers, Cabbage, Lettuce, Burnets, Leeks, and Savory.*

—GERVASE MARKHAM, *THE ENGLISH HOUSEWIFE*, 1615

## From Onion Sets to Green Onions

This is the time of year when you're likely to see onion sets—little onions ready for transplanting, bundled in bunches of 60–80 plants—in your local nursery, feed store, or grocery store. Growing onions from sets is probably the simplest and quickest way to obtain "green onions," small onions that are enjoyed as much for the green tops as the white bulbs. Purchase firm, dormant sets early, before they begin to grow in the heated store. At home, keep them in a cool, dry, dark place until you can set them out in the garden.

You can plant onions as soon as you can till the soil. They will grow almost anywhere, but they appreciate a fertile, moist (but not soggy) soil, and cool temperatures. To produce green onions, plant the sets one inch deep and almost touching. (Green onions are harvested before crowding becomes a problem.) Start pulling your onions when the tops are 6 inches tall. Their flavor will be stronger as they get larger; you can use them in cooked dishes when they're too fiery to eat raw.

The onion has been used medicinally since antiquity. It was also thought to repel evil spirits, and bunches of onions were often hung outside the door or over the manger in the barn to keep witches and bad fairies away.

**Read more about the power of onions:**

*The Onion Book: A Bounty of Culture, Cultivation, and Cuisine,* by Carolyn Dille and Susan Belsinger

*Onions, Leeks, & Garlic: A Handbook for Gardeners,* by Marian Coonse

*Onion skin, very thin,*
*Mild winter's coming in.*
*Onion skin, thick and tough,*
*Coming winter cold and rough.*

—TRADITIONAL

*The onion had many uses. The inside of an onion skin placed on cuts and scratches acted as a type of elastoplast . . . An onion placed on a wasp or bee sting soon took the pain away. A mixture of onions and sugar in water was a cure for whooping cough. Rubbed on the head it was believed a cure for baldness.*

—ROY VICKERY, *OXFORD DICTIONARY OF PLANT-LORE*

*From Dogwood white to Dogwood red,*
*That's the way the summer's fled.*
—SAM RAGAN

## Dogwood White, Dogwood Red

### THE USEFUL DOGWOOD

How did this beautiful little tree get the odd name *dogwood*? Some people think it derives from the use of the bark to brew a wash for mangy dogs; in the seventeenth century, the shrub was called the dog-berry or hound-berry tree. Others think the name grew out of the widespread use of the wood as a dagger or skewer (Fr. *dague*, It/Span. *daga*). It was also called the prick timber tree, "because butchers used to make pricks of it." In fact, dogwood was used for all sorts of tools, especially those that had to resist wear, splitting, and splintering: pegs, pulleys, cogwheels, spindles, bobbins, knitting needles, forks, and spoons. And because it did not contain silica and could be polished smooth, it was used to make specialty tools for watchmakers and opticians.

### THE MEDICINAL DOGWOOD

Dogwood (*Cornus sp.*) was a medicinal staple for Native Americans. The Cherokee chewed twigs for headache, the Chippewa used the bark to treat coughs, the Iroquois used the roots as an eye wash, and the Delaware used the bark as a painkiller. Many tribes used it to treat ague, malaria, and fever, and as a blood cleanser, wound healer, and colic soother. Its use as a chewing stick to clean the teeth and treat toothache and gum ailments led early settlers to use it as a toothpick.

### THE LEGENDARY DOGWOOD

You may have read the legend that the dogwood tree was once as tall and imposing as the oak. Because of the strength of the wood, it was used to make the cross on which Christ was crucified. The dogwood was ashamed of its participation in this horrific event and begged Jesus for forgiveness. He took pity on the tree and decreed that from henceforth, it would be so slender and twisted that it could never be used as a cross. Its blossoms, however, still tell the tale: In the center, there is a crown of thorns, and each petal bears a nail print stained with red.

Since the dogwood is not native to the Mediterranean area, its connection to Christ's crucifixion can only be legendary. The same tale is told of several other small, twisted trees.

**Read more about dogwood:**

*Leaves: In Myth, Magic, & Medicine*, by Alice Thoms Vitale

*The Folklore of Trees and Shrubs*, by Laura C. Martin

*The pretty cosmetic vinegars on that shelf over there—mint vinegar, floral and lavender vinegar—are all made by Verna Roberts, who got her start in a class I taught a few years ago and now markets her delightful vinegars all over central Texas.*

—BLEEDING HEARTS: A CHINA BAYLES MYSTERY

## Cosmetic Vinegars

Cosmetic vinegars have been used as a facial skin tonic for centuries. As we face the dry heat of winter indoors and the blasts of March wind outdoors, this is a good time to take a little extra care. Herbal vinegar skin tonics can help maintain or restore the skin's acid balance, and can tone, soothe, soften, and heal. They are astringent, but since they don't contain alcohol, they don't dry the skin. And for an itchy scalp, part the hair and dab with vinegar-moistened cotton; repeat over the head.

**MAKING AND USING COSMETIC HERBAL VINEGAR**
Start with four cups of high-quality apple cider vinegar and two cups fresh or one cup dried herbs. (See the herbal combinations suggested below.) Steep for several weeks in a dark place, then strain and bottle. To use, mix ½ cup vinegar with 3 cups water, and spritz or splash it on your face after washing.

- Minty Vinegar: equal parts of spearmint, sage, thyme, rosemary
- Sweet Floral Vinegar: equal parts of rose petals and hips, willow bark, chamomile flowers, and dried orange peel. Mix with rose water for use.
- Lovely Lavender Vinegar: lavender flowers, rosemary, thyme

For a rejuvenating facial, follow a facial steaming with refreshing vinegar. For the steam, bring a pan of water to a boil, put 3–4 sprigs of rosemary in the water, boil for one minute, then remove from the heat. Hold your towel-draped head over the pan and allow the rosemary-rich steam to open the pores. Pat with a cotton ball drenched in vinegar. Repeat once or twice. Then spritz with chilled vinegar to close the pores.

If you suffer from frequent headaches, quilt a lavender cap:

*I judge that the flowers of lavender, quilted into a cap and daily worn, are good for all diseases of the head that come of a cold cause . . .*

—WILLIAM TURNER, HERBAL, 1568

**Discover a variety of cosmetic uses of vinegar and other natural products:**
*Natural Beauty for All Seasons,* by Janice Cox

In the floral calendar, today's flower: hearts-ease.

Today is National Potato Chip Day.

*Sauce of the poor man: a little potato with the big one.*

—IRISH SAYING

## The Potato

Throughout history, the potato has had its ups and downs.

In its native Peru, the potato has been a valuable food staple for nearly 8,000 years, and some 4,000 different varieties can still be found there. The Quechua vocabulary included over a thousand words to describe the cultivation and use of potatoes, and "the time it takes to cook a potato" was an important measure of time. The potato was used as a staple medicine and was believed to ensure fertility.

But when the Spaniards brought the potato to Europe in the 1570s, it was a different story. Europeans were suspicious of the plant, partly because they viewed it as a food for the poor and partly because it produced grotesque tubers underground and reproduced itself from those same misshapen tubers. Surely there was some deviltry associated with this! The matter was settled when in 1596 the Swiss botanist Gaspard Bauhin assigned the potato to the *Solanaceae* family: the same nasty clan that included the deadly nightshade, henbane, and tobacco—herbs long used as poisons, narcotics, and magic.

But the potato's prospects brightened again in 1710 when William Salmon, a popular and prolific author, claimed that the cooked tubers stopped "fluxes of the bowel" and could cure tuberculosis and rabies. He also repeated a long-held belief about plants that reproduced themselves below ground: that the potato would "increase seed and provoke lust, causing fruitfulness in both sexes." These claims joined other folk-medicine beliefs: A peeled potato in the pocket could cure a toothache, a dried potato hung around the neck would cure rheumatism, and potato juice rubbed on warts would make them disappear.

The potato rooted itself most firmly and rapidly in Ireland, where by 1800 it was the most important food. Its easy availability led to a rapid population growth, and, when the plant was struck by a blight in the 1840s, to the equally swift deaths of over a million people. In England, the potato was avoided as a symbol of Ireland's unhappy misfortune.

In America, however, the potato was widely appreciated, especially after Thomas Jefferson went to France in the 1780s and gained an appreciation for French cooking. He particularly enjoyed *pommefrites*, and when he became president, had them served at White House dinners—the elegant, tasteful French fry.

Oh, yes, the potato chip. It was invented by George Crum in 1853, when an irate diner sent back the fried potatoes because they weren't crunchy enough.

# MARCH 15

Today is the Ides of March.

*In many cultures, herbal baths are an important ritual. The bathers believe that when certain herbs are added to the bath water, they release not only their scent but their special energies. The bath based on the protective herb rosemary, for instance, was thought to make the bather safe from the forces of negativity and evil. To re-create this ritual for yourself, put a cup and a half of rosemary leaves and one-half cup each of bay leaves, basil, and fennel into a quart jar. Pour boiling water over the herbs and let them steep. Strain into a warm bath. Relax, feeling safe and cared for.*

—RUBY WILCOX, "PERSONAL HERBAL RITUALS," IN *ROSEMARY REMEMBERED: A CHINA BAYLES MYSTERY*

## An Unlucky Day?

Julius Caesar probably did more than anyone else to blacken the reputation of March 15, although for the Romans, there were quite a few other unlucky days. These included the *Kalends* (the first of each month), the *Nones* (the seventh or the fifth, depending on the month), and the *Ides* (the fifteenth or the thirteenth). And we all know what happens when the thirteenth falls on a Friday.

If unlucky days make you nervous, defend yourself with some the traditional protective herbs that have been used for millennia to ward off evil.

- Angelica: Wear it to protect yourself against evil spirits, but beware that it may also keep you from seeing opportunities.
- Borage: If you're concerned about dishonesty, plots, or secrets, place borage leaves or blossoms nearby and listen in. (Borage is said to encourage people to tell the truth.)
- Caraway: Wear the seeds in an amulet to protect against disease and ill health. Put some into your spouse's pocket to protect against infidelity.
- Dill: Hang a bunch of dill over a child's bed to protect against evil fairies.
- Lavender: Use the fresh or dried flowers, oil, perfume, or incense to protect and shield yourself and your home from negative energy.
- Marjoram: Sprinkle it across the threshold for protection against burglars and unwanted visitors.
- Pennyroyal: Burn it as an incense to protect against domestic abuse and violence in the home.
- Rue: Wear the fresh or dried herb in an amulet to protect yourself against illness.
- Rosemary: Bathe in Ruby's protective bath.

**Read more about the protective properties of herbs:**
*Magical Herbalism: The Secret Craft of the Wise*, by Scott Cunningham

*Depend on the rabbit's foot if you will, but remember it didn't work for the rabbit.*

—R. E. SHAY

# MARCH 16

*Laura Kermen is a Papago woman who, at the least, is in her eighties . . . [and] the winters wear hard on her. She therefore keeps a thermos of fresh-brewed creosote tea nearby to drink, and puts its branches in her bath water to ease the ache in her bones. The plant from which she gathers branches is the same one that her father used at the turn of the century.*

—GARY PAUL NABHAN, *GATHERING THE DESERT*

## "The Creosote Bush Is Our Drugstore"

In the deserts of the Southwest, and in Southwestern gardens of native herbs, the creosote bush (*Larrea tridentata*) is blooming now. Its yellow blossoms are a bright accent against the glossy green of its resinous leaves, which are key to its survival through months of heat and drought. When it rains, the plant gives off a strong, tarry odor, which accounts for its common name. The Papago Indians call it greasewood. It is an ancient plant; remains have been found that are some 17,000 years old. Once it puts down roots, it's persistent, sending out satellite shoots—clones—that establish themselves in concentric circles around the original plant, which lives for about 200 years. One such family of cloned plants, called "King Clone" by botanists, has been estimated to be over 9,000 years old, which makes it among the oldest known living creatures.

Creosote bush has a richly diverse history of documented medicinal use by Southwestern Indians, who have used it as a universal remedy to treat colds, lung ailments, intestinal problems, and wounds. Twigs and leaves are dried, powdered, and made into a tea or a poultice; they are also used in baths and sweat lodges. The resinous sap that the plant exudes is used for a variety of purposes. One Papago tribe member remarked that the plant "is our drugstore." Recent scientific studies have indicated that it is antimicrobial, anti-inflammatory, and antioxidant, although researchers caution against overuse.

If your climate is hot and dry, this ancient herbal shrub belongs in your garden. It requires little water and responds to occasional pruning with thicker branching and more foliage and flowers, which attract several species of bees. You can use it as a beautiful specimen plant, or as a hedge. And when you show it off to visitors, tell them that it deserves a great deal of respect. It has survived and thrived in our deserts much longer than humans!

**Explore the variety and usefulness of the native herbs of the Southwest:**
*Gathering the Desert*, by Gary Paul Nabhan

# MARCH 17

Today is St. Patrick's Day.

*May your blessings outnumber*
*The Shamrocks that grow.*
*And may trouble avoid you*
*Wherever you go.*
—IRISH BLESSING

## The Shamrock

Irish legends tell us that when St. Patrick brought Christianity to Ireland, he used the shamrock—the three-leaf clover—to teach the natives about the Holy Trinity, the Three-In-One. The word *shamrock* is derived from the Gaelic word *seamrog*, "summer plant." Long before St. Patrick, however, the herb was used by the ancient Celts as part of their fertility ritual. After the English took over Ireland, it took on still another meaning as a defiant symbol of rebellion: anyone caught "wearing the green" could be condemned to death as a traitor. Today, the shamrock is recognized around the world as a symbol of Ireland, especially on St. Patrick's Day, when everyone is Irish!

In the *Herbal* or *General History of Plants* (1597), John Gerard describes several important medicinal uses of the three-leaf clover, which he called trefoil. "The leaves boiled with a little barrowes grease [the fat of a neutered male pig], and used as a poultice, take away hot swellings and inflammations." To treat the eyes: "Trefoile (especially that with the black halfe Moon upon the leafe) stamped with a little honie, takes away the pin and web in the eies, ceaseth the paine and inflammation thereof. . . ."

In *The English Physician* (1652), the astrological herbalist Nicholas Culpeper says that the plant is ruled by Mercury, and adds: "Country people do also in many places drink the juice thereof against the biting of an adder; and having boiled the herb in water, they first wash the place with the decoction, and then lay some of the herb also to the hurt place."

**Read more about Irish herbs:**

*The Irish Herb Basket: An Illustrated Companion to Herbs*, by Hazel Evans

*Four-leaf clovers were good luck. Children saved these to take home and press in a book or they put them in their shoe:* **Four leaf clover in my shoe, Please to make my wish come true**

—JEANNÉ R. CHESANOW, *HONEYSUCKLE SIPPING: THE PLANT LORE OF CHILDHOOD*

# MARCH 18

*Years ago, I was very impatient with anyone us-*
*ing a long Latin name to designate a common,*
*ordinary plant. . . . I think it was the Pigweed,*
*more than anything else, that cured me of this*
*attitude.*

—EUELL GIBBONS, *STALKING THE WILD ASPARAGUS*

## Good King Henry

Seems like a strange name for a plant, doesn't it? But the stories behind the various names of this popular European herb are even stranger. (Or, as China Bayles would say, there's a mystery here.)

The name came to England from Germany, where the same herb was called *Guter Heinrich*, "Good Heinrich." (The name Heinrich was used to refer to a shrewd or knavish sprite, like the English Robin Goodfellow, or Puck.) Some people say that the herb was called "good Heinrich" to distinguish it from a similar poisonous plant called "bad Heinrich." In Latin, this plant is called *Chenopodium bonus-henricus*. Its folk name "smearwort" refers to its use as an ointment, and to poultices made of the leaves to cleanse and heal chronic sores, which, John Gerard tells us in his 1597 *Herbal*, "they do scour and mundify." The roots were given to sheep as a remedy for cough. The plant was fed to chickens in Germany and was called there *Fette Henne*—or perhaps the leaves were eaten as a vegetable with butter or bacon ("fat"). In any event, it's often referred to in the northern English counties as "fat hen."

### PIGWEED, GOOSEFOOT, AND LAMB'S QUARTERS

In North America, we have our own variety of this useful plant, *Chenopodium album*, which also has a great many common names, among them lamb's quarters, goosefoot, pigweed, and wild spinach. Raw or cooked, it's a tasty spring vegetable. The flower spikes can be eaten like broccoli and the new shoots like asparagus, tossed in butter, while the dried seeds, ground and mixed with wheat flour, make delicious pancakes. The seeds produce a green dye and were also used in the production of untanned leather. Of greater importance, the *Chenopodium* family is used medicinally throughout the world, primarily to treat gastrointestinal ailments.

What's in a name? A little bit of everything!

**Read more about Good King Henry, or whatever name you know it by:**
*A Modern Herbal*, by Mrs. Maud Grieve, 1931
*Stalking the Wild Asparagus*, by Euell Gibbons

*I use lamb's quarters all summer long to add*
*green to a meal, whether cooked or in a salad. I*
*stir-fry onions, garlic, and lamb's quarters into*
*an omelet for breakfast . . . [It] can even grace*
*an elegant dish like quiche [as a substitute for*
*spinach].*

—SUSAN TYLER HITCHCOCK, *GATHER YE WILD THINGS*

# MARCH 19

In the Celtic Tree Calendar, yesterday began the Month of the Alder (March 18–April 14).

> *In Irish legend the first human male was created from alder, as the first female was created from rowan. Alder was anciently regarded as a "faerie tree" able to grant access to faerie realms.*
>
> —JACQUELINE MEMORY PATERSON, *TREE WISDOM*

## The Legendary Alder

According to legend, the fertility gods were holding a feast, and all the plants and trees were invited to join in the party. The alder and the willow, however, stood by themselves, looking out over the water. This annoyed the party's host, who told them that if that's what they wanted to do, they could do it forever. Which is why you will still find the alder and the willow, growing together along the riverside.

### THE MAGICAL ALDER

When an alder tree is cut (it is said), the white inner fibers turn reddish-pink, appearing to bleed. To early people, this made the tree seem magically human. Welsh heroes stained their faces red with the "blood" of the alder, in honor of the god Bran, to whom the tree was sacred. Alder twigs made excellent pipes and whistles, used to call the ravens, Bran's sacred birds, or to "whistle up the wind," as it was said. Druid priests used alder wands to measure the dead; hence, to handle an alder wand invited death, and an alder branch could be used to curse your enemies. The fairies found the alder useful, as well, making a green dye from the flowers for their fairy smocks and breeches.

### THE HEALING ALDER

Thomas Culpeper, the seventeenth-century herbalist, prescribed alder tea as a wash for burns, inflammations, and skin irritations. The leaves were used as a poultice, and the inner root bark as an emetic.

### THE PRACTICAL ALDER

The wood, which resists decay in water, has been much used to build jetties and piles. Easy to work, it was used in cabinetry and to make spinning wheels and cart wheels and wooden clogs. It has been burned to produce charcoal for gunpowder. The bark yielded red and black dye; the leaves green. The leaves were used to tan leather.

**Read more about the alder:**
*Tree Wisdom*, by Jacqueline Memory Paterson

> *Cold March, wet April and hot May,*
> *Will make a fruitful year they say.*
> —BOKE OF FORTUNE 1575

# MARCH 20

Today is National Fragrance Day. The March theme garden: A Fragrance Garden.

> *The walled square contained five gardens, one in each corner and one in the middle. The corner to the right was the kitchen garden, bordered by sprawling thyme, with clumps of marjoram and parsley and sage in the center and a handsome rosemary at the back. One of the back corners was a fragrance garden, with old roses climbing against the stone wall . . .*
>
> —RUEFUL DEATH: A CHINA BAYLES MYSTERY

## A Fragrance Garden

A garden's fragrance gives me enormous pleasure, making the difference between a pleasant garden experience and one that lingers in my mind and my heart. If you're planning to create a new space in your garden this year, think about creating a fragrance garden—or if you've run out of garden room, consider adding a few pots of fragrant herbs and flowers to your deck or sunny porch, preferably near a window, so that the magic of scent can fill your home.

## Herbs for a Fragrance Garden: A Baker's Dozen

**ANNUALS AND TENDER PERENNIALS**
Sweet alyssum (*Lobularia maritima*)
Sweet pea (*Lathyrus odoratus*)
Pineapple sage (*Salvia elegans*)
Rosemary (*Rosmarinus officinalis*)

**PERENNIALS**
Southernwood (*Artemisia abrotanum*)
Dianthus (*Dianthus caryophyllus*)
Day lily (*Hemerocallis sp.*)
Lavender (*Lavandula sp.*)
Thyme (*Thymus vulgaris*)
Violet (*Viola odorata*)

**VINES AND SHRUBS**
Honeysuckle (*Lonicera sp.*)
Passionflower (*Passiflora incarnata*)
Rose (*Rosa sp.*)

**Read more about the fragrant herbs and about creating a theme garden:**
*Herbs and the Fragrant Garden*, by Margaret E. Brownlow
*Theme Gardens*, by Barbara Damrosch

> *In the spring, at the end of the day, you should smell like dirt.*
>
> —MARGARET ATWOOD

# MARCH 21

Zodiac: Today, the Sun enters the astrological sign of Aries. It is also the Spring Equinox.

> *Aries, the Ram, the first sign of the Zodiac, is a masculine sign ruled by the warrior planet Mars. A cardinal sign—suggesting creativity and inventiveness, Aries governs leadership and initiative. Aries people are bold, self-confident, and often impulsive, although they may have a tendency to look before they leap.*
>
> —RUBY WILCOX, "ASTROLOGICAL SIGNS"

## Aries Herbs

Mars-ruled Aries is assertive, energetic, fearless. According to astrologers, Mars rules the circulation of the blood, the muscles, and metabolic processes, as well as the motor nerves and the head. Astrological herbalists assigned "assertive" herbs to Mars: plants that are thorny or prickly, or have a strong, biting taste, or have a red color, to match the planet. Here are three examples:

- Garlic (*Allium sativum*). Garlic has traditionally been used to reduce blood pressure and blood cholesterol, as well as to destroy harmful bacteria. Nicholas Culpeper (*The English Physician*, 1652) cautions that Aries-ruled people with fiery dispositions should be careful how they use garlic.
- Mustard (*Brassica alba* or *nigra*). This favorite Mars-ruled spice is used to stimulate circulation and, in a poultice, to relieve muscle pain. Culpeper and others of his day also used mustard as a cleansing emetic or poultice: "It resists the force of poison, the malignity of mushrooms, and venom of scorpions, or other venomous creatures, if it be taken in time."
- Nettles (*Urtica diocia*). Nettles are rich in Mars-ruled iron and are covered with stinging prickles. As an astringent, nettle is used to relieve nosebleeds or reduce hemorrhage (especially excessive menstrual flow). It has also been used to treat the discomforts of an enlarged prostate.
- Other Mars-ruled herbs: Cayenne stimulates the circulation. Red clover, hops, radish, rhubarb, and sassafras are used to purify the blood. Ginger is a powerful circulatory stimulant and may be used as a poultice to treat muscle sprains.

**Read more about herbs and astrology:**
*Earth Mother Astrology: Ancient Healing Wisdom*, by Marcia Starck

> *It [Nicholas Culpeper's herbal] resorts for every mode of cure to that infallible source prepared by God and Nature in the vegetable system; whence flows spontaneously the genuine virtues of medicine diffused universally over the face of the earth, where nothing grows in vain.*
>
> —PREFACE, *THE ENGLISH PHYSICIAN*, BY NICHOLAS CULPEPER,
> 1789 EDITION

## Mesquite Spring: From Susan's Journal

The leaves are coming out on the mesquite trees, a sure sign of spring. Ranchers in this part of the country hate mesquite with nearly the same passion that they hate prickly pear cactus. The trees (*Prosopis glandulosa*) are deep-rooted and compete with grass for the limited water. And, back in the days when cows were rounded up by real cowboys on real horses, you could lose half your herd in a thorny mesquite thicket. In fact, mesquite is on the Texas list of invasive species, for like most native plants, it is highly adaptable, and when it finds a place it likes, it settles down, makes itself at home, and begins populating the neighborhood with others of its kind.

However, there's not a lot of cattle ranching around here now, and it's harder than it used to be to object to mesquite. The bees adore the flowers, and the

mesquite honey they produce is a finger-lickin' favorite. The tree is perfect for Xeriscaping (as long as you don't let the kids go barefoot where they can step on the thorns). The wood is popular for barbecue (I hear that they love it in New York), and the beans (gathered when they're green) make a delicious jelly. Native Americans processed the dried beans into flour, which was in turn made into flatbread and booze. The leaves and bark are astringent and antibacterial; a tea was used to treat bladder infections and diarrhea. The gum became a glue to mend pottery and a black dye used in weaving.

The tree itself has a lovely shape and color—twisted trunk, pale green canopy, tiny bee-laden flowers in May and clusters of beans in September. And I love the idea that mesquite always knows when spring has come and it's safe to put out leaves. No late freeze, say the dozens of mesquites here at Meadow Knoll. Warm days ahead, and blue skies, and inevitably, summer. And mesquite beans. Oh, yes, and jelly.

**Read more about mesquite:**
*The Magnificent Mesquite*, by Ken E. Rogers

*When in the spring, [mesquite] trees and bushes put on their delicately green, transparent leaves and the mild sun shines upon them, they are more beautiful than any peach orchard. The green seems to float through the young sunlight into the sky. The mesquite is itself a poem.*

—J. FRANK DOBIE, SOUTHWESTERN FOLKLORIST

Today is National Chip and Dip Day.

*Spring is nature's way of saying, "Let's party!"*
—ROBIN WILLIAMS

## The Merryweathers Dip Their Chips

The Pecan Springs herbies are always looking for an excuse for a party, so when Millie Winswell proposed that everybody bring a favorite dip to the March meeting to celebrate Chip and Dip Day, there was instant and unanimous agreement. Things got even more exciting when Bitsie Rae Smith suggested a competition. Who would do the judging? What was the prize? When nobody wanted to take on the politically challenging task of judging, it was decided that everybody would judge, and cast votes for the top three. Bitsie Rae objected that everybody would vote for her own dip as number 1, but Pansy Pride pointed out that since this was true, it wouldn't matter—all those votes would cancel one another out. Pansy also suggested that the prize ought to be a secret until the magic moment when it was awarded. Everybody agreed to this, and they all went home to whip up their dips.

So who won?

Well, it was close, I'll tell you, and the judging took quite awhile. But finally the last chip had been dipped and the last veggie dunked and the final vote was cast. And Denise Dolittle's entry, A Dilly of a Smoked Salmon Dip, came out on top, by the narrow margin of three votes. Which just goes to show, Pansy Pride said, when she rose to award the grand prize, that everybody's dip was a winner. Here's how Denise did it:

**A DILLY OF A SMOKED SALMON DIP**

- 1½ cups flaked smoked salmon
- ¾ cup mayonnaise
- ½ cup sour cream
- 3 tablespoons chopped sun-dried tomatoes
- 3 tablespoons chopped fresh dill
- 2 tablespoons prepared horseradish
- 2 tablespoons finely minced green onion tops
- salt and pepper to taste

Combine all ingredients in a bowl. Cover and chill at least 2 hours. Stir before serving. Makes about 2¾ cups. Serve with chips, crackers, raw veggies, and other dippables.

And the Grand Prize? It was wheeled out in a little red wagon, wrapped and tied with a fancy green bow. Everybody waited expectantly, holding her breath, while Denise pulled off the wrapping paper. And then they let their breath out, all at once, and everybody began to giggle, because the Grand Prize was . . .

Yep, you guessed it.

Harold Thompson's concrete armadillo.

# MARCH 24

*It's not easy being green.*

—KERMIT THE FROG

## French Green

It's time for some green. Green French sorrel, that is. *Rumex scutatus*, that fresh-tasting, tart perennial herb that may be putting up its first green leaves in your garden. (Or you might have a larger-leafed garden sorrel, *Rumex acetosa*, with a not-so-tart taste.) Most cooks prefer French sorrel for that first green soup of spring: lemony-tart, crisp-tasting, and loaded with vitamin C. Here's a recipe for a tasty soup that's easy and quick to make. (See, Kermit? It's actually easy to be green!)

### SPRING GREEN SORREL SOUP

    3 cups vegetable broth
    2 tablespoons instant white rice, uncooked
    1 bunch sorrel, stemmed and rinsed
    ½ cup half-and-half
    salt and pepper to taste

Bring vegetable broth to a boil in a large saucepan over medium heat. Stir in rice, reduce to a simmer, and cook for 8–10 minutes, until rice is nearly done. Stir in sorrel and return to a boil. Remove from heat and puree in two or three batches in a blender. Return to low heat and stir in half-and-half, salt, and pepper. Heat and serve. Makes 6 servings.

Other uses for sorrel:

- mix with other greens for a salad
- add it to potato soup
- include it in a tangy sauce for poultry or fish
- add it to sandwiches with cream cheese and sliced tomatoes
- use as a garnish for salmon and tuna
- use a fresh leaf to soothe a canker sore
- the juice curdles milk, and has been used as a substitute for rennet in cheese making
- was used to staunch bleeding and to treat scurvy

**Read more about sorrel and other spring potherbs:**

*The Greens Book*, by Susan Belsinger and Carolyn Dille

*Our country people used to beat the herb [sorrel] to a mash and take it mixed with vinegar and sugar, as a green sauce with cold meat, hence one of its popular names: Greensauce. Because of their acidity, the leaves, treated as spinach, make a capital dressing with stewed lamb, veal or sweetbread. A few of the leaves may also with advantage be added to turnips and spinach. When boiled by itself, without water, it serves as an excellent accompaniment to roast goose or pork, instead of apple sauce.*

—MRS. MAUD GRIEVE, A MODERN HERBAL, 1931

Today is National Waffle Day.

*The waffle is descended from the oublie, a flat cake cooked between two hot plates and stamped with a crucifix, used in the celebration of the Eucharist. Sometime in the thirteenth century, a craftsman forged the plates in a honeycomb pattern; in Holland, the resulting cake was called a wafel. The word seems to have first appeared in America in 1744, when a lady remarked: "I was not a little grieved that so luxurious a feast should have come under the name of a wafel frolic."*

## A Waffle Frolic

There's no rule that says that waffles are just for breakfast. Why not celebrate National Waffle Day by throwing a waffle frolic? Herbed waffles for brunch, lunch, or supper are bound to get rave reviews from anybody lucky enough to enjoy a plateful.

### WAFFLES WITH SAVORY HERBS
    5 ounces unsalted butter
    1½ cups milk
    2 eggs, lightly beaten
    2 tablespoons minced fresh chives
    1 tablespoon minced fresh thyme
    1 tablespoon minced fresh parsley
    1 tablespoon minced fresh sage
    2 cups flour
    4 teaspoons baking powder
    1 teaspoon salt
    2 tablespoons sugar

Heat butter and milk until butter is melted. Cool slightly. Whisk eggs into butter/milk mixture. Stir in fresh herbs. Sift dry ingredients together and add to liquid ingredients, stirring just to mix. Bake waffles according to waffle iron instructions, greasing iron well. Excellent with creamed chicken. Serves 4.

Four frolicsome toppers for waffles:
- smoked salmon and snipped dill with cream cheese
- chopped tomato, chopped scallions, basil
- avocado, sun-dried tomatoes, pine nuts, oregano
- poached eggs, artichoke hearts, snipped fresh parsley, chives, and thyme

**Cook up some waffles and pancakes:**
*Pancakes and Waffles,* by Lou Seibert Pappas

*A windy and a dry March is good for corn but evil for old folks and child-bearing women.*
—DOVE'S ALMANACK, 1627

## Rhubarb Isn't for Everybody

This truth was impressed upon me as a child, when my mother grew rhubarb in the garden. She called it pie plant, and made it into a pie. I made for my bedroom. I'd rather do my homework than eat rhubarb pie. I thought it tasted like medicine.

No wonder. Some five millennia ago, the Chinese and Russians were using dried, powdered rhubarb root as an effective laxative. They considered this plant enormously valuable, and used it as a cure-all for everything from the plague to the stomachache. When Marco Polo returned from China in the late thirteenth century, he brought back reports of this miracle plant, which whetted everyone's appetite for it. But the dried root wasn't easy to transport and the plant itself didn't thrive in Europe. What's more, the Chinese and Russians didn't take kindly to foreigners who wanted their rhubarb. By the time of Henry VIII, rhubarb—when you could get it—was almost worth its weight in gold.

But the price of rhubarb was about to take a dive. In the 1630s, Sir Matthew Lister brought a Siberian variety to England. For a while, the plant was cultivated only for the root, which was used as a laxative even though it was only a relative of the storied Chinese rhubarb. But in a cold climate where fresh fruits were impossible to obtain in winter, its tart, fresh taste was a treat. And since rhubarb is high in vitamin C, it was a healthy addition to the dinner table. The rhubarb we grow in our gardens is no longer considered a medicinal herb. And the leaves aren't edible, for they contain oxalic acid. But the stalks are used, with plenty of sugar, to make pretty ruby-colored pies, jams, sauces, and even wine.

And now that I'm older and maybe a little wiser, I like rhubarb just fine, especially when China bakes her rhubarb streusel pie.

**CHINA'S RHUBARB STREUSEL PIE**
- 1 unbaked pie shell
- 1½ cups frozen rhubarb, diced
- 1 cup granulated sugar
- 4 tablespoons flour
- 1 egg, beaten
- ½ cup brown sugar
- 1 teaspoon cinnamon
- ½ teaspoon nutmeg
- 2 tablespoons margarine

Mix rhubarb, granulated sugar, 2 tablespoons of the flour, and egg. Pour into pie shell. Mix brown sugar, the remaining 2 tablespoons flour, spices, and margarine, and sprinkle it over the top. Bake at 425° for 15 minutes, then at 350° for 30 minutes longer. Serve warm, with ice cream or whipped cream.

**Read more about the history and migrations of rhubarb:**
*Rhubarb: The Wondrous Drug*, by Clifford M. Foust

When Easter comes in early April, Palm Sunday falls in late March.

*And on the next day much people that were come to the feast, when they heard that Jesus was coming to Jerusalem, took branches of palm trees and went forth to meet him, and cried, Hosanna: Blessed is the King of Israel that cometh in the name of the Lord.*

—JOHN 12:12–13

## "As Many Uses as There Are Days in the Year"

On the Sunday before Easter (the fifth Sunday of Lent), Christians remember Christ's triumphant entry into Jerusalem, when he was greeted by cheering crowds waving palms. Traditionally, in many Christian churches, palm crosses are carried in processions, blessed, and given to be taken home.

The palm tree of the Bible is the date palm, *Phoenix dactylifera*. Its leaves were used to cover the roofs of houses, its trunk was used for timber, rope was made from the fibers of the crown, and the fruit was one of the region's major food staples. Both wine and an intoxicating drink (called "honey" by the Hebrews) was brewed from the flowers, and the leaves were ritually strewn in processions. Dates were used as a healing salve, a cardiac stimulant, and as a treatment in respiratory disorders. The ancient Arab saying that the palm tree has as many uses as there are days in the year seems quite literally true. So if you live in a tropical climate and have palms in your yard or your neighborhood, smile when you see them and remember that these herbal trees have blessed humans since the beginning.

### THE "ENGLISH PALM"

In England and Europe, Palm Sunday was celebrated with other kinds of early-flowering greenery: box, yew, and especially branches of pussy willow, also called the "English palm." In many places, young people went "a-Palming" at dawn, returning to the church with willow boughs and wearing catkins in their hair. (This custom was not always pious. John Aubrey, in his *Miscellanies* (1696) remarked dryly: "This day gives many a Conception.") Once blessed, the greenery was taken home and hung up in the house, where it would protect the family from evil all through the year.

**Read more about palms:**

*Plants of the Bible*, by Harold N. Moldenke and Alma L. Moldenke

*Balls for Lent. Grate white bread, nutmeg, salt, shred parsley, a very little thyme, and a little orange or lemon-peel cut small; make them up into balls with beaten eggs, or you may add a spoonful of Cream; and roll them up in flour, and fry them.*

—E. SMITH, *THE COMPLEAT HOUSEWIFE*, 1736

# MARCH 28

*Feelings, whether of compassion or irritation, should be welcomed, recognized, and treated on an absolutely equal basis; because both are ourselves. The tangerine I am eating is me. The mustard greens I am planting are me. I plant with all my heart and mind. I clean this teapot with the kind of attention I would have were I giving the baby Buddha or Jesus a bath. Nothing should be treated more carefully than anything else. In mindfulness, compassion, irritation, mustard green plant, and teapot are all sacred.*

—THICH NHAT HANH, *THE MIRACLE OF MINDFULNESS*

## Mustard Greens Are Sacred: From Susan's Journal

In our part of Texas, the wild mustard (*Brassica kaber*) has been blooming along the roads for several weeks. This herb—a member of the family that includes broccoli, cauliflower, Brussels sprouts, cabbages, and radishes—grows everywhere, and is generally considered a weed. But I have mustard (*Brassica sp.*) in my herb garden, too. And I treasure Thich Nhat Hanh's gentle reminder: The mustard green is sacred, as are all plants, all people and things, all feelings.

Mustard greens were among my mother's favorite garden vegetables, appearing on our table as soon as the leaves started showing up in our Illinois garden. Mom cooked them with fat back and served them with corn bread, the way her grandmother taught her to do it. Comfort food, simple and good. I can smell it still, and taste it, but just thinking of it makes me smile.

When I grow mustard for greens, I plant it in the fall or in early spring, three weeks before the last frost date. For a fall harvest, I plant from midsummer on; in my warm Texas garden, the fall plantings are better, because the cooler weather delays the inevitable bitterness. I pick the lower leaves while they're young and tender, and get a come-again harvest. Mustard is one of the healthiest plants in the garden, containing the important antioxidants beta carotene and vitamin C. Mustard greens also contain calcium (important to lactose intolerant individuals) and a significant amount of iron.

What I like to do with mustard greens:

- Add the leaves to salads;
- Sauté them with walnuts, water chestnuts, and lemon juice;
- Add them to a warm pasta salad. My favorite: hot cooked pasta, with chopped hot cooked mustard greens, chopped tomatoes, a few nuts, and feta cheese, tossed with hot Italian dressing;
- Cook them the way Mom did; and
- Remember that mustard is every bit as sacred as my teapot and me.

**Read more about cooked greens and other Southern comfort food:**
*The Taste of Country Cooking*, by Edna Lewis

# MARCH 29

*I followed Leatha into the house. She had stopped at Maggie's restaurant and bought a carton of thick tomato soup, Maggie's broccoli salad (she makes it Greek-style, with feta cheese and olives and gives you a separate container of olive-oil dressing), and two walnut and cinnamon-basil cupcakes. While I washed my hands and dug most of the dirt from under my nails, she spread everything on the kitchen table, picnic style. I found two bottles of homemade root beer in the refrigerator, and we settled down.*

—WITCHES' BANE: A CHINA BAYLES MYSTERY

## Beautiful, Bountiful Basil

If you live in the south, you'll find basil plants (*Ocimum basilicum*) in your local nursery now. But most nurseries stock only one or two varieties, so if you're planning to grow different varieties, seeds are your best bet. Start your crop indoors about 4 weeks before you'd put tomato plants into your garden. Sow each variety in a separate container at least 6 inches deep and 18 inches wide. Sift a thin layer of potting medium over the seeds, and water well. When the plants germinate, move the containers into a sunny spot. When they have one or two sets of true leaves, thin with scissors, leaving them spaced an inch apart. In another week, take them outside to harden off, then transplant into your garden.

## FIVE BASIL FAVORITES

- Sweet Genovese Basil. The perfect pesto basil. Full flavor, bright green leaf. Traditional Italian variety.
- Lemon Basil. Culinary, intense lemon flavor, bright green leaves. Great with fish and chicken or fruit salads
- Cinnamon Basil. Culinary, ornamental. Violet stems, lavender flowers. Cinnamon flavor, especially good with Middle Eastern and Asian cuisine. Delicious in fruit salad dressings.
- Purple Ruffles Basil. Culinary, ornamental. Ruffled purple leaves on a compact plant, with a scent of cloves and licorice. Makes a beautiful cranberry-colored flavored vinegar.
- Thai Basil. Culinary, ornamental. Attractive red stems and flowers, green leaves. Licorice-basil aroma. Essential for Thai cuisine.

**Read more about basil:**

*Basil: An Herb Lover's Guide*, by Thomas DeBaggio and Susan Belsinger

*The ordinary Basil is . . . wholly spent to make sweete or washing waters among other sweet herbs, yet sometimes it is put into nosegays. The Physicall properties are to procure a cheerfull and merry hearte whereunto the seeds are chiefly used in pouder.*

—JOHN PARKINSON, A GARDEN OF PLEASANT FLOWERS, 1629

# MARCH 30

*I like to pluck a handful of blossoms and toss them over a spring salad. . . . Redbud's cheery color brightens white desserts like custard or rice pudding: just stir in a handful of blossoms before you set the dish in the oven to bake. And homemade ice cream can be infused with the pastel color and flavor of early redbud blooms.*

—SUSAN TYLER HITCHCOCK, GATHER YE WILD THINGS

## The Many Virtues of Redbuds

The redbud trees (*Cercis canadensis* var. *texensis*) are in bloom this week around the margins of our little woodland, their purple flowers like a cloud of color, brightening the darker oaks and elms around them. Green leaves will replace the flowers in another week or two, and by the end of summer the tree will be hung with purple-brown fruits, pods four inches long, flat and leathery. These lovely trees are worth growing for their stunning beauty, at a time of year when most other trees are still thinking about putting out their first leaves. But loveliness is only one of the many virtues of this little North American native.

### THE MEDICINAL REDBUD

Dried and powdered, the inner bark was an important medicine. Indian healers used it to staunch bleeding, ease skin irritations and poison ivy rash, and treat sores and tumors. Bark tea was drunk to treat diarrhea and dysentery and used (like quinine) to reduce malarial fevers and ease joint and muscle pain and headaches. The flowers were also steeped as a tea and drunk to prevent scurvy, treat kidney and bladder infections, and ease urinary ailments.

### THE EDIBLE REDBUD

The buds can be pickled: Cover with a pickling brine of 1 quart cider vinegar, 1 teaspoon salt, 6 cloves, 1 2-inch cinnamon stick, and ½ teaspoon each allspice and celery seed; ready in about 2 weeks. The flowers are tossed in salads to add tartness and color. The buds, flowers, and tender young pods are sautéed for 10 minutes in butter and eaten as a vegetable. Native Americans roasted the pods in ashes before eating the seeds.

### THE PLIABLE REDBUD

The supple young sprouts, peeled and stripped, can be used in the construction of baskets. Some tribes used the white inner bark or the red outer bark as decorative elements in very sophisticated work. The bark was also used as cordage and coarse twine, and the roots were used in sewing animal skins.

**Read more about redbud:**
*Gather Ye Wild Things: A Forager's Year*, by Susan Tyler Hitchcock

*In the end, there is really nothing more important than taking care of the earth and letting it take care of you.*

—CHARLES SCOTT

## Cattails: The Generous Plant

### CATTAILS, CATTAILS, AND MORE CATTAILS

Even if you don't immediately recognize the cattail's swordlike leaves (green in the growing season, red-brown in the winter), you'll notice its unmistakable stalk, topped with a brown, cigar-shaped flower spike in the summer and a cottony, gray-white seed head in the winter. What you won't see (unless you dig for it) is the rhizome—the thick, fleshy root from which the cattail stalk grows. It's impossible to have just one cattail: A healthy rhizome system, sometimes 15 feet in diameter, produces dozens of stalks, which is why this plant can be invasive.

### STALKING THE COSSACK'S ASPARAGUS

The cattail's generosity begins with its edible roots and shoots. Native peoples dug the rhizomes in winter, because that's when they are crisp and sweet. In the spring, before the flowers began to develop, they stalked the young shoots (in Russia, called "Cossack's asparagus"), which look like leeks and taste something like cucumbers. The edible core is rich in beta carotene, niacin, riboflavin, thiamin, potassium, phosphorus, vitamin C, and plant protein. Cold-weather root- and shoot-gathering is not a picnic, but Indians and settlers couldn't just stop at the local supermarket to stock up on staples.

If you're still hungry when summer comes, you can stalk the flower. The cattail (a primitive plant that was already old when the dinosaurs were young) has a pollen-producing male flower spike (small, always on top) and a seed-producing female (always under the male)—a reasonable (if not politically correct) arrangement. In late spring, the male spike is covered with a saffron-yellow pollen. Bend the flower spike into a paper bag, tap or shake off the loose yellow pollen, and sift out any trash. Substitute up to ¼ or ½ cup of pollen for an equal amount of flour in your favorite pancake or biscuit recipe or use to top yogurt, cereals, and salads.

One Indian tribe's name for cattail was translated as "fruit for papoose's bed," because the fluffy masses of seeds are soft and do not mat. During World War II, several million pounds of seed pods were collected (much of it by children) and used to stuff life jackets, flight suits, mattresses, and pillows.

**More Reading:**
*Identifying and Harvesting Edible and Medicinal Plants in Wild (and Not So Wild) Places*, by Steve Brill
*Stalking the Wild Asparagus*, by Euell Gibbons

April

May

June

Today is April Fool's Day.

*The first of April, of all days in the year, enjoys a character of its own. On this day, it becomes the business of a vast number of people, especially the younger sort, to practice innocent impostures upon their unsuspicious neighbors, by way of making them what in France are called* poissons d'Avril, *and with us April fools.*

—R. CHAMBERS, THE BOOK OF DAYS, 1869

## Fern Seeds Will Make You Invisible!

One of the favorite April Fool tricks of bygone days was to give somebody a packet of fern seed, telling him that if he carried it in his pocket, he'd be invisible. Yes, I know. Ferns can't make you invisible. But that was part of the April Fool trick, and a lot of people fell for it.

The connection between fern seed and invisibility goes back to the times when it was thought that all plants reproduced from seed. Well, then, it was logical. If there are no visible seeds, the seeds must be invisible. And if your logic took you that far, it could take you one step farther: put some of those fern seeds in your pocket, and you would be invisible, too.

Since Midsummer Night's Eve was known to be a magical night, it was obviously the best time to collect these magical, mythical, mysterious fern seeds. On that night in Bohemia, girls spread white cloths under the ferns to catch the seeds, which could not only make them invisible, but lead them to a vein of gold. In Brittany, fern seed collected on Midsummer Night could be kept until the next Palm Sunday, when it would show the way to treasure. And in Austria, fern seed tossed into a cache of money would keep that money from decreasing in value. Quite a reputation for something that couldn't be seen!

It wasn't until 1848 that the real mystery of fern reproduction was solved, and botanists understood the two-phase process that involves both asexual and sexual reproduction. But folklore has a long life. Which is why people could be April Fooled, and why stories about "invisible fern seeds" still appear as late as the beginning of the twentieth century.

Ferns have been used to treat a variety of physical ailments, from wounds and burns to intestinal parasites. The immature, coiled fronds are edible—in New England, the steamed and buttered fiddleheads of the ostrich fern are considered a great delicacy—and the dried fronds are used in basketry and papermaking, and as ornamentals.

**Read more about the secret life of ferns:**
*A Natural History of Ferns*, by Robbin C. Moran

*April, Comes like an idiot, babbling, and strewing flowers.*

—EDNA ST. VINCENT MILLAY

*It is a tradition with many, that a wreath made of Periwinkle and bound about the legs, defendeth them from cramp . . . And Mr. Culpeper writeth, that Periwinkle leaves eaten by man and wife together cause love—which is a rare quality indeed, if it be true.*

—WILLIAM COLES, *THE ART OF SIMPLING*, 1656

## Periwinkle Blue

The periwinkles (*Vinca minor*) are flowering in my Texas garden today, their blossoms like beautiful blue stars scattered among the dark green leaves, brightening the shady places under the oak trees. The generic name of this pretty groundcover derives from the Latin *vincio* ("to bind"), a fact I am reminded of every time I pull weeds in that bed. The long, trailing stems are like tough little ropes. No wonder they have been used for twine!

There are other periwinkles in my garden, too. Beside a rock wall (where this invasive plant can be easily controlled) is a bed of *Vinca major*—same blue flowers, but a larger leaf and longer, arching stems. And I just brought home a dozen *Catharanthus roseus*, the Madagascar periwinkle, for containers on the deck. The blooms run the gamut from white to neon pink to bold purple. This little beauty has been recently reclassified from *Vinca* to *Catharanthus*, but trust me: It's still a first cousin to *Vinca minor*.

In Jamaica, periwinkle was drunk as a tea to ease the symptoms of diabetes. In India and Hawaii, the leaves were used as a poultice to treat wasp stings. In China, the leaves were dried, powdered, and used as an astringent, a diuretic, and a cough remedy. In Central and South America, periwinkle was a staple cold remedy, easing lung congestion and inflammation and sore throats. In the Caribbean islands, an extract from the flowers was used as an eyewash, and the leaves were chewed to ease toothache. Scientists say that the plant contains a host of useful alkaloids, some of which lower blood sugar levels, while others lower blood pressure and still others have anticancer properties. Research is continuing on these useful plants.

The next time you're admiring the periwinkles in your garden, stop for a moment and think about all the things we have to learn about the plants we take so much for granted!

*Through primrose tufts, in that green bower,*
*The periwinkle trailed its wreaths;*
*And 'tis my faith that every flower*
*Enjoys the air it breathes.*

—WILLIAM WORDSWORTH

In the floral calendar, today's flower: white violet.

# APRIL 3

*We carried our lunch trays out to the sunny flagstone patio under my kitchen window, where the late-blooming butterfly weed was attracting the last of the hummingbirds, tanking up for their long haul to Mexico. If you sit out there for lunch in the summer, you'll be barbecued in nothing flat, but on an autumn day like today it was perfect, just the right mix of sun, cloud, and breeze, seasoned with the sweetly pungent odor of the sun-warmed creeping thyme that grows among the paving stones.*

*—THYME OF DEATH: A CHINA BAYLES MYSTERY*

## A Box of Thyme

If you're planning a thyme garden this year, now's the thyme (oh, dear!) to get started. A "thyme box"—a small raised garden (four-by-four feet is a good size) constructed of landscape timbers or boards—is an easy and attractive way to grow a collection of thymes. Use a good garden soil for your mix, with the addition of sand to improve the drainage, and put your garden where it will get a full day's sun. While thyme can be started from seed, beginning with plants will give your garden a head start. Shear the plants in midsummer to make them bushy (you'll have plenty of uses for the snips), and divide every three or four years.

Thyme is one of the basic herbs, grown not just for its culinary uses (it's an excellent seasoning for meat, poultry, and eggs), but also for its medicinal qualities, chiefly as an antiseptic, to combat infection. It was often burned as a fumigant to cleanse the air. As late as World War II, when it was called "Russian penicillin," thyme was used to heal wounds and prevent infections. And if you want to attract fairies, thyme is a must-have. Fairies are thought to be entranced by its wonderful odor, as are bees. Thyme honey is among the most prized honeys in the world.

### SOME THYMELY CHOICES

Thymes come in a wide variety of growth habits, colors, and fragrances. Since it ships well, you can also purchase plants on-line. Here are a few for you to consider:

- Common Thyme: *T. vulgaris*
- Common Thyme: silver, gold, fragrant. *T. vulgaris* cultivars: 'Argenteus,' 'Aureus,' 'Fragrantissimus,' 'Roseus'
- Creeping Thyme: *T. serpyllum*
- Caraway Thyme: *T. Herba-barona*
- Nutmeg Thyme: *T. Herba-barona* v. "Nutmeg"
- Wooly Thyme: *T. pseudolanuginosus*
- Camphor Thyme: *T. camphoratus*
- Lemon Thyme: *T. x citriodorus*
- Coconut thyme: *T. pulegiodes coccineus*

**Read more about thyme:**
*Growing and Using Thyme*, Story Country Wisdom Bulletin A-180, by Michelle Gillett

In some years, this is the Jewish Passover Seder, celebrated on the night of the fourteenth day of Nisan, the first month of the Jewish lunar year.

*The symbolic foods [of the Seder] include those laid down in the Talmud two thousand years ago: bitter herbs—originally wild romaine lettuce—to recall the harsh conditions the Israelites endured; haroset, to remind us of the mortar they had to form; and above all matzah, called* lechem oni, *the unleavened bread of poverty, but also the bread of freedom, for on the night the Israelites left Egypt, their sourdough starter, the yeast of biblical times, had had no time to rise.*

—PHYLLIS GLAZER, *JEWISH FESTIVAL COOKING*

## Bitter Herbs

According to the Talmud, romaine (*Chasa*) is one of the herbs that may be eaten at Seder, with the unleavened matzah. Here are other herbs, native to the Mediterranean area, that may have been available for the Hebrews' use at the time of the first Seder:

• Endive (*Cichorium endivia* and *C. intybus*, also called chicory and radicchio) has a bitter flavor unless it is picked young or blanched.
• Watercress (*Nasturtium officinale*) was used by the Egyptians and early Greeks to increase strength and courage. It has a spicy tang.
• Sorrel (*Rumex acetosella*) was widely available in the spring.
• Dandelion (*Taraxacum officinale*) leaves were also readily available.
• Horseradish (*Cochlearia armoracia*) leaves, rather than the root, would have been eaten at this time of year.
• Nettle (*Urtica dioica*) leaves are rich in minerals.

## HAROSET

Haroset is a fruit-and-nut paste that symbolizes the mortar Jewish slaves used to build for their Egyptian masters. The recipes vary regionally, but all include fruit (dates, apples, figs, raisins, pomegranates), nuts (almonds, chestnuts, walnuts), and spices.

2 medium-size tart apples
½ cup almonds, chopped
1 teaspoon cinnamon
2–3 tablespoons orange juice
1 tablespoon sugar or honey, or to taste

Peel, core, and finely chop or grate the apples. Mix with the rest of the ingredients.

**To learn more about Jewish holiday food:**
*Jewish Festival Cooking: 200 Seasonal Holiday Recipes & Their Traditions*, by Phyllis Glazer with Miriyam Glazer

# APRIL 5

*Gardeners learn by trowel and error.*

—SHARON LOVEJOY

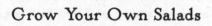

## Grow Your Own Salads

Salads taste better when they come straight from the garden to your salad bowl. What's more, the experience of growing your own may make you appreciate it even more. Here are some considerations for your salad garden.

- Visualize your favorite salad and list all its ingredients: lettuces and other spring greens, plus radishes, carrots, edible flowers, tomatoes, cucumbers, spinach, green onions, mustard.
- Plant your salad fixings close to the kitchen door, or in a collection of containers on your deck, filled with a lightweight potting medium. Plant seeds, water well, and add a solution of fish and/or seaweed fertilizer.
- Add herbs. Basil, cilantro, dill, parsley, and chives will spark any salad. Peppery, aromatic arugula, a trendy salad green, was once called "rocket" or "roquette." About it, one herbalist observes: "In the language of flowers, the Rocket has been taken to represent deceit, since it gives out a lovely perfume in the evening, but in the daytime has none. Hence its name of Hesperis, or Vesper-Flower, given it by the Ancients" (*The Modern Herbal*, 1931).
- Build a teepee trellis in the center and add a climber—Malabar spinach (*Basella rubra*) is nutritious and attractive, as is a climbing tomato. Growing your salads on a deck? Train your climber up a wall trellis.
- Plant an edible border (pretty, too): nasturtium, pansies, Johnny-jump-ups, calendula.
- Plant tight, harvest as you go. You can squeeze four leaf lettuces or four spinach plants into one square foot, or two chards, or a dozen green onion sets. Harvest the young leaves, and finally the whole plant. Then replant.
- Plan for all-season salads. Early Bibb lettuce yields to bush cucumbers. Tomatoes are followed by fall spinach and carrots.

**Read more about salads to grow:**
*The Edible Salad Garden*, by Rosalind Creasy

*The buds of the elder bush, gathered in early spring, and simmered with new butter, or sweet lard, make a very healing and cooling ointment.*

—MRS. CHILD, *THE AMERICAN FRUGAL HOUSEWIFE*, 1833

*Who soweth in raine,*
*hath weedes to his paine,*
*But worse shall he speed,*
*that soweth ill seed.*

—THOMAS TUSSER

*The pedigree of honey*
*Does not concern the bee;*
*A clover, any time, to him*
*Is aristocracy.*
—EMILY DICKINSON

*Don't wear perfume in the garden—unless you want to be pollinated by bees.*

—ANNE RAVER

## Befriending Bees

Plants can't set seed without pollination, and bees are among the best pollinators. Luckily for us humans, there are more than 3,500 native species of bees in the United States, and some of them are bound to live in your neighborhood. They'll drop in for a visit if your garden includes the plants they enjoy. Start planning now for a buzzing garden all year round—and do skip the toxic sprays. The bees will bless you for it.

- Timing is important. To attract different varieties of bees, plan for succession-blooming in spring, summer, and fall.
- Bee-utiful. Bees are attracted to yellow, purple, red, and blue blossoms. But unlike hummingbirds and moths, they can't negotiate long-tube flowers. Members of the *Compositae* family—cosmos, dahlias, zinnias, and sunflowers—are winners, but stay away from hybridized double varieties, which produce almost no pollen.
- Herbs are heavenly. Hyssop, lavender, rosemary, borage, mint, sage, catnip, butterfly weed, horehound, and boneset are especially attractive to bees.
- Weeds are wonderful. From the bee's point of view, any plant that provides nectar and pollen is wonderful—including dandelions and white clover, which we think of as weeds.
- Native is nicer. Wild bees are already adapted to the native plants of your area, so if you want to attract more bees, plant more natives. In many parts of the U.S., this will include wildflowers like coreopsis, gaillardia, basketflowers, toadflax, sunflowers, red clover, black-eyed Susans, and monarda.

**Read more about the secret society of bees:**

*Honey: From Flower to Table*, by Stephanie Rosenbaum

*Letters from the Hive: An Intimate History of Bees, Honey, and Humankind*, by Stephen Buchmann

*The bees have their definite plan for life, perfected through countless ages, and nothing you can do will ever turn them from it. You can delay their work, or you can even thwart it altogether, but no one has ever succeeded in changing a single principle in bee-life. And so the best bee-master is always the one who most exactly obeys the orders from the hive.*

—TICKNER EDWARDS, THE BEE-MASTER OF WARRILOW, 1907

# APRIL 7

*Tansy is very wholesome after the salt fish consumed during Lent, and counteracts the ill-effects which the moist and cold constitution of winter has made on people . . . though many understand [the eating] not, and some simple people take it for a matter of superstition to do so.*

—WILLIAM COLES, *THE ART OF SIMPLING*, 1656

## Tansy: A Lenten Mystery

There's a mystery about tansy. This herb (*Tanacetum vulgare*) tastes bitter and has traditionally been used to expel intestinal parasites, treat kidney ailments, and fever. So why would people use it to flavor a dish that celebrates the end of Lent? Some writers suggest that the tradition began with the celebration of the Jewish Passover and the eating of bitter herbs, adapted to Christian use. Other writers suggest that tansy was used as a blood cleanser after the rigors of Lenten fasting; over time, this reason was forgotten.

The herb was made more palatable by cooking it with other fresh greens in an egg-rich batter, a cross between a pancake and an omelet, strewn with sugar. As time went on, the dish was embellished, first with cream and spices, and then with breadcrumbs and more sugar, until it became a sweet pudding and finally a cake, often called simply "a tansy." The dish might include some symbolic tansy, but it was usually spinach juice that created the traditional green color.

This colonial recipe for tansy pudding comes from Mary Randolph's *The Virginia Housewife Or, Methodical Cook* (1832)—rather like a simple spinach soufflé without the spinach. No tansy? Substitute lemon juice, beating to incorporate.

### TANSY PUDDING

    4 eggs slightly beaten
    1 cup of cream
    ¾ cup of spinach juice mixed with a tablespoon of tansy
        juice
    1 cup of cracker crumbs
    ½ cup of sugar
    ½ teaspoon nutmeg

Mix all together and bake in a buttered dish until firm. It may also be cooked like an omelette. It looks green.

According to Alice Morse Earle (*Old Time Gardens*, 1901), the coffin of Jonathan Mitchell, exhumed, was found to be full of tansy. Mitchell, president of Harvard College, had died in 1668 of "an extream fever." The use of tansy at funerals, Earle reports, "lingered long in country neighborhoods in New England, in some vicinities till fifty years ago."

*Make no mistake: the weeds will win; nature bats last.*

—ROBERT M. PYLE

## The Wayfaring Plantain

If you have plantain (*Plantago major*) in your yard, you're not the only one. They're everywhere. In fact, some 200 species of this plant live in temperate regions around the globe. There's a romantic explanation for plantain's ubiquity. The plantain is said to have once been a maiden who gave her heart to a wayfaring man. Anxious for his return, she waited beside the roadway, weeping. One day, the goddess Demeter walked past and heard the maiden's sad story. "Well, my goodness," Demeter said in a reasonable tone, "if you feel that way about it, why don't you go find the fellow?"

And with that, the goddess transformed the maiden into a small, broadleaf plant, naming her from *planta*, the Latin word for the sole of the foot. And because the plantain would always be underfoot and in danger, Demeter made her immortal. She then sent the plantain on her way, commanding her to follow every road in the world until she found her lover.

The plantain took the goddess's command so seriously that the herbalist John Gerard commended her "great commoditie" for growing anywhere. But the footloose plantain had so many uses that most people welcomed her. The tender green leaves were cooked, or served in salads, or brewed into a tea. The leaf and root were used as a cure-all. Today, herbalists recommend the tea or tincture as a treatment for bronchitis and asthma, while the fresh leaves can be used as a poultice or steeped in an oil that will soothe sunburn, burns, superficial wounds, and skin inflammations.

When Demeter commanded the plantain to follow every road, she also made her immortal, a virtue greatly admired by the ancient Saxons. They included the plant among their nine sacred herbs, giving her the descriptive name Way-broad.

*And you Way-broad, Mother of plants!*
*Over you carts creaked*
*Over you queens rode*
*Over you brides bridled*
*Over you bulls breathed.*
*All these you withstood*
*And strongly resisted,*
*As you also withstand*
*Venomous and vile things*
*And all loathly ones*
*That rove through the land.*

So if you're thinking about spraying something venomous, vile, and loathly on the plantain in your yard, think again. You'll offend the goddess Demeter—and who knows what kind of plant she will turn you into!

*I found some leftover mashed potatoes in the fridge and made a pot of mashed potato soup—hot and tasty, with fresh parsley chopped into it and cheddar cheese grated on top. I was sitting at the table, working on my first bowl when Mc-Quaid showed up. "Want soup?" I asked. "There's some on the stove."*

*He picked up a spoon and tasted mine. "Not bad," he said. "Think I will." He found a bowl, ladled it full, and laced it with catsup.*

—HANGMAN'S ROOT: A CHINA BAYLES MYSTERY

## Parsley: A "Dangerous" Herb

Valued for its zippy taste, its bright green color, and its crisp texture, parsley is an all-around favorite, good in soup, and with vegetables, fish, and eggs. But for all its virtues, parsley has been said to have a darker side. To ensure that this "dangerous" herb would behave, gardeners traditionally planted it on Good Friday. And with the possible exception of basil, parsley may figure in more superstitious beliefs than any other herb. Here's a sample of its mysteries:

- Parsley seeds have to go down to the devil seven times before they can grow.
- Plant parsley only on Good Friday, when it is freed from the devil's influence.
- If a woman other than the mistress of the house plants parsley, she'll get pregnant. If this happens, she should eat parsley three times a day for three weeks, which would take care of the problem.
- If you say a person's name while you're picking parsley, that person will die within a week.
- "Transplant parsley, transplant death." If you move a parsley plant, somebody you know will die.
- "Only the wicked can grow parsley"—and its variant, "Only a witch can grow parsley."

### CHINA'S LEFTOVER POTATO SOUP, WITH PLENTY OF PARSLEY

leftover mashed potatoes

enough milk to thin to soup consistency

1 teaspoon chicken bouillon per cup of mashed potatoes, dissolved in 1–2 tablespoons boiling water

2 teaspoons fresh minced parsley per cup of mashed potatoes

salt and freshly ground pepper to taste

grated cheddar cheese, about 2 tablespoons per cup of mashed potatoes

Heat the mashed potatoes, adding milk to thin. Stir in dissolved chicken bouillon, parsley, salt, and pepper. If you have other leftover vegetables (corn, peas, green beans) or ham or sausage, add them, as well. Heat, ladle into bowls, and top with grated cheese.

**Read more about the dangers of parsley:**
*Oxford Dictionary of Plant-Lore*, by Roy Vickery

*A garden is evidence of faith. It links us with all the misty figures of the past who also planted and were nourished by the fruits of their planting.*

—GLADYS TABER

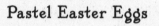

## Pastel Easter Eggs

For Christians, the Easter egg is a symbol of faith, renewal, and rebirth. This year, why not color at least some of them the natural way, using plant materials? It's easy, fun, and interesting, and a great project for the kids.

Start by hard-boiling the eggs, as you usually do. Set them aside, and prepare your dye bath. The general procedure is to simmer the cut-up plant materials in a nonreactive pan for 20–30 minutes, to develop the color. Strain out the plant materials and add a teaspoon of vinegar (except when using onion skins). Then, with a spoon, lower the dry hard-boiled eggs into the bath and let them sit until the color "takes." To obtain a darker color, let the eggs cool in the bath, or remain overnight.

And here's something else you might try: Choose a leaf or a fern frond. Secure it to the egg with a tiny bit of white glue, just to hold it in place. Then wrap the egg with a square of nylon stocking, netting, or cheesecloth, so that the leaf is held firmly against the egg. Gather the material at the top of the egg, tie securely with string, and lower it into the dye bath. When the egg is dyed, the leaf-shape will remain white, and you'll see the soft shadow of the fabric on the egg, as well.

**COLORS FROM NATURE**

- Reds: beets, cooked and allowed to steep for several hours; raspberries, cranberries, or cherries; red onion skins (use LOTS)
- Blues and purples: red cabbage, blueberry juice, cranberry juice and purple grapes, blackberry juice
- Lavender: purple violets, plus 2 teaspoons lemon juice
- Green: spinach, carrot tops
- Orange: yellow onion skins
- Yellows: lemon peel, ground cumin, turmeric, calendula flowers
- Browns: coffee grounds, tea, walnut hulls or bark, cayenne powder

Hint: you may not want to eat naturally-dyed eggs, since they sometimes take on the taste of the dye material.

**Read more about creating colors from natural materials:**
*Wild Color*, by Jenny Dean

*One is nearer God's heart in a garden than anywhere else on earth.*

—DOROTHY FRANCES GURNEY

Indian tribes in the American Northeast gave the name "Planting Moon" to the April New Moon.

*To everything there is a season, and a time to every purpose under heaven: A time to be born, and a time to die; a time to plant, and a time to pluck up that which is planted . . .*

—ECCLESIASTES 3:1–2

## Gardening by the Moon, Part One

### THE FOUR PHASES

As the Moon travels around the earth, its changing angle creates the daily tides and is said to affect, as well, the moisture in the soil. We mark the changes in the Moon's appearance as "phases." Ancient peoples regulated their agricultural practices according to the Moon's passage, and some modern gardeners enjoy experimenting with this age-old tradition. Ruby Wilcox, who keeps an eye on the stars, swears by this gardening practice. She suggests that you give it a try.

- New Moon, First Quarter. During this waxing period, seeds are said to germinate readily. The best time for planting, but especially good for annuals that produce their yield above the ground and their seeds outside the fruit. Examples: lettuce, spinach, celery, broccoli, cabbage, cauliflower, and grain.
- Second Quarter. The second quarter (also a waxing period) produces strong leaf growth. A good time to plant annuals that produce their yield above ground and their seeds inside the fruit, such as beans, melons, peas, peppers, squash, and tomatoes. Also good for vining plants.
- Full Moon, Third Quarter. As the Moon begins to wane, root growth is strong. Time to plant root crops (such as beets, carrots, onions, potatoes, and peanuts) and those that flower and fruit in the second and subsequent seasons, such as perennials, biennials, bulbs, shrubs, trees.
- Fourth Quarter. This waning period is the best time to cultivate, pull weeds, prune plants, and destroy pests.

**Read more about gardening by the moon:**
*Guided by the Moon: Living in Harmony with the Lunar Cycles*, by Johanna Paungger and Thomas Poppe
*The Lunar Garden: Planting by the Moon Phases*, by E. A. Crawford

*Sowe peason and beans in the wane of the moon*
*Who soweth them sooner, he soweth too soone.*
*That they with the planet may rest and arise,*
*and flourish with bearing most plentiful wise.*

—TRADITIONAL

# APRIL 12

## Gardening by the Moon, Part Two

During each lunar month, the Moon moves through the twelve signs of the zodiac, spending two to three days in each sign. The signs are related to the four fundamental elements: earth, air, fire, and water.

- Aries (Fire). Barren and dry. Harvest root and fruit for storage. Cultivate, destroy weeds and pests. Don't bother planting anything.
- Taurus (Earth). Productive and moist. Very good for planting and transplanting, especially for leafy vegetables such as lettuce, cabbage, and spinach. Excellent for root crops and potatoes, biennials, perennials, shrubs. A good time to get your hands dirty.
- Gemini (Air). Barren and dry. Cultivate, destroy weeds and pests, harvest for drying. Stimulate your mind with a good book.
- Cancer (Water). Very fruitful and moist. Excellent for all planting and transplanting. Very good for grafting, and irrigation. Don't forget your umbrella.
- Leo (Fire). Very barren and dry. Cultivate, harvest root crops and fruit for storage. Mow lawns. Destroy weeds and pests. Indulge your creativity with a trip to the art museum.
- Virgo (Earth). Barren and moist. Not generally favorable for planting or transplanting. Cultivate and destroy weeds and pests. Wear a poncho if necessary.
- Libra (Air). Semi-fruitful and moist. Excellent sign for planting flowers, vines (especially melons), and herbs. Enjoy the garden's beauty.
- Scorpio (Water). Very fruitful and moist. Excellent planting sign for shrubs and vines, very good for other planting and for transplanting and irrigating. Said to be good for planting corn, but not for harvesting root crops that may rot, like carrots, potatoes. Keep your feet dry.
- Sagittarius (Fire). Barren and dry. Harvest root crops and fruits for storage, and cultivate. Admire tall trees.
- Capricorn (Earth). Productive and dry. Plant potatoes and other tuber crops. Good for grafting, applying organic fertilizer, and pruning to promote growth. Don't let yourself put down roots.
- Aquarius (Air). Barren and dry. Harvest root and fruit for storage. Cultivate, destroy weeds and pests. Wear a good herbal skin cream to avoid wrinkles.
- Pisces (Water). Very productive and moist. Excellent planting and transplanting sign, especially favoring root growth and irrigation. If the garden is too wet, a good time to go boating.

**Read more about gardening by the moon and stars:**

*Astrological Gardening: The Ancient Wisdom of Successful Planting & Harvesting by the Stars*, by Louise Riotte

*The Farmers' Almanac* (planting information, based on the Moon's sign and phase)

Today is the birthday of Thomas Jefferson, who said, "No occupation is so delightful to me as the culture of the earth, and no culture comparable to that of the garden."

## Garden Pinks

One of the stars of Jefferson's Monticello flower garden is a collection of heirloom garden pinks or carnations (*Dianthus*), a cottage garden favorite. Jefferson sent seeds to a friend in 1786, noting that they were to be sown in March, and were "very fine & very rare."

### THE EDIBLE PINK

The pink most often used in cookery was the clove-scented pink (*Dianthus caryophyllus*), or gillyflower—what we now call the carnation. (Gilly comes from the French *girofle*, or clove, and refers to the spicy scent of the flower.) The blossom was used to make conserves, preserves, syrups, and vinegars, and as a flavoring for wine. The petals add a clovelike flavor to salads and fruit compotes. (Don't use flowers from the florist, for they have been sprayed.)

### CARNATION VINEGAR (FROM THE STORY "VIOLET DEATH," IN *AN UNTHYMELY DEATH*)

    1 cup red or pink carnation (*Dianthus*) petals
    6 cloves
    1 3-inch cinnamon stick
    2 cups white wine vinegar

Pull the petals from the flower heads and snip off the white heels. Wash. Place petals in a jar with the cloves and cinnamon stick, and crush lightly. Add vinegar, and store in a dark place at room temperature until it has reached the desired intensity. Strain into a pretty bottle. Use on crisp greens or on a fruit salad.

### THE MEDICINAL PINK

John Gerard (1597) praised the clove pink as a restorative, which "wonderfully above measure doth comfort the heart." John Parkinson (1640) recommended it for headaches. *Dianthus superbus* has been used in Chinese medicine as a tonic for the nervous system, and to treat the kidneys, the urinary tract, constipation, and eczema.

### THE FRAGRANT PINK

For most of us, the chief reason for including these beautiful plants in our gardens is their spicy-sweet fragrance. Dry the petals for use in sachets, and use the essential oil (purchased) in candles, bath and massage oils, soaps, and as a body oil.

**Read more about Monticello and colonial gardens:**
www.monticello.org, a web site devoted to Monticello, with information about visiting this historic plantation

*Herbs and Herb Lore of Colonial America*, by the Colonial Dames of America

*It gives one a sudden start in going down a barren, stony street, to see upon a narrow strip of grass, just within the iron fence, the radiant dandelion, shining in the grass, like a spark dropped from the sun.*

—HENRY WARD BEECHER

## Dandy Lions

Ever wonder how the dandelion got its name?

The word *dandelion* is an Englishman's pronunciation of the French phrase *dent de lion*, or tooth of the lion. The plant's toothed leaves, perhaps? Or maybe the blossom's color—the same yellow used to picture heraldic lions.

The dandelion's other names are also descriptive. "The devil's milk pail" refers to the sticky white sap that oozes from the broken root, used to remove warts and treat other skin ailments. "Swine's snout" describes the closed blossom. "Puffball" is exactly the right name for the flyaway seeds. And "monk's head" is a good way of describing the smooth, bald head that pokes up out of the grass after the seeds have blown away.

The dandelion's scientific name—*Taraxacum officinale*—has a different ring to it. *Taraxacum* derives from a Greek combination that means "to unsettle," because the plant was used as a stimulating tonic. And the Latin word *officinale*, which is tacked on to the names of so many herbs, refers to the plant's use as a medicinal.

What sort of medicine is it? We can find one clue in the inelegant name "piss-a-bed." The plant produces *taraxacin*, stimulating the kidneys to produce urine. Because the dandelion is high in potassium, a vital nutrient lost when the kidneys do their job, herbalists prefer it to chemical diuretics. The plant also stimulates the liver to produce bile. For centuries, the dandelion has been used to treat heartburn, liver complaints, gall stones, jaundice, and dropsy (what we now call congestive heart failure).

All parts of the dandelion have their uses. The blossoms make a tasty wine. The young leaves are a zesty substitute for iceberg lettuce in a salad or on your tuna sandwich—another folk name for the plant is Wild Endive. And some folks swear by dandelion coffee, which is brewed from the dried, roasted, and ground roots. (But be absolutely sure that your dandelion harvest is organic.)

**Read more about dandelions:**
*The Dandelion Celebration: A Guide to Unexpected Cuisine*, by Peter Gail

*Roses are red,*
*Violets are blue;*
*But they don't get around*
*Like the dandelions do.*

—SLIM ACRES

# APRIL 15

*He who sees things grow from the beginning will have the best view of them.*

—ARISTOTLE

## Good Beginnings: From Susan's Journal

For me, spring hasn't begun until I've sown my first herb seeds outdoors. My herb garden gets sun for most of the day, so the soil is warming up, the nighttime temperatures are in the 50s, and my last frost date is past. (Check your soil, nighttime temperatures, and the frost date in your area.) Here are some of the herbs I grow from seed, with my favorite varieties.

- Catmint (*Nepeta mussinii*). I prefer to grow catmint rather than catnip—the blooms are prettier, and my cat enjoys it just as much. She rarely bothers plants I grow from seed. Sow 4 inches apart, thin to 12 inches.
- Cilantro (*Coriandrum sativum*). My favorite is the "slow-bolt" variety. Cilantro doesn't transplant well, so outdoor sowing is best. Plant 1-2 inches apart, thin to 4 inches. Planting every two weeks will give you cilantro all summer long. The blossoms are nice in salads, the spicy leaves a must for salsa. A staple in Southwestern cuisine.
- Dill (*Anethum graveolens*). Fresh dill leaves are wonderful with grilled salmon, eggs, and salads, and the seeds are an essential ingredient in pickles. I grow

the shorter variety, 'Fernleaf,' although many people prefer the old-fashioned taller varieties for flavor.
- Lemon balm (*Melissa officinalis*). Great for bees, a necessity for herbal teas.
- Parsley (*Petroselinum crispum*). I'm partial to the curly, crispy varieties. Try it as a border plant, and as close to the kitchen door as possible.
- Sage (*Salvia officinalis*). Is a perennial, but starting new plants every year ensures that you will have plenty. The gray-green leaves (or try the attractive tricolor sage) make it an attractive landscape plant. I like a variety called 'Berggarten,' which has larger leaves and a softer taste.
- Nasturtiums (*Tropaeolum majus*). I love the bright, cheerful colors. And did you know that you can pickle the seeds and use them like capers? 'Dwarf Jewel' is a favorite in my garden.

**Read more about good beginnings, from an expert herbalist:**
*Growing Herbs from Seed, Cutting & Root*, by Thomas DeBaggio

*You may yet slip Lavender, Thyme, Peneroyal, Sage, Rosemary etc., and the oftener you clip and cut them, the more will they thrive.*

—JOHN EVELYN, 1620–1706

In the floral calendar, today's flower: greater stitchwort (dead man's bones).

Today is National Stress Awareness Day (appropriate, since yesterday was National Send-in-Your-Taxes Day).

*You're only here for a short visit. Don't hurry, don't worry, and stop to smell the flowers along the way.*

—WALTER HAGEN

## Stressed? Use Some Scents!

Remember those lacy lavender-filled sachets your grandmother tucked under her pillow? And the soft scent of roses from the necklace of rose beads that your great-aunt loved to wear? Now, scientists are learning that roses and lavender don't just smell good, they're therapeutic, and especially helpful in relieving stress. In other words, aromatherapy. Here are some fragrances you can use—in a bath, massage, aroma lamp, compress, or facial steam—to reduce the stress of your everyday life. And if you need to lower the stress of commuting, place a few drops of essential oil on a tissue or scent diffuser and stow it in the car, renewing as necessary.

**FRAGRANCES THAT SOOTHE**

- chamomile, for sleeplessness, depression, irritability
- eucalyptus, for mental fatigue, emotional stress
- jasmine, for anxiety, fearfulness, tension
- lavender, for sleeplessness, nervousness, depression
- orange, for apprehension, nervous tension
- rose, for depression, irritability
- ylang-ylang, for sleeplessness, nervous tension

**Read more about the uses of fragrance:**

*The Aromatherapy Book: Applications and Inhalations*, by Jeanne Rose

*The Aromatherapy Companion*, by Victoria H. Edwards

*If odours may worke satisfaction, they are so soveraigne in plants and so comfortable that no confection of the apothecaries can equall their excellent Vertue.*

—JOHN GERARD, *HERBAL*, 1597

According to some sources, the Celtic month of the Willow began on April 15 (April 15–May 12).

*All a green willow is my garland.*

—JOHN HEYWOOD, 1497–1575

## "All a Green Willow"

Various species of willows (*Salix sp.*) grow around the world. It is a deciduous shrub or tree that can grow as high as 80 feet, producing green tapering leaves and catkins in the spring—pretty to look at, but nothing out of the ordinary. Just another green tree, growing on a riverbank or along the edge of a marsh.

But that's not the whole story, for this nondescript tree has had an extraordinary life. The earliest records of medical use are found in Chinese medical texts from around 500 BCE, prescribing the bark and leaves to relieve pain and fever. In 400 BCE, the Greek physician Hippocrates suggested similar uses, and every physician since has endorsed the prescription. The willow was a staple medicinal herb, used to treat everything from colds and flu to colic, diarrhea, and bleeding gums.

It wasn't until the early 1800s, however, that people began to understand why the willow was such an effective medicine. In 1828, Johann Buchner, professor of pharmacy at the University of Munich, chemically isolated a minute amount of yellow, needlelike crystals, which he called *salicin*. Salicin was not an acceptable substitute for willow, however, because it upset the stomach and left a bitter taste in the mouth.

Ten years later, it was learned that the herb meadowsweet (*Spirea alba*, now called *Filipendula ulmaria*) also contained salicin, and that it was more readily tolerated. The extraction process was improved, salicin was "buffered" with additives, and a compound called acetylsalicylic acid was produced, which had fewer negative side effects.

It took more tinkering, but on March 6, 1899, the Bayer Company was ready to apply for a patent. The new drug was called aspirin: *a* for acetylsalicylic and *spirin* for *Spirea*, the original genus name of meadowsweet. People flocked to buy it, and before long this new variant of an ancient remedy was flourishing in medicine cabinets around the world. It even went to the moon with the Apollo astronauts.

Willow, willow, all a green willow. You've come a long way, baby.

**Read more about the extraordinary life and times of willow:**
*Willows: The Genus Salix*, by Christopher Newsholme

*April weather
Rain and sunshine both together.*

—TRADITIONAL WEATHER LORE

Every year, about this time, the Fredericksburg Herb Farm holds its annual Herbfest.

*The best gardeners I know are those who practice regularly the habit of visiting other gardens.*
—ALAN LACY, *THE GARDENER'S EYE*

## Going Places: The Fredericksburg Herb Farm

If you love herbs and enjoy talking to people who are deeply involved with them, sooner or later you will want to visit a working herb farm. A quick search on the Internet or in a local directory will help you make a list of local places to visit. One of my favorite herb farms is only a couple of hours' drive, so I try to go there at least once a year.

A good time to visit this Fredericksburg, Texas, herb farm is the weekend of their annual Herbfest, where you'll see all kinds of herbal goings-on. A spring tradition in the Texas Hill Country, the annual festival celebrates herbs and their many uses, with gardening workshops, food, wine, art, and entertainment. I always enjoy wandering through the herb gardens and the fields where herbs are grown for the many products made on the farm: vinegars, potpourri, soaps, oils, lotions, and candles.

First established in 1985, this herb enterprise now occupies 14 acres of working fields and gardens, including a Celtic Cross herb garden, a Secret Garden, a Children's Garden, a Kitchen Garden, the Ichtus Garden (a faith garden in the shape of a fish), and a large five-pointed Star Garden centered with a windmill. Each of the sections of the star is home to herbs used for particular purposes: culinary, medicinal, crafts, cosmetics, and bee and butterfly herbs.

A pioneer farmstead home built of limestone houses a gift shop, a tearoom, and a restaurant that features wonderful herbal food: on the menu when I visited was a terrific rosemary-marinated roast beef, sliced thin and topped with a creamy horseradish and chive sauce.

An overnight stay in the Herb Haus (once the home of a Fredericksburg midwife) is a special treat. And if you go in mid-April, you'll enjoy an added bonus: the bluebonnets and wildflowers of the Texas Hill Country.

Visits to herb farms and gardens are a refreshing break in a routine of work and family. I always come home with dozens of photos and a notebook full of ideas for my own garden. There's no better way to spend a weekend!

**Read more about the Fredericksburg Herb Farm:**
*Herbs: Growing & Using the Plants of Romance*, by Bill and Sylvia Varney
Visit the Herb Farm online at www.fredericksburgherb farm.com

# APRIL 19

Today is National Garlic Day.

## Garlic in History

The first prescription for garlic was cut into a stone tablet around 3,000 BCE. The "stinking rose" may have provoked the first labor strike in history, when slaves stopped work on the pyramids because they didn't get the promised garlic. Roman soldiers carried bags of garlic as they marched across Europe. It was a legendary ingredient of Four Thieves' Vinegar, which protected robbers against the plague as they plundered their victims. Modern science has confirmed garlic's reputation as a powerful antibiotic; it can also help to reduce blood pressure and blood sugar levels, decrease cholesterol, and lower the risk of blood clots.

Garlic is easy to grow. All it asks is sun and friable soil. Grow varieties you can't get in the supermarket: rocambole, porcelain garlic, artichoke garlic, or silverskin. Garlic goes with just about anything, from soup to salad to dessert—even garlic ice cream! Maria Sanchez's soup is a Pecan Springs favorite, often served at Bean's Bar and Grill.

**MARIA SANCHEZ'S HEARTY MEXICAN GARLIC SOUP (FROM *LOVE LIES BLEEDING: A CHINA BAYLES MYSTERY*)**

- 3 whole heads of garlic
- 3 tablespoons olive oil
- 1 large onion, sliced thin
- 8 cups rich chicken stock
- 1–2 chipotle chiles, fresh, dried, or canned
- 1 teaspoon cumin or more to taste
- ¼ cup lime juice
- garnish: sour cream or yogurt, sliced green onions, and minced fresh cilantro

Preheat oven to 400°. Separate the cloves of garlic, put into a bowl, and coat with 1 tablespoon oil. Place in a shallow pan and bake about 45 minutes, until soft. Peel when cool enough to handle. Sauté onion in 1 tablespoon oil, then put into a blender with the peeled garlic. Puree, adding a little chicken stock if necessary for a smooth blend. Put the remaining oil in a large saucepan, heat, and add the pureed onion and garlic. Cook the mixture until it begins to dry and brown lightly. Add the rest of the stock, chipotles, and cumin, and simmer 25–30 minutes. Add lime juice and pour into serving bowls. Garnish with sour cream, green onions, and cilantro. Serves 6–8.

**Read more about the "stinking rose":**
*Everything Tastes Better with Garlic*, by Sara Perry
*The New Healing Herbs*, by Michael Castleman

*Waste not a leaf of garlick on your hens.* *

—TRADITIONAL LORE

*Garlic was fed to cocks because it was thought to make them better fighters.

Today or tomorrow, the Sun enters the astrological sign of Taurus.

*The second sign of the Zodiac, Earthy Taurus is ruled by Venus, the planet of love and desire. A fixed (stable, resolute) sign, feminine Taurus governs practicality and security. Earthy, reliable Taureans tend to be conservative, possessive, and sensual. They understand what they need in order to lead the good life.*

—RUBY WILCOX, "ASTROLOGICAL SIGNS"

## Herbs of Taurus

In the ancient world, the planet Venus (ruler of Taurus) was regarded as the female embodiment of beauty, sexual love, and desire, and Taurus is related to those things that we desire. Astrological herbalists assigned soothing, moderating, and balancing herbs to Venus, as well as plants that have lovely flowers.

- Violet (*Viola odorata*). A beautiful flower, violet is also a powerful soother and emollient. Violet leaf tea has been used to ease sore throats and coughs. Candied violet flowers are an edible, delectable garnish for many desserts.
- Daisy (*Bellis perennis*). The flower heads contain mucilage, which make the tea helpful in the treatment of a raw throat. Daisies have also been used to treat kidney problems.

- Plantain (*Plantago major*). Especially useful in the treatment of respiratory ailments. The tea soothes the mucous membranes of the throat and is a specific for bronchitis.
- Other Venus-ruled herbs. Roses are used to treat headaches. Coltsfoot, thyme, and marshmallow relieve the throat. Horehound helps to relieve coughs, soothe sore throats, and ease upper-respiratory ailments. Cowslip has a beautiful yellow flower that was once used as a skin softener. Nicholas Culpeper says: "Our city dames know well enough the ointment or distilled water of it adds to beauty, or at least restores it when it is lost."

**Read more about Culpeper's astrological herbalism, in this edited and illustrated edition:**
*Culpeper's Color Herbal*, by Nicholas Culpeper, edited by David Potterton

*Wonderful tales had our fathers of old—*
*Wonderful tales of the herbs and stars—*
*The Sun was Lord of the Marigolds,*
*Basil and Rocket belonged to Mars.*
*Put as a sum in division it goes—*
*(Every plant had a star bespoke)—*
*Who but Venus should govern the Rose?*
*Who but Jupiter own the Oak?*

—RUDYARD KIPLING, "OUR FATHERS OF OLD"

*Amaranth (the word means "unfading" or "eternal") is the generic name for a number of annual plants that have been used as food, medicines, dyes, and ornamentals. You may recognize the ornamental variety, Love-lies-bleeding. The handsome bloodred flowers look like dangling ropes of fuzzy chenille.*

—*LOVE LIES BLEEDING: A CHINA BAYLES MYSTERY*

## Love Lies Bleeding: About China's Books

*Love Lies Bleeding* is one of the darker China Bayles mysteries. It was one of the harder books for me to write, too, for it is about betrayal: the betrayal of public trust and of the private bonds of love. It is also about the dark side of heroism, and the tragedy of a good cop who goes bad.

Searching for a symbol of this tangle of passion, greed, and betrayal, I came upon the herb love-lies-bleeding (*Amaranthus caudatus*), which is prized for its ropelike, bloodred blossoms. Traditionally used to staunch battlefield bleeding, the plant became symbolic of martial prowess, masculine virility, and heroism. In the Middle Ages, it was worn by knights to symbolize purity and truth, but by the time of the Renaissance, when it was used to treat venereal disease, it had become a symbol of corruption. Love-lies-bleeding provided exactly the signature I needed for this dark tragedy.

But all China Bayles Mysteries are a mix of laughter and tears, and as usual, Ruby Wilcox lightens things up with her optimistic cheerfulness. She also heats things up a bit when she serves her latest cookie concoction, which is liberally spiked with habanero powder. "Soul searing," China mutters. "Cookie monsters. My palate may never recover." But Ruby's hotter-than-Hades cookies have turned out to be the personal favorite of many readers.

### RUBY WILCOX'S HOT LIPS COOKIE CRISPS

1 cup soft shortening
2 cups brown sugar
1 teaspoon vanilla
2 eggs
1½ cups whole wheat flour
1½ cups unbleached flour
½ teaspoon soda
1 teaspoon baking powder
½ teaspoon habanero powder
1½ cups finely chopped cashews

Preheat oven to 325°. Cream shortening and sugar. Add the vanilla and eggs and mix well. In a separate bowl, mix the dry ingredients together with the nuts, and stir into the creamed mixture. Chill. Roll out like a log, about 2 inches in diameter, slice, and bake until golden.

**Read China's sixth adventure:**
*Love Lies Bleeding: A China Bayles Mystery*, by Susan Wittig Albert

# APRIL 22

Earth Day is usually observed on this day.

## Natural Nibbling

In generations past, children growing up in the woods and fields enjoyed a springtime banquet of free natural treats. Alice Morse Earle, remembering what it was like to grow up in the 1860s, writes:

> The children ate an astonishing range: roots, twigs, leaves, bark, tendrils, fruit, berries, flowers, buds, seeds, all alike served for food. Young shoots of sweetbrier and blackberry are nibbled as well as the branches of young birch. Grapevine tendrils have an acid zest as do sorrel.

Here are some of the other healthy, natural treats that children used to gather from the fields and woods throughout the year:

- sunflower seeds (*Helianthus annuus*)
- leaf buds of spruce trees (*Picea*)
- cinnamon fern fiddleheads (*Osmunda cinnamomea*)
- wild mustard (*Brassica sp.*)
- oak apples (oak galls) (*Quercus*)
- wintergreen berries (*Gaultheria procumbens*)
- wild onions (*Allium sp.*)
- honeysuckle blossoms (*Lonicera japonica*)
- wild strawberries (*Fragaria sp.*)
- clover blossoms (*Trifolium pratense*)
- mint (*Mentha sp.*)
- winter cress (*Barbarea vulgaris*)
- cat brier (*Smilax rotundifolia*)
- violets (*Viola*)

Most modern children see food as something that appears on their plates after it has come out of a box or a can. To celebrate Earth Day, take your children or grandchildren into the garden and introduce them to natural nibbling. It might make a difference in the way they approach the world. But it's also wise to caution them against eating anything they're not sure is safe, and encourage them to learn to identify edible plants.

**Read more about natural nibbles:**
*A Field Guide to Edible Wild Plants*, by Bradford Angier

*One rule that every country child knew was: don't put any plant into your mouth until you have been shown by an older child or adult that it is safe to eat. And we found out that some plants had only certain parts that were edible. One friend had a grandmother who played a leaf-matching game with us kids. She would pick five edible leaves, then hold one up and say, "Match this leaf." We had to go find a plant with a matching leaf. Soon, we knew which salad greens to pick.*

—QUOTED IN *HONEYSUCKLE SIPPING: THE PLANT LORE OF CHILDHOOD*, BY JEANNÉ R. CHESANOW

Today is the birthday of William Shakespeare, born in 1564. The theme garden for April: a Shakespeare Garden.

*When daisies pied and violets blue*
*and lady-smocks all silver-white*
*and cuckoo-buds of yellow hue*
*Do paint the meadows with delight.*
—LOVE'S LABORS LOST

## The Blooming Bard

Shakespeare's plays and poems bloom with flowers and gardens. What could be more interesting than a corner of your own garden devoted to the herbs and flowers mentioned in Shakespeare's plays? You might want to add a label to each plant, citing the play or poem in which the plant is mentioned. And if you are a great admirer of the plays, you might want to make a Shakespeare garden album, with pressed flowers and leaves, a note about the plant, and a quotation from the plays.

### SHAKESPEARE'S HERBS AND FLOWERS

Aloe (*Aloe sp.*) *A Lover's Complaint*

Balm (*Melissa officinalis*) *Merry Wives of Windsor* 5:5

Bay laurel (*Laurus nobilis*) *Antony and Cleopatra* 1:3

Sweetbriar or briar (*Rosa eglantine*) *A Midsummer Night's Dream* 2:1

Broom (*Cytisus scoparius*) *A Midsummer Night's Dream* 5:1

Burnet (*Sanguisorba minor*) *King Henry V* 5:2

Chamomile (*Chamaemelum nobile*) *King Henry IV, Part I*, 2:4

Carnation (*Dianthus caryophyllus*) *The Winter's Tale* 4:4

Cowslip (*Primula veris*) *The Tempest* 5:1

Fennel (*Foeniculum vulgare*) *Hamlet* 4:5

Holly (*Ilex sp.*) *As You Like It* 2:7

Honeysuckle (*Lonicera sp.*) *A Midsummer Night's Dream* 4:1

Hyssop (*Hyssopus officinalis*) *Othello* 1:3

Lavender (*Lavendula angustifolia*) *The Winter's Tale* 4:4

Marigold (*Calendula officinalis*) *The Winter's Tale* 4:4

Marjoram (*Origanum sp.*) *The Winter's Tale* 4:4

Mint (*Mentha sp.*) *The Winter's Tale* 4:3

Myrtle (*Myrtus communis*) *Measure for Measure* 2:2

Nettle (*Urtica sp.*) *Othello* 1:3

Pansy (*Viola tricolor*) *Hamlet* 4:5

Parsley (*Petroselinum crispum*) *Taming of the Shrew* 4:4

Poppy (*Poppy somniferum*) *Othello* 3:3

Rose (*Rosa sp.*) *King Henry VI, Part I*, 2:4

Rosemary (*Rosmarinus officinalis*) *The Winter's Tale* 4:4

Rue (*Ruta graveolens*) *The Winter's Tale* 4:4

Savory (*Satureia sp.*) *The Winter's Tale* 4:4

Thyme (*Thymus sp.*) *A Midsummer Night's Dream* 2:1

Violet (*Viola odorata*) *King Henry V* 4:1

Wormwood (*Artemisia absinthium*) *Hamlet* 3:2

**Read more about the Bard's blooms:**
*Shakespeare's Flowers*, by Jessica Kerr

# APRIL 24

*I have pepper and peony seed and a pound of garlic*
*And a farthingworth of fennel-seed, for fasting days.*
—WILLIAM LANGLAND, *PIERS PLOWMAN*, FOURTEENTH CENTURY

## Herb Seeds: Not Just for Planting

Throughout history, many herbs have been valued as much for their seeds as for their leaves, if not more. When you plant your herb garden (either in the ground or on your deck), be sure to include some of the interesting herbs that are valued for their seeds. Or perhaps you'd like to learn how to cook with these seeds. Whether in your garden or in your kitchen, you'll be delighted with the result! Here are five popular choices for you.

- Anise (*Pimpinella anisum*). One of the oldest known aromatic seeds, anise was used as currency in Biblical times. It has long been prized for its scent and its health-promoting properties (it is carminative, expectorant, and anti-spasmodic). It has a licorice taste, and is used to flavor sweet pickles, salads, cakes, cookies, candies, liqueurs, and marinades.
- Caraway (*Carum carvi*). Rye bread is flavored with caraway seed, as are cakes, biscuits, cheese, carrot, cabbage, and potato dishes. It is much used in European and German cuisine. Medicinally, the seed was used to treat digestive ailments. In ancient Egypt, it was used in love potions.
- Coriander (*Coriandrum sativum*). Coriander is men-tioned in the Bible (manna is white, "like a corian-der seed," Exodus 16:31). It was widely used as a cough remedy, an aphrodisiac, and as an incense to summon devils! In cooking, it has been used to flavor beans, onions, potatoes, sausages, stews, pastries, and wine. It is also included in many curry and chili powders.
- Dill (*Anethum graveolens*). Dill has carminative properties and calms intestinal cramps. In Scandinavia, it was given to colicky babies, and derives its name from the Old Norse, *dilla*, meaning "to lull." Dill's most famous culinary use—the dill pickle—has been around for at least 400 years. (And of course, you remember dill as the signature herb in China Bayles' mystery, *A Dilly of a Death*.)
- Nasturtium (*Tropaeolum majus*). Peppery nasturtium flowers are a colorful addition to salads, and their pickled seeds are a good substitute for more-expensive capers.

Pickled nasturtium seeds. Prepare a brine of 1 quart white vinegar, 2 teaspoons pickling salt, a thinly sliced onion, 2 cloves of garlic, 2 peppercorns, and ½ teaspoon each allspice, mace, and celery seed. As your nasturtium blossoms fall, pick the green seed pods, wash, and drop into the pickling mixture. Refrigerate. Stir each time you add more. When you have a cupful, take them out for use, with brine to cover; continue adding to your pickles with fresh seeds until the season is over.

Today is National Zucchini Bread Day.

## Zucchini Bread Day in Pecan Springs

Squashes are among the many plants that Europeans discovered when they arrived in the New World. Although they are now used chiefly as foods, Native Americans also used them as medicines, for such problems as intestinal parasites, kidney ailments, rheumatism, and fevers. Squashes are usually thought of in two groups: winter squashes such as acorn, buttercup, butternut, Hubbard, turban, and pumpkin; summer squashes such as crookneck, and pattypan. And then, of course, there's zucchini.

In Pecan Springs, everybody has a favorite zucchini bread recipe. Mrs. Bubba Harris, the wife of the former chief of police, bakes hers in a slow cooker because she doesn't like to have her oven on during the summer. Bubba retired from the force (Sheila Dawson took his place, as you know if you've been following the Pecan Springs news) and now raises bees, pecans, and zucchini.

**MRS. BUBBA'S SLOW COOKER ZUCCHINI-BASIL BREAD**

- 2 eggs
- ⅔ cup vegetable oil
- ¾ cup honey
- 1⅓ cups zucchini, peeled, grated, drained
- 1 tablespoon minced fresh basil
- 1 teaspoon vanilla
- 2 cups flour
- ¼ teaspoon salt
- ½ teaspoon baking powder
- ½ teaspoons ground cinnamon
- ¼ teaspoon ground nutmeg
- 1 cup chopped pecans

In a mixing bowl with handheld electric mixer, beat eggs until light and foamy. Add oil, honey, zucchini, basil, and vanilla. Mix well. In a separate bowl, mix dry ingredients with nuts; stir into zucchini mixture and blend well. Pour into a greased and floured 2-pound coffee can or 2-quart mold (be sure it fits in your slow cooker). Place crumpled foil in the bottom of the slow cooker and set the can on it. Place in slow cooker. Cover top of can with 6–8 layers of folded paper towels to absorb the steam. Cover and bake on HIGH for 3 to 4 hours. Do not remove cover to check bread until it has cooked for 3 hours. Let stand 5 minutes before turning out of can or mold.

**Got more zucchini? Here are 225 other ways to deal with it:**
*The Classic Zucchini Cookbook: 225 Recipes for All Kinds of Squash*, by Nancy Ralston

## Wild Weeds and Native Herbs

Let's stop thinking that an herb is something we grow in our gardens! Herbs are all around us, but we have to stop calling them "wild weeds" and begin to understand them as "native herbs" before we can see them and appreciate their uniqueness. Start with this quartet, likely to be growing somewhere in your immediate vicinity.

- Chickweed (*Stellaria media*). A zippy addition to salads in early spring, the seeds of this plant are especially loved by birds and poultry. Traditionally used to treat liver and kidney ailments, coughs, rheumatism, and pleurisy. (You may remember this plant from the China Bayles mystery, *Dead Man's Bones*, which features its European cousin, *Stellaria holostea*.)
- Dandelion (*Taraxacum officinale*). You can probably see this plant just outside your window. The young leaves are used in salads; the blossoms are made into wine; and the roots can be dried, ground, roasted, and brewed as coffee. Medicinal uses of this native herb mostly derive from its diuretic properties.
- Milkweed (*Asclepias syriaca*). Native Americans used the fibers of this plant to make twine and netting; collected the latex sap to make chewing gum; collected the fuzzy seeds as stuffing for pillows; and used a decoction of the roots to treat rheumatism, stomach complaints, and gallstones. Don't eat this plant unless you're a monarch butterfly. (Milkweed is the monarch's favorite food plant.)
- Purslane (*Portulaca oleracea*). Purslane migrated here from India, brought by the Europeans who enjoyed it for salads, soups, and pickles. It has plenty of vitamins and minerals, and the seeds can be used like poppy seeds, sprinkled on baked goods and in salad dressings.

**Read more about the many uses of native plants:**

*A Handbook of Native American Herbs*, by Alma R. Hutchens

*I always chew a little chickweed when I find it, to get that burst of vitamins A and C, sunshine for my journey. It adds bright green to salads and sandwiches and ornaments beautiful canapés. Try chickweed chopped into slaw; it adds color and flavor.*

—SUSAN TYLER HITCHCOCK, *GATHER YE WILD THINGS*

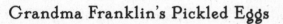

## Grandma Franklin's Pickled Eggs

My grandmother always put up pickled eggs in the spring, because the hens were just starting to lay and the eggs were smaller. Grandma always said that little eggs were prettier, pickled, than big eggs. I remember being fascinated by the pink color and tangy taste, but it was rare that I got more than half an egg. Sunday dinners on the Franklin farm were well-attended, and the menfolk ate before the women and children.

I found Grandma's handwritten recipe not long ago, stuck between the pages of the *Pure Food Cook Book*, which was compiled by the Farm Women of Missouri in 1945—my mother's standby cookbook and recipe file. Here it is, in case your hens are starting to lay. If not, you can buy small eggs at the grocery store.

### PICKLED PINK EGGS

1 dozen small eggs
1 can small beets (not pickled)
2 cups cider vinegar
3 small onions sliced
1 teaspoon salt
1 teaspoon sugar
½ teaspoon pickling spices

Hard boil eggs and peel them. Push a fork into the middle of each egg. Put the eggs in a deep crock. In a pan, heat the beets, vinegar, onions, salt, sugar, and spices until just ready to boil. Cool for 10 minutes. Pour over eggs. Put a plate on top and put in the ice-box for at least a week. Slice in half.

Bill is a chile-head (the affectionate term for somebody who can't go a day without a hot pepper), and likes his pickled eggs hot. Here is my recipe.

### GREEEN CHILE EGGS

1 dozen small eggs, hardboiled, peeled
3 small onions, sliced
2–3 jalapeño peppers
4–5 cloves
bay leaf
2 cups cider vinegar
1 teaspoon ground mustard
1 teaspoon pickling spices

Put the eggs into a suitable jar with onions, peppers, cloves, and bay leaf. Pour a little of the vinegar into the mustard to make a paste; stir paste into the rest of the vinegar, and pickling spices, and heat. Cool 10 minutes and pour over eggs. Refrigerate for 2 weeks.

*It is not the least part of the pleasures of a Garden, to walk and refresh yourself either with your Friends or Acquaintances, or else alone retired from the cares of the World, or apart from company that sometimes may prove burthensome to you.*

—J. WOOLDRIDGE

*I sold out of the "Moth Attack" blend that I grow and mix myself—southernwood, wormwood, rue, and santolina—so I guess it was also a day to think about mothproofing winter woolies.*

—HANGMAN'S ROOT: A CHINA BAYLES MYSTERY

## Chase Those Moths!

It's time to put the woolens away—and you know what happens next. Moths like nothing better for lunch than high-protein animal hair fibers. So they make a beeline for anything made of wool, camel hair, mohair, cashmere, angora, or other animal hair fibers. And if the item has been put away with perspiration on it—well, that's just dessert. Mama Moth stops eating only long enough to lay her eggs, right there on the moth dinner table. And the next time you see that pretty sweater, it's full of holes.

**MOTH FOOLERS**

You can fool moths by putting your woolies down for their summer nap with something that masks the alluring odor of animal fiber. If you don't want your sweater to smell like mothballs and you're averse to toxic chemicals, try strong-smelling herbs, alone or in combination. Stuff the dried herbs into small muslin (or any porous material) bags, and tuck them among your sweaters, scarves, and other winter wear. Here are the herbs China mixes and matches for her "Moth Attack" blend:

Annual herbs: camphor basil, pennyroyal, sweet marjoram

Perennial herbs: rosemary, lavender, patchouli, scented geraniums, pyrethrum daisy, sweet woodruff, tansy, southernwood, wormwood

Shrubs and trees (leaves, needles, shavings): balsam fir, red cedar (try a pet store for shavings), bay laurel, eucalyptus, pine, sassafras

You can also use the essential oils of these herbs. Dab on bits of cotton and place in drawer and boxes.

**More reading about moth chasers:**
*Herbal Treasures*, by Phyllis V. Shaudys

*Poke-root, boiled in water and mixed with a good quantity of molasses, set about the kitchen, the pantry, &c. in large deep plates, will kill cockroaches in great numbers.*

—MRS. CHILD, THE AMERICAN FRUGAL HOUSEWIFE, 1833

*One day, the gardener realizes that what she is doing out there is actually teaching herself to garden by performing a series of experiments. This is a pivotal moment.*

—MARGARET ROACH

## Boon Companions and Bosom Buddies

Companion planting is putting complementary plants together so they can help one another. The idea sounds fanciful? Well, consider these scientific findings:

- Some plants give off odors or chemicals that repel insects.
- Some plants attract beneficial insects.
- Some plants attract insects that will pollinate other plants.
- Some plants lure harmful insects away from valued plants.

Each of these herbs has a special talent. Put it to use in your garden.

- Catnip repels ants and flea beetles.
- Chives suppresses fungal diseases and discourages aphids.
- Coriander can be made into a spray to use against red spider mite.

- Feverfew attracts aphids, which may prefer it to your roses.
- Garlic repels Japanese beetles and aphids and is useful in herbal sprays.
- Nasturtium repels aphids, squash bugs, and striped pumpkin beetle.
- Sage wards off carrot fly.
- Tansy repels Japanese beetles, striped cucumber beetles, squash bugs, ants, flies.
- Thyme deters cabbage worms.
- Yarrow attracts hoverflies, ladybugs, and wasps, all of which prey on aphids.

*Yarrow, yarrow tremble and sway*
*Tiny flowers bright and gay*
*Protect my garden night and day.*

—TRADITIONAL

**Read more about the companionable herbs:**
*Carrots Love Tomatoes: Secrets of Companion Planting for Successful Gardening,* by Louise Riotte
*Great Garden Companions,* by Sally Jean Cunningham

Tonight is May Eve, the night when fairies are about.

## A Fairy Garden

Ruby Wilcox, who is a firm believer in fairies, is planning to spend the evening creating a miniature fairy-garden-in-a-bowl, just for the fairies she hopes will be stopping by for a visit around midnight. Whether you believe or not (of course you do, don't you?), a little magic never hurt anyone.

### THE CONTAINER AND THE SOIL

A wide, shallow terra-cotta bowl (the more weathered and mossy the better) is the best sort of container for a fairy garden, but any sturdy, well-drained container will do. Fill it with a light-weight potting soil. Water when the soil begins to dry (don't keep your garden wet), and add an organic fertilizer every few weeks. Your fairy garden will need plenty of sun, but set it in a protective place so that the wind doesn't tear the fragile plants.

### THE PLANTS

Moss is a must, to cover the soil. But herbs are the real secret to planting a fairy garden. Choose varieties that won't grow more than 8–12 inches high, and clip to keep them the size you want. You can clip some into the shapes of bushes, others into trees. Many different herbs are appropriate. Here are a few suggestions:

- Dwarf boxwood
- Curly chives
- Dwarf curry
- Creeping germander
- Lady's mantle
- Lavender
- Marjoram
- Myrtle
- Oregano
- Dwarf santolina
- Creeping savory
- Scented geranium
- Thyme

### LANDSCAPING AND FAIRY GARDEN FURNITURE

Fairies love a garden that has a "lived-in" look. Add a path of tiny cobbles, a quartz crystal, a pretty shell, a bit of bark or an intricately-shaped branch with lichen growing on it, a reflecting pool made of a small mirror, a Popsicle-stick fence, a bench, an arbor, a wheelbarrow, and other miniature tools and garden accents. A great variety of fairy furniture is available these days—and fairy figures, too. (You might want to add one or two of these, until your garden attracts the real thing.) Garden lighting would be fun, and if you really want to lure fairies, add a miniature fountain, and maybe even a plate of tiny Faerie Blossom Cookies, as a special treat (see May 1). Use your imagination, and be sure to include all the things you'd like to see in your garden if you were a fairy.

*You see children know such a lot now, they don't believe in fairies, and every time a child says, "I don't believe in fairies," there is a fairy somewhere that falls down dead.*

—JAMES BARRIE, *PETER PAN*

# MAY 1

Today is Beltane (meaning "bright fire") the cross-quarter day of the ancient Celtic year, celebrating the beginning of summer. Other cross-quarter days: Imbolc (February 1), Lughnasadh or Lammas (August 1), Samhain (November 1).

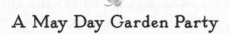

## A May Day Garden Party

The first day of May is the very best day to celebrate our gardens and enjoy them with neighbors and friends. The party doesn't have to be elaborate or involve a lot of work if every guest brings a salad, a casserole, or a dessert. Ask people to use their favorite herbs, and bring a recipe card to display with their offering.

Dress up your table with a bright cloth, cotton napkins edged with pinking shears, flower-wreathed candles, and a few terra-cotta pots filled with rosemary, thyme, parsley, and sage. If your party includes children, they would delight in a miniature May Pole, with bright ribbons and flowers, centered in a large, flat container surrounded by flowers. If yours is a nighttime party, string fairy lights in the trees, hang paper lanterns, and float candles in bowls of water.

Fresh salads are the joy of a garden party, with spring greens, edible flowers, and herbs. Chilled garden soups are always good: tomato, cucumber, avocado. Easy garden casseroles (spinach lasagna, chicken and broccoli, scalloped potatoes with ham, eggplant casserole) are filling. A garden punch with lemon balm and mint is easy (see August 30), or you can serve May wine (see May 24). And dessert tops it off—fresh fruit, cobbler, cheesecake—each featuring an herb, of course. For the kids, Faery Blossom Cookies are sure to be a hit. Here's the recipe from the Fairy Festival Ruby organized in "A Violet Death," in *An Untimely Death and Other Garden Mysteries*:

### FAERIE BLOSSOM COOKIES

2 tablespoons sugar
¼ cup fresh lemon-basil leaves, packed down
¼ cup fresh lemon balm leaves, packed down
¾ cup sugar
½ cup butter or margarine, softened
1 egg
3 tablespoons lemon juice
3 cups flour

Preheat oven to 350°, and lightly grease two baking sheets. In a blender or food processor, process the fresh herbs with 2 tablespoons sugar and set aside. Using your electric mixer, beat butter or margarine until creamy, gradually adding ¾ cup sugar. Add egg and lemon juice and blend. Add herb-sugar mixture, then flour, 1 cup at a time, beating to blend thoroughly. Shape into 1-inch balls and place 2 inches apart on greased baking sheet. Dip the bottom of a glass in sugar and flatten each ball. Bake until golden brown, about 8–10 minutes. Remove to wire racks to cool. Yield: about 3 dozen.

# MAY 2

The first week of May is National Herb Week.

*Mildred obviously enjoyed garden crafts, and the living room was full of her work—bouquets of dried flowers, some small framed pictures made with delicate arrangements of pressed pansies, lavender, and dried herbs, and a sweet-smelling bowl of rose potpourri.*

—"AN UNTHYMELY DEATH," IN AN UNTHYMELY DEATH AND
OTHER GARDEN MYSTERIES

## A Handcrafted Herbal Gift

To celebrate National Herb Week, here is a recipe for a fragrant, old-fashioned rose potpourri that you will enjoy sharing with a friend. It was created by Mildred Rawlins, whom China and Ruby met when they were investigating the unfortunate demise of one of China's gardening friends.

**OLD-FASHIONED ROSE POTPOURRI**

2 cups dried rose petals

1 cup dried lavender

½ cup fresh or dried rosemary leaves

3 bay leaves, fresh or dried, broken

1 tablespoon ground cinnamon

2 teaspoons grated nutmeg

2 teaspoons whole cloves

1 teaspoon powdered cloves

4–5 whole star anise

2 tablespoons orris root powder (a fixative)

6–8 drops essential rose oil

dried rosebuds for decoration

Mix dried materials together. Mix essential rose oil with orris root powder and toss with dried materials. Store in a covered container for 4-6 weeks, gently stirring or shaking every few days, to blend the fragrances. Display potpourri in a pretty bowl or basket, and renew scent with rose oil when necessary.

**Read more of China's garden sleuthing in this collection of short stories:**

*An Unthymely Death and Other Garden Mysteries*, by Susan Wittig Albert

*To make Oyle of Roses—Take of oyle eighteen ounces, the buds of Roses (the white ends of them cut away) three ounces, lay the Roses abroad in the shadow four and twenty houres, then put them in a Glass to the oyle, and stop the Glass close, and set it in the sunne for at least forty days.*

—JOHN PARTRIDGE, THE TREASURE OF HIDDEN SECRETS AND
COMMODIOUS CONCERTS, 1586

*Herbs are our only living connection to past history.*

—DON HAYNIE

## Going Places: Buffalo Springs Herb Farm

The Buffalo Springs Herb Farm, a lovely 220-acre farmstead, is located in Rockbridge County, Virginia, in the Shenandoah Valley, an area of spectacular mountain views, quiet green valleys, and charming towns and villages. Don Haynie and Tom Hamlin bought the eighteenth-century farm in 1989 and began restoring its buildings and fields. They opened the farm to the public in August 1991. Two of their most popular events are the annual May Day celebration on the first Saturday in May—a community-wide event with a May Pole, craft workshops, lectures, food, art, and a ballet performance—and the annual Christmas house tours of their eighteenth-century farmhouse, decorated with holiday herbs and other natural materials.

Don has a special interest in history, and he and Tom have worked very hard to preserve the historical spirit of Buffalo Springs. Their meticulously restored buildings, originally built in the 1790s, will give you a glimpse of life as it was lived by the earliest settlers. But it is the dozen or so theme gardens that will steal your heart. The Celestial Garden, the Fragrance Garden, the Mediterranean Garden, and the Medicinal Garden all give us glimpses of the way herbs have been used over the centuries. The Medieval Garden contains an abbey ruins and is filled with herbs of ritual and worship. You'll smell the sweet scent of strewing herbs—angelica, lavender, rosemary, sage—and hear the muted sounds of Gregorian chants.

May Fest is the farm's most special occasion, with music, wonderful food, beautiful flowers and herbs, and a May Pole. I know, because I was crowned Queen of the May there, in 2006. It was a day of bright flowers and warm friendship, and I'll never forget it.

Buffalo Springs Herb Farm has a plant house, a gift shop, a nature trail with a waterfall and labyrinth, and provides luncheons with selected programs and for groups, by reservation. When you visit the web site (www.buffaloherbs.com), you'll see their current list of workshops, seminars, retreats, special events, hours of operation, and directions. (The farm is three hours from Washington, D.C. and two hours from Richmond.) Treat yourself and your family to a visit!

**Read about creating an Advent garden:**

*The Season of Advent: Herbal Symbolism, Projects, Garden Designs & Recipes*, by Don Haynie (available from the web site or at the farm)

# MAY 4

Tomorrow is National Midwives Day.

*In western tradition, midwives have inspired fear, reverence, amusement, and disdain. They have been condemned for witchcraft, eulogized for Christian benevolence, and caricatured for bawdy humor and old wives' tales.*

—LAUREL THATCHER ULRICH, *A MIDWIFE'S TALE: THE LIFE OF MARTHA BALLARD, BASED ON HER DIARY, 1785–1812*

## A Midwife's Tale

In the 27 years that Martha Ballard kept her remarkable diary, she attended 816 births and served as the apothecary for Hallowell, Maine, crafting and dispensing herbal medications. Her journal gives us a valuable record of a midwife's remarkable service to her community. It is worth reading as the testament of a dedicated herbal practitioner. Laurel Ulrich's appendix detailing Ballard's medicinal plants provides a wealth of information.

Here are a few of the plants Martha Ballard raised in her garden or gathered wild in the woods and fields, with her descriptions of their use in her practice:

• April 5, 1790. For complications following childbirth, "applyd ointment & a Bath of Tansy, mugwort, camomile, & Hysop, which gave Mrs. Cragg relief."
• November 30, 1791. "My daughter Hannah is very unwell this evening. I gave her some Cammomile & Camphor."
• June 5, 1794. For her niece, Parthenia Pitts, "I made a syrup of comphry, plaintain, agrimony & Solomon Seal leaves."
• March 29, 1797. She treated a patient with a "syrup of vinegar and onions and a decoction of gold thread [*Coptis trifolia*] and shumake [sumac] berries."
• August 26, 1799. She was called to treat a young girl with a high fever. "We applied Burdoc leaves to her stomach and feet and gave her a syrrip of mullin and she had some rest."
• May 5, 1807. "Mrs. Nason Calld in to get some Dock root for the itch."
• December 23, 1811. "Sally Ballard is unwell. I made her Sage Tea."

This wonderful book is a tribute to two spirited, persistent, and talented women: Martha Ballard herself, who devoted her life to using herbs to heal; and Laurel Ulrich, the historian who saw the remarkable virtue in Ballard's diary and labored long and hard to bring us this Pulitzer prize–winning work. Both are extraordinary midwives.

**Read more:**
*A Midwife's Tale: The Life of Martha Ballard, Based on Her Diary,* 1785–1812, by Laurel Thatcher Ulrich

# MAY 5

Today is Cinco de Mayo (the Fifth of May). The holiday is celebrated in Mexico and in Mexican-American communities in the U.S. It commemorates the Battle of Puebla (1862), where the Mexican militia defeated the French.

> *Maggie [Garrett] created an open-air dining area under the pecan and live oak trees and I landscaped it with perennial herbs such as Mexican oregano (*Poliomintha longiflora, *a shrub that bears lavender flowers on glossy leaves and has the same scent as Greek and Turkish oregano) and Texas wildflowers—coreopsis, eryngo, gayfeather, bee balm, and several asclepias for the butterflies.*
>
> —WITCHES' BANE: A CHINA BAYLES MYSTERY

## Herbs from South of the Border

If you haven't experimented with the interesting Mexican herbs that are increasingly available, it's time you gave them a try. Here is a quartet of the personal favorites I grow in my Texas garden.

- Mexican Mint Marigold (*Tagetes lucida*). If you live in the sultry South, you know how hard it is to grow tarragon successfully. Try this delightful substitute, which has a stronger anise-licorice flavor than tarragon. It's zippy in vinegars and vinaigrettes, adds zest to herbal butters, and is a delicious addition to pesto. Bonus: the plant repels insects and the blossoms are pretty on your table!

- Cilantro (*Coriandrum sativum*). Throughout the Southwest, you'll taste the fresh pungency of cilantro in salads, salsas, beans, and sandwiches. The leaves look like Italian (flat-leaf) parsley, and best used when the plant is young. Don't try to dry the leaves; you'll lose every bit of the flavor.

- Mexican Oregano (*Poliomintha longiflora*). In my garden, this plant is a 5-foot shrub, with highly aromatic leaves and pretty tubular flowers that attract bees and hummingbirds. Steeped in a robust red wine vinegar, with garlic and chiles, it's a lively marinade. The leaves may be added to soups, beans, and stews (although I like to take them out before serving). Another oregano, *Lippia graveolens*, is used on pizzas and with tomato sauces.

- Hojo Santa, or the root beer plant (*Piper auritum*). When you rub the leaves, your fingers smell like root beer. This tall (6–10 feet) tropical herb likes plenty of humidity, and does well in containers. The leaves are the size of dinner plates, and are often wrapped around tamales. Shredded, they're used to season sauces, chicken, and fish.

**Read more about growing and using south-of-the-border herbs:**
*The Herb Garden Cookbook*, by Lucinda Hutson
*The Essential Cuisines of Mexico*, by Diana Kennedy

May's Theme Garden: A Moon Garden.

*Here at the end of the garden walk is an arbor dark with the shadow of great leaves, such as Gerard calls "leaves round a big like to a buckler." But out of that shadowed background of leaf on leaf shine hundreds of pure, pale stars of sweetness and light,—a true flower of the night in fragrance, beauty, and name—the Moonvine. It is a flower of sentiment, full of suggestion.*

—ALICE MORSE EARLE, *OLD TIME GARDENS*, 1901

## Gardens in the Moonlight

For centuries, people have been enchanted at the sight of the moon in a garden. In medieval Japan, the moonlight was reflected by carefully arranged white rocks and sand, silvery pools of water, and white chrysanthemums. In seventeenth-century India, jasmine, narcissus, lilies, and tuberoses shone in the darkness. Many gray, silver, and white plants are candidates for a cooling retreat, day and night.

Many moon gardens are designed in moon shapes: circles and crescents. You can make your garden large or very small; you can plant it around a pool, or in containers on your deck. Another ideal spot: at the foot of a lamppost, supporting a glow-in-the-dark moonflower.

### HERBS AND FLOWERS FOR YOUR MOON GARDEN

- Artemisia (*Artemisia sp.*). Silver-gray, ferny "Powys Castle," "Dusty Miller," and taller "Silver Queen" are good year round.
- Candytuft (*Iberis sempervirens* "Autumn Snow"). A dainty perennial edging.
- Chrysanthemum (*Chrysanthemum sp.*). There are many decorative varieties, in various heights.
- Hosta (*Hosta plantaginea*). Fragrant white flower spikes appear in late summer.
- Lamb's-Ears (*Stachys byzantina*). Low and silvery, a perfect border plant, and soft to the touch, too.
- Moonflower or Moonvine (*Ipomoea alba*). Perennial in warm climates, this vine will grow to 20 feet. Fragrant, trumpet-shaped white blossoms.
- Nicotiana (*Nicotiana alata grandiflora*). Jasmine-scented ornamental tobacco, elegant, a delight for bees and pollinating insects.
- Shasta daisy (*Chrysanthemum x superbum*). Will fill the garden with white blossoms from early summer to frost.
- Summersweet (*Clethra alnifolia*). A mid-sized rotund shrub, can fill the whole garden with fragrance in July and August.
- White bellflower (*Campanula persicifolia* "Alba"). Flowers in summer.

**Read more about gardens that glow in the dark:**

*The Evening Garden: Flowers and Fragrance from Dusk Till Dawn*, by Peter Loewer

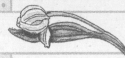

Today is National Roast Leg of Lamb Day.

*"There's an herb sauce for everything, including lamb."*

—MYRA MERRYWEATHER

## The Merryweathers Do Mint

At their regular monthly get-togethers, the Merryweathers celebrate a particular herb. This month, China says, it was mint. Henrietta Henchman kicked off the meeting with a somewhat surprising report on how mint got to be mint: It seems that Pluto was carrying on with a pretty young thing named Mentha. When his wife, Persephone, found out about it, she turned Mentha into a plant and sent her crawling away. Pluto, she banished to the underworld for three-quarters of the year. He could only come up when it got cold enough to freeze the toes off a brass monkey.

Everything that followed this sensational revelation seemed a little anticlimactic, China told me. But Mrs. Henchman gave some good tips on culinary mint, including this one: Store a bunch of mint in the refrigerator, stems down, in a glass of water with a plastic bag over the top. (You can put parsley in the same glass; they'll get along without fighting.) And Fannie Couch came up with several strategies for keeping mint, a notorious garden bully, from taking over the neighborhood. "Plant it in a pot, and plant the pot inside another pot, and plant both in the ground," she said. "When that doesn't work, pull. Growl fiercely and mutter curses while pulling. If all else fails, lock it in the garden shed and throw away the key."

Then there was a recipe exchange—sauces, this time. This is China's favorite.

**SISSY SMILES' CILANTRO-MINT YOGURT SAUCE**
- ½ cup chopped fresh mint, packed
- ½ cup chopped fresh cilantro, packed
- 1 fresh jalapeño or serrano chile, seeded and chopped
- 2 garlic cloves, minced
- 1 tablespoon lemon juice
- 3 tablespoons water
- ¾ cup plain yogurt
- salt to taste
- mint sprig for garnish

Put mint, cilantro, jalapeño, garlic, and lemon juice into a blender. Add up to 3 tablespoons water and process until smooth. Whip yogurt in a bowl until creamy. Fold in cilantro mixture. Add salt to taste, and garnish with a sprig of mint. Makes about 1½ cups. Spoon over grilled chicken, shrimp, or lamb.

And don't miss the Merryweathers' Annual Basil Festival, coming June 14!

**Read more about mint:**
*Growing and Cooking with Mint*: Storey Country Wisdom Bulletin A-145, by Glenn Andrews

On this date in 1886, the first Coca-Cola was sold.

*The cultivation and trade of coca is a very important enterprise and of the greatest significance.*

—JUAN MATIENZO, REPRESENTATIVE OF COCA GROWERS, IN A LETTER TO KING PHILLIP II, 1566

*Coca is a thing without benefit . . . and takes the lives of many.*

—THE SECOND COUNCIL OF LIMA, TO KING PHILLIP II, 1569

## Coca-Cola: The World's Most Popular Herbal Drink

In 1886, in a three-legged kettle in his Atlanta, Georgia, backyard, Dr. John S. Pemberton brewed a carbonated, nonalcoholic, herbal tonic that he called Pemberton's French Wine Coca. Pemberton's formula called for 5 ounces of coca leaf (the source of cocaine) per gallon of syrup. The coca's hefty kick was boosted by a generous dose of the caffeine-rich kola nut; hence: Coca-Cola.

The first glass of Pemberton's tonic was sold to the public at Jacob's Pharmacy on May 8, 1886, for five cents. Originally advertised as "valuable brain-tonic and cure for all nervous afflictions," a glass of Coke contained about 60 milligrams of cocaine. After Asa Chandler bought the company and began distributing syrup for bottled Coke, the drink's popularity soared.

But the dangers of cocaine were recognized, and public disapproval mounted. The drug was removed from the drink by 1903, the company insisting that the "spent leaves" of coca were used for flavoring only.

Coca was first used by the ancient Incas of Peru, where coca-induced trance states were part of their religious ceremonies. The Spanish conquistadors introduced coca to Europe, and in 1853, its active ingredient was isolated and named cocaine. The drug became enormously popular and was used by such notables as Sigmund Freud, Robert Louis Stevenson, Sherlock Holmes, and polar explorer Ernest Shackleton. It was sold over the counter in tonics, toothache cures, and patent medicines; in chocolate cocaine candies; and in cigarettes "guaranteed to lift depression." Cocaine was banned in the U.S. in 1914, and outlawed under The Dangerous Drug Act of 1920.

Those of us who appreciate herbs often think of them as "warm and fuzzy" plants used for good and pleasant purposes. The story of coca's transition from limited use of the whole leaf for religious purposes to the use of the extract as a recreational drug provides us with another view: a sad commentary on humans' misuse and abuse of plants.

**Read more about coca and the drink it made famous:**
*A Brief History of Cocaine*, by Steven B. Karch, M.D.
*For God, Country, and Coca-Cola: A Definitive History of the Great American Soft Drink and the Company that Makes It*, by Mark Pendergrast

On this day in 1914, President Woodrow Wilson issued a proclamation asking Americans to celebrate Mother's Day.

*And so our mothers and grandmothers have, more often than not anonymously, handed on the creative spark, the seed of the flower they themselves never hoped to see—or like a sealed letter they could not plainly read.*

—ALICE WALKER, "IN SEARCH OF OUR MOTHERS' GARDENS"

## Peonies for Mother's Day

The carnation became a symbol of Mother's Day because President William McKinley wore a white one in honor of his mother. White carnations are fine. I have nothing against them. But my mother's peonies always bloomed on Mother's Day, and to me, those extravagant floppy flowers are emblematic of a mother's love.

### THE MEDICINAL, MAGICAL PEONY

In traditional Chinese medicine, the roots and bark of the peony were used to "cool the blood" and treat bacterial infections. In medieval Europe, the peony was a cure-all remedy for gall stones, jaundice, sore gums, and more. Because it was associated with the moon (large, white, round), it was thought to be a remedy for lunacy, as well as for epilepsy, nightmares, and nervous disorders. Peony seeds were swallowed whole to prevent bad dreams, or used in a poultice to relieve stomachaches, while the flower petals were dried and brewed in a tea to ease coughs.

In Europe, peonies were planted near the door to keep evil from entering the house. In England, the seeds were strung and hung as necklaces around children's necks, to keep them from being carried off by fairies and witches. An odd number of flowers on a plant was a sign that death would come before the year was out. In Renaissance England, there was only one way to harvest the root of this dangerous plant: Like the magical mandrake, it had to be pulled out of the ground with a rope attached to a dog.

The peony was one of those flowers that sent a mixed message. White peonies symbolized purity, chastity, and virtue. The red peony, blushing, signified shame. It is said that proper Victorian ladies refused to plant the red peony in their gardens. My grandmother must have been an improper lady; she loved her red peonies above all others.

For me, the peony's magic is never dangerous, only alluring. I can't grow it here at Meadow Knoll (it requires colder weather to bloom). But I will always remember my mother's and grandmother's delight in its wonderful floppy blossoms. When I see it, I think of them.

*A necklace of beads turned from Poeony roots and hung round an infant's neck will prevent convulsions when teething.*

—TRADITIONAL, FROM SUSSEX, ENGLAND

# MAY 10

## Making Paper with Plants, Part One

When Maggie Bruce invited me to contribute to a collection of craft-themed who-dunnits entitled *Murder Most Crafty*, I said yes immediately, and thought of writing about handmade paper. In fact, the research for this short story led me to start making my own paper—and to write a book-length China Bayles mystery, *Spanish Dagger*, featuring a paper artist (available in 2007). I'm hooked!

Papermaking is a fascinating craft, with encouraging results from the beginning. You can use your handmade paper in hundreds of ways: as note paper, holiday cards, calling cards, journal and scrapbook pages, collages, lampshades, gift boxes, book covers, and more. And to add to the pleasure, you'll be using herbs and flowers from your own garden. Love-in-a-mist, pinks, southernwood, borage, thyme, fern, and fennel are among the herbs I've grown and used in paper. Here's an easy project based on recycled paper, from China's adventure, "The Collage to Kill For." (Part One of this topic contains the list of supplies; Part Two, May 11, contains the instructions. Read both before you begin.)

### CHINA BAYLES' HERBS & FLOWERS PAPER PROJECT
*To make the paper pulp, you'll need these items:*
   white copy paper (with no printing)
   rosemary leaves
   bits of fern
   tiny leaves of thyme, savory, southernwood, or other
      small-leaved herbs
   petals from roses, marigolds, borage, pinks, or other small
      blossoms
   liquid starch (an optional sizing, for writing paper only)
   a blender
   a 1- or 2-quart pan
   water

*To make the mold, you'll need:*
   fiberglass window screening, about 10 inches × 12 inches
   a wooden picture frame, about 8 inches × 10 inches
   staples or tacks

*To make the paper, you'll need:*
   a plastic dish pan, to serve as the vat
   6 damp felts (Handiwipes cut in half are convenient and
      cheap)
   a cookie sheet (on which to stack the post of felts and
      paper)
   a damp sponge
   a second cookie sheet (to press the post)

### Read about China's adventure in papermaking:
"The Collage to Kill For," by Susan Wittig Albert, in
   *Murder Most Crafty*, edited by Maggie Bruce

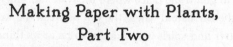

## Making Paper with Plants, Part Two

*To make the mold,* stretch the fiberglass screening over the wooden frame and staple or tack it as tightly as possible.

*To make the pulp,* tear the paper into enough small pieces to fill the blender half full. Add warm water to within 2 inches of the top. Start the blender at a slower speed; increase until the pulp is smooth and thoroughly blended. For writing paper, add 2 teaspoons of liquid starch. (This sizing helps to keep ink from bleeding.) Remove stems from petals and leaves, separate. Bring a quart of water to boil. Add petals and leaves and blanch for 4–5 minutes. Strain. Add petals and leaves to the pulp and stir gently.

*To begin making the paper,* pour the pulp into the vat. Repeat this process twice more, until you have the contents of three blenders in the vat. Now, add enough warm water to fill the vat about three-quarters full. Stir this slurry with your hands to mix. The thicker the slurry, the thicker the paper. Add water or pulp until it is the consistency of pancake batter.

*To create a sheet of paper,* pick up the mold by the short sides, holding it with the mesh side up. Dip the mold into the pulp-filled vat, at about a 45-degree angle. Scoop it under the surface of the pulp. Lift it quickly but steadily out of the slurry, aiming for a smooth, fairly thin layer of pulp on top of the mold. If you're not satisfied, turn the mold over and dump the pulp into the slurry. If the sheet looks okay, shake the mold left to right and back to front to lock the pulp fibers together and produce a uniformly-thick sheet of paper.

Lay a damp felt on the cookie sheet. Place one long edge of the mold on the felt, the wet sheet of paper facing the felt. Gently lay the mold flat, so that the paper is lying directly on the damp felt. With the damp sponge, blot the back of the mold to take up the excess water. Holding down one edge of the mold, slowly lift the other. The wet sheet of paper should remain on the felt. Place another damp felt on top of the sheet of paper.

*To make additional sheets of paper,* stir the pulp with your hands and make another sheet. Stack the sheets of paper and the felts on top of one another as you work.

*To press the paper,* carry the cookie sheet outdoors, or put it in the bathtub, so that you don't have a mess to clean up. Then use the second cookie sheet to press the remaining water out of the post.

*To dry the paper,* gently separate the felts, clip them to coat hangers, and hang them to dry. When nearly so, gently pull off the paper and iron it dry.

*To save your pulp,* dump the remaining slurry into a colander to drain. Put it into a plastic bag and refrigerate or freeze it. NEVER pour pulp down the drain—it will clog!

**Read about making paper with the herbs in your garden:**

*Grow Your Own Paper: Recipes for Creating Unique Handmade Papers*, by Maureen Richardson

In some calendars, the Celtic Tree Month of Hawthorn begins tomorrow.

> *Hawthorn was intimately connected to all aspects of village life, especially that conducted around village wells.*
>
> —JACQUELINE MEMORY PATERSON, *TREE WISDOM*

## The Decorating of the Wells

About this time of year, it was the custom in many English villages to "dress the well," or decorate the village spring from which everyone drew water. This ancient ceremony is thought to have originated from pagan times, a ritual of thanksgiving for the clear, cool water that seemed to magically persist through even the most severe droughts. Another possibility: The custom may have been introduced by the Romans, for the philosopher Seneca suggests that "where springs or rivers flow we should build altars and make sacrifices." However it began, it was banned (as were most pagan rituals) by Catholic priests. The tradition was surreptitiously maintained in some villages, particularly in the county of Derbyshire, where herbs and flowers are inserted in elaborate designs, in shallow frames filled with damp clay and placed beside the well.

The connection of hawthorn and the wells was an important one, for hawthorn was thought to be an herb of fertility and abundance, and many thorns still flourish around old wells. As a magical tree, it was supposed to guard the place where the water sprang forth from the earth, and where the veil between the worlds of matter and spirit was thought to be at its thinnest. Where the hawthorn grew, the friendly fairies gathered, and all was well. Believing that the spirits would live in the well only if they were remembered and respectfully addressed, neighbors from the area brought offerings of flowers to the tree and the well, and celebrated the occasion with stories of the magical happenings there. When the priests came, they revised the stories, so that springs were said to have appeared where saints were beheaded, or had slain dragons, or where the Virgin appeared and left her footprints in the stone.

If you have water in your garden—a pool, a pond, a small fountain—you might like to re-create this ancient celebration of water's power to cleanse, renew, and heal. Perhaps you could plant a hawthorn tree, or decorate your pool or fountain with spring herbs and flowers, or simply sit beside the water and drink a quiet cup of herbal tea, remembering the importance of clean, clear water in our lives, and saying thank you.

**Explore mystic water, powerful plants:**
*Sacred Waters: Holy Wells and Water Lore in Britain and Ireland,* by Janet Bord

# MAY 13

Today is National Tulip Day.

*How could such sweet and wholesome hours*
*Be reckoned but with herbs and flowers?*
—ANDREW MARVEL, 1621–1678

## Tulips on the Menu

Bertha Reppert introduced many of us to the delights of herbs at her Rosemary House, in Mechanicsburg, Pennsylvania. In her book, *Mrs. Reppert's Twelve-Month Herbal*, she describes tulip cups:

. . . I ventured out to gather eight matched red tulip flowers for a luncheon. They will be stuffed with chicken salad . . . to which I plan to add water chestnuts, grated carrot for more color, a touch of new green chives, hard-boiled egg, and black olive halves, and, most importantly, chopped up tulip stems which look and taste like raw peas. This festive platter will draw gasps of admiration because the perky red tulip cups always excite comment. Yes, they are edible, although eating the tulip is each person's option. . . . The pretty salad will be garnished with Johnny-jump-ups. I'll put one of the smiling Johnnies in each goblet of water as well.

If you'd like to impress your luncheon guests with tulip cups, be sure to use only unsprayed flowers from your garden. Cut off the stem at the base of the cup, so that it sits flat, and remove the pistils and stamens. To fill easily, place each tulip cup in a muffin-pan cup. Chill in the pan for one hour before serving, and get ready for those compliments!

### THE TALE OF THE TULIP

The tulip began as a wildflower in western Turkey. A famous legend tells of a prince, whose lover was killed, he mounted his favorite horse and rode off a cliff to his death. From each drop of his blood, a scarlet tulip was said to have sprung up, so that the flower became a symbol of undying love.

In the late 1500s, tulips found their way to Holland. There, an extensive breeding program quickly resulted in exotic flowers that became a status symbol and the center of frenzied speculation. By the 1630s, bulbs were selling for exorbitant prices; one bulb went for 6,000 florins, when the average annual Dutch salary was 150 florins. They were traded on the stock exchanges, and some people, suffering from tulipomania, literally sold everything they possessed to buy tulips. The bubble burst in 1637—an event comparable to the Crash of 1929—and thousands of people were ruined. Luckily for us, the tulip survived.

**Learn about the tulip craze:**
*Tulipomania: The Story of the World's Most Coveted Flower and the Extraordinary Passions It Aroused*, by Mike Dash

On this day in 1607, the first permanent British settlement in North America was established at Jamestown, Virginia.

*In Virginia, there is a plant called the Jamestown weed, whereof some having eaten plentifully became fools for several days, one would blow up a feather in the air, another sit naked, like a monkey, grinning at the rest, or fondly kiss and paw his companions. . . .*

—COTTON MATHER, 1720

## Jimsonweed

The amusing story of the soldiers who ate the hallucinogenic herb Jamestown weed, or jimsonweed, is often told as an example of what not to do: Don't eat plants you're not familiar with. The unwise soldiers, who recovered after eleven days, were lucky, for they had feasted on *Datura stramonium*, a psychoactive member of the nightshade family. Jimsonweed and other related plants contain a narcotic that has been used in many cultures as a poison, a medicine (chiefly as a painkiller and wound healer), and as a ceremonial hallucinogenic: an aid to worship, or to obtaining prophetic dreams or messages. And yes, it can kill you, if you eat enough of it.

**BRUGMANSIA**

Knowing about the dangers of *Datura*, I was surprised to see a beautiful specimen of Brugmansia—called Angel's Trumpet—in the nursery last year, without any warning of its toxicity. When I asked the clerk about it, she just smiled. "Nonsense," she said. "It's completely harmless."

Not so! Like other nightshades, Brugmansia has its darker side. In pre-Conquest Colombia, slaves and wives of dead kings were given a toxic brew of Brugmansia, to sedate them so they wouldn't make a fuss when they were buried alive with their masters and husbands. Nobody's likely to eat it accidentally, since it doesn't taste good. But do keep children (especially adolescents who might be inclined to experiment) away from the plant.

And one other word, while we're on the subject. Many familiar plants are toxic, some of them fatally so. These include oleander, azalea, iris, larkspur, daffodil, crocus, lantana, caladium, dieffenbachia, lupine, castor bean, lily of the valley, poinsettia, bittersweet, boxwood, English ivy, and nicotiana. We don't have to give these beauties up, but we do need to know what they are and how to handle them.

**Read more about plants that have a darker side to their personality:**
*Murder, Magic, and Medicine*, by John Mann

# MAY 15

American poet Emily Dickinson died on this day in 1886.

*My plants look finely now. I am going to send you a little geranium leaf, which you must press for me. Have you made an herbarium yet? I hope you will if you have not, it would be such a treasure to you.*

—EMILY DICKINSON, AGE 14, IN A LETTER TO ABIAH ROOT

## Miss Dickinson's Herbarium

When young Emily Dickinson was a student at Amherst Academy, she began creating an herbarium, a leather-bound collection of pressed plants and flowers. She compiled 66 pages, each page displaying 5 or more specimens. The pressed materials, identified by their botanical names in Emily's small, precise lettering, are attached to the right-hand pages; the left-hand pages, which serve to protect the pressed plants, are blank. The plants, over 450 of them, are mounted on the page with paper bands, glued at each end, allowing the plant to be removed from the page. (Now, of course, the plants are too fragile for removal. Archivists at the Houghton Library of Harvard University, where the collection is held, have prepared photographs of each page for use by researchers; the originals are kept in a special temperature- and humidity-controlled area.)

Emily Dickinson's love of flowers is evident in the more than 1,800 poems she wrote. Only ten were published in her lifetime; the others were not discovered until her sister found them, neatly organized, after Dickinson's death. She is considered one of America's finest poets.

## TO MAKE YOUR OWN HERBARIUM

Collect the whole plant, including the roots, leaves, twigs, blossoms, and seeds. Clean. Spread on newspaper and press in layers, separated by blotting paper and/or pieces of cardboard. Change the blotting papers daily until the plants are dry (a week or more). Arrange the plants on acid-free pages. Mount them with paper strips or acid-free glue. Include the plant's common and botanical names, the place and date of collection, and perhaps a record of your impressions and experiences of the plant. Keep your pages in a binder, or make special covers for them, bound with raffia or ribbon. Shelve in a dark place.

**Read more about Emily Dickinson's herbs and flowers:** *The Gardens of Emily Dickinson*, by Judith Farr

*I hide myself within my flower,*
*That wearing on your breast,*
*You, unsuspecting, wear me too—*
*And angels know the rest.*

—EMILY DICKINSON

Boursin cheese—a mild, creamy cheese flavored with herbs—was originally created in 1957 by François Boursin in the Normandy region of France. Now, the term is used to describe many herb-flavored cheeses.

## Herbs and Cheese

Cheese has been an important part of the human diet for at least 5,000 years, and its smooth texture and (usually!) unobtrusive taste make it a perfect companion for savory herbs. Boursin, an herbed cheese spread that originated in France, makes the best of the natural duo. You can buy it at the supermarket, or make your own taste-alike.

### BOURSIN

- 1 cup farmer's cheese
- 1 cup Asaigo or Parmesan cheese, grated
- 8 ounces cream cheese, softened (don't use "lite" or low-fat)
- 1 stick butter, softened
- 1 teaspoon lemon juice
- 2 tablespoons minced chives
- 3 cloves garlic, finely minced
- ½ cup minced parsley
- 1 teaspoon fresh minced marjoram
- 1 teaspoon fresh minced thyme

In a large bowl, blend the cheeses. Blend in the butter and lemon juice. Add the other ingredients and mix well. Refrigerate to blend flavors. Makes about 30 ounces.

### BOURSIN BASIL ROLLUPS

- 8 ounces Boursin, softened
- 4 8-inch flour tortillas
- 16 fresh basil leaves, washed and dried
- 4 ounces thin-shaved deli roast beef
- 4 teaspoons Dijon mustard

To make this easy appetizer, divide Boursin into fourths and spread one portion over each tortilla. Cover with fresh basil leaves, then layer with roast beef. Spread 1 teaspoon mustard over the meat. Roll up the tortillas tightly and wrap in plastic wrap. Chill 2–3 hours. To serve, cut in slices, straight across or diagonal. Arrange on a platter with fresh greens and herb sprigs.

*If you will have a very dainty Nettle Cheese, which is the finest Summer Cheese which can be eaten . . . as soone as it is drained from the Brine, you shall lay it upon fresh Nettles, and cover it all over with the same, and let it ripen Therein. Observing to renew your Nettles once in two days, and every time you renew them, to turn the Cheese.*

—GERVASE MARKHAM, *THE ENGLISH HOUSEWIFE*, 1615

The first Kentucky Derby was run on this day in 1875.

*. . . the mounds of ices, and the bowls of mint-julep and sherry cobbler they make in these latitudes, are refreshments never to be thought of afterwards, in summer, by those who would preserve contented minds.*

—CHARLES DICKENS, TRAVELING IN AMERICA IN 1842

## Will the Real Mint Julep Please Stand Up?

The mint julep is more than the official Derby Day drink—it's a page of history. Although mint may have been added for the first time in Maryland (or was it Virginia or Carolina?) in the 1700s, the "julep" is an ancient drink known to several cultures. The Persians called it *gulab* and made it with rose water. To the Portuguese, it was *julepe*. And in pharmaceutical Latin, *julapium* refers to any sweetened, aromatic mixture containing a medicated water or an essential oil.

Julep is French, but the mint julep is definitely American. The American South, that is. And if Southern humorist Irving S. Cobb is right, the mint julep may have been a *casus belli* of the War Between the States. It seems to have something to do with nutmeg. "Down our way we've always had a theory," he said. "The war was brought on by some Yankee coming down South and putting nutmeg in a julep. So our folks just up and left the Union flat."

### THE PERFECT MINT JULEP

Beyond the no-nutmeg dictum, there's not much unanimity about how to make the perfect mint julep. The classic Kentucky version: dissolve one lump of sugar in a little water, and add two ounces of bourbon. Pour over shaved ice in a silver mug and stir. Push four sprigs of fresh mint down into the ice and add a short straw. On the other hand, there's the "muddling" school, where the mint is crushed with a spoon in a spoonful of bourbon. And should the mint go in stems up or stems down? Must the ice be shaved, or does crushed ice do as well? Why is the straw short? Do you need a straw at all? What about that silver cup—wouldn't it taste just as good in a glass?

And then there's the recipe developed by an editor of the *Louisville Courier-Journal*, and quoted in Joe Nickell's book, *The Kentucky Mint Julep*. It requires not just one but two glasses, but other than that, it's simple:

Pour the bourbon into the first glass, and mix the mint, sugar and water in the second. Throw out the second and drink the first.

**Read more about the mint, the bourbon, and the Great Horse Race:**
*The Kentucky Mint Julep*, by Joe Nickell

# MAY 18

In some years, today is Hug Your Cat Day.

*"I've always been curious about catnip," Dottie said, watching the melee [cats tussling over a catnip mouse]. "What makes cats go crazy over it?"*

*"It's genetic," I replied. "Nearly all cats are attracted to the volatile oils in the bruised leaves—even the big cats, lions, tigers. But only about two-thirds have the gene that makes them go bananas."*

*"Maybe I should grow some catnip," she said. "Trouble is, the house cats will tear it up."*

*"They will if you set out plants," I said. "But they'll probably ignore it if you grow it from seed."*

—HANGMAN'S ROOT: A CHINA BAYLES MYSTERY

## Hangman's Root: About China's Books Cats vs. Catnip, Round 1

When I settled down to write the third book in the China Bayles series, I already had a character in mind: Dottie Riddle, the Cat Lady of Pecan Springs, who corralled homeless cats in her backyard, thereby setting several nasty neighborhood plots in motion. (Dottie is based on someone I knew years ago: a wonderful woman who could never turn away a homeless kitty.)

Where there are cats, there's bound to be some catnip, so I chose that as the signature herb for the book.

It was a paragraph describing catnip in Michael Castleman's book, *The Healing Herbs*, that gave me an important idea:

> Colonists introduced catnip into North America... [They] believed catnip roots made even the kindest person mean. Hangmen used to consume the roots before executions to get in the right mood for their work.

As I thought about the implications of this, I suddenly knew the title of the book—*Hangman's Root*—and my killer's modus operandi. But more important, I began to understand that every herb has a story to tell, and that the plant's story had the potential of shaping the mystery I wanted to write. It was an ah-ha moment, and from that time on, I began to use herbs in these mysteries in a new way: not just to add texture and interest to the narrative or even to give the mystery greater depth, but to help me find the real story, the story that's hidden in the story of a particular plant.

**Read more:**
*Hangman's Root: A China Bayles Mystery*, by Susan Wittig Albert
*The Healing Herbs: The Ultimate Guide to the Curative Power of Nature's Medicines*, by Michael Castleman

*The sight of a cat in this strange ecstasy over a bunch of Catnip always gives me a half-sense of fear; she becomes such a truly wild creature, such a miniature tiger.*

—ALICE MORSE EARLE, *OLD TIME GARDENS*, 1901

## Cats vs. Catnip, Round 2

Catnip (*Nepeta cataria*) is a perennial member of the mint family, cultivated for centuries for both culinary and medicinal use. In England, the fresh leaves were sprinkled on green salads and the dried herb, mixed with sage and thyme, was used as a seasoning rub for meats. Before China tea became available, people drank tea brewed from the catnip they grew in their gardens. Unlike stimulant teas, catnip tea has a calming effect and was used to induce sleep, quiet upset nerves, and soothe upset stomachs. It was also used to treat colds and flu, reduce fevers, and bring on menstruation—an all-round useful herb.

Now, we use catnip as an ornamental and bee plant, or grow it for our cats. The leaves contain a chemical called nepetalactone, which felines—the tiniest housecats and the largest lions—find irresistible. The chemical induces a harmless physiological reaction that seems to be psychosexual: that is, catnip has both a euphoric and an aphrodisiac effect. Susceptibility is genetic. Some cats just don't get turned on, while others go . . . well, bananas. (Be especially careful if there are lions in the neighborhood.)

When you grow catnip from seed, cats are oblivious to it; when you set transplants, you will inevitably bruise a leaf, releasing the volatile oil, and the cats will come running. Surround it with chicken wire and hope for the best.

### CATNIP VS. MOSQUITOES
Researchers from the University of Iowa have reported that nepetalactone is ten times more effective at repelling mosquitoes than DEET, the synthetic chemical compound used in most insect repellents. You can make some for yourself.

### CATNIP MOSQUITO REPELLENT
　2 cups catnip, washed
　2 cups almond oil

Bruise catnip and pack into a clean jar. Cover with oil, put a lid on the jar and set in a cool, dark place for two weeks. Shake jar lightly every day, and push herbs under the oil to avoid mold. Strain into a clean jar, seal and refrigerate for up to 8 months. To use, rub on exposed skin. (If your mosquitoes are especially ferocious, you can add other strong-smelling herbs, such as rosemary, pennyroyal, basil.)

*May kittens never make big cats.*
*May chicks never grow full size.*

*Many May bugs proclaim a warm summer.*
—TRADITIONAL FARM LORE

# MAY 20

About this time, the ancient Romans celebrated the Rosalia, or Festival of Roses, in honor of the goddess Flora.

> *Delia opened a box, took out a plastic bag, and opened it. "Have you ever smelled anything so sweet?" she asked with a smile, taking out a string of large black beads. "They're rose beads. They'd make a lovely family heirloom."*
>
> —"THE ROSEMARY CAPER," IN *AN UNTHYMELY DEATH*

## An Old-fashioned Treasure

In our grandmothers' time, women were very fond of beautiful black beads made from fresh rose petals. They took a long time to make—two weeks or more—and involved a great deal of work. In her short story, "The Rosemary Caper," China describes an easier way to make this old-fashioned herbal treasure, using a cast-iron pot or large skillet. The iron in the pot helps to blacken the beads. If you can find some rusty nails, add those.

### ROSE BEADS

In a cast-iron cooking container, place a quart of fresh, finely minced red rose petals, a cup of water, a few drops of rose oil to enhance the scent, and rusty nails, if you have any. Simmer for one hour. Remove from heat, stir well with a wooden spoon, and let it stand overnight. The next day, repeat the simmering process, adding water if necessary, until the doughy mixture has turned very dark. Let it stand until it dries to a claylike consistency that can be easily molded. Wet your hands and roll into beads a little larger than a marble. (They will shrink about 50 percent as they dry.) Place on paper towels. When the beads are partly dry, thread a large needle with dental floss, string the beads, and hang them to dry, turning regularly so that they don't stick to the floss. In a week, your rose beads are ready for their final stringing. Alternate them with smaller, pretty beads used as spacers. Add a clasp and store in an airtight container to preserve the scent. As you wear them against your skin, they will warm and give out a sweet fragrance.

### A Bag to Smell Unto, or to Cause One to Sleep

*Take drie Rose leaves, keep them close in a glass which will keep them sweet, then take powder of Mints, powder of cloves in a grosse powder. Put the same to the Rose leaves, then put all these together in a bag, and take that to bed with you, and it will cause you to sleepe, and it is good to smell unto at other times.*

—RAM'S LITTLE DODOEN, 1606

**Read more about old ways to use roses:**

*Rose Recipes from Olden Times*, by Eleanour Sinclair Rohde

Today, the Sun enters the sign of Gemini.

*The third sign of the zodiac, the masculine sign Gemini (the Twins) is ruled by the quick and lively planet Mercury, the messenger of the gods. A mutable sign, fluid and changeable in its purposes, Gemini governs communications and intellectual matters. It is an air sign, suggesting that Gemini people are ingenious, quick-witted, and highly verbal. They may also be restless, easily bored and frustrated when things move slowly.*

—RUBY WILCOX, "ASTROLOGICAL SIGNS"

## Gemini Herbs

Mercury, patron of the art of medicine, was said to rule the respiratory and nervous systems; the ears and hearing; the tongue and speaking; the vocal cords, air passages, lungs, and thyroid, as well as the shoulders, arms, and hands. Plants ruled by Mercury under the sign of Gemini tend to have ferny or divided leaves. Some examples of Gemini herbs:

- Parsley contains high levels of chlorophyll and has been used since ancient times to sweeten the breath, as well as to improve digestion.
- Valerian is a nervine and a relaxant that helps to reduce tension and anxiety, relieve nervous stress, promote sleep, and ease tension-associated pain.

- Licorice has been universally used as a treatment for lung ailments and coughs. It contains glycyrrhetinic acid, a cough suppressant with antiallergenic, antibacterial, and antiviral properties.
- Dill is a nervine and a calmative. In Old Norse, its name means "to lull."
- Other Gemini herbs: elecampane, fennel, flax, caraway. See also the herbs listed for Virgo and Aquarius, both of which are associated with the planet Mercury.

**Read more about herbs and astrology:**

*Healing Herbs and Health Foods of the Zodiac,* by Ada Muir

*There is no single herb without its corresponding star above that beats upon it and commands it to grow.*

—MAIMONIDES, JEWISH PHILOSOPHER, 1135–1204

*White coral bells upon a slender stalk,*
*lilies of the valley deck the garden walk.*
*Oh how I wish that I could hear them ring.*
*That can happen only when the fairies sing.*

—TRADITIONAL

## When the Brownies Sing

I learned this choral round in my Brownie troop, so of course we had our own special version of the last line: "That can happen only when the Brownies sing"— although a friend, years later, informed me that the "right" version belonged to the Campfire Girls.

Over the years, the fragrant spring-flowering lilies of the valley have inspired many poems and legends. In an English tale, St. Leonard went out into the Sussex countryside to battle a dragon, who turned out to be the devil in disguise. After a desperate battle, St. Leonard killed the dragon. Lilies of the valley sprang up from the saint's blood, so that pilgrims to the site could trace the path of the battle. (You'll also find this story in China's mystery *Blood Root*, where lilies of the valley figure in the plot.)

Lily of the valley (*Convallaria majalis*) has long been a medicinal herb. An ointment made from the roots was used to treat burns and prevent scar tissue. More important, the plant had a significant reputation in the treatment of heart complaints, especially congestive heart failure. Modern herbalists recommend its careful use, although the herb's powerful cardiac glycosides can be deadly in inexpert hands. In 1991, Ballantine recalled a cookbook because it suggested decorating a cake with lilies of the valley. (Corrected, the book won a James Beard award.)

In the Victorian language of flowers, this lovely spring-flowering herb symbolized the return of happiness. When you see it, listen for the ringing of the bells, and be on the lookout for Brownies, Campfire Girls—or even fairies.

*The floures of the Valley Lillie distilled with wine and drunke the quantitie of a spoonefull, restore speech unto those that have the dumb palsie and are falne into the apoplexie and are good against the gout and comfort the heart.*

—JOHN GERARD, *THE HERBAL*, 1597

On this day in 1707, Carl Linnaeus was born.

*But these young scholars who invade our hills . . .*
*Love not the flower they pluck, and know it not,*
*And all their botany is Latin names.*
—RALPH WALDO EMERSON, "BLIGHT"

## "All Their Botany Is Latin Names"

The Swedish botanist Carl Linnaeus was not the first to suggest a basic classification for flowering plants, but he was the first to work out the system in detail, basing his system on the number of stamens in the bloom. Most of the time we don't bother to include a plant's full name. But we do use its two basic Latin names: the plant's binomial descriptor. Binomial literally means "two names" and refers to the plant's genus (which is capitalized and may be abbreviated by its first letter) and species (lowercase, may be abbreviated sp.). And in some instances, the binomial becomes a trinomial: some species are further divided into subspecies (subsp.), varieties (var.), and forms (f.). The cultivar begins with a capital letter and is placed inside single quotation marks.

But why in the world do we need all this intimidating Latin? If we're talking about the herb sage, why do we have to say *Salvia officinalis*? Why not just say "sage" and get on it with it?

Because there are a gazillion sages in the world. In fact, I counted 90 different sages in one common-name plant index, not all of them salvias. Take the Jerusalem sage, for instance, which is blooming just outside my window today—not a sage at all, but a *Phlomis fruticosa*. And the Russian sage in my cottage garden is really *Perovskia atriplicifolia* "Blue Spire." You wouldn't ask either one of them to pinch-hit for *Salvia officinalis* in the turkey stuffing.

And then there's the common name puzzle. Say that you wanted to grow mullein in your garden—one of those stalky plants with large, fuzzy leaves that you see growing along the roadsides in summer. Would you look for Aaron's flannel, beggar's blanket, bunny's ears, candlewick, hag's taper, devil's blanket, golden rod, lady's candle, or velvet dock? In England, all of these names refer to one single plant, *Verbascum thapsus*, and tell us something about its many uses. But they won't help you find exactly the plant you want.

If you're passionate about herbs, you'll want to learn their names. But don't be like Emerson's "young scholars." Love the flower, and know its name, as well.

**Read more about the mysteries of Latin binomials and common names:**
*Gardener's Latin*, by Bill Neal

*Hang an ash bough over the door.*
*Put an iron nail in your pocket*
*And a piece of mullein leaf in your shoe.*
—TRADITIONAL PRESCRIPTION FOR PERSONAL SAFETY

In the floral calendar, today's flower: lilac.

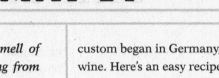

*From my youth I recall that elusive smell of woods in spring—a sweetness ascending from mold and decay but with the breath of young life rising from it. That is the odor that permeates the house when May wine is poured into the May bowl.*

—ADELMA GRENIER SIMMONS, *HERB GARDENING IN FIVE SEASONS*

## Sweet, Sweet Woodruff

We can't let the month of May slip by without a cup of May wine! This drink comes from Germany, where the sweet woodruff (*Galium odoratum*) carpets the spring woodlands with starry white blossoms and whorled leaves. The odd-sounding name woodruff grew out of the earlier *wuderove*, or "wood-wheel" (rove comes from the French *rouelle*, wheel, referring to the circlet of leaves around the stem). The plant contains coumarin, and when it is dried smells like freshly mown vanilla grass. It has long been valued for potpourris and perfumes and is a favorite in sachets. It was once used to stuff mattresses and pillows (hence the name bedstraw). During the Middle Ages, the herb gained a reputation as a wound healer and was used to treat digestive and liver problems. For gardeners with a shady, wooded area, sweet woodruff can be an ideal groundcover.

But it's the herb's centuries-old use as a spring drink that we look forward to every year. Since the custom began in Germany, it's traditional to use Rhine wine. Here's an easy recipe:

**MAY WINE**

1 gallon Rhine wine (use half champagne, if you like)

12–16 sprigs of sweet woodruff, dried overnight in the oven with the pilot light on

1 package frozen strawberries, thawed

1 cup sugar

fresh whole strawberries

Steep the sweet woodruff in the wine for 3–6 days. Chill before serving. Remove the herb and pour chilled wine into a punch bowl over a block of ice. Mash thawed strawberries with a cup of sugar and stir into the wine. Add champagne if you wish, and garnish each cup with a fresh strawberry.

**Read more about sweet woodruff and other herbs:** *The Illustrated Plant Lore*, by Josephine Addison

*To make another herb drinke—Orange-flower Brandy. Take a gallon of French Brandy, boil a pound of orange flowers a little while, and put them in, save the water and with that make a syrup to sweeten it.*

—E. SMITH, *THE COMPLETE HOUSEWIFE*, 1736

*Docke . . . is found almost every where, but especially in gardens among good and wholsome potherbs, being there better knowne, than welcome or desired; wherefor I intend not to spend farther time about his description.*

—JOHN GERARD, *THE HERBAL*, 1597

## A Desirable Dock: From Susan's Journal

Granted, the dock that is growing at the margin of my garden doesn't look like much. It's a weedy green stalk, about three feet high, with clusters of tiny green flowers clinging to the stem and a whorl of large, crumply edged leaves at its base. This is *Rumex crispus*—yellow dock or curly dock or just plain dock—one of the many unruly volunteers making themselves at home in my garden on this spring day.

Dock is no stranger to me, however, and when it shows up in my garden, I let it stay put. The green flowers will turn into reddish-brown fruits as they age; they'll look something like coffee grounds plastered around the stem. In fact, they look enough like coffee grounds that the plant is sometimes called coffeeweed. When I was about ten, my cousin Mary Jean and I "brewed" a coffee can of dock "coffee" in the sun and drank a cup of it. I shudder to think of this now (I could have been drinking jimsonweed tea, for heaven's sake!), although we chose a good herb to experiment with. It's said to be a blood cleanser, to nourish the spleen and detoxify the liver, thus promoting overall good heath. But my ten-year-old spleen didn't need much additional nourishment and my blood hadn't had a chance to get dirty yet, so I'm not sure that the dock had any particular effect.

It certainly did its job a couple of days ago, however. Wearing shorts, I backed into a nettle and got stung good and proper. But since the dock was handy, I grabbed a couple of those big green leaves and rubbed. Hard. And while I rubbed, I chanted a charm that was first recorded in Chaucer's day:

*Nettle out, dock in,*
*Dock remove the nettle sting.*

It worked, of course. Dock's astringent leaf eased the nasty sting just as it did all those long centuries ago. I said a grateful thanks to the dock, and left it, both welcome and desired, among the other good and wholsome herbs in the garden.

In the language of flowers, dock symbolizes patience and shrewdness.

**Read more about dock, nettle, and other valuable herbs:**
*Herbal Healing for Women: Simple Home Remedies for Women of All Ages*, by Rosemary Gladstar

*The love of the desert came to me slowly, for it is a hard-mind place, not a soft-skin place, and concealed in its openness. You cannot stroke it as you would a meadow, you cannot dissemble, nor are there corners in which to hide ... To join it, one must come to know it, and to know it one must walk in it.*

—ANN WOODIN, *HOME IS THE DESERT*

## Prickly Pear: From Susan's Journal

The prickly pear cactus (*Opuntia lindheimeri*) is in bloom now, and the bees are crawling drunkenly over the bright yellow flowers, as large as hollyhock blossoms. Bill has cleared most of the prickly pear from Meadow Knoll because the spines are painful when we carelessly blunder into the plant, or (heaven forbid!) our dogs step on it. But I've safeguarded a few, because they're beautiful and useful and because they remind me that not all plants are easy acquaintances.

The prickly pear's translucent yellow flowers ripen into ruby-red fruits, called *tunas*. These can be made into a beautiful red juice, jelly, marmalade, and syrup. The young, tender pads (*nopales* or *nopalitos*), are sautéed, steamed, or boiled and used in Southwestern cuisine; many supermarkets now carry them in the produce section.

Research suggests that the nutrient-rich fiber in the fruits and pads helps to reduce cholesterol. Traditionally, there were many other medicinal applications. A pad, with the spines burned off, was split and warmed for use as a poultice to relieve chest congestion. A warmed pad was placed over the ear for earache, or over rheumatic or arthritic joints. The gelatinous sap was a soothing skin lotion for rashes and sunburn, and a poultice made of the mashed flesh of the pad was used to heal wounds and burns. Taken internally, the plant treated many gastrointestinal disorders.

And like most native plants, prickly pear served many practical purposes. In rural Mexico, it was used (with water, lime, and salt) to make a waterproof paint for walls, and as a formidable fence—just try getting through that dense, thorny wall! Its fibers were used to make paper and its thorns as needles and pins, while the insect that feeds on its pads and fruit (the cochineal) made red dye. Like many other natives, this durable, adaptable plant has its darker side: free to roam, it can be an invasive pest.

But I'm not thinking about that today, as I revel in those beautiful blooms. I'm thinking about the many native herbs that, like prickly pear, were important to earlier people—the buffalo gourd that grows in the south pasture, the cattails in the marsh, the redbud trees, the willows. They teach me about this place, about the richness and bounty of the land, and remind me that I live in a beautiful wilderness garden.

**Read more about using this at-home-in-the-desert herb:** *The Prickly Pear Cookbook*, by Carolyn Niethammer

# MAY 27

Rachel Carson, writer, ecologist, and marine biologist, was born on this day in 1907.

*For the first time in the history of the world, every human being is now subjected to contact with dangerous chemicals, from the moment of conception until death.*

—RACHEL CARSON, *SILENT SPRING*

## Gardening Green

More than forty years ago, Rachel Carson made it clear that we are endangered by the chemicals in our environment. Most herbalists make it a practice to "garden green"—to follow organic practices of composting, mulching, soil and water conservation—but when it comes to keeping the pests off, we're often not sure what to do. Here are some nonchemical pesticides that are safe to use in your garden.

• Garlic. Interplant garlic with susceptible plants to repel pests. Make an insect-repellent tea: steep 3 ounces of minced garlic cloves in 2 teaspoons of canola oil for at least 24 hours. Mix 1 teaspoons of liquid castile soap or nondetergent soap (this helps the spray cling to the leaves) with 1 pint of water, and add to the garlic oil. Mix thoroughly, strain. To use, mix 2 tablespoons with one pint of water and spray. For greater fire-power, add a teaspoon or two of cayenne pepper.

• Pyrethrum is derived from *Chrysanthemum coccineum*, the painted daisy. You can grow the plant or obtain pyrethrum from your local garden emporium. Dried and powdered, the flower heads are used as direct-contact insecticidal sprays and dusts and are effective against soft-bodied insects.

• Herbal sprays. Make a strong insect-repellent tea by steeping 2 cups of fresh herb leaves in 3 cups boiling water for 2–3 hours. Strain out plant material. Add 1 teaspoon liquid castile soap or nondetergent soap. Dilute with 2 cups water before spraying. Herbs with repellant personalities: painted daisy (see above), sage, mint, thyme, rosemary, tansy, wormwood, feverfew, rue. Experiment to see what works on your particular pest. And do remember that a few bugs aren't going to eat up your entire garden.

• Diatomaceous earth. This is a nontoxic substance made from crushed fossils of freshwater organisms and marine life. The tiny mineral crystals are sharp, and cut through the skin of soft-bodied insects. Dust on plants, sprinkle on the soil surface.

Learn more about the life of Rachel Carson in this definitive biography:
*Rachel Carson: Witness for Nature*, by Linda Lear

*We still talk in terms of conquest. We still haven't become mature enough to think of ourselves as only a tiny part of a vast and incredible universe.*

—RACHEL CARSON

National Pickle Week occurs about this time every year.

> McQuaid drained his coffee cup. "Whatever Phoebe Morgan has on her mind, it's confidential. Which means I won't be able to tell you about it."
>
> "A confidential tête-à-tête with the Pickle Queen?" I snickered. "Sounds like a real sweet dill to me."
>
> McQuaid put down his cup with a loud groan.
>
> I leaned forward. "What's green and swims in the sea?"
>
> "Excuse me," McQuaid said, standing hastily. "I've got to get ready to see Ms. Morgan."
>
> "Moby Pickle," I said with a chortle.
>
> —A DILLY OF A DEATH: A CHINA BAYLES MYSTERY

## A Dilly of a Death: About China's Books

One of the things I like about China's adventures is that each one is different. Sometimes, books in a series can begin to seem repetitive, but I never feel that way about China, primarily because each book is "flavored" differently. Some books are serious, nearly tragic, and are hard (and sometimes painful) to write. Other books are funny. *Chile Death*, for example, and *A Dilly of a Death*, which features the biggest little pickle factory in Pecan Springs, Texas.

The idea for *Dilly* came when Bill and I were visiting the Fredericksburg Herb Farm. We were curious about a big wooden vat, which (it turned out) was full of vinegar, for the herbal vinegars made on the farm. Bill and I exchanged glances, and the idea arrived simultaneously: "The body in the vinegar vat! A pickled victim!"

That isn't the way it turned out, however. In the process of doing the research, I visited the Goldin Pickle Factory. When I told Steve Collett, the owner (and former president of the American Pickle Packers Association) about the body in a vinegar vat, he turned pale. "Don't do that!" he gasped in horror. "People might stop eating pickles!" I had to admit that the idea was a little . . . well, distasteful. Luckily, Steve had an alternative suggestion for disposing of the victim. I don't want to spoil the suspense, so you'll have to read the book to learn what Steve proposed.

There was more fun ahead. Since the book contained a few pickle jokes we decided to have a pickle joke contest on our web site.

The winner: What do you call a pickle lullaby? *A cucumber slumber number.*

**Read more about the mysteries of pickles, and enjoy a few pickle jokes:**

*A Dilly of a Death: A China Bayles Mystery*, by Susan Wittig Albert

www.mysterypartners.com. Click on China Bayles, on *A Dilly of a Death*, and on Pickle Jokes.

# MAY 29

May is National Salsa Month.

## Splendid Salsas!

In Italian and Spanish, salsa is just another word for sauce. But the salsas you can make with the herbs in your garden are out-of-the-ordinary sauces. Here are two fruity salsas, simply splendid enhancements to the flavors of fish, chicken, and other foods. Or layer over cream cheese and serve with crackers. They're at their best when freshly prepared.

### GINGERY-MINT FRUIT SALSA

1 mango, peeled, cut in ½-inch cubes
½ papaya peeled, seeded, cut in ½-inch cubes
1 kiwi, peeled, cut in thin slices
1 8 oz. can chunk pineapple, drained
½ medium red onion, chopped
½ red bell pepper, seeded, chopped
¼ cup chopped fresh mint
2 tablespoons grated fresh ginger
1 tablespoon chopped fresh cilantro
½ cup orange juice
¼ cup lime juice

Combine all ingredients. Refrigerate for 1 hour before serving in a colorful bowl garnished with sprigs of fresh mint. Great with grilled salmon, chicken. Makes about 3 cups.

### A PEACH OF A SALSA

2 ripe peaches, peeled and diced
1 tablespoon lemon juice
½ small red bell pepper, chopped
½ small green bell pepper, chopped
½ red onion, chopped
1 small jalapeño pepper, finely minced
¼ cup pineapple juice
2 tablespoons balsamic vinegar
2 tablespoons chopped fresh mint
1 tablespoon minced fresh cilantro

Dip peaches briefly into boiling water to loosen skins; peel and dice, discarding pits. Toss with lemon juice. Mix in remaining ingredients and refrigerate at least one hour to blend flavors. Makes about 3½ cups.

### A TRIO OF SPLENDID SALSAS

• fresh or frozen cranberries, chopped yellow bell pepper, chopped avocado, diced jalapeño pepper, with minced cilantro and orange juice
• cooked corn kernels (canned or frozen), chopped peaches, red onion, bell pepper, with garlic and white wine vinegar
• white or black beans, sun-dried tomatoes, chopped green onions, garlic, and cilantro, with Italian dressing

**For more salsa inspiration:**
*Nueva Salsa: Recipes to Spice It Up*, by Rafael Palomino

# MAY 30

Memorial Day (originally called Decoration Day) is observed on the last Monday in May.

*In Flanders Fields the poppies blow*
*Between the crosses row on row,*
*That mark our place; and in the sky*
*The larks, still bravely singing, fly*
*Scarce heard amid the guns below.*

—"IN FLANDERS FIELDS," BY LIEUTENANT COLONEL JOHN MCCRAE, CANADIAN ARMY DOCTOR (1872–1918)

## The Memorial Poppy

The first Memorial Day was observed on May 30, 1868, when flowers were placed on the graves of Union and Confederate soldiers at Arlington National Cemetery. The state of New York officially recognized the holiday in 1873, and within 20 years, it was celebrated in all of the northern states. Southern states chose other days to honor their dead until after World War I, when the holiday was changed to honor Americans who died fighting in all the country's wars.

In 1915, moved by the poem "In Flanders Fields," Moina Belle Michael wrote a response:

*We cherish too, the Poppy red*
*That grows on fields where valor led,*
*It seems to signal to the skies*
*That blood of heroes never dies.*

Struck by the symbolism of the red poppy as a tribute to those who were dying in the Great War, Moina Michael wore the flower on Memorial Day. After that, she began selling artificial poppies to her friends and coworkers. All of the money she raised went to benefit needy servicemen and their families.

With energy and dogged determination, Miss Michael worked tirelessly to promote the poppy as a symbol of patriotic sacrifice. In 1920, the flower was officially recognized as a national emblem of remembrance by the American Legion. In 1922, the Veterans of Foreign Wars began selling poppies nationally, and soon the poppies were being made by disabled veterans in the "Buddy Program." Moina Michael died in 1944. Four years later, the United States Post Office issued a commemorative stamp honoring "The Poppy Lady."

The Flanders poppy (*Papaver rhoeas*), also known as the corn poppy, is a hardy annual wildflower native to Europe and naturalized across North America. *Papaver rhoeas* has a long history of medicinal use as an analgesic, a sedative, and an antiasthmatic. While many states prohibit growing its cousin, the opium poppy (*Papaver somniferum*), the corn poppy does not contain enough opium alkaloids to warrant its ban. Corn poppy seeds are safe to use in cooking.

**Read more about Moina Michael and the Flanders poppy:**
*The Miracle Flower, The Story of the Flanders Fields Memorial Poppy*, by Moina Michael

# MAY 31

*And there was the wood, a garden gorilla which some fastidious states have unfeelingly designated as a Class A noxious weed. My woad looked as fierce as the ancient Britons who terrorized the Romans when they painted themselves with it. . . .*

*I sighed. "I think I'd better put in a call to the woad police. Before it goes to seed."*

*"I've got news for you," Ruby said, pulling off a dried seed pod and handing it to me. "What color do you get from woad?"*

*"Blue," Allie replied. "China's got enough woad here to body-paint a whole clan of Picts."*

—INDIGO DYING: A CHINA BAYLES MYSTERY

## From Plant to Dye Pot

Plant dyes are as old as human history. Textile remnants from as early as 3500 BCE show traces of color. Indigo and woad were used to produce the sacred color blue; red by madder; green by a wide variety of plants. Color was used in food (calendula colored cheese, as well as women's hair!) and in cosmetics, brightening lips, cheeks, and eyes. And although it's debatable whether or not the ancient Picts actually painted or tattooed themselves with woad, many other plants are used as body dyes, henna, indigo, and turmeric among them.

If you have an herb or flower garden, you are probably growing several dye plants. All of these have been used to make color and can be grown easily: purple basil, French marigolds, yellow cosmos, hibiscus, coreopsis, marjoram, madder, tansy, Saint-John's-wort, zinnia, weld, and yarrow. (If you're growing woad, watch out. It's wildly invasive.) Many more dye plants grow wild: goldenrod, sunflower, purple loosestrife, broom sedge, nettle, mullein, mustard, sumac, dandelion, and dock, to name just a few. If you have the raw materials and the interest, dyeing is easy and fun. But beware: it can lead to deadly doings, as it does in *Indigo Dying*, which chronicles China's colorful adventure into the dye herbs.

**Read more about dye plants:**
*Colors from Nature: Growing, Collecting & Using Natural Dyes*, by Bobbi McRae
*Indigo Dying: A China Bayles Mystery*, by Susan Wittig Albert

*If the predominating hue of the rainbow is green, more rain may be expected; if red, wind and rain.*

—TRADITIONAL ENGLISH WEATHER LORE

*What is one to say about June, the time of perfect young summer, the fulfillment of the promise of the earlier months, and with as yet no sign to remind one that its fresh young beauty will ever fade.*

—GERTRUDE JEKYLL

## June: Bride's Month

An herbal wedding is wonderful at any time of the year, but a June herbal wedding is a unique and memorable experience for the bride and groom, the family, and all the guests. If there's a wedding in your future—or any other celebration, for that matter—it will be a special delight if it's rich in herbs. Of course, if the wedding is next week, everything is probably already settled, and the most you can do is to tuck rosemary into the bride's bouquet and add some sprigs of lavender and mint to the bridesmaids' flowers. But if you have some time for planning, think about the many ways that herbs can be used as a delightful wedding theme—as China and her friends did, when she and McQuaid got married in *Lavender Lies*.

### ROMANTIC HERBS

We treasure herbs because of the special meanings they have acquired. Here are some herbs that brides over the centuries have included in their weddings, with the loving messages they convey.

- Apple blossom: We choose each other.
- Borage: We have courage for the road ahead.
- Clover (four-leaf): Good luck to us!
- Clover (white): We promise.
- Daisy: We are full of hope.
- Fennel: We will be strong.
- Ivy: We will be faithful, clinging only to each other.
- Lavender: We are devoted to each other.
- Lemon balm: We will comfort each other.
- Marjoram: What a joyful day!
- Mustard seed: We have faith in our future.
- Myrtle: Our love is true.
- Red rose: Our desire is for each other.
- Rosemary: We will always remember this day.
- Sage: We will honor our home and keep it sacred.
- Thyme: We will be constant.
- Yarrow: Our love will be everlasting.

**Read more about how to choose and use wedding herbs:**
*Herbs for Weddings & Other Celebrations: A Treasury of Recipes, Gifts & Decorations*, by Bertha Reppert
*The Language of Flowers*, by Kathleen Gips

*Young men and maids do ready stand*
*With sweet Rosemary in their hands—*
*A perfect token of your virgin's life.*
*To wait upon you they intend*
*Unto the church to make an end,*
*And God make thee a joyful wedded life.*

—OLD BALLAD

Today is the feast day of St. Elmo, the patron saint of sailors.

*The ancient Chinese sailors who used ginger to prevent seasickness were probably right. Ginger's anti-nausea action relieves motion sickness and dizziness (vertigo) better than the standard drug treatment, Dramamine, according to one study published in the British medical journal* Lancet.

—MICHAEL CASTLEMAN, *THE HEALING HERBS*

## Herbs for Travelers

It would be a shame to spoil that honeymoon cruise—or family vacation, or business travel—with a queasy stomach or other minor problem. But herbal help is on the way, with this trio of three tried-and-true remedies. Be sure to pack them in your take-along travel kit.

- Ginger. Commercial ginger capsules are probably the most convenient form of this herb for travelers, but a 12-ounce serving of ginger ale (the real thing, not artificially flavored) should contain enough ginger to do the trick. Another option: take powdered ginger in a small bottle, firmly capped. Use 2 teaspoons in a cup of very hot water. Steep ten minutes and sip. (Do not use ginger during pregnancy or breastfeeding.)

- Peppermint. This age-old remedy hasn't been studied for its efficacy in soothing motion-sickness, but many herbalists prescribe it. Menthol (mint's essential oil) is an antispasmodic, and soothes the smooth muscle lining of the digestive tract. It is an ingredient in many commercial stomach soothers.
- Marjoram. For take-along convenience, try a tincture of this stomach-calming herb. The recommended dose is ½ to 1 teaspoon, up to three times a day.

In addition to stomach-soothers, take along an herbal first aid kit. Include aloe vera for sunburn, minor burns, and chapping. Witch hazel is a natural FDA-approved astringent for scratches, scrapes, and insect bites. Tea tree oil is an effective antiseptic, and can treat athlete's foot and other fungal infections. Arnica helps to ease bruises, sprains, and sore muscles.

**Read more about these and other herbal helpers:**
*The Healing Herbs*, by Michael Castleman

*These plants [marjorams] are easie to be taken in potions, and therefore to good purpose they may be used and ministred unto such as cannot brooke their meate [tolerate their food], and to such as have a sowre squamish and watery stomacke. . . .*

—JOHN GERARD, *HERBAL*, 1597

*The week before Pickle Fest, Fannie Couch usually runs a dozen pickling recipes in her newspaper column. Just for fun, I included a brief history of the cucumber, which found its true calling when it was soaked in salt, vinegar, and water, and turned into a pickle.*

—A DILLY OF A DEATH: A CHINA BAYLES MYSTERY

## "Fit Only for Cows": A Brief History of the Cucumber

Cousin to the Persian melon, the cucumber has been around for at least three thousand years. The plant originated in India, migrated both east to China and west to the Mediterranean and Europe, and discovered America with Columbus, who carried seeds to Haiti in 1494. The Pilgrims planted cukes in their gardens, where they flourished enthusiastically, and the plant was off to a promising new career in North America.

But by the late 1600s, some in England began to worry that eating raw food might lead to illness, and the uncooked cucumber fell from grace. "This day Sir W. Batten tells me that Mr. Newhouse is dead of eating cowcumbers," lamented Samuel Pepys in his famous diary. "Fit only for cows," sniffed another writer.

But you could eat a cooked cucumber and live to tell the tale, especially if you cooked it according to the instructions in Mrs. Raffald's remarkable 1769 cookbook, *The Experienced English Housekeeper*:

### TO STEW CUCUMBERS

Peel off the outer rind, slice the cucumbers pretty thick, fry them in fresh butter, and lay them on a sieve to drain. Put them into a tossing pan with a large glass of red wine, the same of strong gravy, a blade or two of mace. Make it pretty thick with flour and butter and when it boils up put in your cucumbers. Keep shaking them and let them boil five minutes, be careful you don't break them. Pour them into a dish and serve them up.

There. That ought to be safe enough. But wait! There's another option! You might pickle them, for the pickling process was judged to be enough like cooking to redeem the cucumber from its raw sins. Voila! Pickles became the fad food of the eighteenth century, available in barrels in the coffee shops for snacking on the run.

Cucumbers were in great demand at the local apothecary shop, too, where they were an important pharmaceutical. The seeds were employed to treat inflammations of the bowel and urinary tract and to expel tapeworms, and the pulp and juice were used to ease skin inflammations and treat sunburns. Today, beauty consultants in exclusive spas often recommend placing cooling, soothing slices of cucumber over tired and inflamed eyes, and cucumbers are served raw (gasp!) in the very best restaurants.

Samuel Pepys would be amazed.

*Leave cucumbers alone*
*They'll chill you to the bone.*
—TRADITIONAL LORE

# JUNE 4

*Keeping your body healthy is an expression of gratitude to the whole cosmos: the trees, the clouds, everything.*

—THICH NHAT HANH

## Tinctures You Can Make

If you've been reading about herbal healing, you're no doubt aware of tinctures, preparations in which the herbs have been steeped in alcohol. Taking an herb in tincture form is often convenient, especially if you're traveling. Purchased tinctures are usually fairly expensive, but you can make them at home, using herbs you've grown in the garden—and you'll have the satisfaction of using your own herbs to create something that may benefit your health. This recipe recommends alcohol; you can also choose vinegar and glycerin. If that's what you prefer, please consult one of the books below for instructions.

### WHAT YOU NEED:

- a quart glass jar with a lid, and a wooden spoon
- 2 cups alcohol (brandy, vodka, gin)
- plastic strainer and unbleached coffee filter
- bottles (dark amber with droppers preferred)
- labels
- herb of your choice: 4 oz. dry or 6 oz. fresh. Consult a reliable herbal for guidance (see the list below). Be sure to use the recommended part of the plant: i.e. for echinacea, you'll use the root; for Saint-John's-

wort, the leaf.

### HOW TO DO IT:

Fill the jar with the herb you've chosen. Pour the alcohol over the plant material, pushing it down with the wooden spoon until it is completely covered, adding more alcohol if necessary. Cover the jar and label it with the date, the herb, and the kind of alcohol you've used. Put it on a dark shelf for 3–4 weeks, shaking occasionally and checking to see whether you need to add alcohol. Make sure that the plant material remains covered at all times. Strain, using the plastic strainer first, and then the coffee filter. Discard the herbs. Rebottle and label.

**Read more about choosing herbs and making tinctures:**
*Complete Illustrated Guide to the Holistic Herbal*, by David Hoffmann
*Herbal Healing for Women: Simple Home Remedies for Women of All Ages*, by Rosemary Gladstar
*Making Plant Medicine*, by Richard Cech

*It's a wonderful feeling to stock your medicine chest with herbal products you have made yourself. And it's such a good feeling to know you're helping carry on an ancient tradition of healing.*

—ROSEMARY GLADSTAR, *HERBAL HEALING FOR WOMEN*

*If you are not ready to alter your way of life, you cannot be healed.*

—HIPPOCRATES

# JUNE 5

*A garden of herbs is a garden of things loved for themselves in their wholeness and integrity. It is not a garden of flowers, but a garden of plants which are sometimes very lovely flowers and are always more than flowers.*

—HENRY BESTON, *HERBS AND THE EARTH*

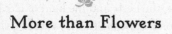

## More than Flowers

Aloe vera is one of our most helpful plant allies, but it's certainly not treasured for its yellow or orange flowers (it only blooms under optimum conditions). It is highly valued because of the healing properties of its leaves, used since the dawn of history to treat infections, burns and wounds, bites and stings, acne, and as a laxative. Aloe even ignited a war. In 332 BCE, Alexander the Great learned that this pharmaceutical treasure was growing on an island off the coast of Somalia and dispatched his troops to capture the island—and the plant.

### GROWING ALOE VERA

Aloe looks like a cactus, but it belongs to the lily family. It is a fine pot plant, ideal for a sunny kitchen window, and it requires little water or extra care. You can grow it outdoors in a well-drained patch of garden, if you'll remember to bring it in when the temperature drops below about 40°F. The aloe will produce offshoots called pups, which you can repot and give to a grateful friend. Make that friends, plural. When an aloe is happy, it pups often.

### THE BAND-AID PLANT

It's the healing gel in aloe's leaves that works its herbal magic. To treat a wound or a scrape, wash it with soap and water. Then cut off one of the aloe's lower leaves, slice it lengthwise (as if you were filleting it) and apply. The gel forms a protective coating on the skin as it dries—hence its name: the Band-Aid plant. Modern scientific research confirms the plant's efficacy as a wound healer. Aloe juice is no longer recommended as a laxative, and the aloe latex (the yellow sap from just beneath the skin) should not be taken internally.

### COSMETIC ALOE

It is said that aloe was one of Cleopatra's beauty secrets, and it is still used in cosmetics and soap. To make a nighttime aloe-enriched moisturizer, blend together thoroughly (use a blender or beater) 3 tablespoons almond oil and 2 tablespoons aloe gel. In a double boiler, melt 2 tablespoons liquid lanolin and blend in the aloe-almond mixture. (You can purchase liquid lanolin in a drugstore. It is a heavy-duty moisturizer with the consistency of petroleum jelly.) Remove from heat and add 2 tablespoons rose water, beating until the mixture has cooled. Spoon into a small jar with a lid.

**Read more about the virtues of aloe:**
*Aloe Vera: Nature's Soothing Healer*, by Diane Gage

*Sometimes the tiniest flowers smell the sweetest.*

—EMILIE BARNES

*The smell of sweet herbs and all kinds of wholesome growth made the whole air a great nosegay.*

—CHARLES DICKENS, *BLEAK HOUSE*

## Tussie-Mussies

The word *tusmose*, or *tussie-mussie*, first appeared in English about 1440. By 1558, it was "tuzziemuzzie, a sweete posie, a nose-gay." Around the same time, it was a "tuttie." But whatever this small, handheld bouquet was called, it was always associated with the "sweet" herbs that warded off the unpleasant smells that offended sensitive noses in the heat of a London summer.

By Victorian times, these little nosegays were not so necessary for "gaying" the nose, but had become popular personal gifts. Every lady who understood the language of flowers (probably a prerequisite to being a lady) would have understood the special, secret meaning of each herb or blossom. The small bouquet was arranged in a circlet of tidy symmetry, with an added ribbon or touch of lace, and presented in a silver holder.

### HOW TO MAKE A TUSSIE-MUSSIE

Start with a single rose or a daisy, or a cluster of violets. Holding the stems, surround it with a circlet of small green leaves, such as rosemary, thyme, fern, or laurel. Tuck in a few forget-me-nots, lilies of the valley, violets, and silvery lambs ears. Other silver-gray sprigs, such as artemisia, add a nice accent, while scented geraniums, basil, and mint lend their sweet scent. Secure the stems with a rubber band or floral tape and push them through a slit in a lacy paper doily. For an elegant touch, use a silvery tussie-mussie holder (available at some florist shops and on-line). If you like, include a card with the meanings of the flowers and herbs. And be sure to point out to the recipient that when the tussie-mussie has dried, it can be used as an attention-getting table decoration.

### SOME SINISTER MEANINGS (PERFECT FOR ONE OF CHINA'S MYSTERIES!)

Clematis: trickery

Dead leaves: melancholy

Hemlock: "You will be my death"

Lettuce: "You have a cold heart"

Monkshood: deceit

Nettle: cruelty

### Read more about floral expressions:

*The Language of Flowers*, by Kathleen Gips

*Tussie-Mussies: The Victorian Art of Expressing Yourself in Flowers*, by Geraldine Laufer

*Since sexual abstinence was supposed to be a part of cloister life, the monks [of the Middle Ages] needed agents that could free them of all desire. What they needed was an anaphrodisiac, an agent that would silence all sexual appetite and transform any paroxysms of desire into chaste thoughts . . . Searching the ancient texts, they finally found what they wanted. . . . And thus, the chase tree, or* agnus castus, *became a common sight in cloister gardens.*

—CHRISTIAN RÄTSCH, *PLANTS OF LOVE*

## Chaste Trees

Here at Meadow Knoll, the chaste trees (*Vitex agnus-castus*) are heavy with purple blooms, to the enormous delight of hummingbirds and bees. Chaste trees are easily rooted from cuttings; we have a dozen, all daughters of a single chaste tree we planted in 1987. In the summer, these tree-herbs form a lovely hedge, about 14 feet high; they lose their leaves in the winter, but their bare branches are a pretty sight. Summer or winter, a fine addition to the garden.

The herbal history and lore of the chaste tree is fascinating. The monks based their belief that the berries would inhibit sexual desire on the testimony of Dioscorides, a famous first-century BCE Greek herbalist whose *De Materia Medica* was the first systematic pharmacopoeia. He reported that "when drunk, [*agnus-castus*] curbs the urge to cohabit," while the Roman naturalist Pliny observed that "the dames of Athens . . . made their pallets and beds with the leaves thereof to cool the heat of lust, and to keep themselves chaste for the time." With that kind of testimony, who can blame the monks for adding a handful of the spicy chaste berries—it came to be called monk's pepper—to a dish of cooked greens, or brewing the ground seeds as a tea? Some monks even carried special protection against unchaste feelings: a knife with a handle made from the wood of the chaste tree.

Through the centuries, the herb was widely used in Europe to treat digestive ailments, colic, and flatulence, and as a "female herb," to treat pain and inflammation of the uterus. Today, it is often recommended as a treatment for PMS.

If you're looking for a pretty herbal tree with an intriguing history of human use, try the chaste tree. The bees will love you for it.

**Read more about the chaste tree:**
*Plants of Love*, by Christian Rätsch
*Vitex: The Women's Herb*, by Christopher Hobbs

*Do you see that lady wearing a crown*
*And dressed all in white?*
*She is Diana, goddess of chastity.*
*She bears a branch of agnus castus in her hand*
*As do all the ladies with her,*
*All wearing chaplets of that herb,*
*For they have kept always their maidenhead.*
—*THE FLOWER AND THE LEAF* (ONCE ASCRIBED TO CHAUCER)

*We had a kettle; we let it leak:*
*Our not repairing made it worse.*
*We haven't had any tea for a week . . .*
*The bottom is out of the Universe.*

—RUDYARD KIPLING, "NATURAL THEOLOGY"

## Tea: The Real Deal

According to Chinese legend, the first cup of tea was brewed about five thousand years ago by Shen Nong, a.k.a. The Divine Cultivator. One day, he was boiling water outdoors when leaves of the tea plant (*Camellia sinensis*) blew off a nearby bush and dropped into the water. The Divine Cultivator tasted the brew and found that it hit the spot. A cup of tea was soon on everyone's table.

The Buddhists explain things differently. The monk Dharuma practiced meditation all day long. One drowsy afternoon, he found his eyelids drooping. So that this would not happen again, he sliced them off and threw them away. A tea plant sprang up where they fell, and after a little trial and error, Dharuma discovered the secret of brewing its leaves into a drink that would keep him awake—although one has to suppose that he learned to sleep with his eyes open.

Tea became known in Europe in the 1600s, as British merchant ships made their way to the Orient and back again. The sprightly stimulant became immediately popular and a brisk trade developed. Tea helped to precipitate at least one war (the American Revolution began with the Boston Tea Party), served several governments as currency, and helped to build the British Empire. Americans have done their fair share, too. They invented iced tea (first served at the St. Louis World's Fair in 1904) and the tea bag (first used in 1908 in New York City by Thomas Sullivan).

Tea is more than just a delicious stimulant, however. In the last few years, scientists have compiled a convincing dossier on the therapeutic virtues of tea. Tea can help to protect the arteries against cholesterol clogs; inhibit the growth of cancers of the colon, stomach, and breast; reduce inflammation; and neutralize many viruses. You can drink black tea or green tea, hot tea or iced tea, with or without caffeine. But do drink brewed tea; scientists say that bottled tea and instant tea don't have as many antioxidants. Herbal teas have different health benefits; you'll want to check them out, as well.

Kipling is right, of course. No tea for a week would turn our world upside down!

**Read more about the mysteries of tea:**
*The New Tea Book: A Guide to Black, Green, Herbal, and Chai Tea*, by Sara Perry

*If on the 8th of June it rain*
*Then foretells a wet harvest, men sayen.*

—TRADITIONAL

*The hair that showed under Ruby's hat was such a vibrant copper that it looked as if she had put on her hat to snuff out a blazing fire.*

*I opened the door and got out, blinking. "What have you done to your hair?"*

*She jammed her hat down on her head. "Why? Is something wrong with it?"*

*"It's very red." At the look on her face, I repented. "But on you, very red is good. Gives you a little extra whoomf." As if she needed it.*

*"I henna-ed it last night," she said. "With paprika and cinnamon."*

*I stood up on tiptoes to sniff. "You're right. Definitely cinnamon. You smell like apple pie."*

*Ruby smiled modestly. "Next time I'm going to try nutmeg and allspice."*

—MISTLETOE MAN: A CHINA BAYLES MYSTERY

## Henna, the Herb

Ruby isn't the first woman in the world to go gaga over henna. This semi-permanent botanical colorant enhances the hair tones of brunettes and redheads (Ruby certainly qualifies!). And because it coats and smoothes each strand, it protects the hair from damage. It is also said that the herb helps to relieve tension around the eyes and forehead, as well as condition the scalp and reduce dandruff and oiliness. And Ruby is right: Spices like cinnamon, nutmeg, and allspice, as well as cloves, tea, and coffee can all alter the basic henna treatment.

Henna (*Lawsonia inermis*) is a tropical shrub whose green leaves are dried and ground into a fine powder, which is graded for color, purity, and fineness. Purchase henna powder from beauty supply houses and on-line.

### VERSATILE HENNA

To color the hair, powdered henna is mixed with water to make a thick paste, which is applied to clean, towel-dried hair. The hair is covered with a shower cap and a towel, which is left on for 2–6 hours.

Women of other times and other cultures have used henna on their fingernails and toenails. The herb colors and conditions the nails as it does the hair. Because henna paste has antifungal and antiseptic properties, it can also soothe damaged cuticles. Ancient herbals recommended using henna as a deodorant, and in Algeria, henna leaves were placed in shoes to sweeten sweaty feet. In the East, henna has been used to treat wounds, ease mild burns and stings, and heal acne. In Malaysia, a henna-leaf tea is gargled for sore throat and drunk for dysentery.

All that from a hair coloring? No wonder that, when Lucy Arnaz thought her building was on fire, she thought first about rescuing her jugs of henna!

**Read more about the magic of henna:**
*Henna, from Head to Toe*, by Norma Pasekoff Weinbert

*"My God, I'm outliving my henna."*

—LUCILLE BALL

# JUNE 10

According to some, the Celtic Month of the Oak begins today.

> *Fairy folks*
> *Are in old oaks.*
> —ENGLISH SAYING

## The Sacred Oak

Because of its great size, age, and dignity, the oak tree has been venerated by many cultures. According to Sir James Frazer, whose *Golden Bough* is a compendium of this sort of thing, the Greeks dedicated the oak to Zeus, the Romans to Jupiter, and the Norse to Thor. The Druids worshipped it too, performing their rites in sacred groves of old oaks. Perhaps, Frazer muses, the reverence these ancient people paid to the oak and the connection they traced to their sky-god was due to the fact that the oak appears to be struck by lightning more frequently than other trees.

### THE MEDICINAL OAK

Many different cultures have used the oak as a source of plant medicine. Throughout Europe, the leaves, acorns, and bark were used as an astringent, tonic, and antiseptic. The inner bark, rich in tannic acid, was harvested in early spring, dried in the sun, and made into a decoction to be used as a gargle for throat and mouth infections. It was also employed as a hot compress for skin ulcers and hemorrhoids. It was drunk as a remedy for diarrhea. An astringent, it was powdered and used like snuff to stop nosebleeds.

In America, Indians used the oak (there are some forty native species) in similar ways. It is mentioned often in accounts of early American medical practice as both astringent and antiseptic. Acorn coffee and acorn meal were also used.

### THE MAGICAL OAK

The oak was often invoked in predicting the weather:

> If the oak is out before the ash, we will surely have a splash.
> If the ash is out before the oak, we shall surely have a soak.

The herbalist John Gerard (1597) reported that the oak gall (*Quercus infectoria*) was predictive, too. If the gall was opened and an ant was found, it foretold a year of plentiful harvests; if a spider, there would be disease; if a worm, disease among the herds and flocks; if the worm crept, a poor harvest; if it turned, plague; if it flew, there would be war.

If you doubt that the oak is magical, I invite you to visit Wistman's Wood, on Dartmoor, in the valley of Devonport Leat. The ancient trees, twisted and bent and no more than 15 feet high, grow out of the granite rocks and are covered with lichen. This enchanted place will make a believer of you.

**Read more about the magic of the oak:**
*Oak: The Frame of Civilization*, by William Bryant Logan

*The tall columns of the Yucca or Adam's Needle stood like shafts of marble against the hedge trees of the Indian Hill garden. . . . In the daytime the Yucca's blossoms hang in scentless, greenish white bells, but at night these bells lift up their heads and expand with great stars of light and odor. . . . Even by moonlight we can see the little white detached fibres at the edge of the leaves, which we are told the Mexican women used as thread to sew with. And we children used to pull off the strong fibres and put them in a needle and sew with them too.*

—ALICE MORSE EARLE, *OLD TIME GARDENS*, 1901

## Spanish Dagger: From Susan's Journal

Yucca will get your attention. When it's not in bloom, it's tall and commanding. When it's in bloom, it's simply stunning: a towering flower stalk, decorated with white flower bells, each with its own resident bee. The whole plant seems to hum. When the crown produces its flower stalk, that's the final chapter. It dies, but its side shoots—its clones—are waiting their turn to bloom.

I've gotten interested in yucca because of one of its folk names: Spanish dagger. Sounds plenty deadly to me, and I've chosen it as the title and the signature herb for the fifteenth China Bayles book. Already, yucca is teaching me some fascinating things. I've learned, for instance, that this is an edible plant; when

I served the blossoms steamed, with a hollandaise sauce, Bill pronounced them as good as artichokes. The Indians ground the dried flat, black seeds into meal and baked them as cakes, but I think I waited too long. When I went to gather them, the bugs had beat me to it. Maybe next year.

The yucca's taproot has other virtues, cleanliness chief among them. Dug, scrubbed, and chipped, the saponin-rich root is boiled in water—three cups of water to one cup of chips—and produces suds. Boil it down by about two-thirds, and you'll have an effective soap that will clean your hair and hands and launder your clothes. Medicinally, the root was used to treat arthritis. One study suggests that it is the saponin that does the work; a cortisone precursor, it is strongly anti-inflammatory.

And then there is the fiber. The Indians soaked the stiff, thick leaves in water, then pounded them with wood clubs until the pulp was soft. The filaments were twisted into thread, cord, or rope and used to construct netting, sandals, baskets, and clothing. The leaves can also be used to make handmade paper. I doubted this, until a friend sent me a sample of some yucca paper she had made. I'm bargaining for more.

**Read more about the yucca and other native herbs:**

*Spanish Dagger*, by Susan Wittig Albert (forthcoming, April 2007)

*Gather Ye Wild Things: A Forager's Year*, by Susan Tyler Hitchcock

# JUNE 12

On this day in 1980, the National Herb Garden was dedicated.

## A National Treasure

The National Herb Garden is now over a quarter of a century old, an enduring tribute both to herbs and to the dedicated herb gardeners who created it. It all started in 1976, when a few determined women from the Herb Society of America (HSA) decided that America was in need of an herb garden, while at the same time, the National Arboretum, in Washington, D.C., was planning several demonstration gardens. Thomas Wirth made the award-winning design, and the women, "armed with tussie-mussies," as one reporter put it, got busy raising the money from HSA members all over the country (when all the pledges were paid, they had collected nearly $420,000!).

Then came the hard work of getting the government to match HSA's contributions. "Herein lies another tale of tussie-mussies and persistence by HSA President Betty Rea," reports HSA historian Dorothy G. Spenser. After a summer of intense Congressional lobbying, the money was finally forthcoming. Spenser writes: "A bulldozer with Betty Rea on board and a tussie-mussie attached to the mirror for good luck started to build the garden." And in the spring of 1980, the garden was dedicated at last—although, as every gardener knows, a garden is *never* finished! HSA continues to support the garden through volunteer work,

consultative help, and monetary contributions. It is fair to say that without the persistence of these gardeners, their hard work and commitment, the National Herb Garden—*our* herb garden—would still be just a dream.

The Herb Garden has three areas: a knot garden, a rose garden; and a group of ten gardens that illustrate the many uses of herbs. The figure-eight shape of the knot garden is outlined with ivy and centered with dwarf juniper, holly, and arborvitae. The rose garden features over a hundred heirloom roses; the focal point is an armillary sundial. The ten gardens include culinary, beverage, and dye gardens, a Colonial garden and a garden featuring the herbs of Dioscorides. One especially "hot" garden is the Pepper Garden, with over a hundred varieties of peppers, hot, hotter, hottest. Asian herbs and Native American herbs are also part of the display, which includes several botanically important collections of rosemary, oregano, lavender, and salvia.

The herb garden is located about ten minutes from the Capitol Building. Visit the web site (http://www.usna.usda.gov/Gardens/collections/herb.html) for directions, times, and announcements of special events.

**Read more about the work of the HSA:**
*The Herb Society of America, 1933–1993,* by Dorothy
   G. Spenser
Visit the Society's web site: www.herbsociety.org

*In the kitchen, I evicted Khat from the rocking chair by the window and Ruby sat down. I put on the copper kettle and measured tea into the blue china teapot McQuaid gave me for Christmas last year—lemon balm tea, with a bit of lemon verbena and dried lemon peel. Besides tasting good, lemon balm is supposed to reduce fevers. I thought it might cool Ruby off a little.*

—WITCHES' BANE: A CHINA BAYLES MYSTERY

## A Zingy, Swingy Lemony Quintet

If you're a lemon-lover, you'll find a lot to love in the lemon herbs. They're easy to grow, fun to use, and each sings its own unique lemony song. Here are five of the most popular. Plant them individually, or group them all together as a lemony ensemble.

- Lemon balm (*Melissa officinalis*). Emphatically citrus, this aromatic herb has a reputation as a sedative that lowers fevers and settles upset stomachs. Essential for summertime iced teas and wintertime hot brews, a tangy addition to steamed vegetables and fruit salads, a happy choice for marinades.
- Lemongrass (*Cymbopogon citratus*). A standby in Asian cooking, lemongrass is a perennial star. Grow it in full sun and take it indoors when the temperature falls below 25°F. Start using the leaves when they're a half-inch wide. Chop and brew with tea, mince and add to salsas, stir-fries, and curries.

- Lemon basil (*Ocimum basilicum* "Citriodorum"). A tender annual, easily grown from seed. Plant it where you can touch it as you pass and listen to it purr. Use in soups, stews, vegetable dishes, pesto (of course!), and desserts, drinks, jellies, and vinegars.
- Lemon Thyme (*Thymus* x *citriodorus*). Low, mounding perennial, great as a container plant. Especially good with grilled fish or chicken, or steamed vegetables.
- Lemon Verbena (*Aloysia triphylla*). A tender perennial shrub with a brash lemony scent, lemon verbena will appreciate being potted up for a winter vacation indoors in all but the deep South. There, left to its own devices, it may grow to 15 feet. Add finely minced leaves to fruit salads, herbed cheeses, or your favorite tea.

### LEMON BUTTER

1 cup unsalted butter, softened
¼ cup fresh lemon juice
2 tablespoons powdered sugar
Grated peel of 1 lemon
3–4 tablespoons very finely minced leaves of any of the lemon herbs

Combine all ingredients and purée until smooth. Cover, refrigerate until firm.

**Read more about these and other herbs:**
*How to Grow and Use 18 Great Plants*, by Ellen Spector Platt

Today is the feast day of St. Basil. There's no historical connection to our favorite herb, but it gives us a good excuse to celebrate!

## Herb Guild Holds Big Basil Bash
### by Fannie Couch, special to the
### Pecan Springs *Enterprise*

The sixth annual Basil Folk-Life Festival, sponsored by the Myra Merryweather Herb Guild and held in the Pecan Springs park last Saturday, came off without a hitch. Guild members brought their favorite basils, nicely potted and on their best behavior—nearly every one of the 60 different varieties! They (the basils, that is) were all lined up on a table and festival-goers were invited to touch and sniff. No tasting, though, or there wouldn't have been any basil left for those who came in the afternoon. You could taste the basils that you bought, at the Merryweather Basil Bonanza Booth. Favorites for sale included pretty "Purple Ruffles" and fragrant "Genovese" along with lemon, cinnamon, Thai (anise), and Mexican spice basils.

Besides sniffing basil, there were other exciting things to do. You could listen to Benny's Barefoot Bluegrass Band, or watch the Cowgirl Cloggers give an electrifying clogging exhibition (interrupted only briefly when Neva Wooster's clogging shoe flew off and hit Mayor Pauline Perkins in the eye). You could buy a chance on a Drunkard's Path quilt, quilted by The Scrappers Quilt Club, and if you were a kid, you could plant basil seeds in take-home pots. And if that wasn't enough, there were all the vendors. And the food, of course.

**BASIL ON THE MENU**
Of course, it's always a challenge to cook for a crowd, but the Merryweathers are up to it. Diners enjoyed a sit-down lunch in the basement of the Second Baptist Church across the street from the park. The menu:

*Vegetable Soup with Basil*
*Basil-Cucumber Salad*
*Lasagna with Tomato-Cheese-Basil Sauce*
*White Beans with Garlic & Basil*
*Spice Cake with Orange-Basil Sauce*
*Myra's Secret Recipe Basil Ice Cream*

(In case you're looking for recipes, Pansy Pride says to tell you that you'll have to wait until the Merryweathers finish *Happy Thymes: A Calendula of Herbal Dillies*. All except for Myra's secret recipe, of course. The Merryweathers have sworn a solemn oath never to reveal the ingredients.)

*To cause basil to grow great, it is good to crop it oft with your fingers and not with any yron thing. Some report a marvellous strange thing of basil, as namely that it groweth fairer and higher, if it be sowen with curses and injuries offered unto it. . . .*

GERVASE MARKHAM, *MAISON RUSTIQUE, OR THE COUNTRY FARME*, 1616

Today is the feast day of St. Vitus. He is invoked on behalf of people who suffer from epilepsy and St. Vitus Dance (Sydenham's chorea, a nervous disorder).

*"Medicinally, bloodroot was used as to treat coughs and stomach and urinary troubles,"* Martha said. *"The Iroquois also brewed a tea that they believed made the heart stronger and cleansed the blood of impurities. And they used it as a love charm."*

*"A love charm," I repeated thoughtfully. "I suppose that was because of its association with blood and the heart."*

*"Perhaps." Martha put her hat back on. "It had an important role in the sacred tradition. The Iroquois burned the leaves as a cleansing smoke to purify someone who had seen a dead person. And tribes in other parts of the country— the Ojibwa, the Ponca, the Potawatomi—used it to paint special identification marks on their faces, so that everyone would know at a glance what clan they belonged to. . . . Bloodroot must have been powerful medicine. . . ."*

—BLOODROOT: A CHINA BAYLES MYSTERY

## Bloodroot: About China's Books

*Bloodroot*, the tenth book in the China Bayles series, takes place at Jordan's Crossing, the Mississippi plantation that belongs to China's great-aunt Tulia. I chose the herb bloodroot as the signature herb because I wanted to explore the idea of "blood relatives" and what happens when we dig for the "root" of something dark in our past, something secret in our family.

Bloodroot—*Sanguinaria canadensis*—is a native American herb, powerful medicine for all the Indian tribes who used it. The genus name refers, of course, to the plant's red juice, which was used by Indians as a skin dye and a powerful medicine. But "sanguinary" also refers to bloodshed, murder, and carnage, while "consanguineous" has to do with blood relationship. To me, bloodroot suggested bloodshed, which is deeply involved with, even caused by, the mysteries of family relationships and the taboos imposed on certain forbidden consanguinities.

Bloodroot was used to treat rheumatism, fever, epilepsy, and St. Vitus' Dance. It is no longer used in these ways, and the Indian cultures that believed in its power no longer survive. But the name, and the history and lore of the plant, still inspire a kind of awe. I can certainly understand why the Iroquois used the herb as an incense to cleanse someone who had seen a ghost. Powerful medicine, indeed.

**Read more:**

*Bloodroot: A China Bayles Mystery*, by Susan Wittig Albert

*The rosehip tea was iced and tasty, with the zing of ginger and a hint of anise. The jam cakes were light and luscious, and Winnie's rose jam, hidden inside each slice of cake, was the color of rubies. We said little as we ate. The taste was too good to spoil with the rattle of words.*

—LAVENDER LIES: A CHINA BAYLES MYSTERY

## Iced Herbal Teas

The days are getting warm, the herbs in the garden are bountiful, and it's time to indulge in a pitcher of iced herbal tea. There are plenty of herbs to choose from, so get out your garden shears and a basket and go for it. But don't just reach for the usual suspects: mint, lemon balm, and lemon verbena. Try these other summer-perfect tea herbs, for a splashy summer flavor.

- Anise hyssop (*Agastache foeniculum*), tastes of mint scented with anise, and its lavender-blue flowers lend a delightful accent. Other anise-flavored herbs: fennel, sweet cicely, and licorice.
- Lemon herbs taste fresh and cool. For a sunny combination, pair lemon balm or lemongrass with lemon verbena, lemon thyme, lemon basil, lemon geranium, the zest of a lemon. Mix and match until your taste is suited.
- All the mints—spearmint, peppermint, and the flavored mints—are delicious in iced teas.

- For a fragrant floral tea, blend lavender, rose petals, rosehips, and the leaves of rose geranium.

**TO BREW A PITCHER OF ICED HERB TEA**

Harvest leaves and flowers and rinse. Put several handfuls into a pitcher and fill with cold water. Refrigerate overnight. Pour over ice, garnish with fresh leaves and flowers, and sweeten to taste.

**Read more about making iced tea:**

*Iced Tea: 50 Recipes for Refreshing Tisanes, Infusions, Coolers, and Spiked Teas*, by Fred Thompson

*Balm's lemony aroma makes it a candidate for the teapot as well as a garnish for summer drinks and salads. Use it in potpourri and flower arrangements, too. It's delicate flavor is lost in cooking or drying, although its mint-and-lemon scent remains.*

—MADALENE HILL & GWEN BARCLAY,
SOUTHERN HERB GROWING

Today is Eat Your Vegetables Day. (No kidding.)

*Life expectancy would grow by leaps and bounds if green vegetables smelled as good as bacon.*

—DOUG LARSON

## Grill Those Veggies

Hamburgers on the grill for supper? Throw on a few herb-marinated vegetables, and your everyday meal will go gourmet. Here's a marinade that will perk up the blandest zucchini:

**HERBED MARINADE FOR VEGETABLES**
This recipe makes enough for 2 pounds of vegetables; it will keep up to 10 days. Vegetables with great grilling potential: pattypan squash, zucchini, eggplant, bell pepper, mushrooms, potatoes, tomatoes, onions.

¼ cup soy sauce
¼ cup balsamic vinegar
¼ cup olive oil
¼ cup water
2 tablespoons honey
1 teaspoon fresh rosemary; chopped, or ½ teaspoon dried
1 teaspoon fresh thyme leaves, or ½ teaspoon dried
1 teaspoon fresh basil, chopped, or ½ teaspoon dried
1 teaspoon fresh oregano, chopped, or ½ teaspoon dried

2 cloves garlic, pressed or finely minced
freshly ground pepper to taste

Whisk all ingredients in a small bowl. Cut the vegetables into pieces about ¼-inch thick, to allow them to cook evenly and quickly. Arrange in a shallow container, pour the marinade over them, cover and refrigerate 2 hours, turning occasionally. (The longer the marinade, the more flavorful the vegetables.) Cook about four inches from the coals, brushing with marinade as they brown and turning to grill both sides. A grilling basket will keep them from diving into the fire.

Herbs that complement vegetables:

| | |
|---|---|
| basil | oregano |
| parsley | rosemary |
| savory | sage |
| marjoram | thyme |

*Vegetables are a must on a diet. I suggest carrot cake, zucchini bread, and pumpkin pie*

—GARFIELD

*I am thinking of the lilac-trees that shook their purple plumes, and when the sash was open, shed fragrance through the room.*

—ANNA S. STEPHENS

## Make Mine Misty

Sometimes just the simple memory of a fragrance is enough to lift our spirits; at other times, it takes something a little more substantial. You can create a daily "spa experience" for yourself if you have a supply of fragrant herbal mists in your refrigerator, ready for a cooling, spirit-raising face and body spritz made of a therapeutic hydrosol, or flower water. Hydrosols are produced from herbal material by a steam-distillation process and preserve many of the healing qualities of the herb or flower. Inexpensive as a facial and body splash, hydrosols are moisturizing, fragrant, and cooling. What's more, you can use them as a base to create your own fragrances.

You can spritz with the flower water alone, or add aloe vera juice (the juice, not the gel) as an additional moisturizer. Here are a couple of easy formulas to help you get started; experiment by adding a few drops of essential oil until you have created a personal favorite. Hydrosols are available from herb shops, or on-line. Aloe vera juice is available at the drugstore.

### LUSCIOUS LEMONY MIST

½ cup lemon verbena hydrosol

2 teaspoons aloe vera juice

5 drops lemongrass essential oil

Pour all ingredients into a 4-ounce glass spray bottle and shake vigorously. Refrigerate. To use, shake, then spray skin lightly, avoiding the eyes.

### INVIGORATING MEADOW MIST

(try this on hot, tired feet at the end of a long day)

½ cup rosemary hydrosol

2 teaspoons aloe vera juice

4 drops orange essential oil

2 drops grapefruit essential oil

### CALMING CHAMOMILE MIST

(just right after a stressful day)

½ cup chamomile hydrosol

2 teaspoons aloe vera juice

4 drops rose essential oil

4 drops lavender essential oil

*To take away freckles: Distil Elder Leaves in June and wash with a Spunge with this Liquor Morning and Evening.*

—THE RECEIPT BOOK OF CHARLES CARTER, COOK TO THE DUKE OF ARGYLL, 1732

**Read more about creating a "spa experience":**
*Secrets of the Spas: Pamper and Vitalize Yourself at Home*, by Catherine Bardey

Father's Day is usually celebrated about this time.

*There's rosemary, that's for remembrance . . . I would give you some violets, but they withered all when my father died.*

—WILLIAM SHAKESPEARE, HAMLET

## Rosemary: Preserving Memories

The knowledge of rosemary's special preserving capabilities goes back a long way. Thousands of years ago, people who lived around the Mediterranean noticed that rosemary leaves slowed spoilage in fresh meat. About the same time, in Egypt, embalmers began using rosemary to make mummies. These demonstrations of the herb's ability to preserve led people to believe that rosemary could also preserve memory. Which is why Greek and Roman students wore garlands of rosemary when they studied.

It wasn't long before the plant became associated with the idea of remembrance. A funeral wreath included rosemary as a sign that the living would always remember the dead. Rosemary in a bridal bouquet symbolized the couple's lifelong remembrance of their wedding vow. During the Middle Ages, this association transformed rosemary into a love charm. If you were tapped by a rosemary sprig, there was no way out: It was love until death. So by the late sixteenth century, when Ophelia hands Hamlet a rosemary sprig "for remembrance," the play's audience understood that Ophelia was in love with him and could guess that his rejection—coupled with her grief at the death of her beloved father—meant her death. The plant was irretrievably linked to love and death, and to the eternal recollection of both.

Modern science has explained rosemary's remarkable preservative properties, and tells us why this herb may actually help us to remember. It turns out that the plant contains powerful antioxidants which slow the cell breakdown that causes decay and spoilage—antioxidants so potent that Japanese researchers have demonstrated rosemary's efficacy as a replacement for chemical preservatives. Importantly, German scientists have found that these same chemicals also help to slow the breakdown of acetylcholine in the brain, and may retard memory loss in early-stage Alzheimer's victims. One American herbalist even suggests that the traditional rosemary rinse that makes your hair shiny may also help you remember to buy shampoo.

So there you are—rosemary, a remarkably helpful herb.

Remember it.

**Read more about rosemary:**

*Growing and Using Rosemary*, Storey Country Wisdom Bulletin A-116, by Bertha P. Reppert

*Make thyself a box of rosemary wood and smell it oft and it will keep thee youngly.*

—BANCKES HERBAL, 1525

# JUNE 20

The summer solstice occurs about this time: the shortest night and the longest day of the year.

*You are a child of the universe, no less than the trees and the stars; you have a right to be here. And whether or not it is clear to you, no doubt the universe is unfolding as it should.*

—MAX EHRMANN, *DESIDERATA*

## Midsummer Magic

On the Summer Solstice, the sun reaches its highest point in the sky and begins its downward plunge into the darkness of winter. For pagan peoples, this was an awe-inspiring event of profound significance, and herbs and flowers gathered at this time were thought to have magical qualities. Fern seeds could make you rich, and maybe even make you invisible. Mugwort could bring you a valuable dream—and whatever you dream on Midsummer's Night is sure to come true. And the sprightly yellow blossoms of chase-devil, or Saint-John's-wort (*Hypericum perforatum*) would shield you from the power of evil spirits during the coming dark.

### CHASING THE DEVIL

Hypericum has been in use for more than 2,000 years. Early people hung it over their doors and above their religious icons to ward off evil spirits. In Northern Europe, it was worn to repel demon lovers and burned in Midsummer ritual bonfires as a protective incense. In some areas, cattle, sheep, and horses were driven through the smoke to protect them, as well. After the Catholic Church established the Feast of St. John as a substitute for the pagan midsummer celebration, chase-devil was still tossed into the ritual flames but under its new and more politically-correct name—Saint-John's-wort. (*Wort* is the Anglo-Saxon word for herb or plant.) During medieval times, the Europeans used Saint-John's-wort to treat melancholia, which they viewed as a form of possession by the devil. A thirteenth-century list of medicinal plants referred to it as *herba demonis fuga*—an herb to chase away devils. In 1630, Italian physician Angelo Sala wrote that Saint-John's-wort had an excellent reputation for treating illnesses of the imagination, melancholia, and anxiety. By the nineteenth century, it was being regularly prescribed as a mood-enhancer, to treat depression.

And of course, that is chiefly why we use it today—and with confidence, for numerous clinical studies have demonstrated its usefulness in treating mild depression. The next time you reach for Saint-John's-wort to banish the blues, remember that people have been using this remarkable herb to chase this particular devil for centuries.

**Read more about the magic of St. John's wort:**
*St. John's Wort: The Mood-Enhancing Herb*, by Christopher Hobbs

*Saint-John's-wort, scaring from the midnight heath The witch and goblin with its spicy breath.*

—TRADITIONAL CHARM

# JUNE 21

Today or tomorrow, the Sun enters the sign of Cancer.

*The fourth sign of the zodiac, the feminine sign Cancer (the Crab) is ruled by the Moon, which governs feelings and the sense of belonging. Cancer is a cardinal water sign, suggesting that Cancer people are sensitive, nurturing, and likely to place a high value on home and family. They may also be occasionally moody, avoid change, and withdraw from painful situations.*

—RUBY WILCOX, "ASTROLOGICAL SIGNS"

## Cancer Herbs

Nurturing, maternal Cancer, ruled by the Moon, governs the breasts, womb, and ovaries, as well as the esophagus and the stomach. It also rules all fluid secretions, including menstrual blood, fluids, and tears. The Moon is often associated with conditions involving irregular periodicity: irregular menstruation and menstruation-related moods, insomnia, hysteria, and epilepsy. Lunar herbs tend to have white or yellow flowers and soft, juicy leaves. The seventeenth-century herbalist Nicholas Culpeper described the following plants as ruled by the Moon. The descriptions are Culpeper's, and reflect the herbs' historical uses.

- Saxifrage (*Pimpinella major*). The root is good for the colic and expels wind. The roots or the seed are used in powder or in decoction to help the mother, procure the courses, remove phlegm and cure venom.
- Lettuce (*Lactuca sativa*). The juice of the plant is mixed with Oil of Roses and applied to the temples to procure sleep and to cure a headache arising from a hot cause. Eaten boiled, lettuce loosens the belly, helps digestion, quenches thirst, increases milk in nursing mothers, and eases griping pains in the stomach.
- Lily (*Lilium candidum*). The root made into a decoction gives delivery to women in travail and expels the afterbirth.
- Chickweed (*Stellaria media*). The juice or distilled water is good for all heats and redness in the eyes if some is dropped into them . . . it is also used in hot and virulent ulcers and sores in the privy parts of men and women, or on the legs or elsewhere.

**Read more about Nicholas Culpeper's astrological herbalism:**

*Culpeper's Medicine: A Practice of Western Holistic Medicine*, by Graeme Tobyn

*In the beginning He formed the Heavens and adorned them with goodly, shining stars, to which He gave power and might to influence everything under heaven . . . so that everything which has its being under Heaven receives it from the stars, and keeps it by their health.*

—ANONYMOUS FIFTEENTH-CENTURY GERMAN PHILOSOPHER

*Our kids are more familiar with computers and cell phones than they are with grass or fireflies. They are seldom outdoors. They think food comes in a box or a bag. It makes me wonder what the future holds for gardeners. Are we a dying breed, soon to become extinct? I like to cook, I like to garden. I just may be a dinosaur.*

—CAROLEE SNYDER

## Going Places: Carolee's Herb Farm, Hartford City Indiana

I love my visits to Carolee's Herb Farm, not just because of its wonderful gardens, or its fields of pick-your-own lavender, or even the big barn, stuffed full of herbal treasures. I love to go there just to visit with Carolee Snyder and hear all about her latest adventure into herbs. When it comes to herbs, Carolee (whom I met when we both served on the board of the International Herb Association) is one of the most knowledgeable and enthusiastic people I know.

Carolee's special passion is lavender. She grows more than sixty different varieties in her lavender field, from the compact, eight-inch "Baby Blue" to the tall, spectacular "Hidcote Giant." And in most years, Carolee and her visiting lavender specialists offer Lavender Daze, a two-day lavender festival, with classes and workshops on cooking, crafting, and growing this delightful plant. You can learn to make a wreath or a sorbet, relax with a lavender massage, or stroll through the lavender fields, warm and fragrant under the Indiana sun.

While you're there, you'll want to browse through Carolee's delightful gardens, twenty of them, each organized around a particular theme: a Sunrise Garden of bright orange and yellow plants, a Cook's Garden, a Cottage Garden, a Thyme Garden. If you live in the vicinity, you can tune in her weekly radio show, where she answers callers' questions and shares gardening information (details on her web site). And if Carolee's life as a gardener and educator tempts you to drop everything and buy a farm, you might check her online personal journal (also on her web site). It will give you an idea of the daily and seasonal challenges she faces and the many different kinds of work she does.

Come lavender time, though, you'll find Carolee in her lavender field, enjoying the scent and sweetness of nature at its finest. Join her.

For Carolee's Cranberry Cordial see November 26.

**Read more about Carolee's gardening life:**
Carolee's Herb Farm web site, www.caroleesherb-farm.com, for directions, photos, recipes, and tips
*Thyme and Thyme Again: Celebrating Good Thymes in the Garden*, by Carolee Snyder (available at the farm, or from the web site)

# JUNE 23

*Flowers are the sweetest things God ever made.*
—HENRY BEECHER (1858)

## Candied Blossoms

So many flowers are in bloom in China's garden right now that she and Ruby are dazzled. It's time to preserve some for summertime sweet treats, so they're planning to get together on Sunday afternoon and spend a few pleasant hours making their flowers even sweeter. Candied blossoms add elegance to cakes, petit fours, cheesecakes, candies, and other dainties. This is a family-friendly project you can do at home, so gather the kids and get started!

### CANDYING FLOWERS AND HERBS

*Gather flowers and herb leaves.* Good choices: Borage flowers, violas (pansies, violets, Johnny-jump-ups), redbud and lilac florets, rose petals, plum and apple blossoms, mint leaves, lemon balm leaves. Nip off the stems, wash them, and dry them on a towel. Transfer to paper towels to ensure that they are thoroughly dry.

*Gather ingredients and equipment.* You will need 2 room-temperature egg whites, water, a cup or more of superfine sugar in a flat bowl or saucer, a clean tweezers, and a waxed paper–lined cookie sheet or tray.

*Candy the flowers.* Beat the egg whites until they just froth. Holding a flower or leaf with the tweezers, dip it into the egg white. Hold it over the sugar, and gently sprinkle sugar over the whole flower, turning it as you work to coat all the surfaces. Place the candied blossom on the wax paper. Repeat until you've candied all your flowers and leaves. Put the cookie sheet in a warm, dry place to dry. If the humidity is high, this may take up to 36 hours. Alternatives: Put the blossoms in an oven with the pilot light lit overnight; or set the oven at 150° and dry them with the door open for several hours; or use a dehydrator. Store in airtight containers (tins or plastic), separating the layers with waxed paper.

**Read more about edible blossoms:**

*Flowers in the Kitchen: A Bouquet of Tasty Recipes*, by Susan Belsinger

*Using flowers in the kitchen is fun, so be creative and experiment. If you think that dill and chives go well together, then try combining their flowers in an unusual vinegar or a savory butter. . . . Sample each bloom to see how it tastes and which foods it goes well with. If you don't like it, don't eat it again; if you do, plant a lot in your garden!*

—SUSAN BELSINGER, *FLOWERS IN THE KITCHEN*

*"Clippers, bags, and wet paper towels?" I asked, startled. I stared at Sheila [the Pecan Springs Chief of Police]. "I think I know what Mrs. Barton was doing in that cemetery! She was a rose rustler!"*

*Now it was Sheila's turn to stare. "A rose rustler? What in the world is that?"*

*"People who want to propagate old roses," I said. "Mrs. Barton brought the clippers in order to take cuttings, and the wet paper towels to wrap around the stems before she put them into the plastic bags."*

—"DEATH OF A ROSE RUSTLER," IN *AN UNTHYMELY DEATH AND OTHER GARDEN MYSTERIES*

## Rose Rustling

Rose rustling? Call the cops!

No, don't. Rose rustling is an honorable profession, engaged in by some of the most law-abiding citizens you'd ever hope to meet. It is the name given to folks who preserve heirloom roses by taking cuttings wherever they happen to find them: in cemeteries, forgotten gardens, abandoned churchyards.

Why old roses? Because their historic interest, color, form, and most of all, their fragrance, make antique roses a valuable addition to contemporary gardens. Early rose cultivars have a much greater adaptability and disease resistance than do modern hybrids. They are especially suited to Southern gardens, where roses sometimes have a hard time of it.

What may be more important, many of these old roses are no longer commercially available. There's enormous excitement, rose rustlers say, in discovering a "found" rose that has not been noticed for a half century or more.

So if you happen to see a rose blooming in a forgotten cemetery, bring clippers, wet paper towels, and a plastic bag, and start rustling!

**HERE'S HOW TO BE A SUCCESSFUL ROSE RUSTLER:**

- Take several six-inch softwood cuttings from this year's growth. Strip the leaves from the lower four inches, leaving one or two leaf-clusters at the tip. (Some rustlers immerse the bottom inch or two in a cup of willow tea for 24 hours, to encourage root growth.)
- Fill six-inch pots with good potting soil and moisten it. Dip the cut end of the cutting into root-stimulating hormone. Make a hole in the potting soil, insert the cutting, firm gently, and water well. Set in a bright indirect light and protect from drying.
- When the cutting has produced its second set of leaves, it has taken firm root and can be moved outside. If your winters are severe, move your rustled roses into the basement for the winter.

**Read more about rose rustlers:**

*People with Dirty Hands: The Passion for Gardening*, by Robin Chotzinoff

## Making Herbal Healing Oils and Salves

For centuries, liniments and salves have been a convenient and effective way to apply healing herbs to a wound, scrape, burn, sting, bruise, inflammation, or skin ulcer. Begin by making an herbal oil for topical use, then make the oil into a salve by adding beeswax, which serves as a hardener and keeps the ingredients from separating.

### MAKE AN HERBAL HEALING OIL

Place three ounces of fresh or dried herbs in a glass jar and cover with a pint of olive oil, making sure that the herbal material is completely covered. Set it in the sun for about two weeks, shaking it daily. Strain through a very fine strainer to remove all of the plant material and store in a labeled, tightly lidded container. A small amount (4 drops per pint) of essential oil may be added for fragrance. You do not need to refrigerate topical oils, but you may add a few drops of benzoin tincture (available from the drugstore) as a preservative, especially if you plan to use the oil to make a salve.

### MAKE AN HERBAL SALVE

Mix ¾ to one ounce of melted beeswax (available from health food stores and on-line) into one cup of herbal oil. To test for consistency, put a spoonful of the melted mixture into a dish and put it in the freezer for 2–3 minutes. Too hard? Add herbal oil. Too soft? Add beeswax. Store salve in a labeled, tightly lidded jar, in a cool place. Salves can be kept in a cool place and replaced every twelve months.

### HERBS FOR HEALING OILS AND SALVES

You can make oils and salves of one herb, or a combination. Be sure to keep a record of the herbs you use in each preparation, and make notes on the use to which it is put, and the observed effect.

- To ease muscular aches: arnica, calendula, cayenne, chamomile, eucalyptus, lavender, marjoram, peppermint, rosemary, Saint-John's-wort, wintergreen
- To treat wounds, skin lesions: chickweed, comfrey, echinacea, elder, golden seal, plaintain, yarrow
- To soothe rashes and itchy skin, treat bug bites and stings: burdock root, chickweed, chaparral, goldenseal, plantain, jewelweed

*Easier than making cookies and just about as much fun, salves are deeply rewarding to create. They require little time and the finished product looks so professional and works so effectively that many people have been inspired to start small businesses with their favorite salve recipes.*

—ROSEMARY GLADSTAR, *HERBAL HEALING FOR WOMEN*

Today is National Chocolate Pudding Day.

## Chocolate: The Pudding Herb

Of course, chocolate has to be the favorite pudding herb, doesn't it?

Culinary herbalist Susan Belsinger adds a surprise to her favorite chocolate pudding: leaves of fresh bay. "Scratch the underside vein of the bayleaf with your thumbnail," Susan instructs. "Close your eyes and sniff. What do you smell? Sniff again. I get spice, nutmeg-like, a little clove-like, maybe allspice, maybe citrus. One more time—keep your eyes closed. I get vanilla at the very end of the aroma. These flavors all go well with chocolate—that's why I use it in desserts. I make bay syrup and bay rice pudding, too. Yum!"

### SUSAN BELSINGER'S CHOCOLATE PUDDING WITH BAY

- 2 cups half-and-half
- 3 large fresh bay leaves or 2 dried bay leaves
- 3 tablespoons cornstarch
- ⅔ cup sugar
- 2 pinches salt
- ¼ cup unsweetened cocoa
- ½ cup milk
- 3 ounces bittersweet or semisweet chocolate, cut into small pieces
- ½ teaspoon pure vanilla extract

Heat the half-and-half with the bay leaves in a heavy-bottomed saucepan over medium heat. When the cream starts to bubble around the edges of the pan, remove from heat and cover. Let stand for 30 minutes. Combine the cornstarch, sugar, salt, and cocoa in a bowl and whisk in the milk. Pour the mixture into the warm bay-infused cream and cook over medium heat, stirring as the pudding thickens. When it begins to boil, stir for one more minute, then remove the pan from the heat and stir in the chocolate pieces until they are melted. Mix in the vanilla. Remove the bay leaves and pour the pudding into six ramekins or custard cups. Best served at room temperature, Susan says, "so you really taste the flavors." Garnish with whipped cream if desired.

**Read more of Susan's herbal recipes:**

*Not Just Desserts: Sweet Herbal Recipes*, by Susan Belsinger, available from www.susanbelsinger.com.

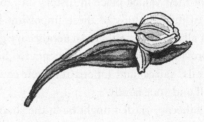

# JUNE 27

The Theme Garden for June: An Apothecary Garden.

*Even the Apothecary Garden, where the plants are grown for their medicinal value rather than their beauty, is pretty at this time of year: the tall stalks of fuzzy-leafed mullein like yellow tapers; the striking blossoms of echinacea, with their drooping purple petals and bright orange centers; and the passionflower, so useful in treating menstrual disorders, clambering happily up its trellis.*

—A DILLY OF A DEATH: A CHINA BAYLES MYSTERY

## Herbs for Healing

One of the most interesting gardens to design and tend is the apothecary garden, which features the medicinal herbs that were so important to the health and well-being of people in earlier times. Medicinal plants were at the heart of medical practice. This garden reminds us of their valued place in history and may inspire you to further study of these important herbs. And it isn't all academic, either! An apothecary garden can also provide you with the ingredients for healing tinctures, oils, salves, and lotions that you can craft for yourself and your family.

Your apothecary garden might be in the shape of a circle, divided into pie-shaped wedges, or in a four-square pattern with small blocks devoted to particular plants. You may also want to incorporate some of the important medicinal shrubs (roses and witch hazel, for instance). An armillary—an ancient style of sundial—will give your garden a medieval look. Of course, before you use any plant therapeutically, you'll want to do your homework. As China always says, she would hate to lose one of her friends due to the uninformed use of herbs!

### A SAMPLING OF APOTHECARY HERBS FOR YOUR GARDEN

- Borage (*Borago officinalis*)
- Catnip or Catmint (*Nepeta cataria*)
- Comfrey (*Symphytum officinale*)
- Echinacea (*Echinacea augustifolia*)
- Horehound (*Marrubium vulgare*)
- Horseradish (*Cochlearia amoracia*)
- Lemon Balm (*Melissa officinalis*)
- Mullein (*Verbascum thapsus*)
- Passionflower (*Passiflora incarnata*)
- Pot Marigold (*Calendula officinalis*)
- Periwinkle (*Vinca major*)
- Saint-John's-wort (*Hypericum perforatum*)
- Valerian (*Valeriana officinalis*)
- Violet (*Viola odorata*)
- Yarrow (*Achillea millefolium*)

**For the history of the apothecary garden, read:**
*History of the English Herb Garden*, by Kay N. Sanecki

**For medical uses of herbs, consult:**
*The Herbal Handbook: A User's Guide to Medical Herbalism*, by David Hoffmann

*Thou pretty herb of Venus' tree,*
*Thy true name it is Yarrow;*
*Now who my bosom friend must be,*
*Pray tell thou me tomorrow.*
—HALLIWELL'S POPULAR RHYMES

## Yarrow, Yea, Yarrow, Nay

Yarrow is so often described as a medicinal herb that its other interesting uses are sometimes overlooked. But it was otherwise in the old days, for yarrow had a reputation as an herb with a dangerously split personality.

**BAD YARROW, GOOD YARROW**
For reasons that aren't quite clear, yarrow was one of the herbs thought to be dedicated to the devil, and two of its early names—Devil's nettle and Devil's plaything—reflect this demonic affiliation. Witches were thought to employ it for spells, and it was considered dangerous to take the flowers indoors: In some parts of England, it was known as "Mother-die" plant. On the other hand, yarrow was worn as an amulet to protect against harm, strewn across the threshold to warn off evil spirits, and hung over the cradle to guard against witches and fairies that might steal the baby.

But it is in divination that the most interesting uses of yarrow appear. Perhaps because of its ambiguous association with the otherworld, the plant was used to predict the future. In China, the yarrow's sacred stems were traditionally used to cast the I Ching, the famous oracle. In Europe, yarrow was placed beneath pillows to invite dreams of the future, and particularly of the future spouse. It was often gathered with specific instructions: "If a maiden wants to know who her be goin' to marry, her must go to the churchyard at midnight and pluck a bit o' yarra off the grave of a young man." Young women split yarrow stems lengthwise to find the initials of their future husband; at the wedding, the two chewed the same yarrow leaf, supposed to ensure faithfulness for at least seven years.

But perhaps the oddest divining charm of all derives from yarrow's use as a snuff to stop nosebleeds (which it might indeed do, given its astringent properties). Here's the charm, from England's East Anglia region, to be chanted while you tickle your nose with yarrow leaves:

*Yarroway, yarroway, bear a white blow*
*If my love love me, my nose will bleed now.*

Get out that hanky and give it a try!

**Read more about the folklore of herbs:**
*Hedgemaids and Fairy Candles: The Lives and Lore of North American Wildflowers*, by Jack Sanders
*Oxford Dictionary of Plant-Lore*, by Roy Vickery

*Hemp-seed I sow, Hemp-seed I hoe,*
*He that is my true love will come after me and mow.*
—TRADITIONAL SONG

Today is the Anglican feast day of St. Peter the Apostle. In some churches in the north of England, the day is still celebrated with the Rushbearing Ceremony.

> *Rushes then were very necessary, not only for warmth to the feet of the worshipper, and thus we find that in olden time, as for example in the Norwich Cathedral, the rush that was sought after was the sweet-scented flag,* Acorus calamus, *which, when bruised, emits the fragrance of the myrtle flower.*

—CANON H. D. RAWNSLEY, 1902

## Strewing Herbs

With all due respect to Canon Rawnsley (one of the founders of England's National Trust), rushes were part of the problem, for the soft-stemmed plants decayed readily and (especially in dining halls) harbored bones, food scraps, insects, and general refuse. When the floor was strewn with herbs, however, the situation was much more hygienic, as a visitor to England remarked: "Their chambers and parlours strawed over with swete herbes," he wrote, "refreshed me."

In the sixteenth century, herbs were grown specifically for strewing. In *Five Hundred Points of Good Husbandry*, Thomas Tusser lists 21 strewing herbs, including basil, balm, fennel, germander, and lavender. At the coronation of King James II in 1685, the Royal Herb Strewer strewed six bushels of herbs in the cathedral aisle, to be trodden on by the king. And as late as the end of the nineteenth century, pews in some English churches were strewn with herbs: costmary, mint, meadowsweet, rue, and sage. Spices were used where they could be afforded.

While you may not be eager to toss herbs on your floors, there are other pleasant ways to use these aromatic plants.

- In a coffee grinder or spice mill, grind cloves, cinnamon, other sweet-smelling spices, and dried rosemary. Mix with baking soda in equal parts (1 cup soda to 1 cup herbs). Sprinkle on your carpet, leave for an hour, then vacuum. (Test an area first, to be sure the material won't stain and that your vacuum will pick it up.)
- Fill sachets and place them in your drawers and cupboards, or under the cushions or pillows on your sofa. Check often for mildew.
- Make potpourri from your garden and place bowls of it throughout your home.
- Hang bundles of aromatic herbs in your cupboards, closets, and attic. Renew as necessary.

**Read more about strewing herbs:**

*Magic Gardens: A Modern Chronicle of Herbs and Savory Seeds*, by Rosetta E. Clarkson

*While wormwood hath seed, get a handful or twain*
*To save against March, to make fleas to refrain*
*Where chamber is swept, and wormwood is strown*
*No flea, for his life, dare abide to be known.*

—THOMAS TUSSER, 1573

# JUNE 30

*Sleep: the golden chain that ties health and our bodies together.*

—THOMAS DEKKER (1572–1632)

## Sweet Snoozes

Sometimes, if you've been busy all day, your body may be tired but your mind can't seem to shut down. You toss and turn and can't fall asleep, or you fall asleep but are wakeful—which makes the next day that much more stressful, which makes it harder to fall asleep the next night, which . . . Well, you get the picture. A third of American adults have trouble sleeping. If you're one of them, try the natural sleep remedy of herbs.

**HERBAL SLEEPY-TIME TEAS**

• Chamomile (*Chamaemelum nobile*) is a relaxing herb that eases digestion and relieves spasms. It is a gentle sedative that is good for anxiety, especially when it is caused by losing one's way in Mr. McGregor's garden. To make the tea, steep one teaspoon of dried chamomile flowers in one cup boiling water for 4–5 minutes. It can be mixed with other sedative herbs.

• Valerian (*Valeriana officinalis*) is relaxing and sleep-inducing, calms digestion, and reduces blood pressure. Long used in folk medicine, clinical studies have validated valerian as a sedative. It can be used without fear of loss of performance the next day. Best taken as a tincture or a tea. Make the tea in the morning—2 teaspoons of valerian root to 2 cups of warm water—and let it steep until evening. Strain, warm, and add honey. Drink 1 cup after dinner and 1 cup before going to bed. Important note: don't confuse valerian with the drug Valium.

• Lemon balm (*Melissa officinalis*) tea is relaxing and sleep-inducing. Steep 2 fresh leaves (or 1 teaspoon of dried leaves) in 1 cup of boiling water for ten minutes. Sip slowly just before bed. Lemon balm can also be mixed with chamomile.

• Lavender (*Lavendula angustifolia*) essential oil has been clinically demonstrated to ease tension and slow beta waves in the brain, suggesting drowsiness. Drink a cup of lavender tea (Steep 1 teaspoon flowers in 1 cup boiling water for 5 minutes.) Use it in a bath before bedtime, and put a few drops on your pillow. Try it in conjunction with one of the other herbal relaxants.

**Read more about herbs that help you sleep:**

*Sleep and Relaxation: A Natural and Herbal Approach,* Story Country Wisdom Bulletin A-201, by Barbara L. Heller

July

❧

August

❧

September

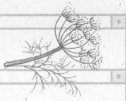

*"Howard!" I exclaimed, irritated. "You dirty dog! Have you been digging up rabbits again?"*

*Howard [McQuaid's elderly basset] regarded me with a guileless grin and a cheerful wag of his muddy tail.*

*"Well, it doesn't matter where you've been," I said firmly. "It's where you're going that counts. You're having a bath."*

—DEAD MAN'S BONES: A CHINA BAYLES MYSTERY

## Dog Days

July brings plenty of sweltering weather, and a sudden increase in the flea population, always a problem if you have pets—and sometimes if you don't. If the dog days are dogging you, here are some herbal solutions.

Start by making an herbal flea repellent oil (see formula below) and use it in the suggested ways. Observe your dog for possible allergies.

- Add 12–14 drops of oil to a quart of pet shampoo, or use the formula for Howard's Herbal Doggie Shampoo (see below).
- Dilute the oil with an equal amount of water, and spray, then comb, your dog's clean coat.
- Spray diluted oil on your dog's clean bedding.

### FLEA REPELLENT OIL

    4 drops eucalyptus oil
    4 drops citronella oil
    4 drops rosemary oil
    3 tablespoons almond or olive oil.

Store in a dry cool place and apply daily until the fleas are gone.

### HOWARD'S HERBAL DOGGIE SHAMPOO (FROM *DEAD MAN'S BONES*)

    1 quart liquid shampoo, any type
    2 drops pennyroyal or peppermint oil
    2 drops lemon oil
    2 drops rosemary oil
    2 drops lavender oil
    2 drops citronella

Mix all together, using amounts listed. Too much of a good thing can irritate a dog's skin. (And do be careful when you use essential oils. Ingested, they are highly toxic.)

**Read more about using herbs for dogs and cats:**
*Herbs for Pets*, by Gregory L. Tilford
*Veterinarians Guide to Natural Remedies for Dogs*, by Martin Zucker

*If the first of July be rainy weather,*
*'Twill rain more or less for four weeks together.*

—TRADITIONAL

In China, July is the month of the lotus.

*There is more pleasure in making a garden than in contemplating a paradise.*

—ANNE SCOTT-JAMES

## The Remarkable Lotus

I can't think of anything prettier than a pool of clear, cool water in a garden, reflecting the moving clouds during the day and the silver moon at night. And there's certainly nothing prettier in a pool than the waxen blossoms of a blooming lotus, an exotic and beautiful herb. If you have a water garden, the richly evocative lotus would be a delightful—and different—addition to your herb collection.

### A PLANT OF PLENTY AND ABUNDANCE

Throughout Asia, the rhizomes, seeds, leaves and flowers of the lotus are all eaten. The rhizomes are roasted, pickled, or dried and sliced for use in curries and soups. The sweet seeds, removed from their bitter covering, are eaten raw, roasted, boiled, or candied. They are also ground into flour. The young leaves, leaf stalks and flowers are eaten as vegetables.

The flowers became symbolic of immortality and resurrection because people observed that they would grow from the bottom of dried-up pools after the monsoon rains. Lotus seeds exhibit a remarkable longevity, apparently due to a special enzyme. In the 1920s, some were recovered from a lake in northeast China, and successfully grown; in the 1990s, when scientists were at last able to determine their age, it was found that they were an astonishing 1,300 years old.

In traditional Asian medicine, the lotus has been used to treat fungal infections, diarrhea, dysentery, fevers, and sexually transmitted diseases. The dried flowers are used in a syrup to treat coughs. The perfume was also thought to be medicinal: It raised the spirits and banished melancholy. The seeds were used as prayer beads, and the fiber was woven into cloth.

Observing the lotus grow from the silt of a long-dried pool when it was filled with monsoon rains, Hindu and Buddhist artists used the plant as a symbol of death and resurrection, and the flowers as symbols of good fortune, plenty, and abundance.

### GROWING LOTUS

Lotus are easy to grow, and hardy in USDA Zones 4–10. They need at least six hours of sun a day. Obtain rhizomes in the spring from your local water-garden plant supplier or from on-line sources. Plant them in enriched soil in shallow pans (a kitty-litter pan is fine), on overturned clay pots stacked at appropriate heights. Check with the supplier for additional culture instructions.

**Read more about waterlilies:**
*Waterlilies and Lotuses*, by Perry D. Slocum

# JULY 3

*Deep in their roots, all flowers keep the light.*

—THEODORE ROETHKE

## Not Just for Headaches

The healing properties of willow are a familiar story to many. But have you heard that this generous plant can help you root cuttings of your favorite shrubs and perennials? Rose rustlers swear by it and rhododendron fanciers recommend it ("rhodies" are notoriously difficult to root). And since it costs nothing to try, you have nothing to lose.

### ROOTING FOR WILLOW

Have you ever planted a budding willow wand in a marsh and watched it put out enthusiastic branches and eagerly stretch itself into a green tree? Willows seem to have a remarkable ability to root themselves almost anywhere. What's more, they seem to be willing to share that ability with other plants. You can take advantage of this generosity by treating your cuttings to a drink of willow tea.

To make this all-natural rooting stimulant favored by generations of gardeners, snip pencil-thin willow wands—budding willow "whips" are best—into one-inch lengths. Put two cups of the snipped wands into a half-gallon jar, fill with boiling water, steep overnight, and strain. To give your cuttings the "root" idea, soak the lower stems overnight in the willow tea, then pot

as usual. The tea you don't use will keep for two weeks or so in the refrigerator.

Good luck, and good rooting!

**Read more about starting plants from cuttings:**
*Growing Herbs from Seed, Cutting & Root: An Adventure in Small Miracles*, by Thomas DeBaggio

*The last week in this month, but not before, you may sow onions to stand the winter. . . . Remember when the plants are come up to let them be weeded in time; for, otherwise, the weeds, which will rise with the onions, will soon get the start of them, and destroy the whole crop.*

—THE GARDENERS KALENDAR, 1777

*Throw aside your Bohea and your Green Hyson Tea,*
*And all things with a new fashioned duty;*
*Procure a good store of the choice Labradore,*
*For there'll soon be enough here to suit ye;*
*Then do without fear, and to all you'll appear*
*Fair, charming, true, lovely and clever;*
*Though the times remain darkish, young men may be*
*sparkish,*
*And love you much stronger than ever.*

—BROADSIDE BALLAD ENCOURAGING THE DRINKING OF NATIVE TEAS

## Sweet Liber-Teas

There'll probably be a pitcher of iced tea on your picnic table today. But for the people who lived during the American Revolution, China tea was not on the menu. The whole affair had, after all, begun with the Boston Tea Party, and one of the patriots' earliest acts was to renounce imported tea in favor of locally grown herbs.

### LABRADOR TEA

The Labrador tea mentioned in the ballad was brewed from *Ledum groenlandicum*. The plant was used medicinally by Native Americans, who shared their knowledge about it with the colonists. In 1768, the *Boston Gazette* reported that the tea had been poured for a "circle of ladies and gentlemen who pronounced it nearly, if not quite, equal in flavor to genuine Bohea tea." The editor added, "If we have the plant, nothing is wanted but the process of curing it into tea of our own manufacture." Labrador teas were a household affair, and every housewife had her own recipe. Most included rose hips, mint, and wild ginger leaves. When available, dried citrus peels, cinnamon, and cloves were added.

### SASSAFRAS TEA, AND OTHER TREE TEAS

This flavorful tea (the original taste of "root beer") was brewed long before and after the Boston Tea Party, for it was thought to be both delicious and health-giving. And since the sassafras tree was an all-American native, it was certainly on the list of politically correct tea plants. Other trees or shrubs used as beverage teas: sweet gum, willow, rose, raspberry, and sumac.

### HERBAL TEAS

Catnip and pennyroyal were easy choices, along with various mints, bergamot, lemon balm, verbena, rosemary, thyme, sage, and wintergreen. Blossoms went into the teapot, as well: elder, red clover, violet, goldenrod, linden.

### YOUR OWN LIBERTY TEA

To make a pitcher of Liberty Tea, pour 10 cups boiling water over these slightly bruised fresh herbs: 5 sprigs spearmint, 3 sprigs applemint, 2 sprigs red bee-balm flowers, 2 sprigs lemon balm, 1 sprig peppermint. Steep 15 minutes. Serve iced. If you don't have these herbs, choose others. Our brave revolutionary foremothers would applaud your experiment!

*It was a hot afternoon, and I can still remember the smell of honeysuckle all along that street. How could I have known that murder can sometimes smell like honeysuckle?*

—FROM THE FILM *DOUBLE INDEMNITY*

## Sweet, Sweet as Honey

Honeysuckle and murder don't usually go together, but Raymond Chandler's line from the famous Fred MacMurray and Barbara Stanwyck film is one of China's favorites, and she insisted that I use it somewhere in this book. Maybe I'd better explain why.

Honeysuckle, as a literary symbol, has long been beloved of poets and novelists. Calling it "woodbine," Chaucer wrote about it in *Troilus and Cressida*:

*When she understood his loyalty and pure intention,*
*She put her arms around him,*
*As about a tree the sweet woodbine twists*
*Encircling and entwining. . . .*

Unfortunately, things don't work out very happily in the end, because Cressida betrays Troilus.

Still, the honeysuckle was clearly alluring and definitely delightful. Hence herbalist William Bullein, in his *Book of Simples* (1562) wrote:

*Ah, how swete and pleasaunt is Woodbinde, in*
*woodes or arbours, after a tender soft rayne; and how frendly doth this herb imbrace the bodies, armes, and braunches of trees.*

There was, however, another side to the story—the tree's side. The poet William Cowper warns:

*As Woodbine weds the plant within her reach,*
*Rough elm or smooth-grain'd ash, or glossy beech . . .*
*But does a mischief while she lends a grace,*
*Slackening its growth by such a strict embrace.*

"Does a mischief" as she "weds"? Well, yes, of course the honeysuckle can do mischief, as any observant gardener knows. In *The Englishman's Flora*, Geoffrey Grigson remarks: "Woodbine, honeysuckle, hugs more like a killing snake than a friend, often squeezing saplings into a spiral."

So perhaps Chandler's line does make sense, after all. In *Double Indemnity*, Barbara Stanwyck plays the role of a dangerous femme-fatale, seducing and entwining and eventually strangling the soul of love-struck, sappy Fred MacMurray, whom she persuades to do murder for her.

Yes, indeed. "Murder can sometimes smell like honeysuckle." And honeysuckle, sweet, sweet honeysuckle, can sometimes smell like murder.

**Read the mystery:**
*Double Indemnity*, by James M. Cain

*The rarity and novelty of this herb, being for the most part but in the gardens of great persons, doth cause it to be of great regard.*

—JOHN PARKINSON, *A GARDEN OF PLEASANT FLOWERS*, 1629

## Santolina

Santolina is one of those plants you may have to look up twice, since some people call it "lavender cotton," and others call it by the first of its Latin binomials: *Santolina chamaecyparissus*. (It's a little hard to get your tongue around the second part of its name, isn't it?) It is a small, silvery perennial with lavenderlike foliage, although its scent is more like wormwood than lavender. Planted close and sheared, it forms a dense, compact, foot-high hedge.

It was the hedging habit of this plant, newly imported from the Mediterranean, that made it so valuable to sixteenth-century English gardeners. They were looking for plants they could use to create the intricate knot gardens that had become popular among the wealthy: a geometric pattern outlined in a low, carefully-clipped hedge of box, lavender, germander, rosemary, or santolina. Of these, santolina was favored, for it grows slowly, is bushy from the base, and is hardier than most of the others. It traveled to Virginia with the wealthy Cavaliers, whose knot gardens imitated those in England, and made itself at home here in America.

We don't plant knot gardens much these days; we no longer employ platoons of gardeners trained to plant, prune, trim, and snip. But we still have santolina. Mine is unruly, for I confess to never having trimmed it; it is growing untidily, but happily, against a dry stone wall, and the yellow flowers that those long-ago British gardeners so carefully trimmed away are bursting into golden bloom. It's handy to have as a moth repellent, the bees enjoy it, and it is a pretty accent in small wreaths of dried plants.

Mostly, though, it is just pretty, an interesting reminder that garden fashions come and go, but that plants come and stay.

**Read more about the design of small formal gardens:**
*Knot Gardens and Parterres: A History of the Knot Garden and How to Make One Today,* by Robin Whalley

*Cresses, mustard, radish, and other small sallad herbs may now be sown. . . . If a constant supply of these small salleting herbs be wanting, a little of the seed should be sown once every week.*

—*THE GARDENERS KALENDAR*, 1777

*By eleven thirty, I had finished planting the flower bed, transplanted a half dozen gray wooly pillows of lamb's ears into various empty spaces, and broke apart several clumps of thyme, replanting them along the path with the creeping phlox and sweet alyssum, where they could spill onto the gravel.*

—WITCHES' BANE: A CHINA BAYLES MYSTERY

## Lamb's-Ears: Surprise!

In the Victorian language of flowers, lamb's-ears (*Stachys byzantina*) meant surprise—and no wonder. When you bend to touch this lovely little plant, you'll find that it is as soft and supple as gray velvet. Once used as a poultice and wound bandage and first cousin to the medicinal betony (*Stachys officinalis*), it can soothe a garden cut. And it's charming in the garden, too, although it has a disconcerting tendency to die out in the center after it stretches up to its full height (about 18 inches) and puts up lavender bloom stalks. Plant it in the driest part of your garden, for it is native to the dry, rocky hills of Turkey and Iran. Let it reseed (it loves to do this), and you will be surprised at the delightful little clumps of lamb's-ears that will appear.

### A SILVER WREATH
But lamb's-ears is at its most charming in a silvery garden wreath. You can purchase various wreath forms at craft stories—my favorite is an eight-inch loosely-woven vine wreath into which I can easily insert plant stems. Make a hanging tie for the back of the wreath. In the garden, choose stems of silver, gray, and gray-green plants: artemisias "Silver King," "Silver Queen," and "Powys Castle," lavender, pussytoes, statice, speedwell, wooly oregano, yarrow, santolina, and lamb's-ears. Place your wreath form flat, insert the plants' stems into it in a decorative pattern that suits you, and add a silver bow. Let it dry flat for a few days, then hang. Make one for yourself and one as a surprise gift for a friend, who will be just as charmed by those lamb's-ears as you are.

**Read more about wreathmaking:**
*Country Living Handmade Wreaths*, by Arlene Hamilton Stewart

*When a toad crosses the road on a summer afternoon, rain is at hand.*

—TRADITIONAL WEATHER LORE

Today is the feast day of St. Elizabeth of Portugal, known as the Peacemaker. She is often depicted with an olive branch, a symbol of peace. In some calendars, today is also the beginning of the Celtic Tree Month of Holly (see December 3).

*The necessary ingredients of civilization are wine and olive oil.*

—ANCIENT SAYING

## The Legendary Olive

In Greek and Roman mythology, the olive was the symbol of Athena, and of the city of Athens. In fact, Athens was named for Athena in a competition between Athena and Poseidon, each of whom gave a gift to humankind. Because of its oil, its fruit, and its wood, Athena's olive tree, emblematic of domestic industry and peaceful agriculture, was judged to be of greater use to the people than Poseidon's horse, which represented conquest and war. The oil was used to anoint the statues of the gods, priests and kings, and Olympic athletes. Throughout the Mediterranean region, an olive branch hung over a door is supposed to keep out devils, witches, and other evil spirits.

In Egypt, it was believed that Isis, goddess of fertility, had taught humans how to extract oil from olives. Olive branches were placed in the tombs of the pharaohs and olive oil was applied to their mummies. The oil was used in cosmetics and in medicine, where it was used to treat everything from kidney and chest complaints to fevers, plague, and dropsy.

### THE HEALTHY OLIVE

The beneficial health effects of olive oil are due to its monounsaturated fatty acids and its antioxidants. Research has demonstrated that it protects against heart disease by controlling LDL ("bad") cholesterol while increasing HDL ("good") cholesterol. Olive oil has a beneficial effect on ulcers and gastritis, activates the secretion of bile and pancreatic hormones, and lowers the incidence of gallstone formation. If you're using olive oil for health reasons, you want to purchase *extra virgin* oil, which is less processed and therefore contains higher levels of antioxidants, particularly vitamin E and phenols.

One important note: If you're frying or sautéing food, use another oil. Excessive heat may cause olive oil to change into a "transfat," negating most of its health benefits.

**Read more about olives:**
*The Passionate Olive*, by Carol Firenze

# JULY 9

Today is National Sugar Cookie Day.

*C is for cookie, it's good enough for me; oh cookie cookie cookie starts with C.*

—THE COOKIE MONSTER

## Creative Herbal Sugar Cookies

I collect herbal cookbooks from herb guilds around the country. I love them because they exhibit the kind of creative cookery that herbs inspire. In honor of National Sugar Cookie Day, here are three sugar cookie recipes, dreamed up by creative cooks. Thanks, gals, for allowing me to share these!

### CURRY COOKIES
1 cup butter or margarine
2 cups brown sugar
2 teaspoons vanilla extract
2 eggs
1½ cups chopped walnuts
1½ cups whole-wheat pastry flour
1½ cups unbleached flour
½ teaspoon baking soda
1 teaspoon baking powder
2 teaspoons curry powder
½ teaspoon salt

Preheat oven to 325°. Cream butter and sugar. Add the vanilla and eggs; continue to cream the mixture. Mix together the walnuts, flours, baking soda, baking powder, curry powder, and salt. Stir these dry ingredients into creamed mixture. Refrigerate until dough is chilled. Roll into a log and slice. Bake in preheated oven until golden. —Bettye Boone, *Collected Herbal Favorites*

### MINT BUTTER COOKIES
1½ cups flour
⅛ teaspoon salt
½ teaspoon baking powder
1 stick butter
⅔ cup sugar
1 egg
2 tablespoons milk
4 tablespoons chopped fresh mint
¼ teaspoon vanilla

Cream butter, gradually add sugar and beat until fluffy. Add the egg, milk, and vanilla and beat thoroughly. Mix dry ingredients and chopped mint. Let dough chill overnight. Drop by teaspoonfuls 2 inches apart on greased cookie sheet. Bake at 350° for 10–12 minutes. —Calista Trembath, *Lemon Verbena Herbal Cookbook*

To obtain these books, contact: *Lemon Verbena Herbal Cookbook*, Lemon Verbena Herb Society, 6049 Skyline Dr., East Lansing, MI 48823; *Collected Herbal Favorites*, The Herb Bunch, 205 Hermitage Road, Lexington, SC 29072.

# JULY 10

*To a Gallon of water put a quart of honey, about ten sprigs of Sweet-Marjoram; half so many tops of Bays. Boil these very well together, and when it is cold, bottle it up. It will be ten days before it is ready to drink.*

—THE CLOSET OF SIR KENELM DIGBY OPENED, 1669

## Marjoram, Oregano— Which Is Which?

If you're confused about this herb, you're not alone, for the words *marjoram* and *oregano* are almost interchangeable common names given to some thirty-six species of small perennial shrubs or tender perennials in the genus *Origanum*. The parent species, *Origanum vulgare*, originated in the mountains of the Mediterranean area. In Greece, newlyweds wore wreaths of marjoram. It was planted on graves for good fortune in the afterlife. And in England, witches who repented of their practices were said to bathe in oregano and thyme to wash off the guilt.

*Origanum vulgare* (the word *vulgare* means "common") has very little of that magical oregano flavor. Its full-blooded Greek cousin, on the other hand, will make you stand up and shout Pizza! So if it's flavor you're after, look for the white-flowered Greek oregano, *O. vulgare hirtum*. If sweet and subtle is your pleasure, try *O. marjorana*, valued for its milder, warmer taste and gentle aroma.

## WHAT COLOR IS YOUR OREGANO?

Taste, of course, isn't everything. If you're a gardener, you're looking for color—and oregano has plenty. Try these colorful cultivars in raised beds, window boxes, or containers, where you can enjoy their arching blossom-sprays.

- Go for the gold with "Areum" or "Norton's Gold"
- Think pink with "Kent Beauty," "Showy Pink," or "Barbara Tingey"
- Plan on purple with "Hopleys Purple," "Herrenhausen," or "Rosunkuppel"

## OREGANO FOR GOOD HEALTH

- To relieve the muscular ache that comes with colds and flu, use 10–12 drops of oregano essential oil in a hot bath. Breathe deeply.
- As a massage oil, add 6–8 drops to ⅛ cup almond or olive oil. Massage onto the chest to ease respiratory ills, or into a sprain or bruise.
- For stomach upsets, sip a cup of oregano tea. Pour 1 cup of boiling water over 1–2 teaspoons dried oregano, steep for 5 minutes, strain.
- For inflamed gums, steep the tea for 10 minutes and swish around in your mouth.

**Read more about oregano:**

*Growing and Using Oregano*, Storey Country Wisdom Bulletin A-157, by Sara Pitzer

# JULY 11

## Prairie Doctor

The echinacea (*Echinacea purpurea*) is blooming in my garden just now, its drooping purple petals a colorful contrast to its bright orange centers. On this hot July afternoon, it is the prettiest thing in the garden. The bees and butterflies pausing happily to enjoy it obviously think so, too.

Echinacea is native to the Great Plains of North America, and the peoples of the region, skilled herbalists as they were, understood its effectiveness long before white people came into their territory. In their larder of plant medicines—ginseng, goldenseal, slippery elm, chickweed, milkweed—echinacea held the highest place. It was used to treat toothaches, coughs, infections, sore throats, and just about anything else. Preparation was simple: They dug a fresh root and sucked on it.

European botanists heard about the coneflower in the early 1700s, but it was not until the Indians shared their knowledge with the settlers that word of this American treasure, often called "prairie doctor," got around. It was a German named H.C.F. Meyer, of Pawnee City, Nebraska, who made it famous, incorporating echinacea with herbs such as hops and wormwood in "Meyer's Blood Purifier." Meyer was so persuaded of the efficacy of his preparation that he offered to demonstrate—on his own person—how quickly it would cure the bite of a full-grown rattlesnake. Nobody took him up on his grandstanding offer, but it brought echinacea to the attention of physicians and patients, and its use began to grow steadily. But while European interest remained strong, echinacea dropped out of sight in its native country in the 1940s, and did not reemerge until the 1990s. Now, it is one of the best-selling herbal remedies on the market, recommended as a treatment for colds, flu, and related ailments. There's a great deal of literature on this herb; while there are no known safety issues, it's a good idea to read about it before using it.

Herbalist Steven Foster suggests making your own herbal tea with the fresh flowering tops of *E. purpurea*. Pick a flower, he says, chop it fine, and put it into a tea bag or nonreactive strainer. Steep in hot water for 15 minutes, and sip to combat flu and colds.

Prairie doctor tea. Sounds right to me.

**Read more about echinacea:**

*Echinacea: The Immune Herb*, by Christopher Hobbs, L.Ac.

*Echinacea: Nature's Immune Enhancer*, by Steven Foster

*I do not know whether I was then a man dreaming I was a butterfly, or whether I am now a butterfly dreaming I am a man.*

—CHANG TZU

## Milkweed and Monarchs: From Susan's Journal

Out for the morning walk with the dogs today, I have to stop and admire the neat globular pastel flower clusters of the green milkweed (*Asclepias viridis*), blooming across our meadows. The green milkweed comes along about a month after the antelope-horn milkweed (*Asclepias asperula*), which bloomed earlier. There's a problem, though. I've looked at a dozen plants of both species this morning, and I don't see any damage on any of them. Flowers intact and nary a leaf nibbled.

What's wrong with that? Perfect plants are nice, aren't they?

Yes, usually. But not in this case, for the milkweeds are the foraging food of the monarch butterfly, which lays its eggs exclusively on this plant. In earlier years, I could watch the striped caterpillars feeding on the leaves, absorbing the bitter taste of the latex sap that protects them from predators. Having lunched and munched for two or three weeks, the caterpillars pupate, spinning jewel-like green chrysalides ornamented with gold spots. If I am lucky, I may even see an adult monarch as it emerges from its chrysalis, stretches its wings to dry, and flies away.

But not this year. Several black swallowtail caterpillars have chewed the garden fennel to tatters (I grow it mostly for them), but the milkweed in the fields is picture perfect. No monarch mothers, no munching monarch caterpillars, no chrysalides, no emerging adults. Of course, this is only one small corner of Texas; I'm hoping it's not typical. But last year's monarch migration was sparse, according to published reports, and this year's may be sparser. Bad weather and habitat destruction in Mexico, chemicals in the United States. Those butterflies may look carefree, but their lives aren't all milkweed and sweet breezes.

So you can see why I'm not celebrating all those perfect leaves and flowers.

I'm rooting for the monarchs.

**Read more about monarchs**

*Four Wings and a Prayer: Caught in the Mystery of the Monarch Butterfly*, by Sue Halpern

*I have a garden of my own*
*But so with roses overgrown*
*And lilies, that you would it guess*
*To be a little wilderness.*

—ANDREW MARVELL, 1621–1678

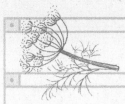

*Come buy my mint, my fine green mint!*

—LONDON STREET CRY

## Mint Mythology

The Greeks had a myth for it. Pluto, the god of the underworld, indulged in a passionate fling with a haughty, beautiful nymph named Menthe. His jealous wife, Persephone, transformed the proud girl into a small plant that grew underfoot, so it would be trodden by all. Pluto was heartbroken when he found out. He couldn't undo Persephone's magic but he worked some of his own, endowing Menthe with a sweet, spicy fragrance, so that those who trod on her would love her as he did.

### MULTIPLE MINTS

The best-known mints are spearmint (*Mentha spicata*) and peppermint (*Mentha piperita*). To confuse the matter, there is also water mint (*Mentha aquatica*), horse mint (*Mentha longifolia*), and pennyroyal (*Mentha pulegium*). And then there are the flavored mints: apple mint, pineapple mint, chocolate mint, orange mint, and ginger mint. Mints are almost too easy to grow, so unless you plant them behind a barrier, you'll have mint in your marigolds. They crossbreed easily, too, so if you want your chocolate mint to remain true to its divine nature, give it a separate garden spot of its own.

### MEDICINAL MINT

Menthol (mint's essential oil) soothes the digestive tract, hence its use as a digestive aid and its starring role in the after-dinner mint. American Indians used mint as a rub to treat pain, headache, and coughs, and menthol still appears in many ointments and creams that relieve pain, clear chest congestion, and heal cold sores. Peppermint has also been used as an abortifacient, and pregnant women should avoid this herb. And never, *never* ingest peppermint oil—it is decidedly, definitively fatal.

### CRAFTY MINT

Got mountains of mint? Make mint soap. Brew a strong tea (1 tablespoon dried mint to ⅓ cup boiling water, steep 15 minutes). Grate two large bars of castile soap. Reheat the mint tea and add 4 drops peppermint oil. Mix well, knead, and form into balls. Place on waxed paper and air-dry 2–4 days. Gritty? Wet, smooth with your hands, and dry again.

**Read more about mint:**

*Mints: A Family of Herbs and Ornamentals*, by Barbara Perry Lawton

*But if any man can name the full list of all the kinds and all the properties of Mint, he must be one who knows how many fish Swim in the Ocean, how many sparks Vulcan Sees fly in the air from his vast furnace in Etna.*

—HORTULUS, ABBOT WALAFRID STRABO, 809–849

## Going Places: Shady Acres Herb Farm, Chaska, Minnesota

If you live in the Upper Midwest and want some help getting started with herbs (that winter climate is challenging!), you must make a visit to Shady Acres, the dream farm of Jim and Theresa Mieseler. There, you can stroll through the herb gardens and greenhouses settled across a green and pretty landscape, meet helpful people who know their herbs, and learn how you can take home both plants and knowledge, so you can grow your own.

Jim and Theresa's 25-acre farm is located in the rolling farmlands of Carver County, just 30 miles southwest of Minneapolis–St. Paul. The couple has been there since 1977, long enough to put down roots in the Minnesota soil, to learn the habits and needs of all the herbs they grow and sell, and see their dream grow. And grow it has. From a small beginning, the Mieselers' farm now includes eight greenhouses, display gardens, classroom space, a gift shop—and a full calendar of events from late March through mid-December.

There's always something to learn at Shady Acres. Want to create a fairy garden? Theresa will provide the plants, accessories, and materials that you and your child can use to create a charming landscape. If it's container gardening you're interested in, you can go home with three terra-cotta containers full of plants! Or if you'd like to learn about scented geraniums, or topiaries, or edible wild plants, those classes are available, as well.

And crafts, too—soap-making, for instance. You'll not only see the herbs growing in the garden, you'll see how they're used in soap, and when you go home, you'll take with you eight ounces of your own custom blended soap. Or you can learn to make a holiday wreath of fresh balsam, or a holiday window box. And kids can paint gourds and make wreaths and pomanders.

Special events are on the Shady Acres menu, as well: a bus tour of area gardens; an outdoor supper fresh off the grill; an afternoon of herbal sorbets; a morning crafts workshop followed by a delicious lunch; and a delightful seven-course dinner in the garden, with live music.

All of the plants the Mieselers sell are produced from seeds, root division, or cuttings grown at the farm. Herbs are available for nation-wide shipping from April through September. Check out the on-line store at the web site: www.shadyacres.com, where you'll also find gift shop items, books, oils, and herbal supplies. And be sure to subscribe to the farm's newsletter, so you can keep up with all the goings-on!

# JULY 15

Today is St. Swithin's Day.

*St. Swithin's Day if thou does rain*
*For forty days it will remain;*
*St. Swithin's Day if thou be fair*
*For forty days 'twill rain na mair.*

—TRADITIONAL WEATHER LORE

## The Weather in Your Garden

We have satellites and Nex-rad radar and the TV weatherman to tell us what sort of weather to expect. But in past centuries, farmers and gardeners could only look to the skies and depend on folk wisdom for their meteorological forecast. The St. Swithin's Day rhyme is a good example.

Saint Swithin was a Saxon bishop of Winchester in the ninth century. According to legend, he asked to be buried outdoors, so that "the sweet rain from heaven" could fall on his grave. For nine years, that's where he stayed—until the Winchester monks decided to move him to a splendid shrine inside the cathedral. The ceremony, planned for July 15, 971, was rained out, or so the story goes, and the rain continued for 40 days. Hence the prediction: foul weather on St. Swithin's Day will bring 40 days of rain—but not often enough to make it a reliable prognosticator, according to British meteorologists.

But there are other weather proverbs that might help:

- If the leaves show their undersides, beware of foul weather.
- When the dew is on the grass, rain will never come to pass.
- When you hear the rain crow call, the rain will fall.
- When the wind's in the south, the rain's in its mouth.

If these don't work, try looking at your garden. Clover, chickweed, dandelions, morning glories, anemone, and tulips are said to fold their petals prior to a rain. If the calendula blossom opens before seven, you'll soon hear thunder; if it stays open all day, you're in for sunshine. Most reliable, perhaps, is the bog pimpernel (*Anagallis tenella*), also called shepherd's weather glass and poor man's barometer. It is immortalized in this quatrain:

*Pimpernel, pimpernel, tell me true*
*Whether the weather be fine or no;*
*No heart can think, no tongue can tell,*
*The virtues of the pimpernel.*

And for predicting the temperature, try your local rhododendron, which furls its leaves as the temperature rises and falls: completely closed at 20°F, completely open at 60°F.

Who needs the weather man?

**Read more about weather lore:**
*The Farmer's Almanac*

*My garden is an honest place. Every tree and every vine are incapable of concealment, and tell after two or three months exactly what sort of treatment they have had.*

—RALPH WALDO EMERSON

*A doctor can bury his mistakes but an architect can only advise his clients to plant vines.*

—FRANK LLOYD WRIGHT

## Vining Herbs

Most of us think of herbs as relatively small plants—until we stand in the shade of a ginseng tree. To broaden your herbal repertory even further, consider these herbal vines, all of which are as honest as Emerson says they are, but are capable of concealing a multitude of architectural crimes.

• English Ivy (*Hedera helix*). Perennial evergreen vine. According to herbalist Maud Grieve: "Ivy was in high esteem among the ancients. Its leaves formed the poet's crown, as well as the wreath of Bacchus, to whom the plant was dedicated, probably because of the practice of binding the brow with Ivy leaves to prevent intoxication, a quality formerly attributed to the plant. We are told by old writers that the effects of intoxication by wine are removed if a handful of Ivy leaves are bruised and gently boiled in wine and drunk." Also used in divination.

• Hops (*Humulus lupulus*). Robust perennial vine, may grow 30 feet in one season. Antibiotic and anti-inflammatory, hops have been used in salves and wound compresses. The plant has a sedative action and has been used in teas, as well as sleep pillows. Used in brewing beer.

• Passionflower (*Passiflora incarnata*). Vigorous perennial vine. Widely used to treat sleep disorders, nervousness, headache; it is favored because it is effective without narcotic after-effects. Native to South and Central America and first documented in the 1560s, this plant is available in most nurseries. Not reliably hardy in colder climates.

• Love-in-a-puff (*Cardiospermum halicacabum*—see February 6). A fast-growing annual or tender perennial. In Chinese medicine, a tea brewed from the leaves is used to treat skin ailments and promote wound healing. In India, the leaves are mixed with castor oil and used to treat rheumatism and joint stiffness. The leaf juice soothes earaches.

**Read more about native vines, many of them herbal:**
*Native Trees, Shrubs, and Vines: A Guide to Using, Growing, and Propagating North American Woody Plants*, by William Cullina

*Ivy, ivy, I love you, in my bosom I put you.*
*The first young man to speak to me*
*My future husband he shall be.*

—TRADITIONAL LOVE CHARM

*With all the rain we've been having, the Hopi dye sunflowers were taller and larger than usual, their orange-rimmed heads plump with purple-black seeds. The safflowers too, were vigorous and woody, while the unruly madder (a distant cousin of that all-important cinchona tree) was thigh-high and sprawling.*

—INDIGO DYING: A CHINA BAYLES MYSTERY

## Seeing Red

I didn't know much about the dye herbs until I began doing the research for *Indigo Dying*, China's full-color mystery. Then, as I usually do with these novels, I did as much hands-on research as I could find time for. I discovered that many of the plants in my herb garden are good to dye with—goldenrod, tansy, mint, mullein, marigold, and yarrow—and that a great many of the wild plants growing at Meadow Knoll yield natural dyes: coreopsis, Joe-Pye weed, dock, burdock, black-eyed Susan, milkweed, osage orange, and sumac. I also planted two dye herbs that were new to me: coltsfoot and madder.

Madder (*Rubia tinctorum*) really likes my garden. Really. China wasn't kidding when she described it as "thigh-high and sprawling," although she might have added "plain-Jane and homely," to boot. Madder would probably like your garden, too, but do think twice before you plant it. Once it has put its roots down, it's here to stay. If you don't want it to colonize your entire neighborhood, be ruthless.

But this plain-Jane plant has a secret personality. It can make you see red. Literally. Dried and chopped, that tangle of woody roots yields a clear, bright, gorgeous red, which has been treasured for centuries. A fragment of madder-dyed cloth found in India is some 5,000 years old; a belt found in Tutankhamun's tomb was put there in 1350 BCE and the whole of the ancient world was mad for madder. In the Far East, it was a major cash crop and, by the mid-1600s, it was being planted across Europe. In 1865, worldwide production had risen to about 70,000 tons a year. But in 1869, German chemists synthesized alizarin, the pigment that turns madder red, and the new chemical dye became available at half the price of madder. The madder market crashed, and madder plantations around the world were abandoned.

Madder is more difficult to use than to grow, and it may be a challenge to get that clear, bright color. But once you've seen madder red, you'll want more of it. For instructions and encouragement, read the section on the plant in *A Dyer's Garden*.

**Read more about the colorful herbs:**
*A Dyer's Garden*, by Rita Buchanan

*Beware of wearing red in the garden*
*For bees dislike that color.*

—TRADITIONAL LORE FROM THE CHANNEL ISLANDS

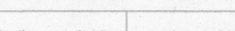

# JULY 18

On this day in 1861, the Battle of Bull Run was fought.

*Now, if we only had some china-berry trees here, we shouldn't need any other grease. They are making splendid soap at Vicksburg with china-balls. They just put the berries into the lye and it eats them right up and makes a fine soap.*

—LETTER, CITED IN *CIVIL WAR PLANTS & HERBS*

## Making Do and Doing Without

In 1861, when the Civil War began, people in the North and the South began a time of making-do and doing without. For Southerners, however, the times were exceedingly difficult, and the women—many of whom had been accustomed to fine foods, clothing, and plenty of household help—discovered resources in themselves and in the land that they had not suspected.

- Coffee (that all-important herbal stimulant) rose to fifty dollars a pound. Roasted and ground rye, wheat, corn, sweet potatoes, beans, groundnuts, chestnuts, chicory, okra, sorghum, and dandelion—all were used as substitutes. One woman reported that sliced potatoes were dried, toasted, and ground, and made into a "really delicious" beverage.
- The leaves of currant, raspberry, and blackberry bushes, and of willow, holly, sage, and garden herbs were dried and substituted for tea.

- Sorghum molasses, honey, and even a syrup of watermelon juice were substituted for sugar.
- Parthenia Hague also reported that dogwood berries were substituted for quinine, while the bark of the wild cherry, poplar, and wahoo tree were used to treat dysentery. A syrup made of mullein, globe flower (*Trollius Europaeus*), and wild-cherry bark was a cough remedy. Sassafras treated bronchitis and pneumonia, and boneset (*Eupatorium perfoliatum*) was administered to malaria patients.
- Ladies grew poppies to make laudanum and made a painkiller from jimsonweed.
- The North had problems, too. "I will not move my army without onions," General Grant wired the War Office in 1864, perhaps in a double entendre: Onions were another prized laxative. The War Office sent him three boxcar loads.

From the *Confederate Receipt Book*, 1863:

Table Beer: To eight quarts of boiling water put a pound of treacle, a quarter of an ounce of ginger, and two bay leaves, let this boil for a quarter of an hour, then cool, and work it with yeast as other beer.

Acorn coffee: Take sound ripe acorns, wash them while in the shell, dry them, and parch until they open, take the shell off, roast with a little bacon fat, and you will have a splendid cup of coffee.

**Read more:**
*Civil War Plants & Herbs*, by Patricia B. Mitchell

# JULY 19

*I believe that if ever I had to practice cannibalism, I might manage if there were enough tarragon around.*

—JAMES BEARD

## Tasteful Tarragon

I'm not sure I'd go as far as the esteemed Mr. Beard, but of all the artemisias, tarragon (*Artemisia dracunculus* var. *sativa*) is without a doubt the tastiest. In fact, its distinctive taste—a complex amalgam of anise, licorice, mint, grass, and pepper, with a resinous tang—is the reason that tarragon is still around, since it is one of a very few culinary herbs that never made a medicinal name for themselves. Tarragon is congenial with vegetables, salads, fish and chicken, and especially happy in vinegar. In your northern garden, you'll want to start with plants, for the true tarragon rarely flowers and hence does not set seeds. At the nursery, give them the pinch test, and only buy plants that have the distinctive tarragon taste. Avoid Russian tarragon (*Artemisia dracunculoides*); it doesn't have much taste. Tarragon sulks in Southern gardens, so if you live where the summers are very warm, try Mexican Mint Marigold (*Tagetes lucida*), which has a bonus of pretty yellow flowers.

If you're experimenting with tarragon, try this easy recipe.

### GRILLED TARRAGON CHICKEN

    1 tablespoon chopped fresh or ½ tablespoon dried
        tarragon
    2 teaspoons Dijon mustard
    2–3 minced garlic cloves
    1 tablespoon honey
    2 tablespoons lemon juice
    salt and pepper
    2 tablespoon olive oil
    4 boneless, skinless chicken breasts

In a small bowl, place all ingredients except chicken. Whisk together. Pound chicken to about ¾-inch thickness. Arrange in a shallow pan and pour marinade over it, coating both sides. Refrigerate for 2–3 hours. Grill chicken until cooked through, turning to brown all sides. Serve immediately. Serves 4.

*Tomatoes and oregano make it Italian; wine and tarragon make it French. Sour cream makes it Russian; lemon and cinnamon make it Greek. Soy sauce makes it Chinese; garlic makes it good.*

—ALICE MAY BROCK

# JULY 20

*Where there are herbs even the smallest of gardens has a human past and is a human thing.*

—HENRY BESTON

## A Wheelbarrow Herb Garden

My favorite small herb garden is planted in a wheelbarrow, instantly gratifying to create and easy to maintain. I made mine from an old wheelbarrow that had outlived its usefulness and has several rusted-out spots in the bottom, perfect for drainage! I covered the bottom with old window-screening, to prevent the soil from washing out, and half-filled the barrow with a light, fast-draining potting medium.

I chose herbs that have the same requirements for water and sun (with herbs, that's fairly easy) and set the purchased plants or transplants into the half-filled wheelbarrow, putting the taller plants at the back, the shorter ones in front, and tilting the smaller plants in front so that they drape over the rim. I layered in a slow-release fertilizer and finished filling in the soil, then watered it well and stood back to admire. One important asset of this garden: you can wheel it into the sun, into the shade, or simply park it outside the kitchen door.

**PLANTS IN MY WHEELBARROW HERB GARDEN**

- Onions. I've chosen Egyptian Walking Onions, which are perennially green in my Texas garden.
- Sage doesn't have much of a chance to grow tall, because I keep snipping off the top-most leaves!
- Dill. "Fernleaf" is slow to bolt (set seed) and fairly short, topping out at 18 inches. It has a long taproot, so I plant it in the deepest part of the barrow.
- Lemon thyme is planted at the front, where it can spill over the edge.
- Lemon balm, a favorite tea herb, basks in the middle.
- Chives. I grow them for their edible blossoms and spicy green leaves.
- Pansies, Johnny-jump-ups, and violas provide cool weather color, and are pretty in a spring salad.
- Nasturtiums. "Dwarf Jewel" is my favorite, a summery accent in my mostly green garden. I pickle the seeds.

Basil? It grows in pots on my deck. Parsley? In the border, along with the lavenders, fennel, marjoram, lemon verbena, chervil, coriander, and garlic. The bay tree and lemongrass live in a barrel, and the mint is magically multiplying under the cypress trees along Pecan Creek. But that wheelbarrow garden is overflowing with just about everything I need to make supper special.

*I never had any other Desire so strong, and so like to Covetousness, as that one which I have had always, that I might be Master at last of a small House and large Garden, with very moderate Conveniences joined to them, and there dedicate the Remainder of my Life to the Culture of them, and study of Nature.*

—ABRAHAM COWLEY, 1618–1667

*I never set eyes on a clover-field now,*
*Er fool round a stable, er climb in the mow,*
*But my childhood comes back jest as clear and*
*as plane*
*As the smell of the clover I'm sniffin' again . . .*

*And so I love clover—it seems like a part*
*Of the sacredest sorrows and joys of my hart;*
*And wharever it blossoms; oh, thare let me bow*
*And thank the good God as I'm thankin' Him*
*now. . . .*

—JAMES WHITCOMB RILEY, "THE CLOVER," 1901

## "And So I Love Clover . . ."

The Indiana poet, James Whitcomb Riley, was one of my favorites when I was a child. I checked his books out of the Carnegie library in Danville, Illinois, and can remember reading "The Clover" aloud to myself, swinging with its Midwestern cadences and its familiar colloquial dialect. To this day, I think of Riley's poem when I see clover—which is often, because we can hardly walk across the lawn or through a meadow without seeing one of the many *Trifolia*, all of which are much beloved by bees. Clover honey is one of the most popular honeys. And red clover (*Trifolia pratense*) is one of our most useful herbs.

Red clover has been used as a pot herb for eons; the young leaves and new flowers have appeared in both salads and soups; and the sprouted seeds add a crisp texture and robust flavor to salads. It has been used medicinally for centuries in many cultures. Recently, researchers from the National Cancer Institute have found that red clover contains four antitumor compounds, and it is being recommended as a complementary cancer treatment by some herbalists.

To make a medicinal tea, put a handful of clean red clover blossoms and leaves into a teapot, add two cups boiling water, cover and steep for 10 minutes. For additional flavor, add lemon balm or mint and sweeten with some of that delicious clover honey.

### RED CLOVER REMEDY FOR CHAPPED LIPS

Combine 1 tablespoon dried red clover flowers, 2 teaspoons honey, and ¼ cup water. Bring to a boil and simmer 2 minutes. Remove from heat and strain. Add ½ teaspoon cornstarch. Cool, stirring occasionally. Use to moisten lips.

**Read more about clover and other wild herbs:**
*Herbal Remedies from the Wild: Finding and Using Medicinal Herbs*, by Corinne Martin

*If the down flyeth off coltsfoot, dandelion and thistles when there is no winde, it is a signe of rain.*

—SIXTEENTH-CENTURY ENGLISH WEATHER LORE

*The marigold, whose courtier's face*
*Echoes the sun, and doth unlace*
*Her at his rise, at his full stop*
*Packs and shuts up her gaudy shop.*

—JOHN CLEVELAND, 1613–1658

## The Calendula

The marigold of John Cleveland's poem is the orange flowered *Calendula officinalis*, sometimes said to be named for the Virgin Mary. Here's what Maud Grieve (an avid collector of herb tidbits) had to say about this in her *Modern Herbal* (1929):

> The Common Marigold . . . is said to be in bloom on the calends of every month, hence its Latin name. It was not named after the Virgin, its name being a corruption of the Anglo-Saxon *merso-meargealla*, the Marsh Marigold. Old English authors called it Golds or Ruddes. It was, however, later associated with the Virgin Mary, and in the seventeenth century with Queen Mary.

Calendula (also called pot marigold*) was used as a stimulant and wound treatment. An infusion of dried petals was said to raise the spirits and to "bring out" measles and chickenpox. In the kitchen, the leaves and petals were added to salads and soups for flavor, and baked goods, puddings, butter, and cheeses were col-ored with the dried petals. Hence, Marigold Custard, in *Gardening with Herbs for Flavor and Fragrance*, by Helen Morgenthau Fox.

### MARIGOLD CUSTARD

- 1 pint milk
- 1 cup of marigold petals*
- ¼ teaspoon salt
- 3 tablespoons of sugar
- small piece of vanilla bean
- 3 egg yolks
- ⅛ teaspoon nutmeg
- ⅛ teaspoon allspice
- ½ teaspoon rose water

Pound the marigold petals in a mortar, or crush them with a spoon, and scald with the milk and vanilla bean. Remove the vanilla bean, and add slightly beaten yolks of eggs, salt, and sugar mixed with the spice. Cook until the mixture coats the spoon. Add rose water and cool. This makes a good sauce for a blanc mange [white pudding]. It may be poured into a dish without cooking, and then baked like a custard. Serve with beaten cream, and garnish with marigold blossoms.

*Don't confuse calendula or pot marigold with the French marigold (*Tagetes sp.*). Although *Tagetes* is used for the same culinary purposes, it has a very different taste; it does not have a history of medicinal use in the West.

Today, the Sun enters the sign of Leo.

*The fifth sign of the zodiac, the masculine sign Leo (the Lion) is ruled by the Sun. A cardinal sign, Leo is associated with creativity, authority, achievement, and executive ability. It is a fire sign, suggesting that Leo people are energetic, commanding, self-assertive. They may also be occasionally blind to the effect their energies have on others.*

—RUBY WILCOX, "ASTROLOGICAL SIGNS"

## Leo Herbs

Traditionally, Sun-ruled Leo is associated with the cardiac system, but also with the spine, the thymus gland, and the eyes. Herbs related to Leo are said to strengthen and tone the heart, regulate blood pressure, and raise the spirits. Some plants and herbs have been traditionally associated with Leo because of their color (orange or bright yellow) their shape (radiating, like the sunflower), or their association with victory (bay laurel). Some of the Leo herbs:

• Rosemary (*Rosmarinus officinalis*). Rosemary is one of the most beloved herbs, and is sacred to the Sun. During the Middle Ages, a twig of blossoming rosemary given to a sweetheart preserved love. Now, we know that the powerful antioxidants in the herb make it a preservative. Drunk as a tea, it is also a pleasant picker-upper. Enliven your solar spirit with a cup of hot rosemary tea each morning.

• Calendula (*Calendula officinalis*). This is not the French marigold, but the old-fashioned pot marigold found in cottage gardens. Antiseptic and antifungal, it is used in salves to heals wounds and in tinctures to treat athlete's foot and ringworm, and cold sores. Internally, it has been used to treat digestive problems. (See July 22)

• Hawthorne (*Crataegus oxyacanthoides*). Perhaps the best and certainly the safest tonic remedy for the heart and circulatory system. The tea has been used to ease stress and insomnia.

• Other Leo herbs. Motherwort (*Leonurus cardiaca*) is another heart-toning herb whose Latin name suggests its connection to Leo. Saint-John's-wort has a symbolic connection to the heart, perhaps because of its bloodred sap; to dream of your true love, pick it at Midsummer's Eve and hang it over your bed. Angelica is used to make a stimulating, aromatic tea. Bay laurel is a symbol of victory and triumphant achievement.

*It [Angelica archangelica] is an herb of the Sun in Leo; let it be gathered when he is there, the Moon applying to his good aspect; let it be gathered either in his hour or in the hour of Jupiter: let Sol be angular: observe the like in gathering the herbs of other planets, and you may happen to do wonders.*

—NICHOLAS CULPEPER

### Daylily Delights

The daylilies are blooming in my garden now, and on the sunny bank of Pecan Creek, where they mix and mingle with native grasses in sunny profusion. The garden is home to the colorful hybrids, but the daylilies along the creek are the old-fashioned orange ones—not so impressive as individual blooms, perhaps, but en masse, a delight.

#### THE MEDICINAL DAYLILY

This beautiful perennial has been valued for centuries in Chinese and Japanese medicine, where it is considered antibiotic and diuretic, and used to treat for urinary tract disorders, vaginal yeast infections. John Gerard (*The Herbal*, 1597) was the first to mention the name *daylily*, which refers to the fact that the blooms stay open for a single day (although you'll find as many as a dozen blooms on one stalk). Gerard recommended the plant's use (like that of true lilies, with which it was confused) to cool inflammations.

#### THE CULINARY DAYLILY

But it's in the kitchen that this plant shows its stuff. Sautéed or stir-fried, the buds taste something like asparagus; serve them with pasta, other vegetables, and poultry. Add the fresh flowers to salad, soups, or vegetables, or dip in batter and fry like a fritter. Stuffed with a delicate seafood salad, the flowers are nothing short of stunning. Dried, the flowers are used in stir-fries and soups; in Oriental markets, the dried buds are sold as "Golden Needles." The fresh tubers are crisp and nutritious, with a nutty taste, and can be added raw to salads or boiled or stir-fried and served as a side dish. (Always check for possible allergies before you eat a new vegetable, and never consume anything that may have been sprayed.)

#### GINGERY DAYLILY BUDS WITH RICE

    2 cups daylily buds
    1 tablespoon oil
    2 shallots, finely minced
    1 teaspoon freshly grated ginger
    1 tablespoon fresh chopped Italian parsley
    1 tablespoon rice wine vinegar
    1 tablespoon tamari or soy sauce
    1 tablespoon water
    2 cups cooked rice (a mix of wild and brown rice is nice)
    ⅓ cup slivered almonds

Steam buds until tender (10–15 minutes). In heavy skillet, heat the oil. Add shallots and sauté for about a minute. Add ginger and parsley and cook, stirring, 1–2 minutes more. Add vinegar, tamari, and water. Stir to mix. Toss in daylily buds. Serve over hot rice, topped with slivered almonds. Serves 4.

**Read more about daylilies and other edible flowers:**
*The Daylily: A Guide for Gardeners*, by John P. Peat
*Flowers in the Kitchen*, by Susan Belsinger

# JULY 25

Today is the feast day of St. Christopher, the patron saint of (among many other vocations) fullers.

## Fullers and Teasels

You don't meet many fullers these days, but when cloth was made by hand, fulling (fleecing, or raising the nap of a fabric) was an important part of the cloth-making process. It was the messiest part of the process, actually, for in past centuries, it involved washing the cloth in human urine (a rich source of ammonia) and dusting it with fuller's earth. The cloth was then rewashed and suspended to dry on double-ended hooks in a frame called a tenter—the origin of the phrase "on tenterhooks."

That's where the teasel came in. The name is from the Anglo-Saxon *taesan*, to tease. The stiff, spiny flower heads were fixed to a cylinder that revolved against the cloth, raising the nap. The teasel was grown for the purpose, and there was a substantial demand. As late as the 1920s, one woolen manufacturer was using 20,000 teasel heads a year. In 1530, the Worshipful Company of Clothmakers was granted a new coat of arms, which featured a prominent gold teasel. It still does.

The root of the teasel was used medicinally, according to Nicholas Culpeper, as a cleansing herb and eye-wash; an ointment made from the roots, he adds, is good for warts, cankers, and fistulas. The plant was used as a protection against witches, who apparently didn't much like its sharp spines.

A teasel might be an interesting plant for the garden, if you could have just one. However, a single teasel plant can produce some 2,000 seeds. If even ten percent of these germinate (half generally do), you're in trouble.

> *Cut thistles in June, they'll come again soon;*
> *Cut in July, they may die*
> *Cut in August, die they must.*
>
> —ENGLISH AGRICULTURAL LORE

215

*The recorded history of the genus Capsicum begins with Columbus, who undertook his voyage of discovery in search of (among other things) black pepper. Columbus did not find what he was looking for, but in many people's opinion, he bit into something much better. He became the first European to blister his tongue on a hot pepper.*

—CHILE DEATH: A CHINA BAYLES MYSTERY

## Chile Death: About China's Books

*Chile Death* began with something I saw on television back in 1997, about the legal liabilities that restaurant owners face when their patrons are allergic to something in the food. The specific case under discussion involved a fatal peanut allergy—a perfect modus operandi for murder, it seemed to me, especially since the book I wanted to write involved a chili cook-off, and the victim was one of the judges. What if he was allergic to peanuts? What if the murderer knew this? And just how hard could it be to slip a peanut into one of the chili samples the judge had to taste?

The previous book in the series, *Love Lies Bleeding*, is a dark story that ends with McQuaid being very seriously wounded. In fact, when *Chile Death* begins, he is depressed at the prospect of long-term therapy—so I wanted a cheerful book. A funny book, actually. And there is something undeniably funny about chiles. I

seem to have been a little defensive about this, for in the Author's Note, I feel compelled to quote George Bernard Shaw: "Life does not cease to be funny when people die any more than it ceases to be serious when people laugh."

Bill's habanero peppers are fruiting just now, in pots on our deck. He dries and powders these very, very, VERY hot peppers and concocts a salsa that is hot enough to melt teeth. The recipe goes something like this, although it varies from batch to batch, depending on how he's feeling at the moment.

### BILL'S INCENDIARY SALSA

2 tomatoes, chopped
1 carrot, grated
½ onion, chopped
4 canned chipotle peppers, minced
3 cloves garlic, minced
¼ cup chopped cilantro
some vinegar
as much powdered habanero as you dare

Throw everything into a bowl and stir violently. Serve with chips. Stand by with a fire extinguisher and a box of tissues.

**Read more about chiles and chili:**

*Chile Death: A China Bayles Mystery*, by Susan Wittig Albert

*Great Bowls of Fire! Hot and Spicy Soups, Stews and Chiles*, by Dave DeWitt

Today is Take a Plant for a Walk Day.

*You don't have a garden just for yourself. You have it to share.*

—AUGUSTA CARTER

## The Merryweathers' Passalong Plant Sale

Every few months, the Merryweathers get together and trade plants. The plant swap is quite an occasion, as you might imagine, for most members' gardens are full of passalong herbs. For example, old Mrs. Barnscape got her Egyptian walking onions from Alice Gomme, who traded them to Letty Funk for a root cutting of angelica, which Letty got from her cousin in Indiana. Unfortunately, the angelica didn't survive the Central Texas summer, which made Alice very sad, because she'd always wanted an angel in her garden. She had to console herself with some comfrey that Al Hottes gave her, with a warning. "Keep it in a pot on the porch," he said. "Once those roots go down, you'll never get them up again."

The passalong plant swap has proved a roaring success for the Merryweathers, but they have had to make a few rules, since there are inevitably a few people who take advantage. Here is the latest version:

1. Put your plant in a pot. Do not bring it in a paper bag, a cardboard box, a napkin, or an old shoe.

2. Do not bring a buggy plant. (Leave your aphids at home!) Do not bring a plant with dormant bindweed seeds in the soil, ready to germinate with joy when they are settled in their new home.

3. Do not bring a plant that is at death's doorway.

4. Your plant must have roots. (Do not stick an unrooted cutting in a pot and call it a plant.)

5. It is not okay to bring 10 garlic bulbs and take home 10 pots of herbs.

6. There's no limit on the number of plants you can bring. Just be sure to label each one, correctly, please. Nobody wants to take home a hardy perennial, only to have it give up the ghost at the first kiss of frost. Put your name on it, too. Your REAL name.

7. Bring fresh seeds in a sealed, labeled envelope. The fair exchange is 25 seeds for a plant, **NOT 5!** (You know who you are.)

8. Do not bring seeds that nobody took last year. Do not bring seeds that people can rake up off their lawns: mesquite seeds, acorns, or grass seed.

9. If you bring a garden bully, for heaven's sake label it BULLY. Some people are silly enough to give bullies a home, but they at least ought to be warned. (A bully: Any plant that hops out of the bed the minute your back is turned.)

10. No trading in the parking lot. No insider trades. And no wire tumbleweeds.

**To learn more about taking plants for a walk, read:**
*Passalong Plants,* by Steve Bender and Felder Rushing

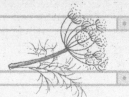

# JULY 28

Beatrix Potter was born on this day in 1866. She wrote *The Tale of Peter Rabbit* and other immortal books for children. July's theme garden is a Peter Rabbit Garden.

*My news is all gardening at present, and supplies. I went to see an old lady at Windermere and impudently took a large basket and trowel with me. She had the most untidy garden I ever saw. I got nice things in handfuls without any shame, amongst others a bundle of lavender slips . . . and another bunch of violet suckers.*

—BEATRIX POTTER, LETTER TO MILLIE WARNE, OCTOBER 12, 1907

## A Peter Rabbit Garden

A Peter Rabbit Garden would be a lovely project for you and your children (or grandchildren) to share. It could be a container on the deck or a corner of your garden, or a larger area with a piece of garden art in the middle: Peter himself, perhaps, or a wheelbarrow with his coat on it. You might want to put a little wooden fence around it (like the fence around Mr. MacGregor's garden), or perhaps a low stone wall, such as the one that Tom, Moppet, and Mittens sat on in *The Tale of Tom Kitten*. And certainly you'll want to read Miss Potter's "little books" (as she liked to call them) and pick out the flowers you see growing in the pictures she painted with such care—some of them in her very own garden at Hill Top Farm.

## PETER'S PLANTS

These plants are all mentioned in the Little Books. These would all be appropriate for Peter's garden.

| | |
|---|---|
| Lemon balm | Strawberry |
| Mint | Lettuce |
| Chamomile | Beets (try "MacGregor's Favorite") |
| Tansy | Radish |
| Lavender | Rhubarb |
| Sage | Onions |
| Thyme | Roses |
| Rosemary | Pinks |
| Parsley | Pansies |

## MISS POTTER'S GARDEN

Miss Potter's garden at Hill Top Farm included a great many herbs and flowers, many of them passalong plants. "I have been planting hard all day—thanks to a very well meant but slightly ill-timed present of saxifrage from Mrs. Taylor at the corner cottage." In the hedgerows, she found violets, daffodils, primroses, wild strawberries, and wood anemones, and wall-rue fern from an old bridge. She completely redesigned the garden, making it what it into a beautiful cottage garden brimming with color and fragrance.

**Read more about Miss Potter:**
*At Home with Beatrix Potter*, by Susan Denyer
*The Tale of Hill Top Farm: A Cottage Tale Mystery Featuring Beatrix Potter*, by Susan Wittig Albert

Today is the feast day of St. Martha, the patron saint of homemakers, housewives, and cooks.

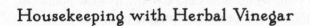

## Housekeeping with Herbal Vinegar

Every now and then, Fannie Couch (talk-show host at Radio KPST-FM in Pecan Springs) talks housekeeping. Today, in honor of St. Martha (no, not that Martha) she invited people to phone in their tips for using herbal vinegars. Fannie's top five choices each won a bottle of Fannie's homemade lavender vinegar:

- Emily Thackway says she polishes her mother's walnut table with a soft cloth moistened with a mixture of 3 tablespoons linseed oil, 3 tablespoons malt vinegar, and ½ teaspoon lavender oil. "Mama would be proud," Emily says.
- Fannie's cousin Minnie Watson gets the mildew off her shower curtains with full-strength vinegar, mixed with a few drops of lemon essential oil.
- Minnie's daughter-in-law Agnes makes her own floor cleaner. She pours ⅛ cup of liquid soap into a bucket, adds ½ cup white vinegar and ½ cup herbal tea (she likes peppermint, for the clean smell). She fills the bucket half full of water and mops her floor. "Clean as a whistle," says Agnes. "Gets the germs, too."
- Hank Litton's wool jacket reeked of Bubba Harris' cigar smoke after Saturday night's poker game. Lila filled the bathtub with hot water, added two cups of vinegar and a cup of strong rosemary tea, and hung the jacket to steam. She reports that it passed the sniff test.
- Mae Ruth Robbins had ants in the kitchen. "But I fixed 'em good," she crows. "I made me up a cup of real strong tansy tea, mixed it with a cup of vinegar, and sprayed 'em. Figure if they're brave enough to come back, I'll hit 'em again." Go for it, Mae Ruth!

**VINEGAR OF THE FOUR THIEVES\***
*Take lavender, rosemary, sage, wormwood, rue, and mint, of each a large handful; put them in a pot of earthen ware, pour on them four quarts of very strong vinegar, cover the pot closely, and put a board on the top; keep it in the hottest sun two weeks, then strain and bottle it, putting in each bottle a clove of garlic. When it has settled in the bottle and become clear, pour it off gently; do this until you get it all free from sediment. The proper time to make it is when the herbs are in full vigour. This vinegar is very refreshing in crowded rooms, in the apartments of the sick; and is peculiarly grateful when sprinkled about the house in damp weather.*

—MARY RANDOLPH, *THE VIRGINIA HOUSEWIFE OR, METHODICAL COOK,* 1860

\*This famous vinegar (the recipe exists in many versions) takes its name from its legendary use as a plague-preventative. Thieves were said to wear vinegar-soaked rags over their mouths as they robbed corpses.

# JULY 30

In some years (not all) today is Deviled Egg Day.

## Some Divine Deviltry

No doubt about it, deviled eggs are perfect for picnics, barbecues, and the Sunday church social. The tradition of stuffing eggs goes back to Roman times, while the word *deviled* came into use around 1800 to denote food prepared with piquant seasonings, such as cayenne and mustard. China says that Brian, McQuaid's son, wolfs down three or four of her Classic Devils without taking a breath.

### CHINA'S CLASSIC DEVILS

6 hard-boiled eggs

2 tablespoons mayonnaise

1 teaspoon Dijon mustard

1 teaspoon cider vinegar

2–3 leaves of fresh Italian parsley, finely chopped

white bulb of 1 green onion, minced

green leaves of onion, thinly sliced, opened out to make rings

freshly ground black pepper

salt to taste, or Savory Blend (August 29)

paprika for garnish

Halve eggs; scoop yolks into a small bowl. Mash well; add mayonnaise, Dijon, and vinegar. Stir in minced onion and chopped parsley. Add salt and pepper to taste. Fill egg white halves, using a table knife or small teaspoon. Sprinkle with paprika and sliced green onion rings. May be doubled or tripled to serve a gang.

To jazz up those Classic Devils, try these herbal additions, or experiment with your own:

- **Red-Hot Devils**: ½ teaspoon grated horseradish; 1 teaspoon minced cilantro; pinch cayenne; pinch chili powder; 1 small jalapeño pepper, finely chopped. Reserve half the jalapeño for garnish.
- **South of the Border Devils**: 2 tablespoons sour cream; ½ teaspoon cumin; 1 clove garlic, minced; 2–3 tablespoons shredded cheddar cheese. Garnish with pimentos.
- **Pesto Devils**: 2 tablespoons minced fresh basil, 1 tablespoon minced fresh thyme; 1 tablespoon minced fresh parsley; 1 clove garlic, minced. Garnish with a caper in a green onion ring.
- **Dilly Devils**: 2 tablespoons pickle relish; substitute dill pickle juice for vinegar in Classic Devils recipe. Garnish with a bit of relish and a green onion ring.
- **Bleu Devils**: 2 tablespoons bleu cheese; 1 tablespoon minced fresh parsley. Garnish with a green onion ring.

**A bouquet of garden proverbs:**

Fine words butter no parsnips.

A book is a garden carried in the pocket.

Tickle it with a hoe, and it will laugh into a harvest.

God does not subtract from the allotted span the hours spent hoeing.

In some years, today is National Cheesecake Day.

## Cheesecake: Not Just for Dessert

Savory cheesecakes are delightfully versatile. Here's one you can serve as a brunch entrée, an appetizer, or a late-night snack.

**MARGE CLARK'S BASIL PESTO CHEESECAKE**

*Crust*
- 1 tablespoon butter, softened
- ¼ cup Italian seasoned bread crumbs

*Filling*
- 2 8-ounce packages cream cheese, softened
- 1 cup ricotta cheese
- ½ cup grated Parmesan cheese
- 3 large eggs
- ½ cup pesto (recipe follows)
- Chopped fresh basil and sun-dried tomatoes for garnish
- Rounds of French or Italian bread, toasted

*Make the crust*: Rub the butter over the bottom and halfway up sides of a 9-inch springform pan. Sprinkle the bread crumbs evenly over the bottom. Set pan aside.

*Make the filling*: Preheat oven to 350°. Combine cheeses in a food processor and process until very smooth. Add eggs and mix thoroughly. Pour half of cheese mixture into a small bowl. To the half remaining in the food processor, add pesto and mix well. Pour pesto-cheese mixture into prepared pan. Carefully pour plain mixture over pesto mixture and smooth to cover the entire surface. Bake 35–40 minutes, or until set in the center. Cool. Cover and refrigerate overnight. To serve, loosen from sides of pan with a knife. Remove pan sides. Chop some fresh basil and sprinkle over the top, with sun-dried tomatoes. Invite guests to slice cheesecake and spread it on rounds of toasted bread. Adapted with permission from *The Best of Thymes: An Herbal Cookbook*

**MARGE CLARK'S BEST BASIL PESTO**
- 4 cups fresh green basil leaves, coarsely chopped
- 1 cup pine nuts
- ½ cup extra virgin olive oil
- 1 cup grated Parmesan cheese
- ¼ cup butter, softened
- 2 cloves garlic, crushed
- salt

In food processor or blender, purée basil with pine nuts, oil, cheese, butter, garlic, and salt to taste. Place in a glass jar. Pour a thin layer of olive oil over top. Screw on lid and refrigerate. When ready to use, stir the olive oil into the pesto.

**More reading from Marge Clark (1934–1999):**
*It's About Thyme*, 1988
*Christmas at Oak Hill Farm*, 1994
*The Best of Thymes*, 1997

# AUGUST 1

Today is the Celtic festival of Lughnasadh (pronounced *loo-na-sa*), anglicized as "Lammas." It is the third of four seasonal cross-quarter days. Others: Imbolc (February 1), Beltane (May 1), and Samhain (November 1).

*The ancient mid-summer celebration of Lammas (Old English for "loaf mass") consecrated the first loaves of bread baked from the new harvest. In honor of Lammas, I planned to teach a class on herbal breads.*

—ROSEMARY REMEMBERED: A CHINA BAYLES MYSTERY

## The Lammas Loaf

A braided or twisted bread is traditional for Lammas celebrations. China makes hers with herbs fresh from the garden. If you're using dried herbs, use half of the amount suggested for fresh herbs.

**CHINA'S BRAIDED HERB LOAF**
- 1 envelope active dry yeast
- 1 teaspoon sugar
- ¼ cup warm water
- 2 tablespoons melted butter, divided
- 2 ½ to 3 cups bread flour
- 1 teaspoon salt
- 2 tablespoons minced fresh chives
- 2 tablespoons minced fresh thyme
- 2 tablespoons minced fresh rosemary
- 2 tablespoons minced fresh oregano
- 2 teaspoons poppy seeds

In a large bowl, sprinkle yeast and sugar over ¼ cup warm water. Stir to dissolve. Add 1 cup water and 1 tablespoon melted butter. Mix 2½ cups flour with salt and chives. Stir into the yeast mixture, adding a half-cup at a time, to form a slightly sticky dough. Add the additional ½ cup flour only if necessary. Turn dough out onto a floured surface and knead until smooth and elastic (5–6 minutes). Spray a large bowl with cooking oil. Place the dough in the bowl and turn to coat. Cover with clean, damp cloth and let rise in a warm place until doubled, about 90 minutes. Punch dough down. Divide into thirds. Into each third, knead a single herb: thyme in one, rosemary in the second, thyme in the third. Roll dough into three 20-inch ropes. Arrange ropes on a greased cookie sheet, side by side. Starting at the middle, braid toward each end, pressing together at the ends. Cover and let rise 45–50 minutes, until doubled. Brush with remaining butter and sprinkle poppy seeds over braid. Bake 25–30 minutes, until golden. Cool on a rack 30 minutes. Serve hot, giving thanks for the great joy of eating nutritious fresh bread! (Hint: You might want to bake two of these beautiful herb bread braids; National Friendship Day is coming soon.)

**Read more about Lammas and other holidays:**
*Celebrate the Earth: A Year of Holidays in the Pagan Tradition*, by Laurie Cabot

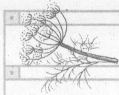

# AUGUST 2

National Friendship Day is celebrated on the first Sunday in August.

*Friendship: Ivy. Denotes something true and lasting, and not to be changed by the beating of the winter winds.*

—ROBERT TYAS, *THE LANGUAGE OF FLOWERS, OR FLORAL EMBLEMS OF THOUGHTS, FEELINGS, AND SENTIMENTS,* 1869

## Friendship, Herbs, and Flowers

We can guess just how much friendship meant to the Victorians by glancing through the various herbs and flowers that were used to describe and define it.

- Friendship—acacia, acacia rose, balsam, cedar, ivy, marigold, yellow rose,
- Early and sincere friendship—periwinkle, honeysuckle
- True friendship—oak-leaf scented geranium
- Unchanging friendship—arborvitae
- Warm friendship—pine
- "I'm thinking of an absent friend."—zinnia
- "A great deal is to be gained by good company."—rose in a tuft of grass
- "I rejoice in your friendship."—yellow rose
- "I will always be a true friend."—azalea
- "I will be your friend in adversity."—snowdrop
- "My time with you is a pleasure."—lemon thyme
- "Friendship warms old hearts."—chervil
- "You are the light of my life."—feverfew

**FRIENDSHIP GIFTS**
On this Friendship Day, your friends will appreciate knowing how much they have meant to you. Send them a card or a note with a small friendship gift:

- a packet of herb seeds or dried herbs from your garden (see August 3)
- a tussie-mussie (June 6)
- a jar of herb jelly (August 8)
- a passalong plant (July 27)
- a bottle of floral vinegar (March 13)
- a copy of *An Unthymely Death & Other Garden Mysteries* (China's short story collection, full of herb lore, crafts, and recipes)

**Read more about the language of flowers:**
*The Meaning of Flowers,* by Claire Powell

*The Common Rosemary is so well knowne through all our Land, being in every womans garden, that it were sufficient but to name it as an ornament among other sweete herbes and flowers in our Garden . . . Inwardly for the head and heart; outwardly for the sinewes and joynts: for civill uses, as all doe knowe, at weddings, funerals, etc. to bestow among friends.*

—JOHN PARKINSON, *A GARDEN OF PLEASANT FLOWERS,* 1629

*Gathering and drying home-grown herbs is one of the great pleasures of herb gardening. It is rewarding to use your own fresh seasonings, and if you dry them, you will doubly appreciate each savory leaf.*

—ADELMA GRENIER SIMMONS, *HERB GARDENING IN FIVE SEASONS*

## Your Herbal Harvest: Part I

You've probably already begun harvesting and using the herbs in your garden. If you haven't, plan now what you're going to do—above all, don't wait until the day before your first freeze to gather and preserve your herbs!

You can begin harvesting your herbs for daily use when the plant has enough foliage to ensure continued growth. Successive harvests throughout the season encourage bushy plants with stronger leaf growth, so plan to cut back your plants and preserve your harvest frequently.

Harvest in the morning, after the dew dries but before the temperature climbs, to ensure that you've caught the plant when its essential oils are strongest. Here are some things to remember:

• Herbs are at their best when they're fresh-picked. For daily use, pick just what you need. Wrap herbs in a damp paper towel and put them in a tightly closed plastic bag in the refrigerator.

• Long-stemmed herbs (thyme, rosemary, oregano, savory, dill, fennel) can be kept on the kitchen counter for a few days. Strip lower leaves for immediate use and put the stems in a narrow-necked vase filled with water, out of the sun.

• Herbs produce their most intense oil concentration and flavor after the flower buds appear but before they open. Harvest at this time for most uses. Blooming plants such as basil and oregano may still be suitable for vinegars, however.

• Harvest annual herbs until frost, making as many successive harvests as possible without damaging the plant. Don't cut too near the ground, for lower foliage is necessary for strong, continuing growth. At the end of the season, harvest the entire plant.

• Harvest perennial herbs until about one month before the frost date. Late pruning encourages tender growth that may be killed by the frost, and plants need the regrowth to see them through the winter.

• Harvest tarragon or lavender flowers in early summer, then cut the plants to half their height to encourage fall flowering.

• Harvest herb seeds (mustard, fennel) as the seed pods darken and dry, but before they burst. Secure a paper bag over the seed head to complete ripening, then cut the stem and hang the bag for further drying.

• Harvest herb roots (bloodroot, chicory, ginseng, goldenseal, horseradish) after the foliage fades.

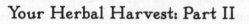

## Your Herbal Harvest: Part II

For centuries, drying was the only means of preserving the herbal harvest. It still remains a reliable way of keeping herbs on hand through the winter months. Now, however, we have other means available. Here are options:

• **Freezing**. This method best preserves flavor. Rinse the herbs and chop coarsely. Place about one or two teaspoons in each ice cube tray compartment, cover with chicken or vegetable stock, olive oil, or plain water, and freeze. Transfer frozen cubes to plastic bags. Alternatively, spread herbs loosely on a cookie sheet and freeze. Transfer frozen herbs into a plastic bag and seal. Thawed herbs are suitable for cooking.

• **Air Drying**. Remove dead or damaged foliage. Rinse only if necessary and shake. Spread out to dry until surface moisture has evaporated. Make small bundles, secure the stems with twine or twist ties, and hang in a warm, dry, shaded place, allowing for good air circulation. Alternatively, spread herbs on window screens resting on sawhorses or chair backs. Stir often to ensure even drying. When leaves are crumbly-dry, separate from the stems without crushing. Store in glass or plastic bottles in a cool, dry place away from sunlight, moisture, and heat.

• **Drying with Heat.** Air drying (which retains better flavor and color) may be difficult in some high-humidity situations. Your food dehydrator does a good job of drying herbs; follow the manufacturer's directions. For oven drying, spread the herbs on cookie sheets and dry with the pilot light, or at the lowest possible temperature setting. For microwave drying, layer clean, dry leaves between dry paper towels and microwave on high power for 1 to 2 minutes. Cool. If the leaves are not brittle, microwave for 30 seconds and retest. Repeat if necessary.

**Read more about harvesting the herbs in your garden:**
*The Rodale Herb Book*, edited by William H. Hylton

> *Gather Herbs in the Full to keep dry; they keep and retain their vertue and sweet smell, provided you take the same care as you do in Hay, that you expose them not in too thin, but competent Heaps, which you may turn and move till they be reasonable dry, not brittle; and the sooner it be dispatch'd, the better. For there is very great difference in the Vertue of Plants, according as they are dried.*
>
> —JOHN EVELYN, *ELYSIUM BRITANNICUM*, 1660

# AUGUST 5

According to some, the Celtic month of the Hazel Tree begins today (August 5–September 1).

> *I went out to the hazelwood,*
> *Because a fire was in my head . . .*
> —W. B. YEATS, *THE SONG OF WANDERING AENGUS*

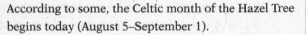

## The Sacred Hazel

The hazel tree (*Corylus avellana*) was revered as a sacred tree, the Celtic tree of knowledge, growing at the heart of the Otherworld, over the Well of Wisdom. The hazel was associated with poetry and magic, and those who ate the nuts might be rewarded with poetic, prophetic, and divinatory power. (Or perhaps it was the highly intoxicating hazel-mead, frequently mentioned in early Irish literature, that did it.)

### THE MAGICAL HAZEL

Hazel's magic was usually connected with its divinatory powers. Druid priests wielded hazel rods, and dowsers preferred forked hazel sticks to indicate where underground water might be found. As late as the nineteenth century in the south of England, young brides were given a bundle of hazel sticks to ensure fertility, and a fine show of catkins in the spring predicted a fine crop of babies: "A plenty of catkins, a plenty of prams."

Hazel was considered a protective herb. A wattle fence made of hazel kept witches out. Cattle were driven through the smoke of Midsummer Night's hazel bonfires, and hazel wands passed through the flames were used as protection against disease and witches' spells. In East Anglia, hazel wands were gathered on Palm Sunday (see March 27) and blessed for protection the rest of the year. In some places, however, the hazel was thought to bring bad luck. Gathering hazelnuts on Sunday, for instance, would attract the devil's attention. In one ballad, a "foolish young maid" went nutting on Sunday, encountered a "Gentleman all in black who laid her on her back" (no gentleman, he), with the predictable outcome: a babe with horns and a tail.

### THE USEFUL HAZEL

Only a few medicinal uses of hazel are recorded: the nuts, mixed with honey, were used to treat coughs; mixed with pepper, they cleared the head. The wood itself, however, found many uses. The tree was coppiced to produce pliable wands for basket-making, hoops and hurdles, wattles and hedge-stakes, fishing rods and walking sticks. Like willow, hazel was used to make light, one-man boats called coracles and temporary woodland shelters.

**Read more about the folklore of hazel:**
*The Oxford Dictionary of Plant-Lore,* by Roy Vickery

*The sun shines on both sides of the hedge.*

—TRADITIONAL

The Shakers arrived in New York Harbor on this day in 1774, on a ship called *Mariah*.

> *Behold the Flowers that deck the Field,*
> *The Gentle breeze perfuming,*
> *and Tender Herbs their Fragrance Yield*
> *Are Health and Life Diffusing*
> —HARVARD SHAKER COMMUNITY HERB CATALOG, 1843

## Shaker Medicinal Herbs

The Shakers were the among the first commercial purveyors of herb seeds and dried herbs in America. At first, they gathered the plants in the areas where they settled—eleven Shaker communities had been established in the northeastern states by 1800—but they quickly began to exploit the potential of the pharmaceutical market. Even as late as 1889, when the industry was waning, the community in Enfield, New Hampshire, reported shipping some 44,000 pounds of dried dock root, in one season, to a single pharmaceutical firm.

Here are five of the herbs offered in the Shakers' 1837 catalog, with their descriptions:

- Bugle (*Lycopus virginicus*). In spitting of blood and similar diseases, it is, perhaps, the best remedy known. It is a sedative, and tonic, and appears to equalize the circulation of the blood.
- Button Snake-Root (*Liatris spicata*). A powerful diuretic.
- Golden Seal (*Hydrastis canadensis*) Tonic and gently laxative. Promotes the biliary [gallbladder] secretions and removes jaundice.
- Gravel Plant (*Epigaea repens*) Diuretic. . . . Has often cured where the catheter had to be habitually used.
- Pleurisy Root (*Asclepias tuberosa*) In all inflammations of the chest this is an invaluable medicine. It is sudorific, anodyne, and expectorant.

In addition to growing and selling dried herbs, the Shakers also produced and marketed a variety of medicinal preparations, and by the 1880s, some eighty different proprietary medicines were being sold. The herbal medicine business declined steadily after the Civil War, however, as did the appeal of the Shaker religion. But because the Shakers kept careful records—community journals were required by rule, and business documents were rigorously maintained—we can still see and marvel at their wide-ranging efforts to build a better life, not only for themselves but for others.

**Read more about Shaker gardens:**
*Shaker Medicinal Herbs: A Compendium of History, Lore, and Uses*, by Amy Bess Miller

> *'Tis a gift to be simple, 'tis a gift to be free*
> *'Tis a gift to come down where we ought to be*
> *And when we find ourselves in the place just right*
> *'Twill be in the valley of love and delight.*
> —SHAKER HYMN

In some years, today is National Mustard Day.

*A tale without love is like beef without mustard, an insipid dish.*

—ANATOLE FRANCE

## Pass the Mustard

Homer Mayo, the seventysomething geezer who won the Adams County mustard competition last year (his story is told in "Mustard Madness," in *An Unthymely Death and Other Garden Mysteries*), insists that there's nothing like mustard to turn on your taste buds—and he's right. Whether you prefer the yellow ballpark-and-hot-dog mustard, a gourmet Dijon, or the fiery kick of Chinese mustard, you can't go wrong.

It's not hard to make your own from mustard seeds or powder. (Check out the recipes on pages 149–141 of *Unthymely Death*.) But if you want to experiment with herbal mustards, here's an easy way to get started.

### MAKE-IT-YOURSELF GOURMET MUSTARD

1 cup of Dijon-style mustard

¼ cup dried herbs (or about one-half cup finely chopped fresh herbs)

1 ½ tablespoons dry white wine

Combine all ingredients in a lidded jar and refrigerate for a week before using, so that the flavors mellow and mingle. Keep for up to three months. Some zesty combinations:

- Minced thyme, parsley, and marjoram, with one clove garlic
- Minced tarragon with basil and thyme
- 1–2 tablespoons prepared or freshly grated horseradish, one clove garlic, ¼ cup grated fresh ginger root, 2 tablespoons honey

### MEDICINAL MUSTARD

Like pepper, mustard stimulates appetite and digestion. It also stimulates blood circulation, and is traditionally used in chest poultices to ease lung congestion and as a rub to warm chilly hands and feet. Native Americans found the herb useful for headaches and colds (they sniffed the powdered seeds as an inhalant); and as a poultice to ease back pain.

### MAGICAL MUSTARD

Mustard had its magical qualities, too. In northern Europe, mothers sewed mustard seeds into their daughters' wedding dresses to encourage the groom's passion. In India, mustard seeds were spread on doorsteps to repel evil spirits. In Denmark, mustard was sown around barns to keep fairies and spirits away from the animals.

**Read more about mustard:**

*The Good Cook's Book of Mustard,* by Michele Anna Jordan

# AUGUST 8

## Sweet, Savory, Sparkling Herb Jellies

You might not think of jelly as a means of preserving your herb harvest, but that's certainly one way to look at it. Pretty, too, all those sparkling jars of pale lavender or rich wine-colored jelly lined up on a shelf: savory jellies to be served with cheeses or meats, sweet jellies for desserts and treat. Nothing makes a nicer gift for a friend, either.

### HOW TO MAKE HERB JELLY

Herb jelly begins with a strong herb infusion brewed with water, fruit juice, or wine. Fruit juice is nice for sweet jellies; wine for savory jellies. The tea is then added to the other ingredients: sugar for sweetening, vinegar or lemon juice for tartness, pectin to set the jelly.

1 cup chopped fresh herbs, or ⅓ cup dried (for ideas, see below)

2½ cups boiling water, juice, or wine

¼ cup lemon juice or cider vinegar

4½ cups sugar food coloring (optional)

3 ounces liquid pectin

*To make the infusion:* Pour boiling water, juice, or wine onto the herbs. Steep until cool. Strain infusion and measure 2 cups into a large nonreactive pot.

*To make the jelly:* Add sugar and vinegar or lemon juice to the herb tea and cook over high heat, stirring constantly. When sugar is dissolved, add coloring (if desired). When mixture boils, add pectin. Return to a full rolling boil and continue boiling and stirring for 1 full minute. Remove from heat, skim off foam, and pour into half-pint sterile jars and seal. Store in refrigerator. For longer storage, process for five minutes in a boiling-water bath, and seal with a thin layer of melted paraffin.

Suggested combinations:

- For sweet jellies: Apple, orange, or pineapple juice with scented geraniums, rose petals (white heels removed), rosemary, lavender, pineapple sage, lemon balm, mint
- For savory jellies: White wine with dill, tarragon, lemongrass, lemon geranium, parsley; red wine with garlic, rosemary, thyme, savory, bay

**Read more about preserving your herbal harvest:**
*Good Gifts from the Home: Jams, Jellies & Preserves,* by Linda Ferrari

Today is Izaak Walton's birthday. He is known for his book *The Compleat Angler*, and for this remark about lavender-scented sheets: "I long to be in a house where the sheets smell of lavender."

*"Whoever heard of anybody having a normal week just before her wedding?" Ruby demanded. "Why, things haven't even started to get difficult. We haven't heard Sunday's weather forecast yet."*

*More headaches. I held the lavender to my nose and sniffed.*

—LAVENDER LIES: A CHINA BAYLES MYSTERY

## Lavender Lies: About China's Books

Lavender was a natural choice when it came to selecting a signature herb for that all-important book in which China and McQuaid would finally (after many trials, tribulations, and setbacks) get married. Lavender is, after all, the favorite of most brides, and China is no exception. It's a traditional headache remedy, too—and who doesn't suffer from a headache or two when they're planning a wedding?

Before China and McQuaid can get married, they have headaches to fix and mysteries to solve. There's the who-killed-Edgar-Coleman mystery, about a local real estate shark found shot to death in his garage. With the small-town gossip mill turning at top speed, it doesn't take long for China to learn that Coleman was blackmailing several City Council members—did one of them do him in? Then there's the mystery of a missing child, and a mother's agonized search. The final mystery, of course, has to do with whether the long-anticipated wedding will actually come off, for while China, Ruby, and their friends are making wedding arrangements, McQuaid has been appointed as Pecan Springs' interim police chief, and it's his job to solve a murder. China can forget about a honeymoon—unless she can help McQuaid catch Coleman's killer.

Whether you're helping with a wedding or solving a murder, lavender will provide sweet, welcome relief from headaches and stress. Take a basket to the herb garden and pick the flower spikes just as the buds are opening. If that headache is really getting you down, sniff lavender often, or try some lavender tea. You can add the fresh or dried flowers to homemade soaps, cosmetics, potpourris, and sachets, or use them in cookies, vinegars, jellies, and teas.

**More Reading:**
*Lavender Lies: A China Bayles Mystery*, by Susan Wittig Albert

*One of the country names for meadowsweet is bridewort because this was the favourite plant for strewing at wedding festivals.*

—KAY SANECKI, *HISTORY OF THE ENGLISH HERB GARDEN*

# AUGUST 10

## The Fragrant Rose

There's no greater pleasure than to walk through the garden on a bright morning when the sweet, summery fragrance of roses fills the air. Wouldn't it be wonderful if we could preserve that scent for always? You could make a necklace of rose beads (see May 20); or you could try another of the many old-fashioned ways of capturing that glorious fragrance.

### ROSE OIL

Make your own delightful rose massage oil with this simple recipe. Pack 4 cups of fresh scented rose petals into a glass jar. Cover with 1 cup almond oil and let stand for two days. Strain the oil into another jar, pressing the oil from the petals. Discard the petals. Repack the jar with fresh petals, and pour the scented oil over it. Repeat several times, until the fragrance has reached the desired intensity.

### ROSE WATER

Put 2 cups of scented rose petals into a nonreactive saucepan. Add 4 cups of distilled water, and simmer over low heat until the liquid is reduced by about half. Cool. Strain and discard the petals. If you'd like a stronger scent, repeat, using fresh petals and enough water to make 4 cups. Keep in a spray bottle to use on your hair and skin—even nicer when it's cooled in the refrigerator.

### ROSE SUGAR

Make this fragrant sugar to sprinkle over strawberries and add to herbal tea. Bruise ½ cup clean, scented rose petals in a mortar. Stir petals into 1 cup superfine granulated sugar and store in a lidded container for 3 weeks. Sift the sugar from the petals. Use immediately or store in a clean, dry container.

**Discover more delightful things to make with roses:**

*Rose Recipes from Olden Times*, by Eleanour Sinclair Rohde

*Bags to Scent Linen. Take Rose leaves dried in the shade, Cloves beat to a gross [thick] powder and Mace scraped; mix them together and put the composition into little bags.*

—THE TOILET OF FLORA, 1779

*An addiction to gardening is not all bad when you consider all the other choices in life.*

—CORA LEA BELL

## Taste-Tempting Fruit Vinegars

The peaches are ripe and luscious, and the market is displaying beautiful raspberries, blueberries, and cherries. Use them, along with a variety of herbs and spices, to make a vinegar, and you'll have a shelf of wonderful taste-tempters all winter long.

### HOW TO MAKE A FRUIT VINEGAR, WITH HERBS

Pit the fruit if necessary, cut up or mash it lightly. Wash the fresh herbs and bruise lightly. Put fruit and herbs into a quart or half-gallon jar and cover completely with vinegar. Put on the lid and set the container in a dark, cool place for at least a week, shaking every day and making sure that the vinegar covers the fruit and herbs. Steep as long as a month, checking for flavor. For the most intense taste, strain out the fruit and herbs, pour the flavored vinegar over fresh, prepared fruit and herbs, and steep again. When you're satisfied, strain into a nonreactive pan. Add sweetener (up to ½ cup sugar or ¼ cup honey to each 2 cups of vinegar). Simmer for 3 minutes, stirring. Skim off any foam, let cool, and pour into sterilized bottles. Cap and label. (You'll want to experiment with sweeteners; some people prefer none at all.)

### SUGGESTED COMBINATIONS

Use red wine vinegar with these fruits and herbs:
> Raspberries, lemon thyme, and rosemary
> Cherries, tarragon, and anise hyssop
> Cranberries, mint, orange peel, cinnamon stick

Use white wine vinegar with these combinations:
> Peaches, opal basil, cinnamon stick
> Raspberries, fragrant rose petals, rose geranium
> Strawberries, mint, candied ginger
> Strawberries, peaches, opal basil, candied ginger

**Read more about making and using fruit vinegar:**
*Gourmet Vinegars: The How-tos of Making and Cooking with Vinegars*, by Marsha Peters Johnson

*If the sage tree thrives and grows*
*The master's not master and that he knows.*

—ENGLISH HERB LORE

The Theme Garden for August: A Tea Garden.

*Do you remember during hot summer days you would pause by the lemon balm in a tour of the garden and draw the leafy tips through your lightly closed, warm, moist hands? What a fragrance would be released. You no doubt did this to the bee-balm, the peppermint, applemint or many another herb which makes a fragrant tea.*

—ROSETTA E. CLARKSON, *MAGIC GARDENS*

## A Garden of Herbal Teas

In our busy lives, let's not forget the pleasure of taking tea in the garden, with the birds singing, the roses buzzing with delirious bees, and the air sweet with the scent of honeysuckle. Sounds delicious, doesn't it? Easy, too. All we need is a teapot, a teacup, tea herbs, fresh or dried, and the time to sit quietly and sip.

Creating a garden of tea plants doesn't have to be difficult, either. For an instant tea garden, try clustering pots of tea herbs on your deck, beside a small table and pair of chairs. No room for pots on the floor? Hang them, or line them up on your deck railing. Or put cushions and a low table beneath a luxuriant trailing vine—hops, for instance, which will bring the scent of fresh-mown hay to a pot of tea. If you have the space, you might want to place a sundial in the center of a square or circular plot and arrange the plants around it, the taller ones in the center or the back, low plants around the edge. Add a small fountain, and the falling water will play a soft musical accompaniment to your own private tea ceremony.

### SOME MUCH-LOVED TEA HERBS FOR YOUR GARDEN

| | |
|---|---|
| roses | calendula |
| lavender | thyme |
| borage | basil |
| lemon balm | chamomile |
| rosemary | angelica |
| sage | sweet cicely |
| mint | |

### SERVING TEA IN THE GARDEN

Serving tea in the garden is easier if you're organized for it. A handsome china teapot or glass pitcher, delicate cups and saucers or glasses for iced tea, a pretty tray, a spotless tea cloth, a small vase of flowers, a plate of sweets or savories—if you keep what you need in one place, you're more likely to use it. And if you've already arranged your tea garden to include a place for several chairs, you'll want to invite a friend or two and make an event of it. There's nothing nicer on a warm summer afternoon!

**Read more about tea gardens:**

*Herbal Tea Gardens: 22 Plans for Your Enjoyment & Well-being*, by Marietta Marshall Marcin

*Tea Gardens: Places to Make and Take Tea*, by Ann Lovejoy

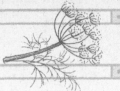

My new herbal calendar arrived today!

*Gather ye rosebuds while ye may*
*Old time is still a-flying.*
—ROBERT HERRICK

## Time Is Still A-Flying: From Susan's Journal

Every year, my friend Theresa Loe sends me her herbal wall calendar—always a beauty, filled Theresa's notes on gardening, crafting, and cooking with herbs and Peggy Turchette's gorgeous drawings. (Peggy has also done the drawings for this book.) Theresa has been creating her calendar since 2001, and she's still spilling over with delightful ideas to mark and measure time, herbally speaking.

I love garden calendars, and collect them by the dozen. But I also love the old "books of days"—the book you're reading now is a modern example of the genre. My favorite was published in 1862: *The Book of Days. A Miscellany of Popular Antiquities in Connection with the Calendar*. Robert Chambers, the author, tells me that tansy cakes are an important custom at Easter, that the herb horsetail was used as a "children's bottle brush," and that "A swarm of bees in May is worth a load of hay." And then there is Charles Kightly's *The Perpetual Almanack of Folklore*, whose entry for tomorrow . . . well, you'll see, when you get to August 14. Another personal favorite: *A Country-man's Daybook: An Anthology of Countryside Lore*, compiled by C. N. French in 1929 and "Dedicated to Cottage Gardeners." For today, I read this meteorological admonition:

*If the moon show a silver shield,*
*Be not afraid to reap your field,*
*But if she rises haloed round,*
*Soon we'll tread on deluged ground.*

I am also reminded to "never offer your hen for sale on a rainy day" and "Day and night, sun and moon, air and light, everyone must have, but none can buy."

I'll keep these wise words in mind. I hope you will, too. Meanwhile, I really must do something about my rough hands. On her October, 2006, calendar page, Theresa offers a great suggestion:

**THERESA LOE'S CHAMOMILE SPA OIL**

¼ cup jojoba oil
6 drops of Roman chamomile essential oil
4 drops lavender essential oil
2 drops tea tree essential oil

Combine all oils in a glass jar or bottle with a tight-fitting lid. Store in a cool dry place. Use within 1 year.

**Enjoy an herbal calendar:**
*The New Herbal Calendar*, by Theresa Loe, with illustrations by Peggy Turchette

# AUGUST 14

*The flowers of harvest-time—Harvest Bells, Harvest Daisies and Harvest Lilies—all now in bloom.*

—CHARLES KIGHTLY, *THE PERPETUAL ALMANACK OF FOLKLORE, AUGUST 14*

## Flowers and Herbs

It's not at all unusual for us to drive down a country lane and recognize not one plant of the hundreds that grow along the roadside. In earlier generations, however, people had a name—and a use—for every plant. Here is what country people in England knew about the "harvest flowers" that Kightly mentions.

### HARVEST BELLS
Kightly's harvest bells are the harebells (*Campanula rotundifolia*) of folklore, also known as the "bluebells of Scotland." If you picked this dangerous flower, its bell might ring, summoning one of the plant's magical protectors who could carry you off. The "hare" of "harebell" referred to the legendary shape-shifting magical hare, an ally of this plant. Other names: Witch-bell, Witch-thimble, Fairy Ringers, Granny's Tears.

### HARVEST DAISIES
Kightly's harvest daisy is the familiar ox-eye daisy that brightens the meadows and pastures. About it, John Pechey (1694) had this to say: "The whole Herb, Stalks, Leaves and Flowers, boyl'd in Posset-drink, and drunk, is accounted an excellent Remedy for an Asthma, Consumption, and Difficulty of breathing. . . . A Decoction of the Herb cures all Diseases that are occasion'd by drinking cold Beer when the Body is hot." And if your hot body is not afflicted by drinking cold beer, here's another way you can use this valuable herb: In Germany, harvest daisies were hung around the house to ward off lightning.

### HARVEST LILIES
The herbalist John Gerard turned up his nose at the invasive harvest lilies—"Bell-bind" or wild morning-glory (*Calystegia sepium*)— dismissing them as "unprofitable weedes and hurtfull unto eche thing that groweth next unto them." But country folk ate the nutritious roots, stalks, and young shoots, carefully, because the plant is also purgative. They used the roots to make a wound poultice and brewed a decoction to increase the flow of bile. The flexible stems became a useful and readily available twine. And harvesters' children played a game with the flowers, squeezing the green calyx so that the white petals popped off. It was called "Granny Jump Out of Bed."

**Learn more about plant lore:**
*The Englishman's Flora*, by Geoffrey Grigson

*When snails climb up the stalks of grass, wet weather is at hand.*

—COLONIAL AMERICAN WEATHER LORE

# AUGUST 15

Today is the Feast of the Assumption, celebrating the Virgin Mary, first celebrated in 529.

## Mary's Plants

Before the rise of Christianity, many plants were dedicated to pagan goddesses. But as the Catholic Church expanded its political territory and Christian priests began to convert pagans, the flower names were converted as well. Mary (and other saints) took the place of Venus, Diana, and Juno. The tables were turned at the Reformation, however, and many of the plants whose names had been changed were converted again, not back to their pagan names, but to "lady," without the "our lady" reference. Political correctness in the garden. Now, both styles occur.

The best-known of these Mary-herbs is lady's-mantle, a graceful, frothy chartreuse plant prized as a wound healer. In medieval times, alchemists believed that the dew that collected in its pretty, pleated leaves had magical properties. The plant's genus name, *Alchemilla*, refers to the alchemical use of the plants.

Other "our-lady" herbs:
- Our lady's bedstraw (*Galium verum*). The name comes from the Christian legend that this was one of the Bethlehem manger's "cradle herbs," and also from the plant's use as a fragrant herb (like its cousin, sweet woodruff, it contains coumarin) for stuffing straw mattresses. Medicinally, bedstraw was used as a diuretic and to treat bleeding. The herb has the interesting property of curdling milk; Tuscan dairy farmers used it to make cheese.
- Our lady's thistle, or milk thistle (*Silybum marianum*) took its name from the story that the Virgin's milk fell on its leaves when she hastened to conceal the infant Jesus from Herod's soldiers. The plant has a long history of medicinal use, mostly as a protection for the liver; contemporary herbalists recommend it for liver ailments, a use which is supported by recent pharmacological studies.
- Our lady's smock (cuckoo flower, meadowcress); our lady's tears (lily-of-the-valley); our lady's bunch of keys (cowslip); our lady's gloves (foxglove).

**Read more about Mary's plants:**
"Flowers of the Madonna," by Harold N. Moldenke, *Horticulture Magazine*, December, 1953

*The Blessed Virgin Maries feast hath here*
*her place and time*
*Wherein departing from the earth, she did*
*the heavens climb.*
*Great bundles then of hearbes to church the people*
*fast do bear*
*To which against all hurtful things the*
*priest doth hallow there.*
—SIXTEENTH CENTURY HYMN

Yesterday was the birthday of Julia Child, who was born on August 15, 1912, in Pasadena, California.

*Find something you're passionate about and keep tremendously interested in it.*

—JULIA CHILD

## The French Chef

Fannie Farmer may have made us aware of our "American cuisine" and led us to practice the science of cookery, but Julia Child seduced us from our casseroles and gave us France—and became an American icon in the process. Her profound and far-reaching influence on American cookery earned her the title of "Mother of the American Food Renaissance," while her sparkling joie de vivre turned cooking into an exciting adventure and focussed our attention on the pleasures of the table. As food correspondent Sara Moulton says, it was Julia (St. Julia, Our Lady of the Ladle) who urged us all to march into our supermarkets and "demand leeks and shallots." And it was Julia who brought the phrase "herbes de Provence" into the vocabulary of American cooks.

### HERBES DE PROVENCE
Herbes de Provence is the name given to a group of herbs that are favorites in southern France: bay, rosemary, thyme, summer savory, cloves, lavender, tarragon, chervil, sage, marjoram, basil, fennel seed, and orange zest. They are available in a dried mix, or you can create your own fresh blend (as Julia always recommended) to complement the dish you're making.

For the fresh blend, simply mix together 1 tablespoon each of finely chopped fresh oregano, savory, thyme, marjoram, rosemary, and lavender. Or you can use your harvest of dried herbs for gifts, with the basic recipe below. Package the herbs in colorful calico bags tucked into small terra-cotta pots and tied with a raffia bow.

### HERBES DE PROVENCE
3 parts dried rosemary, crushed fine

3 parts dried marjoram

3 parts dried thyme

2 parts dried summer savory

2 parts dried lavender flowers, crushed

2 parts dried orange peel, crushed to a powder

2 parts dried bay leaves, crushed fine

1 part dried mint

1 part fennel seed

½ part ground cloves

½ part coriander

Blend thoroughly. Store in an airtight container.

**Read more about Our Lady of the Ladle:**
*Appetite for Life: The Biography of Julia Child*, by Noel Riley Fitch
*Mastering the Art of French Cooking*, by Julia Child

*Our lives are dyed the color of our imaginations.*

—MARCUS AURELIUS

## *Indigo Dying*: About China's Books

Each one of China's mysteries teaches me something new about herbs, but when it came to *Indigo Dying*, I had a lot to learn. As you might guess by the title, the signature herbs all have to do with dyeing, a craft I hadn't yet tried. Pretty soon I was out in the fields collecting dye plants and rooting through dozens of sources, collecting information about the colorful herbs. (See May 31 and July 17 for additional background.)

I was most fascinated by indigo, however, a shrubby herb whose leaves produced a rich, clear blue, much prized by all cultures. Dying with indigo traditionally involved fermenting the leaves with human urine, then drying the residue and forming it into large cakes. Indigo was so valuable that it created an incentive for direct trade between Europe and the Orient, leading to international conflict over the "Devil's Dye." Here are a few of the interesting tidbits I discovered in my reading and used as chapter headings in the book.

- If we go far back in time and space we find the colour blue associated with power, magic and divinity. . . . [The historian Pliny] describes the Roman legions' unusual encounter with blue-dyed Celts in AD 44 and 45: "Omnes vero se Britanni vitro inficiunt, quod caeruleum efficit colorem, atque horribiliores sunt in pugna aspectu." [All Britons dye themselves with woad which makes them blue, in order that in battle their appearance may be the more terrible.] —Gosta Sandberg *Indigo Textiles: Technique and History*

- One drop of indigo is enough to spoil a whole bowl of milk. —Japanese proverb

- I would rather wear my own indigo wrapper than a rich red cloak that isn't mine. —African proverb

- On the island of Sumba, the art of indigo dyeing is part of a larger traditional practice involving the mysteries of divination, magic, and herbal medicines. This complex body of occult knowledge is possessed only by a few Kodi women who understand the dangerous practices of moro, or "blueness," and are known as the "blue-handed women" (warico kabahu moro). Because of their association with indigo dyeing, they are viewed by the Kodi as intimately associated with death. —Paraphrased from Janet Hoskins, "Why Do Ladies Sing the Blues?" in *Cloth and Human Experience*, edited by Annette B. Weiner & Jane Schneider

**Read more:**

*Indigo Dying: A China Bayles Mystery*, by Susan Wittig Albert

*Whereas in our times the Art of Simpling is so farre from being rewarded, that it is grown contemptible and he is accounted a simple fellow, that pretends to have any skill therein. Truly it is to be lamented that the men of these times which pretend to so much Light should goe the way to put out their owne Eyes, by trampling upon that which should preserve them, to the great discouragement of those that have any mind to bend their Studies this way.*

—WILLIAM COLE, *THE ART OF SIMPLING*, 1656

## The Household Simple-Closet and Still-Room

Herb gardens weren't just for pretty in our foremothers' days; they were a necessity. Every good wife and mother had an herb garden to supply her domestic pharmacopoeia, and most practiced the art of "simpling": using one or two herbs at a time in salves, lotions, teas, and tinctures, rather than creating complex recipes as the physicians did, often with outlandish ingredients. "Simplers" grew their own medicinal herbs, harvested and stored them carefully, and used them with a full understanding (as much as was permitted at that time) of their properties and effects.

The simple-closet (the place where herbs were stored) and the still-room (where medicines were made) were the special provinces of the mother and daughters of the house, and were never entrusted to servants. The shelves contained things like ivy berries, ash "keys," daisy root, the inner bark of oak, goldenrod, and yarrow, thyme, motherwort, and peony roots. From these supplies the good wife prepared herbal wines and waters, syrups, juleps, and vinegars, as well as tinctures, conserves, confections, and treacles. For external use, she prepared oils, ointments, liniments, compresses, poultices—and of course, scent bags and potpourris. And then there were the magical purposes of herbs: love philters and charms, protection, cleansing, good luck. Yes, of course, superstition and folklore was part and parcel of the process, but there was also careful thought, methodical preparation, and meticulous observation—more than we can say, perhaps, about our consumption of pharmaceuticals today. Perhaps it's time to restore the simple-closet and the still-room to our homes.

**Read more about simpling:**
*The Art of Simpling*, by William Coles

*With what rare Colours, and sweet Odours do the flourishing Fields and Gardens entertain the Senses. The usefulness of it no judicious man can deny, unless he would also deny the virtues of Herbs, which experience itself doth daily approve. For how often do we see, not only men's Bodies, but even the Minds of those that are even distracted, to be cured by them?*

—WILLIAM COLES, *THE ART OF SIMPLING*

## Going Places: The Herbfarm, Woodinville, Washington

It all began with a wheelbarrow and a bunch of chives.

In 1974, Lola Zimmerman had a few extra chive plants in her garden. She put them in a wheelbarrow and parked them on the road in front of the old dairy farm that she and her husband Bill owned in the foothills of the Cascades. She put up a hand-lettered sign: HERBS FOR SALE. The chives went fast—and so did the other herbs that Lola began offering for sale. It was just one skip and a jump from the wheelbarrow to the nursery, and before long, the Zimmermans' herb farm was a blooming business.

The next skip and a jump took the Herbfarm in a different direction. In 1986, the Zimmermans' son Ron and daughter-in-law Carrie remodeled part of the home and garage into a charming little restaurant that seated just 24 diners—enthusiastic diners, as it turned out. The excellent herbal cookery got rave reviews, and there was never an empty seat. And when chef Jerry Traunfeld, noted for his innovative multi-course dinners, became the Herbfarm's chef in 1990, the restaurant took another huge leap forward. An expert in culinary herbs, Jerry has been featured in the *New York Times Magazine*, *Food and Wine*, *Bon Appétit*, *Gourmet*, and many other publications. He has appeared on numerous television shows and is a regular guest on National Public Radio's "The Splendid Table." Under his guidance, The Herbfarm Restaurant was ranked fifteenth in the nation by *Gourmet*. Jerry is the author of *The Herbfarm Cookbook*, a must-have for every cook who would like to adventure into herbal gourmet cookery. You'll know why when you've tried his recipe for stinging nettle, lovage, and mussel soup.

But the journey has not been without its disasters. In 1997 the Herbfarm burned to the ground. It took four years to reopen in a new site, and when it finally happened, everyone breathed a sigh of relief. Jerry returned to the kitchen, Hamlet the pig returned to the garden, and the Zimmermans' old farm tractor went back to work. Want to drop in for dinner? Better make your reservation today. You might have to wait 8 or 9 months for a table.

And while you're waiting, imagine what you might do with a wheelbarrow and a few extra herb plants.

**Read more about The Herbfarm:**
*The Herbfarm Cookbook*, by Jerry Traunfeld
For directions and reservations and lots more, visit the Herbfarm's web site: www.theherbfarm.com

In some years, today is National Potato Day.

*My idea of heaven is a great big baked potato and someone to share it with.*

—OPHRA WINFREY

## But It Doesn't Have to Be Baked!

Baked potatoes are nice, especially with fresh snipped chives, minced cilantro, a generous dollop of garlic butter, and sour cream, of course. But if you're not in the mood for baked, here are some delicious alternatives, made with herbs from your garden.

### LILA JENNINGS' GREATER GARLIC MASHED POTATOES

Lila owns the Nueces Street Diner in Pecan Springs, where her Greater Garlic Mashed Potatoes are featured in a comfort-menu that includes fried okra, meat loaf, coleslaw, and apple pie.

    16 cups peeled white potatoes, quartered
    4 heads peeled garlic cloves (Lila says this is right.)
    2 cups milk
    ½ pound butter
    salt and pepper to taste

Simmer the potatoes until tender. Drain and mash with the butter. While the potatoes are cooking, simmer the garlic and milk in a saucepan until soft. Puree in a blender. Beat the puree into the mashed potatoes, and season with salt and pepper. Lila says this recipe makes enough for 16 people. If you're feeding four, divide by four.

### ROSEMARY-GARLIC POTATOES

China microwaves these potatoes on those Texas summer evenings when it's hot enough to fry eggs on the patio and she doesn't want to turn on the oven.

    4–5 red potatoes, cut into eighths
    1 tablespoon olive oil
    3 cloves garlic, minced
    ½ teaspoon salt, or Savory Blend (August 29)
    ¼ teaspoon black pepper
    3 sprigs rosemary
    2 teaspoons chopped parsley

Toss potatoes with oil, garlic, salt, pepper. Turn into a microwave baking dish and lay rosemary sprigs on top. Cover and microwave on high for 15 minutes or until potatoes are tender. Remove rosemary. Garnish with parsley. Makes 4 servings.

**Learn all about potato cookery:**
*Potato*, by Alex Barker

*What I say is that, if a fellow really likes potatoes, he must be a pretty decent sort of fellow.*

—A. A. MILNE, AUTHOR OF *WINNIE-THE-POOH*

# AUGUST 21

Today is St. Stephen's Day. On this day, Hungarians celebrate King Steven (born about 970) and the founding of the Hungarian state.

*One of the Krautzenheimer granddaughters, costumed in a perky red skirt, suspenders, and embroidered Bavarian apron, danced over and took our orders: sauerbraten for McQuaid and a bowl of Hungarian goulash for me.*

—DEAD MAN'S BONES: A CHINA BAYLES MYSTERY

## Paprika

Without paprika, Hungarian goulash would be . . . well, plain old beef stew. Paprika is the mild, rich-tasting red pepper that gives the dish—and Hungarian cuisine—its distinctive flavor. Peppers didn't arrive in Europe until Columbus got home. It was another two hundred years before the first peppers arrived in Hungary, probably brought by Balkan refugees fleeing from the invading Turks. (It's amazing how many plants were borne on the winds of war.)

Paprika is the powder ground from dried ripe peppers, sweet or hot, depending on the peppers, and variously bright red or rusty brown. When you're cooking with paprika, remember that it releases its flavor only when it's heated; if it's burned, it turns bitter. However, it's often used as much to dress up food as for flavor. Who wants to eat a naked deviled egg?

The next time you visit Pecan Springs, drop in at the Krautzenheimer's Restaurant, which is located on the square, next to the Sophie Briggs Historical Museum. The goulash is China's favorite.

### MRS. KRAUTZENHEIMER'S HUNGARIAN GOULASH

2 pounds beef stew meat, cut in 1-inch cubes

½ teaspoon salt

2 tablespoons paprika (best: imported sweet Hungarian paprika)

1 large onion, chopped

2 tablespoons shortening

4 cups water

2 carrots, scraped, sliced

2 potatoes, cubed

1 large ripe tomato, quartered and seeded

2 cloves garlic, minced

½ teaspoon dry mustard

2 bay leaves

Mix beef cubes with salt and paprika. Over medium heat, brown chopped onion in shortening. Add beef cubes and brown, stirring. Reduce heat and simmer for 1 hour. Add water and remaining ingredients. Cover and simmer until vegetables are done and meat is tender. Remove bay leaves. Serve over hot noodles. Serves 6–8.

**Learn about Eastern European cuisine:**

*All Along the Danube: Recipes from Germany, Austria, Czechoslovakia, Yugoslavia, Hungary, Romania and Bulgaria,* by Marina Polvay

# AUGUST 22

Today or tomorrow, the Sun enters the sign of Virgo.

*The sixth sign of the zodiac, the feminine sign Virgo (the Virgin) is ruled by Mercury. A mutable sign, Virgo is associated with altruistic service to others. It is an earth sign, suggesting that Virgo people are methodical, thoughtful, conservative, and concerned about matters of health and finance. They may also be highly self-critical and feel that they are unable to live up to their own high standards.*

—RUBY WILCOX, "ASTROLOGICAL SIGNS"

## Virgo Herbs

Virgo rules the sinuses, respiratory system, abdomen, digestive process, and lower intestinal tract. Herbs associated with Virgo often assist in digestion (as do Cancer herbs) and help to reduce flatulence.

• Fennel (*Foeniculum vulgare*). Fennel is an excellent stomach-settler and intestinal soother. It stimulates the digestion and relieves gas. A traditional remedy for flatulence: Steep 1–2 teaspoons of crushed fennel seeds to 1 cup of boiling water for 8–10 minutes. Fennel also has a reputation as a weight-reducer. The seeds and the plant are used in salads and cooked as a vegetable. High in calcium, iron, potassium, and vitamins A and C.

• Anise (*Pimpinella anisum*). John Gerard says that anise seed "wasteth and consumeth wide, and is good against belchings and upbraidings of the stomacke." Its volatile oils ease intestinal cramps and gas. The seeds are featured in many breads, cookies, cakes, candies, and liqueurs. An aromatic tea of the seeds is said to break up bronchial mucus.

• Liquorice (*Glycyrrhiza glabra*). According to Nicholas Culpeper, "the root boiled in water with some Maidenhead and figs makes a good drink for those who have a dry cough." It was traditionally used to treat constipation in children.

• Other Virgo herbs. Dill seeds are another traditional remedy for gas and intestinal cramps. Recent research suggests that the plant's essential oils may inhibit cancer formation. Cranesbill is helpful in relieving diarrhea and dysentery. Oregano has long been used to treat indigestion and diarrhea; its oils have fungicidal and vermifugal properties.

*The admirable Harmony of the Creation is herein seen, in the influence of Stars upon Herbs, and the Body of Man, how one part of the Creation is subservient to another and all for the use of Man.*

—NICHOLAS CULPEPER

**Read more about astrological herbalism:**
*Llewellyn's Herbal Almanac*, published annually by Llewellyn publications

# AUGUST 23

The Herb Society of America (HSA) was founded on this day in 1933.

❧

## "Something More Worthwhile..."

The Herb Society of America began because a small group of women wanted to do "something more worthwhile than the ordinary garden club." In 1932, they began a serious study of herbs with Dr. Edgar Anderson, a botanist at the Arnold Arboretum at Harvard. The group chose rosemary as their focus, and met each week, growing, drying, and mounting specimens for detailed microscopic examination and library research. When they were finished, they went on to horehound and other herbs. And in 1933, they began the challenging work of organizing an herb society, reaching out to people who shared a serious interest in plants that had served humankind through the centuries.

The first officers were elected at the September 1933 meeting in Wenham, Massachusetts. The members of the small group—ambitiously calling themselves the Herb Society of America—immediately set about making their influence felt by creating a public herb garden in Franklin Park, in Boston, and shortly after, a garden at the National Cathedral in Washington. Busy, dedicated ladies, they began a regular publication called *The Herbarist*, placed an exhibit called "A 17th Century Still Room" at the Boston Flower Show, and incorporated their organization on May 17, 1935. The New York and Pennsylvania Groups were created in 1936, and the organization continued to grow. By 1945, in spite of the difficulties created by the war, there were six units, and the growth made reorganization necessary.

From that time forward, like a well-tended garden, HSA continued to grow and flourish. It wielded the tussie-mussie power that blossomed into the National Herb Garden (see June 12) and established its national headquarters in an 1841 house adjacent to the Holden Arboretum in Kirtland, Ohio. Projects of the national organization and its units include gardens, plant collections, a members' seed exchange, regional symposia, and an annual national conference.

At this writing, there are 45 units in 23 states, and a membership of 2,300. But the commitment expressed by the Society's seven founders—those dedicated women who wanted to "do something more worthwhile"—remains the same: to promote the knowledge, use, and delight of herbs through educational programs, research, and shared experience. If you're interested in becoming a member, contact The Herb Society of America, 9019 Kirtland Chardon Road, Kirtland, OH 44094 (440-256-0514), or visit the web site: www.herbsociety.org.

**Read more about the Society's history:**
*The Herb Society of America, 1933–1993*, by Dorothy G. Spencer

*The true gardener, like an artist, is never satisfied.*

—H. E. BATES

*Pruning helps you grow.*

—EMILIE BARNES

## Making an Herb Topiary

We're all familiar with the art of training plants: espaliering a vine or a tree against a wall or pruning a rowdy rose into a more congenial garden companion. Herbs—rosemary, lavender, santolina, and bay are good plants to start with—can be pruned into ornamental shapes, too, and it's fun and easy to transform them into topiaries. What's more, the trimmings can go into potpourri bowl or the soup pot!

### A ROSEMARY TOPIARY

The simplest topiary is a single-stem "round-head standard," which you can train in a single or a double pom-pom. To get started, collect a potted rosemary plant (an upright cultivar 12–18 inches tall, with good growth), an appropriate container with a drainage hole in the bottom, a bamboo or wooden stake, clip-

pers, and raffia. Push the stake into the pot beside the main stem, then remove all the stems but that one and tie the stem to the stake. If the stem has grown crooked, gently straighten it as much as possible, tying it at several points to the stake.

Then decide where you want to develop the ball, and strip the leaves below that point, being careful not to damage the stem. Prune the plant to approximate the shape you want, cutting just past the growth nodes to encourage bushiness. As new growth appears on the stem, pinch it off; retie the stem as necessary to ensure straight growth. As new growth shoots out from the nodes in the ball, keep shaping it. If you want to create a double-ball standard, train the central stem to grow straight up, shaping the higher ball some six inches above the lower. If you like, add moss or rocks to cover the soil surface. Care for your plant as you would for any potted rosemary.

**Design, plant, trim, and enjoy a topiary:**
*Herb Topiaries,* by Sally Gallo

*Plantain and house-leek, boiled in cream, and strained before it is put away to cool, makes a very cooling, soothing ointment. Plantain leaves laid upon a wound are cooling and healing.*

—MRS. CHILD, *THE AMERICAN FRUGAL HOUSEWIFE,* 1833

*A tree grows which they call "the fever tree" in the vicinity of Loxa [Ecuador], whose bark, of the color of cinnamon, made into powder of the weight of two small silver coins and given as a beverage, cures the fevers and tertians [malaria]; it has produced miraculous results in Lima.*

—FATHER CALACHA, 1633

## The Powder of the Devil

Malaria, as old as recorded history, was dreaded by everyone, for even if the mosquito-borne disease did not kill, it shattered the victim's health. We might still be helpless against it if it were not for a tree with yellow bark, and people with the courage to try what must have seemed like a Peruvian witch doctor's barbaric powder—which is exactly what Oliver Cromwell called it when he lay dying of malaria, preferring the physicians' bloodletting to "the powder of the devil," as he called it.

In fact, as William Cook wrote in 1869, seventeenth-century physicians angrily opposed the use of *Cinchona* powder, calling it "absolutely pernicious"; their rejection was, he says, "a marked illustration of the astounding bitterness with which learned men will oppose the progress of knowledge." The remedy might never have been accepted if a former apothecary's apprentice named Robert Talbor had not treated King Charles II of England with an infusion of cinchona powder in white wine. When the king was cured, demand for the bark shot up, and within the next century, the trees—growing on remote mountains at altitudes up to 10,000 feet—had been harvested to the point of extinction. Clearly, the *Cinchona* had to be grown in plantations. However, the Indians believed that if the trees were ever successfully grown elsewhere, the native *Cinchona* would die, and did everything they could to prevent that from happening.

But in 1865, an adventurous British trader named Charles Ledger managed to smuggle out a pound of seeds. Inexplicably, the British government was not eager to acquire them, but the Dutch were more than happy to oblige. By 1881, nearly three-quarters of a million *Cinchona* trees were growing on plantations in Dutch-held Java, and quinine—the Devil's Powder—was available to the world.

**More about quinine:**

*The Fever Bark Tree: The Pageant of Quinine*, by Marie Louise Duran-Reynals

# AUGUST 26

*The heart that has truly loved never forgets,*
*But as truly loves on to the close,*
*As the sunflower turns on her god when he sets*
*The same look which she did when he rose.*

—THOMAS MOORE, "BELIEVE ME IF ALL THOSE ENDEARING YOUNG CHARMS"

## Sunflowers

These sun-worshippers are blooming now in meadows, along roadsides, and in gardens, pleasing butterflies, birds, and people. These plants, which belong to the genus *Helianthus* and are named for their habit of following the sun's movement, are as useful as they are pretty, providing nutritious seeds to eat, fiber for materials, medicine, a golden yellow dye, and an all-purpose oil. Domestically cultivated by Native Americans as long ago as 5,000 years, the plant was introduced into Europe in the sixteenth century.

### THE ORNAMENTAL SUNFLOWER

Sunflowers are among the easiest—and most impressive—annuals. They love the sun (naturally!), require plenty of water, and the taller varieties need some protection from the wind. In spring, plant the seeds in rich, well-drained soil, about twelve inches apart. Expect blooms in 10–12 weeks, and stake where necessary. Harvest the heads before the birds do and hang in paper bags to dry. The head is dry when you can rub the seeds loose.

### THE EDIBLE SUNFLOWER

Sunflower seeds are packed with healthy unsaturated fats, protein, and fiber, plus important nutrients like the antioxidant vitamin E. Since they have a very high oil content, they are a valuable source of polyunsaturated oil. Raw or roasted, whole or ground, they can be used in recipes in place of other nuts—in your favorite pesto recipe, for instance, as a substitute for pine nuts. To roast your harvest, spread on cookie sheets and roast at 150–200° until completely dry (about 3–4 hours), stirring once or twice. Store in a lidded jar in the refrigerator.

### THE APOTHECARY SUNFLOWER

The leaves and seeds have been used as an expectorant and a diuretic, and (in a decoction) as a treatment for bronchitis. In Russia, the leaves were used as a treatment for malarial fevers. The oil is high in linoleic acid; in lotions and salves, this fatty acid helps the skin to retain moisture.

**All about sunflowers:**
*Sunflowers*, by Debra M. Mancoff

*What a desolate place would be a world without flowers! It would be a face without a smile, a feast without a welcome.*

—CLARA L. BALFOUR

# AUGUST 27

*The whole toppe with its pleasant yellow floures sheweth like to a wax candle or taper cunningly wrought.*

—HENRY LYTE, 1578

## A Plant of a Hundred Names

The folk names of herbs often reflect their uses. Take mullein, for example, the tall, erect plant that is blooming bright yellow along dry, gravelly roadsides in many parts of the country just now. Roman soldiers stripped off the leaves and flowers, bundled the resinous stalks together, and dipped them in tallow: they called it *candelaria*. In England, the stringy fibers of the stalk were twisted and used as wicks for candles: candlewick plant. Because the plant was thought to be burned by witches, it was sometimes called the hag's taper. And during the last century, miners in the American West burned the stalks as torches in their mines. They called it miner's candle.

The stalk itself resembled a rod, and because it was so strong and straight, it was sometimes connected with authority: Aaron's rod (which "was budded, and brought forth buds, and bloomed blossoms," Numbers 17:8), or Jupiter's staff (perhaps it might be used to ward off lightning?). Alternatively, it was beggar's staff, presumably because a beggar couldn't afford a staff made of stouter material.

And then there are the large, soft, fuzzy, flannel-like leaves at the base of the plant, making it poor man's flannel, flannel-flower, flannel-jacket, flannel petti-coats, Adam's flannel. In other places, it took its name from a slightly different resemblance: Donkey's Ear or Bunny's Ear. And in modern America, some wilderness campers call it Hiker's Toilet Paper!

Over the centuries, herbalists have found many uses for mullein. The fresh flowers were steeped in oil and used as earache drops, while a tea was thought to relieve the symptoms of gout. The juice of the leaves and flowers was said to remove warts, and the leaves, as a poultice, treated coughs and bronchitis.

P.S. To be botanically correct, we should also point out that mullein, by any other name or not, remains *Verbascum thapsus*.

**Read about the hidden history of plants:**
*The Illustrated Plant Lore*, by Josephine Addison

*When rain is coming, frogs change color.*

—TRADITIONAL WEATHER LORE

*The lightnings and thundring will do no harme, if there be buried in the midst of the garden a kinde of toad called a hedge toade, closed up in a pot of earth.*

—GERVASE MARKHAM, *MAISON RUSTIQUE, OR A COUNTRY FARME*, 1616

# AUGUST 28

## Lyle Bippert and His Bug-Bee-Gone

At the close of the Merryweathers' Herb Guild meeting yesterday, Lyle Bippert handed out take-home samples of his herbal bug repellant, Bug-Bee-Gone. It's good to keep the bugs off, Lyle says, and it also works pretty well as a bass bait. Last month, he claims, while fishing in Canyon Lake, he caught a four-pound bass on a purple plastic wiggle-worm he accidentally dunked in his Bug-Bee-Gone.

Now, Lyle is famous for his fish stories, and you don't want to believe everything he says. But it's a fact that Hank Etzel, of Hank's Worms & Minnows, has offered to take a dozen bottles on a trial basis. Maybe Lyle (who recently retired from his career at Filbert's Feed Store) will be the next Texas millionaire, or maybe he'll just catch a lot of fish. Either way, here is his formula, which will soon appear in the Guild's new book, *Happy Thymes: A Calendula of Herbal Dillies.*

### BIPPERT'S SUREFIRE BUG-BEE-GONE
- 2 cups rubbing alcohol
- 12 drops rosemary oil
- 12 drops pine oil
- 12 drops lemon oil
- 12 drops juniper oil
- 12 drops citronella

Mix together in a clean peanut-butter jar with a lid. Shake before you splash it on or dunk your fishing lure in it. (Not guaranteed against killer bees.)

Lyle contributed another formula to *Happy Thymes,* this one called "Fisherman's Foot Formula." After he's been wearing his fishing boots all day, he brews up a strong herbal tea: 2 quarts boiling water, ⅓ cup dried thyme, ⅓ cup dried rosemary, and ⅓ cup dried peppermint. "When this has cooled off some," Lyle says, "I pour it in a pan and soak my tootsies in it. When I'm done, I pour it back in the jar and put it in the fridge to keep for next time." His wife, Hazel, adds this caution: "Make sure you label the jar. Lyle's stuff works good on feet, but it's just not real tasty."

When the Foot Formula has gone around a second time, Lyle heats it to boiling, takes it outdoors, and pours it onto the nearest fire-ant mound. "Kills 'em deader 'n your average doornail," he reports. "No chemicals, neither. I'm gonna take a sample over to Texas A&M and see if the Aggies want to do some research with it."

Go for it, Lyle. The Merryweathers are rooting for you.

# AUGUST 29

Today is National More Herbs, Less Salt Day.

*"China, do you have any more rosemary-tarragon vinegar?" Helen asked. "And while you're at it, Mother wants some of that no-salt seasoning blend you make. She sneaks it on her food when the nurses are looking the other way." Helen's mother lives in a nursing home in Waco. If she can't get along without that season-ing, it must be good.*

—WITCHES' BANE: A CHINA BAYLES MYSTERY

## Getting the Salt Out

If you're one of the many people who need to reduce salt, here are recipes for the herbal blends China sells in her shop. Mix the ingredients thoroughly, pulverize them in a coffee grinder, spice grinder, or blender, and store in a tightly lidded jar in a cool, dark place. Each makes about ⅓ cup. You can also stir them into sour cream (I use low-fat) or yogurt for a zippy dip.

### SAVORY BLEND

2 tablespoons dried dillweed

2 tablespoons dried chives

1 tablespoon dried oregano

1 tablespoon dried basil

2 teaspoons celery seeds

1 teaspoon powdered lemon peel

½ teaspoon dried thyme

½ teaspoon ground black pepper

### ZIPPY BLEND

2 tablespoons dried winter savory

1 tablespoon dried mustard

1 tablespoon dried chives

2 teaspoons curry powder

1½ teaspoons ground white pepper

1½ teaspoons ground cumin

1 teaspoon powdered orange peel

1 teaspoon garlic powder

### SPICY BLEND

2 tablespoons paprika

1 tablespoon black pepper

1 tablespoon crushed coriander seeds

1 tablespoon powdered cloves

1 teaspoon dried mustard

1 teaspoon dried winter savory

½ teaspoon garlic powder

½ teaspoon powdered orange peel

**For more help in getting the salt out:**

*The American Heart Association Low-Salt Cookbook*, by the American Heart Association

*Herb Mixtures & Spicy Blends*, edited by Deborah L. Balmuth

*Balm with its delicious lemon scent, is by common consent one of the most sweetly smelling of all the herbs in the garden. Balm-wine was made of it and a tea which is good for feverish colds. The fresh leaves make better tea than the dry.*

—FRANCIS A. BARDSWELL, *THE HERB GARDEN*, 1911

## Balm for the Soul

Lemon balm (*Melissa officinalis*) has been beloved since long before Homer spoke of "sweet balm and gentle violets" in the *Odyssey*, or Theocritus mentioned (in *The Idyll*) that his sheep loved to browse it in the meadows. Virgil grew it especially for his bees (*melissa* is from the Greek word for "bee"), and Thomas Jefferson included it in his 1794 list of herbs at Monticello. It has calmative properties, and is widely used in tea and other drinks.

In your garden, use lemon balm as a border plant, or in a container. Plant it along a path, where you can reach down and touch it, and cut it back to encourage bushiness. You'll find plenty of uses for those cuttings!

### BALM FOR THE THIRSTY

This delicious garden punch is easy to make, and it will be the star of your garden party. Thanks to Lucinda Hutson, for allowing me to reprint it from her book, *The Herb Garden Cookbook*.

### GARDEN PUNCH

- 2 generous bunches of lemon balm sprigs, on long stems if possible, *plus*
- 2 generous bunches mild-flavored mints (also on long stems if possible) to loosely fill the pitcher
- 1 large can (46 ounces) unsweetened pineapple juice or equivalent pure unfiltered apple juice
- juice of two lemons
- 1 lemon, cut in thin slices
- sparkling water or champagne to taste

Gently wring the bunches of lemon balm and mint to release their flavor. Place in a large glass pitcher, cover with the juices and the lemon slices. Chill overnight, occasionally stirring and pressing down on the herbs with the back of a wooden spoon. Pour into iced glasses with a splash of sparkling water (or champagne) and a sprig of fresh lemon balm and/or mint. Serves 8–10.

**Read more of Lucinda Hutson's garden cookery:**
*The Herb Garden Cookbook,* by Lucinda Hutson

*To make a nourishing drink for harvest laborers: Take a gallon of water, and put a little of it into a pan with half a pound of oatmeal, a pound of sugar, the juice of an orange and lemon and their rind sliced small. Boil them for ten minutes, then add the rest of the water, take from the fire, and stir well until it is cold.*

—MISTRESS CLARK'S BOOK, EIGHTEENTH CENTURY

Yesterday was the Feast Day of St. Fiacre, the patron saint of gardeners, florists, and herbalists.

If your garden is doing particularly well this year, you can thank St. Fiacre, the patron saint of gardens. If it isn't—well, perhaps you could ask this helpful saint to lend a hand.

## The Tale of St. Fiacre

Fiacre lived in the seventh century. He was raised in an Irish monastery, where he learned to use healing herbs. He wanted to be a hermit, but his skill and knowledge brought people to him, so he went to France in search of solitude, taking up residence in a cave near a spring. He needed a garden (who doesn't?) so he asked a nearby bishop, St. Faro of Meaux, for land. The bishop gave him as much garden space as he could plow in a day. The next morning, it is said, Fiacre chose his spot and began to walk around it, dragging his spade behind him. Magically, wherever his spade touched, trees toppled, bushes were uprooted, the soil was turned over, and the rocks were plucked out. The local folk, frightened, called it sorcery, but the bishop declared Fiacre's garden a miracle. (Personally, I suspect that the bishop had some gardening work of his own that needed to be done.) Fiacre's garden, always in bloom and always beautifully tended, became a place of pilgrimage. His healing herbs were eagerly sought, and his culinary herbs were used to flavor food that was offered to the poor.

To invite blessings to your garden, you might purchase a small statue of this gardener's saint and put it in a quiet corner where you can enjoy the meditative silence Fiacre sought in his own garden. Surround it with such healing herbs as sage, thyme, mint, fennel, dill, and Saint-John's-wart—herbs that Fiacre would have known and used.

*The growing of the first few herbs is the discovery of a whole new world of garden pleasure and human meaning, but it is when a gardener has tried a few, liked them and been liked by them, and would go on that the full adventure begins.*

—HENRY BESTON, *HERBS AND THE EARTH*

September is National Honey Month.

*I broke open a biscuit and drizzled honey on it with a spoon. The honey had the scent of lavender, and when I tasted it, the flavor of lavender, warmed by the sun.*

—BLOODROOT: A CHINA BAYLES MYSTERY

## Herbal Honey

Flavored honeys are among the easiest and most delicious herbal treats—and they make wonderful gifts, too. Many different herbs, spices, and herbs and spices in combination can be used to flavor honey. Make sure that none of the herbal material has been sprayed.

Here are some ideas to experiment with. To each cup of honey, use one of the following herbs, in the approximate amounts suggested. Or you can combine herbs—if you do, reduce the amounts proportionally (for example, 2 cinnamon basil leaves and 2 cinnamon sticks):

½ cup fragrant rose petals

4 tablespoons fresh lavender flowers

3–4 lemon or rose geranium leaves

3 sprigs rosemary

3 sprigs thyme

4 cinnamon basil leaves

4–5 cinnamon sticks

3 teaspoons orange zest or lemon zest

In a nonreactive saucepan, heat the honey gently. Put the herbs in a clean jar and pour the honey over them. Cap tightly and let sit for a week or two before using. Wonderful on waffles, pancakes, toast, ice cream, and fruit.

**Learn more about bees and honey:**

*Honey: From Hive to Honeypot: A Celebration of Bees and their Bounty*, by Sue Style

*The neatest way to separate beeswax from honey-comb is to tie the comb up [when the honey has been removed] in a linen or woolen bag; place it in a kettle of cold water, and hang it over the fire. As the water heats, the wax melts, and rises to the surface, while all the impurities remain in the bag. It is well to put a few pebbles in the bag, to keep it from floating.*

—MRS. CHILD, THE AMERICAN FRUGAL HOUSEWIFE, 1833

*Isn't it funny*
*How a bear likes honey?*
*Buzz, buzz, buzz,*
*I wonder why he does.*

—A. A. MILNE, WINNIE-THE-POOH, 1926

In some calendars, the Celtic month of Vines (Brambles) begins today (September 2–29).

*The bramble trees were: the dog-rose; bramble; broom; heather; ivy; vine. . . .*

—JACQUELINE MEMORY PATERSON, *TREE WISDOM*

## Brambles

The bramble "trees" were not the most lordly of the Celtic trees, but one—the dog rose (*Rosa canina*)—was useful, as well as beautiful. It is said that this beautiful wild rose derived its name from the ancient tradition that the root would cure a bite from a mad dog. More likely, it was originally called the dag rose (*dag* meaning "dagger"), for its sharp thorns, and the name was changed to "dog" by people who did not understand the reference.

The dog rose produced a valuable fruit, the rose hip (the seed pod that forms when the flower has dropped away), which was esteemed for its flavor, its medicinal qualities, and its magical properties. When fruit was not readily available, the tart, spicy rose hip would have been a tasty treat, especially steeped in a tea. Dried and powdered and taken as a medicine, rose hips were used to treat a variety of ailments, among them diarrhea and dysentery and "weak stomachs." (Now, we know that they are a superb source of vitamin C.) Magically, rose hips were strung and worn as a necklace to attract love, while rose hip tea was believed to increase one's prophetic powers.

If your roses produce hips (many modern roses do not), they can be made into a delicious jam, jelly, marmalade, puree, syrup—and even soup! And of course, you can add them (chopped) to that cup of herbal tea you're brewing, especially if you're expecting to make a few prophesies.

**ROSE HIP SYRUP**
    4 cups rose hips
    2 cups water
    1 cup sugar

Wash rose hips and remove stems. Boil hips and water for 20 minutes in a covered glass or enamel saucepan. Strain, and return the juice to the pan. Add sugar, and stir until dissolved. Bring to a gentle boil and boil for five minutes. Cool and store in refrigerator. An especially tasty treat: ½ cup rose hip syrup stirred into 3 cups applesauce!

**Explore other old-fashioned things to do with roses:**
*Rose Recipes from Olden Times*, by Eleanour Sinclair Rohde

*If seeds in the black earth can turn into such beautiful roses, what might not the heart of man become in its long journey toward the stars?*

—G. K. CHESTERTON

## September's Theme Garden: A Zodiac Garden

There are several ways to design and plant a Zodiac Garden. You might, for example, choose to create a small garden of just those herbs that are ruled by your Sun sign. If you're a Taurus, for instance, you might have violets, roses, daisies, plantain, horehound, and thyme—the herbs listed for Taurus in the entry for April 20. If your Moon is in Aries, add one or two of the Mars-ruled Aries herbs; if your rising sign is in Cancer, add another herb from that group! You could also design and make, or purchase, a special symbol designating your Sun sign: a large flat rock or a brick, painted with your sign, works beautifully for this. If your garden is planted against a fence or a wall, your Sun sign could be painted on the wall.

Another kind of Zodiac Garden—one you might see at an herb farm or horticultural center, for instance—is larger and more ambitious. A large circular garden is divided (with planks, bricks, rocks, or narrow pathways) into twelve wedge-shaped sections, one for each of the signs of the zodiac: Aries, Taurus, Gemini, Cancer, Leo, Virgo, Libra, Scorpio, Sagittarius, Capricorn, Aquarius, and Pisces. Each of the sections contains herbs that are associated with that sign. A birdbath, a gazing globe, a sundial, or an armillary (an upright sundial) are all perfect centerpieces for such a garden. If you plant a garden of this design, you could designate your Sun, Moon, and rising signs with markers of your choice.

Even if you don't believe (as earlier peoples did) that the stars influence our lives, a Zodiac Garden honors the historical and traditional associations of herbs, the planets, and human experience, and acknowledges the important belief that all things are connected in a universe in which we are all parts of some larger whole.

**Read more about herbs and astrology:**

*Herbs of the Zodiac*, by Bertha Reppert, available from Rosemary House, Mechanicsburg, PA, www.rosemaryhouse.com

*A morning-glory at my window satisfies me more than the metaphysics of books.*

—WALT WHITMAN

*I forked the bacon out of the skillet onto a plate covered with a paper towel. We don't often eat bacon at home, but I operate on the hypothesis that when you're dining under an open sky, fat grams don't count. I poured out most of the grease, cracked a couple of eggs into the little that was left, let them cook for a minute, then slopped a glug of water into the hot skillet and clapped on the lid. Eggs cooked this way are steamed, sort of. If I'd been at home, I would have added fresh parsley and garlic chives, but McQuaid's camping pantry doesn't include such niceties.*

—INDIGO DYING: A CHINA BAYLES MYSTERY

## Garlic Chives

There's garlic (*Allium sativum*), and there are chives (*A. schoenoprasum*)—and then there are garlic chives (*A. tuberosum*, also called Chinese chives), which are brightening my garden with pretty globes of starry white flowers, dearly loved by the bees. For months now, I've been snipping the flat, narrow green leaves into salads, omelets, soups, and mashed potatoes, where they add color and a subtle garlic taste. The tender young leaves are best to cook with, so it's a good idea to shear the entire clump back to the ground every three or four weeks, to make sure that the leaves don't get tough and bitter. You can dry the snipped leaves for wintertime use, or pop them into small plastic bags and freeze them.

Now, about those tiny black seeds that will inevitably be produced by those pretty white flowers. You can collect them by tapping the drying seed head onto a plate, then sprout the seeds for spicy salad sprouts. Or you can clip the seed heads while they're still flowering, dry them in paper bags, shake out the seeds, and add the pretty heads to your herbal wreaths. Or you can let Nature take its course, in which case you will have more garlic chives than you know what to do with. (Of course, they do make lovely passalong plants.) In cold regions, they'll die back to the ground and pop up again in the spring. Every two or three years, dig and divide the clump.

Oh, by the way: Chinese herbalists use garlic chives to stimulate the appetite, improve digestion, and fight fatigue—another reason to plant and enjoy this ornamental culinary herb.

**Read about the Allium allies:**

*Garlic, Onion, and Other Alliums*, by Ellen Spector Platt

*The juice of Onions mix't with the decoction of Penniroyal . . . anointed upon a pild [bare] or bald head in the sun, bringeth the haire againe very speedily.*

—JOHN GERARD, *THE HERBAL*, 1597

# SEPTEMBER 5

*"Oh, wow!" Ruby gasped. "Ivy, these are beautiful!"*

*I pulled in my breath. Before us lay a dozen different botanical prints, in exquisite shades of greens and pastels, all on fine ivory paper. I picked up a print and studied it carefully. "Why, this looks as if it were made from an actual sprig of yarrow!" I picked up another. "And here's thyme. How gorgeous!"*

*"Do you think so?" Ivy asked, looking pleased. "I really enjoy making them. And yes, they're plant prints, made by inking the plant material and pressing it on paper. It's a very old art—the earliest example I know of is found in one of Leonardo Da Vinci's books."*

—"IVY'S WILD, WONDERFUL WEEDS," IN *AN UNTHYMELY DEATH AND OTHER GARDEN MYSTERIES*

## Plant Printing

Plant printing, described by Laura Donnelly Bethmann in her book, *Nature Printing with Herbs, Fruits & Flowers*, is a lovely way to preserve the herbs you've grown in your garden. Start by collecting some of your favorite garden plants. Fern, rosemary, sage, thyme, parsley, dandelion, oregano—these and others make beautiful prints. Once you've collected them, press them in a plant press or between the pages of a phone book for a week or so. When you're ready to print, assemble these items:

newspapers

water-soluble ink such as Speedball (it's best to start with one color, say, green)

a flat plate or piece of glass or tile

the pressed plants (make sure they're clean)

an artist's brush

tweezers

a few sheets of printmaking or art paper (your handmade paper would be nice!)

a few sheets of non-textured paper towel

Then do this:

- Spread newspapers over your working area. Squeeze or scoop a small blob of ink onto the plate, glass, or tile and brush it out evenly.
- Lay the plant material on the inked plate, veined-side up. With the brush, paint the ink evenly on the leaf, beginning at the center and working outward.
- Use the tweezers to gently lift the inked leaf and place it on the printing paper, veined-side down. Place a paper towel over the inked plant and gently press outward from the center. (Don't rub—you'll move the plant and smear the ink.)
- Remove the paper towel and use the tweezers to lift the plant. Let your print dry, frame it, and hang it where others can admire it.

Some project ideas: giftwrap, notecards, invitations, holiday cards, herbarium, calendars, printed fabric. Once you've begun creating your garden of nature prints, you'll think of dozens of other exciting things to do!

# SEPTEMBER 6

*Maggie and I landscaped the patio and the lot beside it with pots and beds of annual and perennial herbs—a large bay tree in an old wooden wine cask and low hedges of chives, parsley, and winter savory for the kitchen; fennel and lavender and thyme for the bees; borage and catnip and monarda for the hummingbirds.*

—LOVE LIES BLEEDING: A CHINA BAYLES MYSTERY

## Blue Stars

The blooming borage is full of happy bees this morning. The bright blue blossoms, star-shaped, make this one of the prettiest herbs. It's not fussy about soil, but it does like a spot that gets plenty of sun. And once you have it, you're likely to have more of it, for it reseeds readily, pollinated by the bees and hummingbirds, which adore the starry blossoms.

### CULINARY BORAGE
The leaves and starry flowers have a lovely cucumber-like taste. Use borage fresh; it loses its flavor when dried.

- Garnish cold summer drinks with borage flowers, and freeze them in ice cubes and ice rings.
- The flowers are pretty in salads and cold soups. Garnish cold tomato soup with thin slices of lemon, cucumber, and bright blue borage stars.
- The young leaves are a complementary garnish to cucumber soups.
- Sauté the very young leaves like spinach, or toss (raw) with other salad greens. Older leaves are tough and bitter.
- The flowers can be candied and used decoratively.

### MEDICINAL AND COSMETIC BORAGE
"Borage for courage" people used to say, and the plant belongs to a group of herbs called "cordials," which have a reputation for being "heartening." (Since borage was traditionally steeped in wine, perhaps it was the wine that imparted the courage.) Borage is also a valuable diuretic, for it is high in potassium. Applied to the skin, the sap soothes itches and insect bites. Borage oil is used in cosmetics; you might try using the leaves as a facial steam for improving dry skin. Pour boiling water over 1 cup fresh leaves in a bowl. Drape a towel over your head and allow the steam to penetrate your pores.

**For more about borage and all your other herbs:**
*The Rodale Herb Book*, edited by William H. Hylton

*Sprigs of Borage are of known virtue to revive the hypochondriac and cheer the hard student.*

—JOHN EVELYN, 1699

# SEPTEMBER 7

*Sage never looks better, I think, than when I come upon it in the early morning and find the pebbled leaves silvered over with a summer dew. In its way there is nothing more quietly individual in all the garden.*

—HENRY BESTON, *HERBS AND THE EARTH*

## A Sage Choice

If we voted for our favorite herbs, sage (*Salvia officinalis*) would probably come out very near the top. In the garden, sage grows into a low, rounded bush about 3–4 feet in diameter, so give your plant plenty of elbow room in a well-drained soil with lots of sun. It's a natural for a deck planter or an outside window box, if you trim it regularly. And of course, you'll be using those trimmings!

The seventeenth-century herbalist Culpeper said that sage "is of excellent use to help the memory" and "profitable for all pains in the head coming of cold rheumatic humours, as also for all pains in the joints." In fact, the herb's name comes from the word *salvere*, "to save." Sage is antibacterial, anti-inflammatory, and antioxidant. Modern research confirms many of its traditional uses.

Sage is a favorite seasoning for soups, vegetables, meats, fowl, and fruit. For a stunning appetizer, try these savory sage fritters, a modern version of a recipe that first appeared in a cookery book published in 1518, written by a cook who worked for wealthy families in Italy's northern provinces. The first English version may be the one for "Clary [Sage] Fritters" in Elizabeth Raffald's *Experienced English Housekeeper*, 1769. She suggests serving with "quarters of Seville oranges laid round them."

### SAGE FRITTERS

36 whole sage leaves, washed and dried (leave stems on, for easier handling)
1 cup beer
⅔ cup flour
¼ teaspoon cinnamon
salt and pepper, to taste
1 egg white, at room temp
vegetable oil for frying

Select whole, unblemished sage leaves with stems left on, for easy handling. Combine beer, flour, cinnamon, salt, and pepper, making a smooth batter. Let stand 15 minutes at room temperature. In a large skillet, heat 1 inch of oil to about 360°. Beat the egg white until it is stiff but not dry. Fold it into batter, and pour into a shallow dish. Lay a dozen of the leaves on the surface of the batter. Using tongs or large kitchen tweezers, turn to coat both sides. Fry in hot oil until crisp and golden brown on both sides. Drain on paper towels; serve hot.

**Read more about sage:**

*Growing and Using Sage: A Storey Country Wisdom Bulletin,* by Patricia R. Barrett

*"Of course it's real money."* Ruby was nettled. *"What do you expect to pay architects and contractors with? Vanilla beans?"*

—CHILE DEATH: A CHINA BAYLES MYSTERY

## Vanilla: Worth Its Weight in Silver

Vanilla (*Vanilla planifolia*) is so flavorful and fragrant that it's hard to imagine dessert without it. And in its native Mexico, it was so valuable that the Totonac Indians (the first to cultivate it) thought that it sprang from the blood of a princess, who was captured and slain when she fled with her lover. When the Totonac were conquered by the Aztecs, they were required to pay taxes and tributes with vanilla beans. Vanilla was literally worth its weight in silver.

The Spanish first became acquainted with vanilla as an ingredient in the bitter Aztec aphrodisiac drink, *xocolatl*, which was brewed with cacao beans and chile peppers. The tropical plant, a member of the orchid family could only be cultivated in Mexico, for the tubular flowers could be pollinated only by a tiny bee and a humming bird. In 1836, a twelve-year-old African slave in Madagascar figured out how to hand-pollinate the blossoms with a bamboo splinter, a method that is still used today. Vanilla is widely grown throughout the tropics, but it is still highly valuable. Some two thousand tons are produced each year, but that is still not enough to satisfy people's desire for it, and many have to be satisfied with synthetic vanillin.

China enjoys making her own vanilla extract, using vanilla beans. This is her recipe:

### CHINA'S FAVORITE VANILLA EXTRACT

Using a funnel, pour 1 cup brandy or rum into a small-diameter bottle. Split 2–3 vanilla beans lengthwise, then cut the split pieces into halves, retaining the aromatic seeds. Drop pieces and seeds into the bottle and cap it tightly. Set on a dark shelf for several weeks, shaking frequently (and sniffing deeply whenever possible). Use when the flavor suits you, topping off each time you remove some. Every now and then add a piece or two of split vanilla bean, to enrich the flavor.

**Read more about vanilla:**

*Vanilla: The Cultural History of the World's Favorite Flavor and Fragrance*, by Patricia Rain

*Vanilla: Travels in Search of the Ice Cream Orchid*, by Tim Ecott

*Ah, you flavor everything; you are the vanilla of society.*

—SYDNEY SMITH, 1771–1845

# SEPTEMBER 9

*Roses to be used for potpourri should be the most fragrant ones. First in choice is the old cabbage or Provence rose (Rosa centifolia), large and, true to its name, has at least a hundred petals of a rich pink hue.*

—ROSEMARY E. CLARKSON, *MAGIC GARDENS*

## The Sweet Pot

There are two ways of making potpourri: the "moist" method and the "dry" method. Dry potpourri is a quick, easy way to create a pretty bowl of fragrant dried floral buds, petals, and other pretties. The moist method is the true potpourri, however, for the word *pourri* literally means "rotted" or "fermented": hence, a pot of fermented flowers, sometimes called a "sweet pot." This traditional method takes more time and the result isn't pretty enough to display. So it is usually kept in an opaque container, with the lid removed to allow the fragrance to diffuse. The fragrance is more subtle, however, and it lasts longer.

**TO MAKE A SWEET POT**
What you need:
a half-gallon wide-mouthed glass jar or crock with a lid
a wooden spoon
about a cup of coarse salt (kosher or sea salt, mixed half-and-half with noniodized table salt)
6 cups of fragrant flower petals, dried until leathery
¼ cup vodka

essential oil of rose, lavender, orange (if the flowers are not sufficiently fragrant)
3–4 tablespoons of mixed spices: nutmeg, cloves, cinnamon, allspice, crushed anise, coriander, or cardamom seeds, crushed vanilla bean, orange or lemon curls

How to do it: Put a ½-inch layer of petals in the bottom of the jar and cover with 1–2 tablespoons of salt. Over this, sprinkle a teaspoon of vodka and a drop or two of essential oil (if desired). Repeat. With the wooden spoon, press down the mass and put on the lid. Set aside to cure for 10 days, stirring daily. At the end of the 10 days, add the spices and stir thoroughly. Put the lid back on and set aside for six weeks. To use, put into pretty china or an earthenware pot with a lid; remove the lid to scent the room with the fragrance of your summer garden.

**Read more about using the fragrance of flowers:**
*Potpourri and Fragrant Crafts*, by Betsy Williams

*Take a glassful of Rose Water, Cloves well beaten to a powder, a penny weight; then take the fire panne and make it red hot in the fyre, and put thereon of the said Rose water with the sayd powder of Cloves making it so as to consume little by little, but the rose water must be muskt [musk], and you shall make a parfume of excellent good odour.*

—*A QUEEN'S DELIGHT*, 1665

# SEPTEMBER 10

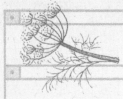

## The Merryweathers Pick a Peck of Pestos!

At their September meeting every year, the Merry-weathers set out a big basket of mini-crostini, line up their pots of pestos, and have a pesto-tasting, with each one voting for her favorite. This is always an exciting event, because nobody can predict what fantastic new recipes people are likely to come up with. "Pesto isn't just for pasta," Patsy Pride always says. "And basil is definitely not the only pesto herb." To which Fannie Couch always adds: "Whoever said 'The soul of pesto may be basil, but its heart is garlic' has a limited number of taste buds!"

In Italian, the word *pesto* simply means "paste"—and many herbs can be "pasted." For the classic basil pesto, check out Marge Clark's recipe in the July 31 entry. But there are many other pesto possibilities. The Merryweathers picked three pestos as top of the pack:

First place: Felicity Firestone's Fennel and Tomato Pesto (recipe below)
Second place: Ethel Gramling's Caraway Thyme Pesto
Third place: Sandy Kinky's Pistachio Mint Pesto
Voted too hot to handle: Cilantro Habanero Sunflower Seed Pesto

## FENNEL AND TOMATO PESTO

2 tablespoons fennel seeds
1 cup hot water
1 large fennel bulb, chopped
1 cup fresh parsley
2 medium cloves garlic
¼ cup freshly grated Parmesan cheese
¼ cup pecans
½ cup olive oil
freshly ground pepper and salt or Savory Blend (August 29)
½ cup sun-dried tomatoes, finely chopped

Cover fennel seeds with hot water and set aside. Steam chopped fennel bulb 4–5 minutes, or microwave 3 minutes. Put into food processor with drained fennel seeds, parsley, garlic, cheese, and nuts. Process to mix. With machine running, slowly add olive oil. Season to taste with salt and pepper. Add chopped tomatoes and let stand for 10 minutes before serving. If serving over pasta, add a little hot pasta water or milk to thin.

**Pesto isn't just for pasta. Learn how to use it:**
*Pestos! Cooking with Herb Pastes*, by Dorothy Rankin

*He who eats pesto never leaves Genoa.*
—ITALIAN PROVERB

# SEPTEMBER 11

*I should like to enjoy this summer flower by flower, as if it were to be the last one for me.*

—ANDRÉ GIDE

## Forever Herbs and Flowers

The garden is in full flower, the herbs are lush and fragrant, and you'd love to capture and hold those delightful shapes and colors forever. You can, simply by picking and pressing the plants in a phone directory or other large book and using them for flower crafts. (For ideas, see December 20.)

### PRESSING HERBS

Pick the herbs on a dry morning, at their peak. Arrange them on a sheet of paper, giving some thought to how they will look when they've been pressed. Place a second sheet over the first and insert the sandwich into a large book (the phone book is traditional), stack more books on top, and do something else for a week or so. If you're in a hurry, try the microwave method. Place the plant-paper sandwich between the pages of a hardcover book. (Avoid books that contain metallic materials.) Put the book in the microwave and weight with another book or heavy glass dish. Set at medium-high for two minutes. Repeat as necessary, letting the book cool before removing the herbs.

### THE PRESSED FLOWER GARDEN

You'll have your own favorite garden and wayside plants. These are some of the flowering herbs I enjoy growing and using in pressed flower projects. Parsley, dill, and fern are indispensable.

| ANNUALS | PERENNIALS |
|---|---|
| Queen Anne's lace | Yarrow |
| Calendula | Daisy |
| Cornflower | Carnation |
| Cosmos | Goldenrod |
| Candytuft | Violet |
| Sweet Pea | Passionflower |
| Honesty | |
| Salvia | |
| French marigold | |

**Read more about pressing herbs and flowers:**
*Pressed Flowers*, by Pamela Le Bailly
*Forever Flowers: A Flower Lover's Guide to Selecting, Pressing, and Designing,* by Bernice Peitzer

*In this month the Gardener has great variety of Business and must employ his Head as well as his Hands toward furnishing his Kitchen Garden with everything necessary for Winter Use.*

—THE GENTLEMAN'S AND GARDENER'S KALENDAR, 1724

# SEPTEMBER 12

*"Guess it's time to make some more vinegar," I said. Making and bottling herb vinegars is one of my favorite evening tasks, and I love looking at the rows of sparkling bottles. It must be the same satisfaction that country women have when they look at the rows of canned green beans on the cellar shelves.*

—THYME OF DEATH: A CHINA BAYLES MYSTERY

## Herb Vinegars

If you've made fruit vinegars, you'll find that making herb vinegars is even easier. Start now, and in the next two or three weeks, you'll be able to present each of your friends with a unique handmade gift.

What you need:
purchased vinegars: red-wine, white-wine, sherry, cider
herbs: choose among basil, garlic, tarragon, dill, chives, fennel, salad burnet, borage, mint, sage, lavender, nasturtium flowers and leaves, thyme, rosemary, parsley, chervil, marjoram, chiles
recycled, sterilized wide-mouthed jars (quart, half-gallon, gallon), with lids
glass or plastic measuring cups
plastic funnels
coffee filters
cheesecloth
plastic and wooden spoons
labels
pretty bottles with caps or corks

How to do it:
   Put the fresh, clean herbs into a jar (1 cup fresh herbs to 1 quart vinegar) and add vinegar. Label the jar and place on a sunny windowsill, where the heat of the sun will help extract the oils from the herbs. Turn frequently, and test for flavor in two weeks. Strain herbs, then filter the vinegar through a coffee filter into a pretty bottle. Add a sprig or two of fresh herbs, cap or cork, and a label. For gift-giving, use raffia or ribbon to tie on a gift card made with pressed herbs.

Some zesty combinations:
· Red-wine vinegar with basil, garlic, and savory; rosemary, sage, bay, and garlic; cilantro, rosemary, bay, and chile peppers; thyme, rosemary, oregano, and basil.
· White-wine vinegar with dill, lemon basil, lemon balm; orange mint, orange zest, cardamom seeds, and garlic; chives, chive blossoms, elder flowers, lemon balm.
· Sherry vinegar with allspice berries, cloves, cinnamon, rosemary; basil, tarragon, and garlic.
· Cider vinegar with horseradish, garlic, and chile peppers; garlic, dill, pickling spices.

**More Reading:**
*Herbal Vinegar: Flavored Vinegars, Mustards, Chutneys, Preserves, Conserves, Salsas, Cosmetic Uses, Household Tips*, by Maggie Oster

# SEPTEMBER 13

## Going Places: Long Creek Herb Farm, Blue Eye, Missouri

It takes a little doing to get to Jim Long's herbal homestead, hidden away in the oak-and-hickory woods along the Missouri-Arkansas border, but the people who make their way there know that it's worth the effort. The gardens are lovely, the woods are delightful, and a sweet, fragrant silence lies over all. The place is so beautiful that it has been featured in such national magazines as *Southern Living*, *Country Living Gardener*, and *Gourmet*.

Jim Long worked as a landscape architect before he bought Long Creek and retired to the life of an herb farmer, but "retired" is not a word you'd use to describe him. Throughout the warm season, he and his partner, Josh Young, welcome guests (individually and in groups) to the gardens where they grow the herbs that they transform into soaps, insect repellents, dream pillows, herbal seasoning blends, pet products, and much more. When you visit the farm, you'll find these in the rustic Herb Shop, where herbs hang from the ceiling and fill the shelves (you can also find them on the farm's web site, at www.longcreekherbs.com) Jim and Josh are always busy tending their Ozark farmstead, cultivating and working with herbs, and enjoying every minute of every day.

But Jim is also a talented speaker and writer, and many people consider themselves friends of the farm because they know it through his lectures, numerous books (some 28 to date), and magazine and syndicated newspaper columns. He's also an herbal historian. Among his books, three are my personal favorites: *Herbal Medicines of the Civil War*; *Herbal Medicines on the Santa Fe Trail*; and *"It will do no harm to try it": The Home Remedies Diary of Elias Slagle, 1859*. Jim found Slagle's diary in a museum and has spent six years studying it. He writes:

> Hidden within the pages of the crumbling old diary are bits of humor, insights into fear of diseases of that time, and hope found in the plants that might deter or cure a particular illness. He records the use of ginger, pine tar, cayenne pepper, cinnamon, horseradish, rhubarb, myrrh, wild cherry bark, camphor, quinine, mullein, cabbage, lemons, mustard and many more. (From "Mysteries in the Old Diary," *Herb Companion Magazine*)

It is Jim's knowledge and appreciation of the past and his generosity in sharing it that makes him such a special person and Long Creek Herb Farm such a special place. Be sure and check the web site—www.longcreekherbs.com—for open hours. Advance reservations are required to visit the gardens and the shop. While you're on the web site, take a few minutes to look at garden photos and read some of Jim's columns, and bookmark the page so you can go back often.

*It is commonly called saponaria, of the great scouring qualitie that the leaves have: for they yield out of themselves a certain juyce when they are bruised, which scoureth almost as well as sope.*

—JOHN GERARD, *HERBAL*, 1597

## My Lady's Washbowl

Before the invention of alkali-based soap, many peoples used natural soaps: the saps and juices of plants rich in saponins, which produce lather and have cleansing properties. On America's western plains, the root of the yucca plant was regularly used as soap, while in Mexico and South America, it was the leathery brown leaves of the soapberry tree (*Sapindus saponaria*). In California, five species and five varieties of the "soap lily" (*Chlorogalum*) grow in the coastal shrub community. In the Andes, the dried inner bark of the soapbark tree (*Quillaja saponaria*), is used for soap and has also been employed in fire-extinguishing solutions. And in the Far East, the soapnut tree (*Sapindus mukorossi*) is used to clean silver and as a detergent for shawls and silks. The saponins in these plants are toxic, and indigenous peoples have often thrown them into the water to stun fish for easy catching.

### BOUNCING BET

But it's the soapwort, or Bouncing Bet (*Saponaria officinalis*) that you're likely to have in your herb garden.

The plant is indigenous to Western Asia and Europe but was cultivated in colonial gardens of North America and is now widely naturalized. The lather is obtained from all parts of the plant, which is blooming a bright pink just now, in my Texas garden, very pretty among the darker green leaves.

Bouncing Bet is a country name for "washerwoman," and the plant's other folk names—my lady's washbowl, latherwort, crow's soap, and fuller's herb—all reflect its long use as a cleansing agent. The herb was grown around woolen mills, where fullers used it to clean and thicken woolen fabric, and in Switzerland, where it was used to wash sheep before shearing. Soapwort was employed as a treatment for eczema, psoriasis, and acne, and used by Native Americans in a poultice for abdominal pain. Like other saponaceous plants, soapwort is mildly toxic, but that didn't keep the Germans (and the Pennsylvania Dutch, as well) from adding it to beer to create a foamier head. Now, museum curators use it to clean delicate antique fabrics.

In the language of flowers, Bouncing Bet means (what else?) cleanliness.

*The easiest way to discover soapwort's soap is to pick a handful of leaves and flowers. Wet them and rub them between your hands. A fresh, grassy scent and cool green lather will arise. Try it on dirty hands and faces—it cleans.*

—SUSAN TYLER HITCHCOCK, *GATHER YE WILD THINGS*

# SEPTEMBER 15

*It is, indeed, a jewel. Upon the approach of twilight each leaf droops as if wilted, and from the notches along its edge the crystal beads begin to grow, until its border is hung full with its gems. It is Aladdin's lantern that you see among a bed of these succulent green plants, for the spectacle is like a dream land.*

—WILLIAM HAMILTON GIBSON, *OUR NATIVE ORCHIDS*, 1905

## A Jewel of a Weed

Gibson's description may be . . . well, a little extravagant. Still, jewelweed *(Impatiens capensis)* has a beautiful orchidlike flower, and the plant's widely known ability to take the itch out of poison ivy and insect bites does give it a special status.

People who live in jewelweed's range (the Eastern seaboard, west to Oklahoma) know this herb by two other common and self-explanatory names: touch-me-not and snapweed. The ripe seed pods burst at a touch, snapping their seeds for distances of up to four feet—a habit that explains why this plant is so invasive. In the garden, one jewelweed will quickly lead to dozens, so unless you're fond of pulling seedlings, you might want to pass on this one. Enjoy the plant in its woodland haunts, where it grows in moist, shady areas.

You can easily use jewelweed to solve your poison ivy problems. On the spot, just rub the affected area with the fresh leaves. Gather additional leaves—better yet, the just-flowering tops—and use them to brew a strong bath tea: four cups of boiling water poured over a cup of the fresh herb, steeped for 15 minutes. Strain and pour into your bath for a fragrant, cleansing soak. Keep the extra tea in the refrigerator for a month or more, or freeze the tea in ice cube trays for those days in early spring when poison ivy is at its most potent. You can also use it to make an ointment or a salve.

**Find out more about jewelweed and other native herbs:**
*Hedgemaids and Fairy Candles: The Lives and Lore of North American Wildflowers,* by Jack Sanders

*About the edges of the yellow corn,*
*And o'er the gardens grown somewhere outworn*
*The bees went hurrying to fill up their store;*
*The apple boughs bent over more and more . . .*

—WILLIAM MORRIS

# SEPTEMBER 16

*Almost all connoisseurs*
*Savor anise liqueurs,*
*Perhaps amiss. It's anise*
*And not licorice,*
*Giving licorice liqueurs their allures.*
—JAMES DUKE, *LIVING LIQUEURS*

## Anise

Licorice-flavored anise (*Pimpinella anisum*) is an herb that is undistinguished in the garden but calls attention to itself when it appears on the plate. In Roman times, aniseed was used as a spice, especially in the *mustacae*, the spiced cake served after banquets to ease indigestion; it may be a precursor of the modern wedding cake. It is mentioned in the Bible (Matthew 23:23) as a payment of taxes and land rents, although most scholars think this is a mistranslation, and that dill is meant. Aniseed was believed to ward off evil.

The aromatic seed was especially prized in northern Europe, where it had to be imported because the plant doesn't readily set seed in northern climates. In the thirteenth century, the repair of London Bridge was funded by a tax on imported condiments, including aniseed. Edward IV's royal linen was scented with "lytill bagges of fustian stuffed with anneys," and there was a heavy import duty on the seed until the 1700s.

Even if your anise refuses to set seed, the foliage makes a deliciously licorice-flavored tea and vinegar, and can be added to fruit salads. Aniseed is a favorite flavoring for liqueurs; to make your own, steep six tablespoons of crushed aniseeds in a quart of brandy.

Interestingly, aniseed (once used as a mouse bait) is employed in the sport of "drag-hunting" in England. In the early 1900s, the drag was described as "a red herring in a hare-skin with a little aniseed." Foxhounds are familiar with anise, according to Elizabeth Hayes, in *Spices and Herbs*, for they are trained to follow a trail made by dragging a sack saturated with anise oil.

To grow in your garden, plant the seeds in early spring, in rich soil and full sun, well away from the local hounds.

**Read more about the lore and uses of spices:**
*Spices and Herbs: Lore & Cookery*, by Elizabeth S. Hayes

*The decayed Flower-stems of Hyssop, Savory, Lavenders and other aromatic Plants of that kind, should be cut down, and all the straggling and other young Shoots should be shortened. . . . But remember to do this in a moist Time, if possible.*
—THE GARDENERS KALENDAR, 1777

*As a child, Lunaria was a favorite flower, for it afforded to us juvenile money. Indeed, it was generally known among us as Money-flower or Money-seed, or sometimes as Money-in-both-pockets. The seed valves formed our medium of exchange and trade, passing as silver dollars.*

—ALICE MORSE EARLE, *OLD TIME GARDENS*

## Honesty, Honestly

My mother grew honesty in her garden. It would have bloomed about now, its translucent, silvery seed disks shimmering like full moons. It is an old-fashioned plant that was once common to English cottage gardens—there is one growing in the garden of Beatrix Potter's Hill Top Farm. In a letter to a friend, she tells how she got the plant: "Mrs. Satterthwaite says stolen plants always grow, I stole some 'honesty' yesterday, it was put to be burnt in a heap of garden refuse!" Honesty blooms in early summer, with lavender, pink, or white flowers. The translucent seed pods that follow are perfect in dried bouquets.

This is another of those plants-with-a-dozen-names. Its Latin name, *Lunaria*, is derived from "moon," and one of its names—moonwort—refers to its shimmering moonlike seed disks. But because the seeds resemble coins, it is also called money flower, money plant, or penny flower. In *Old Time Gardens*, Alice Morse Earle tells a poignant story about an old man named Elmer, who was (in the language of the times) addle-pated. He slept in barns, proffered the seeds of the money plant in return for the loaves of bread and jugs of milk he "bought" in the village, and was fond of saying that he had hundreds of silver dollars put away for the winter. The villagers understood what he meant by this and humored him, but one day some tramps overheard him talking about his wealth and killed him for it. "Scattered around him," Earle writes sadly, "were hundreds of the seeds of his autumnal store of the money plant; these were all the silver dollars his assailants found."

No one—not even the Oxford English Dictionary, that font of linguistic wisdom—seems to know where the name "honesty" came from. All we have is John Gerard's report, in his *Herbal* of 1597: "We cal this herb in English Pennie Flour . . . and among our women it is called Honestie." I wonder whether poor old Elmer was the only man ever killed for his honesty.

**Read more of Alice Earle's fascinating recollections:**
*Old Time Gardens*, by Alice Morse Earle

*"Mrs. Satterthwaite says stolen plants always grow, I stole some 'honesty' yesterday . . . I have had something out of nearly every garden in the village."*

—BEATRIX POTTER, IN A LETTER TO HER FRIEND
MILLIE WARNE, OCTOBER 12, 1906

*Mints are like stray cats; you take them in, give them some food, and they are yours forever.*

—ART TUCKER

## The Ubiquitous Mint

Mint is so universally valued that it is grown by cooks and herbalists everywhere. If you don't already have mint in your herb garden (for heaven's sake, why not?), this is a good time to remedy that deficiency. Transplanted now, mint will have time to settle in before the winter.

Of course, you'll want to take precautions. Mint is like the proverbial camel: Once it has its nose under the tent, the rest arrives shortly. Control its spread with metal or wooden barriers, and be ruthless about removing stolons. If you don't want the extra work, grow it in a hanging basket or large, shallow pot.

Peppermint (*Mentha piperita*) is the medicinal mint. Its menthol soothes digestive troubles, freshens the breath, relieves chest congestion, and has a calming effect. A steaming cup of peppermint tea not only tastes good but also works wonders when you're coming down with a cold. Spearmint (*Mentha spicata*)— the "Wrigley's Spearmint" herb—is more often used as a culinary herb. It's a standby for mint jelly, mint sauce, mint julep, and mint punch. Both plants can be dried, but their flavor is much more pronounced when they're fresh. Some other mints you will enjoy: apple mint, lavender mint, chocolate mint, pineapple mint, banana mint, lemon bergamot mint, and wooly apple mint. These flavored mints should be renewed every year, since they are easily cross-pollinated and the seedlings do not come true.

And then there's pennyroyal (*Mentha pulegium*). It has long had a reputation as a flea-fighter; *pulegium* means flea. It was used in bedding, as a strewing herb, and as an insect spray. However, it is also a powerful abortifacient, and can be toxic. You'll sometimes find it recommended as a culinary herb, but it's safer to avoid internal use, especially during pregnancy.

**MINTED WATERMELON AND CUCUMBER SALAD**

4 cucumbers, peeled, halved, seeded, sliced

8 cups watermelon, seeded, cubed

¼ red onion, sliced thin

salt

Slice cucumbers and toss with 1 teaspoon of salt. Let sit in colander about 30 minutes, then pat dry. Just before serving, place cubed watermelon in large bowl and sprinkle with salt to taste. Toss with cucumbers, red onions, and mint dressing.

**Learn about mint and other herbs of the Southern garden:**

*Southern Herb Growing,* by Madalene Hill and Gwen Barclay

*Dead man's bones is the folk name given to the herb Greater stitchwort (Stellaria holostea) . . . The name was perhaps derived from a confusion with another plant that was traditionally used to treat fractures, or because the stems were brittle and easily snapped, like the dried bones of the dead.*

—DEAD MAN'S BONES: A CHINA BAYLES MYSTERY

## Dead Man's Bones: About China's Books

*Dead Man's Bones* is about . . . well, bones. There's a skeleton in a cave, and skeletons in several closets, and a great many hidden things that must be discovered. The signature herb (*Stellaria holostea*) is only tangentially connected to bones, but many of the other herbs that appear in the book play a role in helping to treat skeletal disorders.

Declining estrogen is one of the causes of bone loss. Herbs that have estrogenic effects include black cohosh, dong quai, burdock root, Chinese ox knee root, alfalfa, and motherwort. Red clover has been shown to increase cortical bone, while numerous studies have confirmed that soy slows bone loss. Nettle, alfalfa, oatstraw, horsetail, and slippery elm have been traditionally recommended to enhance the body's minerals.

Other herbs are prescribed to reduce inflammation and relieve the pain of rheumatoid arthritis and osteoarthritis. Turmeric, Devil's claw (an African herb), and boswellia (a tree native to India, Africa, and the Middle East, which yields a resin known as sallai guggal) are among these. Recent scientific studies have confirmed the traditional use of willow bark, ginger, Saint-John's-wort, evening primrose, borage, and black current as effective inflammation suppressors. The remedy most thoroughly studied is capsaicin, the highly regarded pain-reliever in chile peppers.

Foods play a therapeutic role in maintaining strong bones. Green leafy vegetables such as kale, parsley, collard greens, and mustard greens offer significant protection against osteoporosis, "brittle bone disease." Ruby Wilcox (who believes that every little bit helps) came up with a soup that includes some of these phytomedicines. You'll find her recipe in *Dead Man's Bones*.

**Learn more about better bones:**
*Healthy Bones & Joints: A Natural Approach to Treating Arthritis, Osteoporosis, Tendonitis, Myalgia & Bursitis*, by David Hoffman

# SEPTEMBER 20

## Sweet Annie Wreaths

When I first began crafting with herbs, I took a class in wreath-making that inspired me to design and create my own herbal wreaths. I like to work with grapevine wreath forms. To cover the form, I use sweet Annie (*Artemisia annua*), which has also been used extensively in China as a treatment for malaria.

Valuable as sweet Annie is medicinally, I prize the decorative properties of its feathery, fragrant foliage, which is as attractive dried as fresh. Used fresh, when it's pliant, it's a perfect filler material for my wreaths. I simply let it dry on the wreath, along with the fresh decorative and accent herbs I've tucked among its ferny branches. It turns a lovely brown, a perfect background. If you prefer a silvery wreath, you'll want to choose Silver King or Silver Queen artemisia; if a pale green, try oregano.

**YOU'LL NEED:**

filler herb: sweet Annie, Silver King or Silver Queen artemisia, or oregano

decorative herbs: lavender, rosemary, statice, baby's breath, ornamental oreganos, vitex, butterfly weed

accent herbs: roses, lamb's-ears leaves and flowers, gold yarrow, gold tansy buttons, strawflowers, bay

a wreath form, 12"-16" in diameter (grapevine is my favorite)

a wire coat hanger, to make the hanging loop

flexible florist's wire

wire wreath pins

needle-nosed pliers and wire nippers

glue gun (optional)

decorative ribbon bow (optional)

newspaper to cover working surface

**HOW TO ASSEMBLE YOUR WREATH:**

Collect herbs (filler, decorative, and accent) on a dry, cool day. Cover your working surface with newspaper, and lay the wreath form flat. With the nippers, cut the coat hanger into an 8-inch length, bend it into the shape of a hanger hook and insert it firmly into the grapevine form. Beginning at the bottom and working in both directions, push the stiff stem ends of the filler herb into the form, covering it very thickly. (All herbs shrink as they dry.) If the filler seems loose, secure with wire pins. Then hang the wreath and begin inserting the decorative herbs, pinning or gluing where necessary. Finally, insert the accent herbs. If you're using a bow, add it now. Hang and admire!

**Read more about wreath-making:**

*The Complete Book of Wreaths,* by Chris Rankin

In some years, this is the joyous Jewish holiday, Rosh Hashanah, celebrated on the first day of the month of Tishri.

## Rosh Hashanah

Over the centuries, the first dinner of this harvest festival celebrated God's gift of food in abundance, the seven blessed species that are cited in Deuteronomy 8:8: wheat and barley, vine and fig trees and pomegranates, olive trees, and honey. The celebration begins with a festive meal at which these foods are eaten, and always includes the *challah*, a loaf of bread that commemorates the offerings of the High Priest in the Temple at Jerusalem.

There are as many recipes for *challah* as there are Jewish families, but most include wheat flour, yeast, oil, honey, salt, and eggs. Raisins are often included, and in some families, there is a tradition of using seven seeds, echoing the theme of seven blessings. Here are the seeds frequently used:

- Sesame seeds are among the oldest condiments, dating to 1600 BCE. Tiny, flat oval seeds with a nutty taste, they may be white, yellow, black, and red. They are pressed to release a valuable oil.
- Poppy seeds were used as a condiment as early as the first century CE. It is derived from the opium poppy, but the seeds contain none of the narcotic.

- Nigella's black seeds are spicy with a licorice fragrance, like anise or fennel. A favorite of early Egyptians, they have been used as a digestive aid, an appetite stimulant, and a cure-all remedy.
- Caraway, distinctively aromatic, is often recognized as the most typical spice of German-speaking countries, used in baked goods, as well vegetables, especially cabbage. The "seeds" are really small fruits.
- Anise seeds (fruits) are mostly used to flavor baked goods and liqueurs.
- Fennel seeds (fruits), native to the Mediterranean, were known to the earliest peoples. It is used in breads, sauces, and in pickling.
- Coriander seeds (fruits) taste like lemony sage. In Exodus 16:31, the manna that fell from heaven is described as "white like coriander seed."

**Read more about Jewish food:**
*Eat and Be Satisfied: A Social History of Jewish Food*, by John Cooper

*I am sorry to say that Peter was not very well during the evening. His mother put him to bed, and made some camomile tea; and she gave a dose of it to Peter! "One table-spoonful to be taken at bed-time."*

—BEATRIX POTTER, *THE TALE OF PETER RABBIT*

## Comforting Chamomile

Chamomile (*Matricaria chamamilla*) is a sweet-smelling herb that has been used for centuries to heal and soothe, both inside and out. Even though the plant is small, its pervasive, long-lasting fragrance—it smells like ripe apples—made it a favorite strewing herb. It was often planted around benches in pleasure gardens, so that the scent filled the air and comforted the weary garden-goer. And a sprig of apple-sweet chamomile tucked into the lapel or carried in a tussie-mussie provided a good antidote to the uglier smells of the city.

Although chamomile was never used as a culinary herb, it has had a long reputation as a medicinal plant. The Egyptians and Romans made it into a wound ointment and drank it as a tea to treat liver and bladder ailments. In England, the Saxons used it to ease the eyes and to treat toothache. But chamomile's most important medicinal application does not appear until the sixteenth century, when it began to be used for children's colic, for dysentery, and as a calmative—just what poor Peter needed, after his exhausting adventures in Mr. McGregor's garden!

Chamomile is also valued as a cosmetic. In a facial steam, Ruby Wilcox finds that it soothes and refreshes tired skin. She places a half cup of dried flowers in a bowl and covers them with boiling water. Then she drapes her head with a towel and sits for ten minutes over the bowl, as she listens to her favorite country-western music. Other herbs she sometimes adds to this reviving facial steam: comfrey, fennel, sage, peppermint.

And in case you're wondering, there are various ways to spell the word: chamomile and camomile—and camomella, camayle, canalilla, and canamille. However you spell its name, the herb still smells sweet!

**Read more about chamomile and other herbs:**
*Old Time Herbs for Northern Gardens*, by Minnie Watson Kamm

*If acorns abound in September, snow will be deep in December.*

—TRADITIONAL WEATHER LORE

Today, the Sun enters the sign of Libra. It is also the Fall Equinox, and the first day of autumn.

*The seventh sign of the zodiac, the feminine sign Libra (the Scales) is ruled by Venus. A cardinal sign, Libra is associated with aesthetic beauty, balance, culture, harmony, and enjoyment of social pleasures. It is an air sign, suggesting that while Libra people may be urbane, diplomatic, and charming, they may also be indecisive, changeable, and unreliable.*

—RUBY WILCOX, "ASTROLOGICAL SIGNS"

## Libra Herbs

Venus-ruled Libra has traditionally been related to the endocrine system, the thyroid, kidneys, urinary tract, and bladder. Venus (which also rules Taurus) is responsible for the harmonious interrelationships among the various body systems. Here are some Libra herbs:

- Thyme (*Thyme vulgaris*). Thyme is a powerful antiseptic used in many medicinal preparations. A tea may relieve menstrual cramps and help relax the muscles of the gastrointestinal tract. Thymol (thyme's powerful phytochemical) has valuable antioxidant, antibacterial, and antifungal properties. It is currently used as an ingredient in mouth-care products and feminine douche powders.
- Goldenseal (*Hydrastis canadensis*). A native American herb, goldenseal was first used by the Cherokees. It is particularly useful in toning the glandular system. It has been used as a general tonic to treat inflamed mucous membranes of the mouth, throat, vagina, and digestive system, as well as a treatment for jaundice and ulcers.
- Cranberry (*Vaccinium macrocarpon*). Research shows that cranberry juice helps to prevent urinary tract infections. The berries are high in vitamin C.
- Other Libra herbs. Corn silk tea is a soothing diuretic and has been used to sooth urinary irritations. Stone root and gravel root both have a centuries-old history of use in the treatment of gall stones and gravel. Barberry and Oregon grape are used to treat bladder diseases.

*We who have seen men walk on the moon are not likely to recover so much faith in the stars that we would entrust our health to them, yet we can still find fascination and significance in astrology, even in this skeptical, scientific age.*

—JOHN LUST, *THE HERB BOOK*

# SEPTEMBER 24

## Garden Whimsies

If you're fortunate enough to share your garden with children (your own, your grandchildren, or a neighbor's), you know the pleasure of sharing the child's enjoyment of herbs and flowers—and you may play a role in shaping that child's understanding of the natural world. Do you remember your own childhood delights in the garden? These are some of mine, gathered from hours spent playing with my cousin Mary Jean in our grandmother's Missouri garden.

- Hollyhock dolls. Grandma's hollyhocks were ruffled beauties that made the most marvelous dolls. An upside-down bloom made the doll's frilly skirt. Two closed buds, speared on a toothpick, made her bodice and head, and we pushed a short piece of wire through her bodice (ouch!) to serve as her arms. Bent, her tiny "hands" could hold tinier blossoms, and she wore a petal apron and hat, with pretty blades of grass for ribbons and bits of fern for lace. Sometimes our dolls carried purses made of bleeding heart blossoms, or pulled little boats made of nutshells.

- Aunt Daisy. We pinched the petals into the shape of bonnets, with two long ones for ties, and drew eyes and a smile on the yellow center. Sometimes we impaled the faces on sticks stuck in the ground, making dozens of Aunt Daisies!

- Clover, clover, come over. We picked clover flowers and slit the stem just below the head. Then we pushed another stem through the slit, continuing until we had a five-foot chain we could use as a jump rope (carefully). We'd jump, calling out "clover, clover, come over!"

- Hideaways. We always had hideaways in the garden, under a rosebush or at the end of a row of cucumbers or in a pretty tent made of autumn leaves. We filled small cardboard boxes with treasures—snail shells, acorn cups, a butterfly wing, a piece of lichen—and hid them, with confidential notes written to our favorite fairies.

**Gardens and kids are a natural combination:**

*Roots, Shoots, Buckets & Boots: Gardening Together with Children*, by Sharon Lovejoy

# SEPTEMBER 25

The fourth Sunday in September is Good Neighbor Day.

> *As for Rosmarine, I lett it runne all over my garden walls, not onlie because my bees love it, but because it is the herb sacred to remembrance, and, therefore to friendship.*
>
> —SIR THOMAS MORE, 1478–1535

## Rosemary and Friendship

If you're wondering what you might give your neighbors and friends in token of Good Neighbor day, here are a few suggestions using rosemary, the herb of friendship.

- a rosemary plant in a decorative pot
- a pretty bottle of rosemary and opal basil vinegar
- notepaper printed with rosemary (see September 5)
- a living wreath made with rosemary (see September 20)
- a rosemary bubble bath (see January 8)
- a plate of Rosemary Friendship Squares, with sprigs of rosemary and a bow

### ROSEMARY FRIENDSHIP SQUARES

This recipe is reprinted with permission from *Cooking with Herbs*, by the Goose Creek Herb Guild in Leesburg, Virginia. I spent a memorable morning with the Guild a few years ago, helping to celebrate their 25th anniversary. I remember their friendly welcome with a great deal of pleasure.

2 eggs
1 cup brown sugar
2 teaspoons vanilla
1 cup flour
½ teaspoon salt
1 teaspoon baking powder
1 heaping tablespoon minced fresh rosemary
1 cup candied fruit and raisins
⅔ cup chopped pecans

Preheat oven to 350°. Grease and flour an 8 × 8-inch baking pan. Beat eggs vigorously, adding brown sugar gradually. Add vanilla. Sift flour and add with salt and baking powder. Stir in rosemary, fruit and nuts. Bake about 30 minutes. Remove from pan while warm. Cool and cut into squares.

**Other recipes from the Goose Creek Herb Guild:**
*Cooking with Herbs*, by the Goose Creek Herb Guild.
  To purchase, send a check for $10 (price includes postage) to The Goose Creek Herb Guild, PO Box 2224, Leesburg, VA 20177.

> *The leaves of the Bramble boiled in water, with honey, alum and a little white wine added thereto, make a most excellent lotion or washing water.*
>
> —JOHN GERARD, *THE HERBAL*, 1597

Today is National Pancake Day.

*Sunday morning dawned bright and shiny, the cedar elms glowing gold against a cornflower blue sky, the clean, crisp scent of cedar in the air, the sort of day that is Texas at its best. McQuaid and I were lazy and slept late, then had a leisurely breakfast of bacon, eggs, and pancakes.*

—DEAD MAN'S BONES, A CHINA BAYLES MYSTERY

## Herbal Syrups

Maple is fine, but for a tasty change of pace on your breakfast pancakes, China suggests herbal syrups. These delicious taste treats aren't just for pancakes, either! Easy-to-make herbal syrups are equally luscious on ice cream, in dessert sauces, or frozen and served as a sorbet. Or for a zippy drink, you can pour syrup over crushed ice and add ginger ale, sparkling water, or lemonade.

All these tasty delights start with a very simple syrup, made from your choice of herbs: mint, rosemary, lemon balm, lemon verbena, lemon basil, lavender blossoms, rose petals, slices of ginger, cinnamon sticks, and more. You can mix them, too. Experiment and develop your own favorite recipe.

### CHINA'S BASIC HERBAL SYRUP

3 cups boiling water
1 cup fresh herbs
2 cups sugar

Make a strong tea by pouring the boiling water over the herbs and steeping until cool (1–2 hours, at least). Strain out the plant material and mix the tea with the sugar in a nonreactive saucepan over medium heat. Bring to a boil, stirring. Reduce heat and simmer for 10–12 minutes, until the syrup thickens. Store in a lidded jar in the refrigerator for up to three months. (It never lasts that long at China's house!) Makes about 1 ½ cups syrup.

**Learn how to make more herbal syrups and other confections:**
*Fancy Pantry,* by Helen Witty

# SEPTEMBER 27

Today or tomorrow is Native American Day.

*Civilization has taught us to build empires for Life Insurance Companies, numerous research, welfare, old age organizations, etc. In comparison, the Indians' protection came from Nature, the "Mother Earth" being the most important. They learned to treat lives with plant life, the medicine from the earth.*

—ALMA R. HUTCHENS, *INDIAN HERBOLOGY*
*OF NORTH AMERICA*

## Native American Herbs

A great deal of our herbal knowledge and lore was brought to this continent by settlers from England and Europe. Because of the long written tradition of use, we often pay more attention to these herbs, and think of them as more important than our native plants. But our indigenous medicinal herbs should have a special interest for us—not perhaps, to treat our ailments, but to broaden our awareness of the value of the plants around us. As an example, here are ten plants that various Native American tribes used to treat colds, coughs, and respiratory ailments, depending on where they lived and what was seasonally available.

- Creosote bush (*Larrea divaricata* or *tridentata*)
- Pleurisy root (*Asclepias tuberosa*)
- Wormwood (*Artemisia sp.*)
- Boneset (*Eupatorium perforatum*)
- Wild cherry (*Prunus serotina*)
- Willow (*Salix sp.*)
- White pine (*Pinus strobus*)
- Sarsaparilla (*Aralia nudicaulis*)
- Skunk Cabbage (*Lysichiton americanum*)
- Yerba santa (*Eriodictyon californicum*)

Here is a good project for you and your children. Make a list of the 10 most important indigenous herbs in your region, collect specimens (where the plant is not endangered), and study their various uses. But please don't experiment with medicinal plants until you've done your homework!

**Read more about the herbs used by Native Americans:**
*Native American Ethnobotany*, by Daniel E. Moerman

*The landscape changes shape when you start noticing which plants grow where, which plants are good for what. Good-for-nothing backlots turn into fruitful havens. Weeds in the garden look as good as the vegetables. Forest underbrush begins to tell a story as intricate as an illuminated manuscript, once one takes the time to read it.*

—SUSAN TYLER HITCHCOCK, *GATHER YE WILD THINGS*

# SEPTEMBER 28

Tomorrow is the beginning of the Celtic Month of Ivy, according to some sources. Its power to cling and to bind was thought by many cultures to be magical. Ivy was associated with the moon.

> *The custom of decorating houses and churches with Ivy at Christmas was forbidden by one of the early Councils of the Church, on account of its pagan associations, but the custom still remains.*
>
> —MRS. GRIEVE, *THE MODERN HERBAL* (1931)

## Living Ivy Wreath

Because ivy was associated with many pagan rituals, it was often considered to be a "dangerous" plant. In England, for instance, holly was brought into the house for the Yule season, but not ivy.

But for most of us, ivy is perfect for holiday decorations. And if you start now, you can have an elegant living ivy wreath as a centerpiece for your holiday parties. As you work with this familiar plant, remember that through the centuries, ivy (*Hedera helix*) has been an important herb. European healers described ivy leaves as useful in treating intestinal parasites and lowering fever, as well as healing burns. In ancient Greece, ivy leaves were simmered in wine and drunk to reduce intoxication.

To make the wreath, you'll need:
a wire wreath box frame 16" diameter
sphagnum moss
10–12 ivy plants in 4" containers (there may be several
 plants in one container)
potting soil
slow-release fertilizer pellets
flexible copper wire

How to do it:

Lay the wreath frame flat, open side up. Soak the sphagnum moss until it is moist. Cover the inside of the frame, pressing the moss against the outside. Remove the ivy plants from the containers and settle them into the frame, spacing equally and tilting the plants slightly to cover the root ball of the adjoining plant. Add potting soil where necessary and sprinkle slow-release fertilizer pellets, following package directions. Wrap the copper wire (it will be nearly invisible) around the frame and between the plants to secure them in place. Lay sphagnum moss between the plants. Keep moist and shaded, and water when the bottom of the wreath feels dry. Indoors, place on a tray. (You can use this same technique with many other herbs. Some possibilities: prostrate rosemary, thyme, dwarf nasturtium, mint, hen-and-chicks.)

**Learn how to use many live herbs and plants in wreaths:**
*The Living Wreath*, by Teddy Colbert

Today is the feast day of St. Michael the Archangel.

*According to one legend, Angelica was revealed in a dream by an angel to cure the plague. Another explanation of the name of this plant is that it blooms on the day of Michael the Archangel (May 8, old style), and is on that account a preservative against evil spirits and witchcraft: all parts of the plant were believed efficacious against spells and enchantment. It was held in such esteem that it was called "The Root of the Holy Ghost."*

—MRS. GRIEVE, *THE MODERN HERBAL*, 1931

## Angelica

Angelica (*Angelica archangelica*) was held in high reverence in medieval Europe, when healing plants were viewed as very nearly sacred. The religious names of many plants indicate their importance and value—Saint-John's-wort (*Hypericum sp.*), St. George's herb or valerian (*Valeriana officinalis*), and Our Lady's thistle or blessed thistle (*Cnicus benedictus*)—but angelica was valued even more than these, perhaps because of its reputation for dispelling the plague. Described by an herbalist of the 1570s as "that happy counterbane against contagions, sent down from heav'n," angelica came to be regarded with great reverence and even greater superstition.

Angelica can grow to six feet in height, with large, tropical-looking leaves and hollow stems 2–3 inches in diameter. In addition to its medicinal uses (as a remedy for colds, pleurisy, rheumatism, urinary tract infections, and typhoid fever), it has been widely used in perfumes, candies, and sweets. In the 1600s, the juice was distilled and used as a flavoring, the root and stalks were candied, and the thin-sliced stalks were used to decorate pastries. The oil is still used as a flavoring for liqueurs.

If you live where the summers are relatively cool and moist, the plant would be an unusual and impressive back-of-the-border herb. And perhaps you would like to use the stems in Martha Washington's recipe.

### TO CANDY ANGELICO STALKS

About A weeke in aprill, take of ye stalks of Angelico, & boyle them in faire water till they be tender, then pill ye thin scin of them [pull the thin skin off them] & squees them betwixt 2 plates till all ye water be out, then brayd [abrade] them If you like it, & boyle them to A candy in sugar as other roots be done. Then dry them in a stove.

—MARTHA WASHINGTON'S COOKBOOK

**Read more about "old-fashioned" herbs:**
*Gardening with Herbs for Flavor and Fragrance*, by Helen Morgenthau Fox, 1933

*Never eat a blackberry after Michaelmas Day, for the devil spits on them all.*

—ENGLISH LORE

Sukkot, the Jewish Feast of Tabernacles, may be celebrated about this time. The "tabernacles" are the tiny makeshift huts in which the Israelites stayed as they journeyed through the wilderness. They may also represent the temporary huts in which ancient farmers stayed while they harvested their crops.

❦

## The Four Herbs of Sukkot

On the first day you are to take choice fruit from the trees, and palm fronds, leafy branches and poplars . . . Leviticus 23:40, New International Version

In Jewish practice, the choice fruit from the trees is interpreted as the *etrog* or *Citrus medica*—familiar to us as the citron, a lemonlike fruit native to the Holy Land. The palm fronds, called *lulavim* in Hebrew, are supposed to be at least two feet long; palms are a symbol of victory. "Leafy branches" are represented by a branch of the myrtle tree—a symbol of divine generosity—with leaves in clusters of three. Jewish tradition interprets "poplars" as willows. In the Temple, the *etrog* is carried in the left hand and the palm, myrtle, and willow (bundled together) are held in the right, as the congregation sings psalms and hymns of praise.

The Sukkot's festival menu would include stuffed dishes made with chopped fillings, such as these traditional stuffed mushrooms, filled with herbs:

## HERB-STUFFED MUSHROOMS

- 12 large mushrooms
- 2 tablespoons grated Parmesan cheese
- 1 garlic clove, minced
- ¼ cup finely chopped green onion tops
- 1 tablespoon roasted sunflower seeds, chopped
- ¾ cup dry bread crumbs
- 1 tablespoon chopped fresh parsley
- 1 teaspoon minced fresh oregano
- 2 tablespoons butter, melted
- 4 tablespoons olive oil

Preheat the oven to 350°. Clean mushrooms and remove stems (save for another use). Mix remaining ingredients, except for olive oil. Stuff the mushroom caps, pressing the filling firmly with a spoon. Place mushrooms in a casserole dish greased with 2 tablespoons olive oil. Pour the remaining oil over the mushrooms. Bake 20 minutes. Serve warm.

The citron was the first cultivated citrus fruit, with records dating back to 4000 BCE. It was a common fruit in the Mediterranean region, and today is cultivated primarily in Sicily, Corsica, and Crete, Greece, and Israel. The peel is candied and used in a variety of desserts.

**You might also want to read:**

*In Search of Plenty: A History of Jewish Food*, by Oded Schwartz

October

❧

November

❧

December

In China and Japan, today begins the Month of the Chrysanthemum.

*I closed up both shops at the usual hour, then drove over to the theater to add a few last-minute plants to the landscaping: more rosemary, some lemongrass, and several santolina, and another dozen of chrysanthemums. In my opinion, it is theoretically possible to have too many chrysanthemums, but I have personally never reached that point. When they're in bloom, they're bronze and red and gold and pretty; when they're not, they're green and pretty. Such a deal.*

—DEAD MAN'S BONES: A CHINA BAYLES MYSTERY

## Chrysanthemum: The Royal Flower

As a flowering herb, chrysanthemums were cultivated in China around 1500 BCE. A decoction of the roots was used to soothe headaches, the young leaves and petals were eaten in salads, and a tea was made from the leaves. In Japan, the Imperial court held its first chrysanthemum show in 910 CE, when the plant was declared the national flower and adopted by the ruling family as its symbol. National Chrysanthemum Day is still celebrated there. For many, the flower typifies the East in the same way that the rose typifies the West.

The flower was brought to Europe in the seventeenth century. It was named by Karl Linnaeus from the Greek prefix *chrys-*, which means "golden" (the color of the original flowers), and *-anthemon*, "flower." When it began to appear in England in the late 1700s, it became popular as a bedding plant. It never caught on as a medicinal herb, however. In Europe, the chrysanthemum is mostly used as a funeral flower and connotes sadness and grief; in contemporary America, it is a celebratory flower, summoning up thoughts of football games and homecoming dances.

The colorful petals of garden chrysanthemums add a festive touch to salads and vegetable dishes. (Never use florist varieties, which may have been sprayed.) According to Susan Belsinger (*Flowers in the Kitchen*) some varieties may be bitter. In China, the greens are stir-fried with garlic, ginger, and dried chile peppers and served over noodles.

**Learn more about chrysanthemums:**
*Chrysanthemums: The Complete Guide*, by Baden Locke

*If the new moon appear with the points of her crescent turned up, the month will be dry: if the points are turned down it will be wet.*

—ENGLISH WEATHER LORE

*There is an old tradition that the Elder tree must on no account be burnt or even cut down without the permission of Hylde-Moer, the Elder tree mother.*

—MRS. C. F. LEYEL, *HERBAL DELIGHTS*, 1937

## Elderberry-Sumac Rob: Susan's Journal

When I was a girl growing up on the farm in Illinois, I remember early October as a time of crisp, cool days: the skies clear and blue, the sumac berries turning scarlet, and the elderberry bushes heavy with ebony berries—a time for jellies and jams, certainly. But I was reading Bertha Reppert's *Twelve Month Herbal* the other day, and found that in early October, Bertha's thoughts are turning to elderberry-sumac rob. "They claim there's a witch residing in every elder tree," she says, "and rob is surely a witch's brew, turned into pure ambrosia."

Rob? It's not a noun I know, but a quick search through the Oxford English Dictionary yields this definition: "the juice of a fruit, reduced by boiling to the consistency of a syrup and preserved with sugar; a conserve of fruit." The word, we're told, is Arabic: *robb* or *rubb,* meaning fruit syrup.

Ah, yes, fruit syrup. That, I understand. And Bertha's instructions for her rob are understandable, as well. She harvests sumac berries (she doesn't say which variety, but here in Texas we have *Rhus trilobata,* better known as the lemonade-bush, the fruits of which produce a lovely, tart juice). She cooks them with water, strains them, and uses the sumac juice to cook her elderberry harvest. She tosses in cloves, nutmeg, and a cinnamon stick, and boils it all together for half an hour. Then she adds a cup of sugar for each quart, stirs until it dissolves, strains it again, and bottles it. "Served with great ceremony in tiny glasses, it is the most elegant of drinks," she says.

It would be an elegant jelly, too, with the addition of pectin and more sugar. And healthy, I must add, for the elder's flowers and fruit are respected as remedies for colds and flu, and sumac has a reputation as an aid to digestion. It's nice when something delicious and elegant is also good for you. And doubly nice when reading about it brings back those crisp October days of bright sumac and dark, rich elderberries.

**Read about Bertha's adventures with elder:**
*Mrs. Reppert's Twelve-Month Herbal,* by Bertha Reppert

*There is no better reason for preferring this elderberry bush than that it stirs an early memory, that it is no novelty in my life, speaking to me merely through my present sensibilities to form and colour, but the long companion of my existence that wove itself into my joys when joys were vivid.*

—GEORGE ELIOT, *THE MILL ON THE FLOSS*

*There is apparently no truth to old tales that the fiery horseradish (Cochlearia armoracia) is so named because it was once used to cure horses of colds, or because it made a good seasoning for horse meat. Horse is used as an adjective before a number of plants to indicate a large, strong or coarse kind. Other examples include the "horse cucumber," "horse mint" and "horse plum."*

—ROBERT HENDRICKSON, *LADYBUGS, TIGER LILIES & WALLFLOWERS*

## Horseradish: Rooting for Flavor

If you have horseradish in your garden, it's time to think about harvesting your crop. Dig the roots carefully, cut off the foliage about an inch above the crown, and store them in a cool, dark place. Process by grating or grinding, mixing with vinegar (¼ cup vinegar to 1 cup ground horseradish), and packing into small jars. Ground horseradish will keep in the refrigerator for 4–6 weeks, or may be frozen.

### HORSERADISH IN THE MEDICINE CABINET

Like mustard, horseradish has long been recognized for its medicinal properties: stimulant, laxative, diuretic, and antiseptic. The juice was used to relieve coughs and colds; a syrup treated sore throats; and the root itself staved off scurvy. (Horseradish is a source of vitamin C.) It was also used as a vermifuge. William Coles [1656] observes: "Of all things given to children for worms, horseradish is not the least, for it soon killeth and expelleth them." (The worms, not the children.) The leaves were used as a rubifacient for sciatica and as a compress to relieve toothache.

### HORSERADISH ON THE MENU

Horseradish is hailed as a spicy sauce for meats or fish. But the zippy flavor makes it a natural for other dishes, as well. Try adding a spoonful of grated horseradish to coleslaw, beans, chicken salad, deviled eggs, meatballs—the possibilities are endless. Of course, it works as a dip, too—a healthy, versatile, all-round good-for-you herb.

### ZIPPY HORSERADISH DIP

    1 pint nonfat sour cream
    16 ounces cream cheese, softened
    6 tablespoons grated horseradish
    2 teaspoons finely chopped green onion
    1 teaspoon red pepper flakes
    parsley, for garnish

Combine all ingredients in mixer bowl, with mixer on slow speed. Refrigerate 1 hour. Garnish with parsley and serve with vegetables for dipping.

*If the oak wears his leaves in October, you may expect a hard winter.*

—GERMAN WEATHER LORE

# OCTOBER 4

October's Theme Garden: A Garden of Old Roses.

*Oh, no man knows*
*Through what wild centuries*
*Roves back the rose.*

—WALTER DE LA MARE, "ALL THAT'S PAST"

## Old Rose Charm

Remember your grandmother's roses? Large, loose, floppy blossoms, delightfully fragrant—and very different from today's neat, compact, scentless roses. A garden organized around a collection of antique roses will not only be beautiful, but will take you back in time, as well: "through what wild centuries," as de la Mare says. Here are five old roses, representative of the five classes of important European roses: Alba, Centifolia, Damask, Gallica, and Moss. Each is cold-hardy, with a spectacular spring bloom, and each one has a past. If roses interest you, perhaps it would be fun (and enlightening) to dig up the stories behind each one.

- Félicité Parmentier, 1834 (Alba). Sweetly scented, delicate pink blossoms, gray-green foliage, and a small bush (4–5') that is ideal for a smaller garden.
- Autumn Damask, before 1819 (Damask). A repeat bloomer with richly fragrant, ruffled, deep pink flowers. Prized for its superb scent, wonderful in potpourri. Damask roses were brought to Europe from the Middle East during the Crusades; they are named for the Syrian city of Damascus.
- Henri Martin, 1863 (Moss). Crimson buds, fragrant crimson flowers, a prolific spring bloomer. Heat tolerant in my Texas garden. The mosses take their name from the prickly fuzz of the bud.
- Shailer's Provence, before 1799 (Centifolia). Hundreds of lovely lilac-pink petals, in clusters of three, delightfully scented—the old-fashioned cabbage rose (4–5').
- Belle Isis, before 1845 (Gallica). Shell-pink, with a strong scent of myrrh, rose, and anise, Belle Isis is a landmark in rose breeding. Gallicas set hips readily, and figure in most medicinal and herbal lore.

**Explore the world of old roses:**
*Growing Old-Fashioned Roses*, by Brent G. Dickerson
*Roses: Old Roses and Species Roses*, by Paul Starosta
*The Love of Roses: From Myth to Modern Culture*, by Graham Rose and Peter King

*To pickle Rosebuds: Pick Rosebuds and put them in an earthen Pipkin, with white wine Vinegar and Sugar and so you may use Cowslips, Violets or Rosemary Flowers.*

—MURRELL'S *TWO BOOKS OF COOKERIES & CARVING*, 1650

# OCTOBER 5

*We lay under our tent, having pitched it more prudently with reference to the wind and the flame, and the usual huge fire blazed in front. Supper was eaten off a large log, which some freshet had thrown up. This night we had a dish of arbor-vitae, or cedar-tea, which the lumberer sometimes uses when other herbs fail: "A quart of arbor-vitae, To make him strong and mighty." But I had no wish to repeat the experiment. It had too medicinal a taste for my palate.*

—HENRY DAVID THOREAU, *THE MAINE WOODS*, 1847

## The Tree of Life

Arborvitae (*Thuja occidentalis*) may not have pleased Thoreau's palate, but it was certainly a life-preserving tree for a great many Native Americans. As a decoction, infusion, poultice, tincture, or salve, it was used to treat rheumatism and menstrual disorders, (Algonquin, Quebec); headaches and infections (Chippewa); urinary and bladder ailments (Cree, Woodlands); cuts, bruises, sores, fever, stimulant (Iroquois); and swellings (Menominee). Many tribes used it in their sacred rituals, and burned it as a purifying and exorcising smudge. Others employed the bark and fiber in the making of baskets, tools, weapons, and canoes. The leaves were used as insect repellent, and the bark as a tanning agent.

The first news of arborvitae's health-giving properties came to Europe via the report of French explorer Jacque Cartier, who was taught by an Indian guide to use the decoction to treat his men, who were suffering from scurvy. Vitamin C was not yet known, but the Indians understood the therapeutic nature of this important tree. Scientists have learned that one of its constituents is thujone (also found in artemisia, lavender, sage, and juniper); a stimulant, thujone acts on the heart and central nervous system. Today, arborvitae oil is used in insect repellents, soaps, and room deodorizers.

Want to grow it? It thrives in Zones 3–7, in both tall and dwarf cultivars. "Prostrata" (a prostrate cultivar) is good in rock gardens; "Little Gem" is a hardy dwarf; and "Globosa," a globe form, grows to five feet in diameter. Plant it now or in the spring, give it plenty of room, water deeply during the first year, and watch for bagworms (its only serious pest). If you don't want to repeat Thoreau's experience with arborvitae tea, try using the fresh bark and needles to brew an invigorating tea to add to your bathwater.

*Aromatherapist Jeanne Rose (*The Aromatherapy Book*) mentions the scent of arborvitae as useful in smoothing transitions and grieving loss, which may cause both emotional or physical disharmonies of the heart.*

**Read more about the Tree of Life:**
*Leaves: In Myth, Magic & Medicine,* by Alice Thoms Vitale

# OCTOBER 6

## The Tale of the Priscilla Hollyhock

Flowers tell stories, and stories can teach us something important about ourselves. This story teaches me about faith and hope and renewal. My sixth-grade teacher read it in the *St. Louis Post-Dispatch* and told our class about it—about the handful of hollyhock seeds that came to Southern Illinois in the pocket of a slave-child named Priscilla.

Priscilla's trek had been a long one. Born on a Georgia plantation, she had been sold to a Cherokee chief. Shortly thereafter, the Indian band was evicted from their homes and forced to take the terrible journey that came to be called the Trail of Tears. On Dutch Creek, near Jonesboro, Illinois, a wealthy Southern Illinois farmer named Barzilla Silkwood encountered the Indians, who were being sent under military escort to Oklahoma. Priscilla, by that time about 12 years old, was with them. With surprise, Silkwood recognized her as the very same child, an orphan, whom he had seen earlier working as a house servant on a Georgia plantation. Moved by her plight, he bought her—for a thousand dollars in gold, it is said—but not as a slave. He freed her and took her to his inn near Mulkeytown, Illinois, to join the fifteen other orphaned children to whom he and his wife had given a home. Priscilla lived at the Silkwood Inn until she died at the age of 75 and was buried in the Silkwood family plot.

And the hollyhocks? They are a small variety, almost a dwarf, the flowers a dark-veined rose-pink, the leaves dark green. Priscilla had brought the seeds from the plantation where the little hollyhocks had blossomed, to her home with the Cherokee Indians, and then on the Trail of Tears. In 1838, when she made her new home with the Silkwoods, she planted the hollyhocks in the garden, where they have flourished ever since. In 1950, to complete the journey, some of Priscilla's seeds were gathered and sent to the daughter of the last chief of the Oklahoma Cherokees, where they were planted around the Indians' homes—the gift of a little girl who had faith in a flower.

**Read more about Priscilla's journey, and about hollyhocks:**

"Priscilla," *St. Louis Post Dispatch*, April 8, 1953, by John W. Allen, Curator of the Southern Illinois University Museum

*A Contemplation Upon Flowers: Garden Plants in Myth and Literature*, by Bobby J. Ward

*The Hollyhock, first brought to this country from China, was once eaten as a pot-herb, though it is not particularly palatable. Its flowers are employed medicinally for their emollient, demulcent and diuretic properties, which make them useful in chest complaints.*

—MRS. GRIEVE, *MODERN HERBAL*, 1931

# OCTOBER 7

In some years, this is Yom Kippur, the Jewish Day of Atonement, a day of fasting and reflection.

## Break-Fast

Fasting, whether for religious or health reasons, can be an important part of our lives. People who fast regularly suggest that pre-fast meals should be simple and nourishing, low in carbohydrates and salt. And the break-fast meal is also important, to replenish both the body and spirit. This lemon-herb-egg soup is traditional throughout the Mediterranean region.

### EGG SOUP WITH LEMON AND HERBS

½ cup uncooked rice or orzo

6 cups chicken or vegetable broth

3 teaspoons parsley, chopped

2 teaspoons dill, chopped

6 egg yolks

1 cup lemon juice

In a medium pot, bring the broth to a boil. Add rice or orzo and cook until done, adding herbs in the last few minutes. In a medium bowl, thoroughly beat the egg yolks. Add the lemon juice slowly, continuing to beat. Then very gradually add about 2 cups of the hot broth to the eggs, beating constantly to incorporate and prevent curdling. Add the egg-lemon-broth mixture to the soup, stirring. Serve hot.

### ORANGE-MINT FRUIT SOUP

3 cups hot water

½ cup raisins

¼ cup small pitted prunes

¼ cup dried apricots

¼ cup uncooked quick-cooking tapioca

1 cup apple juice

1 cup orange juice

1 can Mandarin orange sections

2 tablespoons snipped mint

yogurt

nutmeg, sprigs of mint, orange peels for garnish

In large saucepan, over medium heat, combine water, dried fruit, and tapioca. Stir until smooth. Reduce heat and simmer 30–35 minutes, until the tapioca is transparent and the soup is thick and clear. Add apple juice, orange juice, Mandarin orange sections, and mint and heat to desired serving temperature. Serve with dollops of yogurt, dusted with nutmeg and garnished with sprigs of mint and orange peel. Serves 6.

# OCTOBER 8

Today is the day we've all been waiting for: National Frappe Day! It's also National Flower Day: In 1986, the rose became the national flower of the United States.

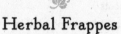

## Herbal Frappes

Frappes, frozen fruit desserts, fruit shakes, smoothies—whatever you choose to call them, these concoctions are marvelous. And they're even nicer when they're flavored with your favorite herb. These recipes make one serving.

### GINGER-PEACHY BREAKFAST FRAPPE
Ginger is valued in Eastern cultures as a metabolism booster, while Western research shows that the herb stimulates the digestive process, prevents nausea, and relieves cold symptoms. Start your day with a ginger-peachy frappe. Pour half a cup of boiling water over a one-inch piece of fresh ginger root (peeled and crushed) and let steep for five minutes. Strain and stir in 2–3 tablespoons of honey to make a syrup. Refrigerate. At breakfast time, place one peeled, pitted, chopped peach and one sliced banana in a blender and whir. Add the syrup and process until smooth. Delish!

### LUNCHTIME VANILLA POWER FRAPPE
Protein powder (available in groceries) is a good basis for meal-substitute frappes; flaxseed is a heart-healthy herb, and vanilla an all-time herbal flavoring favorite. For lunch on the run, blend together ½ cup ice water, 1 tablespoon flaxseed oil, 2 teaspoons pure vanilla ex-

tract, ½ teaspoon cinnamon, ½ cup protein powder.

### DINNERTIME BERRY-MINTY DESSERT FRAPPE
Made with soy milk, this frappe is good for your bones. Tasty, too! In a blender, combine 1 cup soy milk, 1 teaspoon sugar, 1 cup fresh strawberries, ¼ teaspoon mint flavoring extract, 4 ice cubes. Blend until thick and foamy. Garnish with mint sprig.

### BEDTIME BANANA-YOGURT FRAPPE
Researchers tell us Calcium can help you go to sleep and lemon verbena has a sweetly sedative effect. For a bedtime frappe, try this calcium-rich treat:

- ¾ cup yogurt (plain or fruit-flavored)
- ¾ cup milk
- ½ cup sliced banana
- 1 tablespoon lemon verbena
- 1 tablespoon honey (optional)

Combine all ingredients in blender and process until smooth. Dust with nutmeg.

**Learn how to make other frappes:**
*Smoothies, Shakes, and Frappes: 750 Refreshing, Revitalizing, and Nourishing Drinks,* by Sally Ann Berk

***If you pull up your kale today and dirt clings to the roots, good fortune lies ahead.***

—GARDEN LORE

# OCTOBER 9

Pomegranates are in season now.

## Celebrating the Pomegranate

The pomegranate is one of the earliest cultivated fruits, planted in Northern Iran or Turkey between 4000 BCE and 3000 BCE. The first archaeological evidence is found in Jericho, dating from around 3000 BCE. An important food, it has played many other roles in various cultures. In China, the pomegranate with its numerous seeds symbolizes fertility, posterity, and royalty, while in Hebraic tradition, it represents fullness and confidence—again, because of the many seeds. (In Jewish lore, the pomegranate is said to contain 613 seeds.) Medicinally, the seeds were used by the Greeks and Romans as a vermifuge (to remove intestinal parasites), the rind treated complaints that had to do with the blood, such as menstruation or hemorrhage; and the leaves and rind were used as a poultice for ulcers and eye ailments. In Sri Lanka, the flowers made a red dye; in Morocco, the bark, used in tanning, gave Moroccan leather its distinctive yellow hue. The rind was an ingredient in ink, and throughout the Middle East, the plant was used in needlework and architectural design to symbolize abundance. And some scholars say that the fruit was the original "apple" from the Tree of Knowledge.

**POMEGRANATE MUFFINS**

    2 cups flour
    ⅔ cup sugar, plus 2 teaspoons for sprinkling
    1 tablespoon baking powder
    ¼ cup minced candied ginger
    1 tablespoons grated orange peel
    1½ cups pomegranate arils and seeds
        (the yield of 2 medium pomegranates)
    1 cup milk
    1 egg
    ¼ cup butter or margarine, melted and cooled
    ½ teaspoon salt

Preheat oven to 400°. Place paper cups in a 12-cup muffin pan. In a large mixing bowl, combine dry ingredients. Stir in ginger, orange peel, and pomegranate seeds. Make a well in the center of the dry ingredients. In a small bowl, combine milk, egg, and butter or margarine. Pour into the well and stir with a fork until just blended. Spoon into muffin cups and bake 12–14 minutes. Sprinkle tops with sugar. Serve warm.

*To seed a pomegranate*: Cut off the blossom end of the pomegranate and cut the fruit into sections. Soak the sections for 5–10 minutes in a large bowl of water. Working in the water, pull out the arils (juice sacs) with your fingers. Strain out the water. (Beware: pomegranate juice stains—permanently.)

**More Reading:**
*Pomegranates*, by Ann Kleinberg

# OCTOBER 10

Columbus Day is celebrated on the second Monday of October.

> *We found a man in a canoe going from Santa Maria to Fernandia. He had with him some dried leaves which are in high value among them, for a quantity of it was brought to me at San Salvador.*
>
> —CHRISTOPHER COLUMBUS, *JOURNAL*, OCTOBER 15, 1492

## Tobacco

While minor quantities of nicotine may be found in some Old World plants (belladonna and *Nicotiana africana*), the habitual use of *Nicotiana tabacum* began in the Americas and was widespread by the first century CE. Rodrigo de Jerez, exploring Cuba, adopted the natives' smoking habit. Back home in Spain, however, his neighbors were so terrified by the smoke coming out of his mouth and nose that the local Inquisitor sentenced him to seven years in jail. By the time de Jerez got out, everyone in Spain was smoking, and tobacco was on its way to becoming one of the most prized herbs in history.

The dried leaves of tobacco were smoked for the feeling of well-being. But it was the herb's medical properties that were most often touted. It was claimed to be a panacea, especially effective in the treatment of headaches, toothache, worms, bad breath, lockjaw, and cancer. In 1603 in England, the physicians wrote an urgent letter to King James I, complaining that the drug was being used without a prescription; the king promptly levied a large import duty on tobacco imports. A few years later, though, Sir Frances Bacon wrote that more people than ever were smoking, and that it was next to impossible to quit. And in the American colonies, where a would-be husband was required to fork over 120 pounds of tobacco for his chosen wife's passage, tobacco rapidly became the monetary standard. It helped to finance the American Revolution, subsidized the practice of slavery, and contributed enormously to the new country's growing wealth.

It wasn't until the 1950s that the significant health risks of tobacco consumption were officially recognized. The first tobacco lawsuit, filed by a man who lost his larynx to cancer, was won in 1962; the first secondhand smoke suit was won in 1976. In 1995, the FDA finally declared nicotine a drug.

**More Reading:**

*Tobacco: A Cultural History of How an Exotic Plant Seduced Civilization,* by Iain Gately

> *Tobaco is a remedy for the Tooth-ache, if the Teeth and Gumbs be rubbed with a linnen Cloth dipp't in the juice, and afterward a round ball of the leaves laid unto the place.*
>
> —JOHN GERARD, *HERBAL*, 1597

# OCTOBER 11

*Culinary note: To cook chili, you have to know how to spell. Chiles are peppers, ranging in temperature from mild to incendiary. Chili is a thick stew made with meat, peppers, herbs, sometimes tomatoes, and (if you live north of the Red River) beans. If you live in Springfield, Illinois, or other northern or eastern locations, you might spell chili with two l's: chilli. Texans never spell chili with beans, unless they're looking for a fight.*

—CHILE DEATH: A CHINA BAYLES MYSTERY

## Chiles and Chili

Tobacco wasn't the only thing Columbus exported from the New World, of course. Most people would probably agree that the chile pepper has contributed a great deal more than tobacco to human civilization. While it's not official, chili has to rank right up there with ballpark hotdogs and movie popcorn as the Great American Dish. And yes, where I grew up, the word is spelled *chilli* and the pot is full of beans. Red beans. Red kidney beans.

China's favorite chili recipe is named for the Pedernales River (that's pronounced *Purd-nal'-is*, folks), which flows through President Lyndon Johnson's Texas ranch. This no-frills, no-fuss chili was said to be Johnson's favorite, and the recipe comes from a card Mrs. Johnson used to hand out. "It has been almost as popular as the government pamphlet on the care and feeding of children," she once remarked. You will notice that there are no beans.

**PEDERNALES CHILI**

 4 pounds ground lean beef
 1 large onion, chopped
 2 cloves garlic, minced
 1 teaspoon ground oregano
 1 teaspoon ground cumin
 3 tablespoons chili powder
 2 cans tomatoes
 2 cups hot water
 salt to taste

Brown ground beef in heavy iron skillet. Add onion and garlic and cook 4–5 minutes. Add remaining ingredients and simmer one hour. When cool, skim fat. Better on the second day, when the flavors have mellowed.

**Discover the secrets of chili cookery:**
*The Ultimate Chili Book: Connoisseur's Guide to Gourmet Recipes and the Perfect Four-Alarm Bowl,* by Christopher B. O'Hara

*I once absent-mindedly ordered Three Mile Island dressing in a restaurant and, with great presence of mind, they brought Thousand Island Dressing and a bottle of chili sauce.*

—TERRY PRATCHETT, BRITISH SATIRIST

# OCTOBER 12

*But those which perfume the Aire most delightfully, not passed by as the rest, but being Trodden upon and Crushed, are Three: That is, Burnet, Wilde-Time, and Water-Mints. Therefore you are to set whole Allies of them, to have the Pleasure, when you walke or tread.*

—FRANCIS BACON

## Salad Burnet

If you haven't yet set out Bacon's fragrant Allies—burnet, thyme, and mint—now is the time. Mint and thyme are most easily started from cuttings and transplants, but you can sow the seeds of salad burnet (*Sanguisorba minor*) seeds now, in full sun and well-drained soil, for harvesting in early spring. If you already have burnet in your garden, you're probably using it regularly, now that the weather is cooler. The pretty, cucumber-flavored young leaves, lacy and delicate-looking, are the most delicious now and in early spring, perfect for salads, as its name suggests. Burnet also lends an interesting flavor to vinegars, sauces, salad dressings, and creamy soups. Added to a pitcher of iced punch, the leaves are decorative and cooling.

Like its larger medicinal cousin (*Sanguisorba officinalis*), salad burnet has been used for more than two thousand years, primarily as an astringent. *Sanguisorba* means "blood-absorbing," so called for the plant's ability to contract small blood vessels. Roman soldiers drank burnet tea before battle, hoping it might reduce bleeding if they were wounded; soldiers in the American Revolution drank New Jersey tea (*Ceanothus americanus*) for a similar purpose. Burnet was also used (with some two dozen other herbs) in wine and vinegar as an deterrent to plague infections.

### BURNET VINEGAR

1 cup burnet leaves, packed
2 cups white wine vinegar

Pack leaves into a clean jar and cover with vinegar. Put on a tight lid and set on a sunny shelf, turning frequently. Taste in two weeks. Continue steeping (if it's not quite intense enough) or strain and rebottle. Not necessarily helpful in preventing plague, but super on salads.

### A DILLY OF A BURNET BUTTER

½ pound unsalted butter
1 teaspoon Dijon mustard
½ cup chopped burnet leaves
3 tablespoons minced fresh dill

Blend all ingredients thoroughly. Use on steamed vegetables, fish, or sandwiches.

*To make water for washing hands at table: Boil sage, then strain the water and cool it until it is a little more than lukewarm. Or use chamomile, marjoram, or rosemary boiled with orange peel. Bay leaves are also good.*

—*LE MENAGIER DE PARIS, C. 1393*

# OCTOBER 18

*Things chick'ny and mutt'ny*
*Taste better with chutney,*
*Which leads to the mystery eternal:*
*Why didn't Major Grey make Colonel?*

—UNKNOWN

## Major Grey's Chutney

The word *chutney* derives from the Indian *chatni*, a fresh, fine-ground paste of coconut, spices, chiles, and herbs (often ginger, garlic, coriander, and mint), served as an accompaniment to rice and curries. Chutney first appeared in English around 1800, after British colonial officers returning from India began bringing home their newly acquired tastes for spicy curries and flavored rice. The most famous of the commercial British chutneys is called Major Grey. The major himself seems to have been a fiction (there is no copyright or trademark on the name), but his mango-based chutney has had a strong appeal for the past two centuries. Unlike the uncooked Indian *chatni*, chutney is usually made of mangos, apples, or pears, simmered in vinegar with onions, raisins, brown sugar, spices, and chiles.

This is my adaptation of the chutney that Bill enjoys. Shortly after I made it for him, he proposed. Of course, the two events may not have been related, but there it is.

### MAJOR GREY'S MANGO CHUTNEY: SUSAN'S VERSION

6 cups mangos, peeled, chopped
1 onion, chopped
1 cup raisins
½ cup peeled, diced fresh ginger
1 lemon, sliced thin and seeded
2 large cloves garlic, minced
1–2 teaspoons chile powder
1¼ cups granulated sugar
1 cup brown sugar
2 cups cider vinegar
1 teaspoon whole cloves
1 teaspoon nutmeg
1 cinnamon stick, about 2 inches
1 teaspoon salt
½ teaspoon whole peppercorns

Combine all ingredients in a heavy pot. Bring to boil. Lower heat to simmer and cook about 2 hours or until thick, stirring often to keep from sticking. Seal in sterilized jars. Refrigerate after opening. Makes about 3 pints.

**More Reading:**

*Hints and Pinches: A Concise Compendium of Aromatics, Chutneys, Herbs, Relishes, Spices, and Other Such Concerns*, by Eugene Walter

# OCTOBER 14

Today is National Dessert Day.

*Cake is one of the luxuries of the table, and, like all luxuries, must be sparingly indulged in order to be enjoyed, its value depending chiefly on its rarity.*

—SARAH JOSEPHA HALE, *THE GOOD HOUSEKEEPER*, 1841

## Let Them Eat Pears

The evenings are shorter and crisper, fall is in the air, fresh pears are in the market, and there's still some cinnamon basil in the garden. On Dessert Day, what could be more elegant and easier than this fruit-and-herb delight?

### OVEN-POACHED PEARS WITH CINNAMON BASIL CRÈME FRAÎCHE

6 ripe pears
¾ cup light brown sugar, mixed with 1 teaspoon cinnamon
2 tablespoons butter
½ cup dark rum
garnish: slivered almonds, sprigs of basil or basil blossoms

Peel pears, quarter, and core. Arrange in a baking dish. Sprinkle brown sugar/cinnamon mixture on top and dot with butter. Pour rum over pears, and cover with foil. Bake at 350° for 15 minutes. Remove foil, baste, and bake until pears are cooked and tender, about 10–15 more minutes. Divide among six dessert bowls and serve with cinnamon basil crème fraîche, garnished with slivered almonds and sprigs of basil or basil blossoms.

### CINNAMON BASIL CRÈME FRAÎCHE

Mix together in a small bowl:

1 cup crème fraîche
½ cup minced fresh cinnamon basil leaves (sweet basil can be substituted)
Pinch of nutmeg

### TO MAKE CRÈME FRAÎCHE

Crème fraîche can be purchased, or you can make it yourself. Heat 1 cup heavy whipping cream to 105°. Stir in 1 tablespoon buttermilk. Cover and set in a warm place for 8–36 hours, stirring and tasting every 8 hours or so. The crème is ready when it is thick, with a slightly sour, nutty taste. It can be kept in the refrigerator for about 10 days. Use to top berries, fruit, puddings.

**For more herbal dessert treats:**
*Not Just Desserts: Sweet Herbal Recipes*, by Susan Belsinger, available from www.susanbelsinger.com.

*Just think of all those women on the* **Titanic** *who said, "No, thank you," to dessert that night. And for what!*

—ERMA BOMBECK

# OCTOBER 15

## A Great Bear of a Burr

Walk along an untrodden path this weekend, and when you get home, you may find your sweater studded with burrs. You've had a brush with burdock: *Arctium lappa*. Burdock is aptly named, for the Greek word *arctos* means "bear," while *lappa* derives from the Celtic word for "to seize." In 1948, George de Mestral, looking at the tenacious burrs under a microscope, noticed the tiny hooks that the plant has developed to hitch a ride on passersby. The result of de Mestral's observations? Velcro, a fastener with stiff hooks on one tape and soft loops on a matching tape.

The burdock has inspired a great many other uses, as well. Over the centuries, herbalists from many cultures have recommended it as a blood purifier, helpful in the treatment of gout and gallbladder and liver ailments. An infusion of the leaves eases indigestion, and a poultice heals burns and bruises. The root is used to treat skin disorders such as eczema and psoriasis. It has both anti-inflammatory and antibiotic properties. And if you ever run short of vegetables—or if you just want to try something different—burdock is a good choice. The young stalk, leaves, and flowers, steamed, taste like artichoke. In Russia, the leaves are used to wrap fish for steaming. In Japan, the taproot (called *gobo*) is a common vegetable, served raw or in soups and stir-fries.

And that Shakespeare bit about "holiday foolery"? The bard may be referring to an ancient custom in the Scottish town of South Queensbury in which a flannel-clad man is completely covered with burrs from head to toe. It's thought that the "burryman" may represent the spirit of the harvest, or that the ritual was a kind of catharsis, the burrs symbolizing evil.

**More Reading:**
*Healing Wise*, by Susun S. Weed

# OCTOBER 16

## Sprightly Saffron

If you're growing saffron (*Crocus sativus*) in your garden, this perky purple crocus is probably blooming just now. If you're not, now is the right time to purchase and plant the corms, which are about the size of a garlic clove. Planted now, your crocus will put up leaves in the spring and will flower the following autumn. They need a half-day's sun and well-drained soil, since the corms have a tendency to rot.

Saffron consists of the dried stigmata of *Crocus sativus*, which have to be picked by hand—laboriously, as you'll discover if you've done it. Since these filaments are threadlike and only an inch long, it takes a lot of stooping to collect even a teaspoon. One ounce of saffron is said to require 4,000 crocus blooms. No wonder it's the most expensive spice in the world!

Originally from ancient Persia, saffron has been used as a flavoring, a coloring agent, and a medicine. It has an earthy, bitter-honey taste, and is used in Mediterranean and Asian cuisines. It goes well with fish and seafood. In England, it's best known for its use in saffron buns. An Essex town—Saffron Walden, where it was grown—is named for it. As a dye, it produces a distinctive yellow-orange color; Buddhist priests' robes are dyed from it. Medicinally, it has been used topically to treat skin ailments; internally, it is said to improve blood circulation, reduce fever and inflammation, calm anxiety, and relieve depression. Francis Bacon wrote that saffron "maketh the English sprightly."

To dry your garden saffron, lay the filaments on paper and put in the oven (pilot light only). When dry, fold the paper and rub to a powder. To use, steep in hot, acidic, or alcoholic liquid (depending on the recipe) for about 20 minutes, to extract all the aroma, flavor and color. Add to your favorite paella recipe, to sautéed scallops, or to biscuits.

**Explore the exotic mysteries and adventures of saffron:** *Secrets of Saffron: The Vagabond Life of the World's Most Seductive Spice*, by Pat Willard

*It is reported at Saffronwalden that a Pilgrim purposing to do good to his Countrey, stole an head of Saffron, and hid the same in his Palmers staffe, which he had made hollow before of purpose, and so he brought this Root into this Realme, with Venture of his life: for if he had bene taken, by the Law of the Countrey from whence it came, he had died for the fact.*
—RICHARD HAKLUYT, *PRINCIPAL NAVIGATIONS, VOYAGES, TRAFFIQUES AND DISCOVERIES OF THE ENGLISH NATION*, 1582

In the floral calendar, today's flower: yarrow.

## Going Places: Willow Pond Farm, Fairfield, Pennsylvania

Willow Pond Farm will linger long in your memory. You'll recall with pleasure the many bright gardens and the fragrant lavender fields, home of the Pennsylvania Lavender Festival, a joyous June affair held each Father's Day weekend. But once you've tasted Madeline's splendid herbal jellies, you'll never, ever forget them.

Tom and Madeline Wajda (pronounced *Vy-da*) have owned Willow Pond since 1994. Tom grew up on an Ohio farm and is happy to return to his roots after spending 30 years in the U.S. foreign diplomatic corps. While the Wajdas lived in Paris, Madeline studied classical French cookery, receiving her coveted Certificate of Excellence in French cuisine. You can sample her culinary talents at the "boardinghouse lunches" held on the farm's patio or in the eighteenth-century stone farmhouse and followed by a workshop on herbs. Then visit the old summer kitchen (now the farm's gift shop) and step back to a time when jam and jelly was cooked in an iron kettle over an open fire.

Madeline's sweet and savory jellies are a farm specialty, and worth all the praise they get. "The most satisfying thing about making herbal jellies is watching people discover a new way to use herbs," Madeline says. "Nearly everyone's tried hot pepper jelly, but it's a giant leap to garlic or horseradish jelly, used as condiments! Jellies bring out people's creativity. Some use them with chicken and beef, but one inventive cook brushes garlic jelly over skewered shrimp on the grill, while another adds basil tomato jelly to a goat cheese–focaccia sandwich."

Madeline reports that the best-selling jellies change with the seasons: lavender in spring and summer, spicy rosemary and sage cranberry in fall. She loves to experiment with unusual combinations, like her new lavender-kissed fruit jams: blueberry, strawberry, and peach, each with an irresistible lavender fragrance and flavor. "When the season allows," she adds, "I make other flower jellies: rose petal, violet, apple blossom, and lilac. They are truly unique gifts."

You'll want to visit the farm in person, but you can also visit on-line, where you can purchase Madeline's delightful jellies, honeys, vinegars, and teas. Willow Pond Herb Farm, just 20 minutes west of Gettysburg, is open April through December. You'll find hours and directions at the web site: www.willowpondherbs.com. While you're there, check out the helpful articles and recipes in the Potting Shed and Madeline's Kitchen. (You'll find Madeline's recipe for Rosemary Walnuts in this book, on December 24.)

Oh, and don't forget the Lavender Festival. China and I have definitely put it on our calendar!

# OCTOBER 18

The English herbalist and astrologer, Nicholas Culpeper, was born on this day in 1616. He died in 1654, at the age of 38.

> *It is a base dishonourable unworthy part of the College of Physicians of London to train up the people in such ignorance that they should not be able to know what the Herbs in their Gardens be good for.*
>
> —NICHOLAS CULPEPER, *A PHYSICAL DIRECTORY*, 1650

## The People's Herbalist

Nicholas Culpeper may be responsible for giving medical herbalism its reputation for quackery. Vilified for his opposition to the powerful Royal College of Physicians, he is seen today as a proponent of herbal superstition. But if it had not been for Culpeper, the physicians and surgeons of his time might have succeeded in replacing herbal self-healing with their own "expert" forms of health care. We owe a great debt to this herbalist, who preserved the traditional uses of plant medicines in a clear and readable way.

Culpeper lived in a time when it was politically dangerous for anyone but licensed physicians to dispense medical knowledge. Trained as an apothecary and motivated by a desire to make medicines available to common people, Culpeper translated into English the Latin *London Pharmacopoeia*, a closely held handbook of medical preparations. He published his work as *The London Dispensatory* (1651), naming and ridiculing the exotic "pharmaceuticals" that the Royal College prescribed: thirteen kinds of dung, the brains of sparrows, the hearts of stags, the horns of unicorns, powdered earthworms, fox lungs, horse testicles. Of one preparation, he says, "'Tis a mess altogether." It's no wonder that the enraged College put Culpeper on trial for witchcraft!

Culpeper followed the *Dispensatory* with the first English textbook on midwifery and childcare, emphasizing nutrition and cleanliness and recommending herbal remedies for common problems of pregnancy and childbirth. After that came his most famous work: *The English Physician*. The book listed the medicinal uses of plants found in the garden, hedgerow, and field, and indexed these to common illnesses, using astrological terms that his readers already understood. He recommended "simples," rather than elaborate compounds, and wrote his recipes in a readable, humorous style. He sold his book for a mere three pence, so that even the poorest could buy a copy—and they did. *The English Physician* has appeared in more than 100 editions in the 350 years since its first publication.

**More Reading:**

*Culpeper's Medicine: A Practice of Western Holistic Medicine*, by Graeme Tobyn

"The People's Herbalist: Nicholas Culpeper," by Susan Wittig Albert, *The Herb Companion*, June/July 2002, pp. 35–39

*On those foreign hillsides where wild herbs grow, they reproduce themselves naturally. . . . When the plants' underground roots or rhizomes branch off and send up new plants, we say the plants have spread by their roots. A little farther along our hillside there is a colony of plants that multiply from their bases; every year each plant has a larger base with more shoots coming from it; we say these herbs multiply from their crowns.*

—THOMAS DEBAGGIO, *GROWING HERBS FROM SEED, CUTTING & ROOT*

## Divide and Multiply

Dividing your herbs to multiply them is good for you (dividing gives you more plants, for free!) and good for the plants (dividing discourages disease by thinning foliage). The best candidates for division are the perennial herbs that die back in the winter and return, larger than life, in the spring. In the southern half of the U.S., dividing these plants now will give them time to settle in for vigorous new growth in the spring. In the north, you may want to mark the plants now (before their tops die back) for division in early spring.

Whenever you do the work, you'll need a shovel and a sharp knife. Dig around the circumference of the clump, then lift the root mass out of the ground. Shake off the soil or wash it off with a hose. Pull the clump apart, or divide the mass into pieces with the knife, trying to keep a large root system with each division. (Sometimes a clump will yield a dozen or so new plants; the larger the divisions, the less transplant shock the plant will suffer.) Dig a hole for your new plant, put it in, and water thoroughly.

**HERBS TO DIVIDE**

| | |
|---|---|
| bee balm | lemon balm |
| catnip | lemongrass |
| most artemisias | oregano |
| mints | tarragon |
| sorrel | chives |
| day lilies | sweet woodruff |

**More Reading:**

*Growing Herbs from Seed, Cutting & Root*, by Thomas DeBaggio

*Is not October the first of the Months of the Spade—the month when one ought to start trenching and double-trenching, planting and transplanting, and doing back-aching things all day?*

—WILFRID BLUNT, *A GARDENER'S DESIGN*

*Who can endure a Cabbage Bed in October?*

—JANE AUSTEN, *SANDITON*

# OCTOBER 20

*Witch-hazel blossoms in the faal,*
*To cure the chills and Fayvers all.*
—EARNEST THOMPSON SETON, *TWO LITTLE SAVAGES*

## Witch Hazel

When you see a witch hazel (*Hamamelis virginia*) in its spectacular late-autumn dress, you may understand how Native Americans felt when they encountered this native golden beauty. Is it any wonder that native peoples believed that the plant was a gift from the Great Spirit?

### POWERFUL MEDICINE

Witch hazel was an important ceremonial herb. The Penobscot and the Potawatami used the twigs in cleansing sweat baths and drank witch hazel tea to encourage sweating. The Menominee used the seeds as sacred beads, and to predict the recovery of an ailing person. The Mohicans used forked witch hazel sticks to locate underground water, and colonists eagerly did the same. But while "witching" for water may sound spooky, the name "witch hazel" has nothing to do with the supernatural. In England, small trees (ash, elm, hazel) were cut, or coppiced, to encourage the growth of pliant shoots, or *wyches*, for bows and woven fencing. Witch hazel shrubs reminded colonists of the coppiced trees back home.

Because it is soothing, cooling, and astringent, witch hazel is used as an ingredient in many skin lotions. Try some for yourself.

### CUCUMBER-MINT AFTER-BATH SPRITZER

    2 tablespoons fresh mint leaves
    ½ cup boiling water
    2 cucumbers
    ¼ cup witch hazel
    1 teaspoon aloe vera gel

Pour boiling water over mint leaves, cool, strain. In a blender, puree cucumbers and strain juice. Mix ½ cup cucumber juice with mint infusion, witch hazel, and aloe vera gel. Pour into a clean spray bottle and store in refrigerator for up to a week. Shake before using.

### More Reading:

*New England Natives: A Celebration of People and Trees*, by Sheila Connor

*The bark affords an excellent topical application for painful tumors and piles, external inflammations, sore and inflamed eyes. . . . A tea is made from the leaves and employed for many purposes, in bowel complaints, pains in the sides, menstrual effusions, bleeding of the stomach. In this last case, the chewed leaves, decoction of the bark or tea of the leaves, are all employed with great advantage."*

—CONSTANTINE RAFINESQUE, 1830, DESCRIBING CHEROKEE,
CHIPPEWA, AND IROQUOIS USES OF THE HERB

# OCTOBER 21

## The Comfrey Controversy

Comfrey, a revered herb-garden perennial, has large leaves and a stout root that is mucilaginous even after it is dried. Its use in the treatment of fractures has given comfrey the long-lasting reputation indicated by its name, which is related to the Latin verb *confervere*, to grow together. Its genus name, *Symphytum*, comes from the Greek, "to cause to grow together." Other names: knitbone, knitback, boneset.

Both the leaves and the root were a popular remedy in earlier times. The Greeks used the root to treat wounds, believing that it encouraged the torn flesh to grow back together. A comfrey poultice hardens like plaster, and was often used as a cast for broken bones. A tea was brewed of the leaves and drunk for respiratory and intestinal ailments. By the Renaissance, it was being used for everything from bruises to sore throat and whooping cough, and in nineteenth-century America, it was prescribed for diarrhea, dysentery, and menstrual discomfort, as well. It was also eaten as a vegetable in Ireland and northern England, and the leaves were sometimes dried and added to flour.

Scientific studies have affirmed comfrey's "grow-together" properties. Both the leaves and the root (but especially the root) contain allantoin, a chemical that promotes the growth of new cells. However, some studies have indicated that excessive amounts of the herb, taken internally over an extended period, can cause liver dysfunction. It has been argued that comfrey is so unsafe that it should never be used; however, in a study published in the journal *Science*, the researcher pointed out that a cup of comfrey tea posed about the same cancer risk as a peanut butter sandwich.

Comfrey poses the same questions for us that are posed by all phytomedicines—in fact, by any medicine. What are the benefits of its use? What are the negative side-effects? Is it safe? Am I likely to be sorry? Whether we're taking something prescribed by a doctor or grown in our gardens, these are good questions to ask.

**More Reading:**
*The Healing Herbs*, by Michael Castleman

*It is extolled above all other herbes for the stopping of bloud in . . . bleeding wounds.*

—JOHN GERARD, *HERBAL*, 1597

## Golden, Golden, Goldenrod: From Susan's Journal

Today is one of those days when the Texas prairies outshine my garden, for the goldenrod is in bloom, its golden glory blazing across the fields.

The genus name of this remarkable plant is *Solidago*, which means "to make whole." It has been used as a healing herb since ancient times and grew throughout Europe, but the goldenrod market perked up when the Old World discovered that the New World had it in great plenty. The plant was baled, loaded onto ships, and taken to England to be sold in the apothecary shops, where two ounces might fetch a gold crown.

For Native Americans, goldenrod was a staple medicine, and since there were some two dozen species growing across the continent, at least one was in reach of nearly every tribe. It was used as a wound healer, but also employed in the treatment of headaches, fevers, diarrhea, coughs, stomach cramps, and kidney ailments, as well as rheumatism and toothache. They chewed the roots, brewed the roots and stems, and made poultices of the leaves. Calling it "sun medicine," some tribes used it in their steam baths, but it was also made into a charm, smoked with other tobaccos, woven into baskets, burned as an incense, and made into a dye.

Oh, yes, a dye. It *does* make beautiful colors, especially for wool. Using different mordants with different parts of the plant, I have obtained lovely shades of gold, orange-flushed tan, burnished olive, and shimmering gray.

And if that's not enough to convince you of this value of this golden plant, consider this: Discovering that its sap contained a natural latex, Thomas Edison bred the plant to increase the rubber yield and produced a resilient, long-lasting rubber that Henry Ford had made into a set of tires. Edison was still experimenting with his goldenrod rubber when he died in 1931. His research was turned over to the U.S. government, which apparently found it of little importance, even when rubber became almost impossible to get during World War II.

Goldenrod rubber. Imagine that.

**Read more about goldenrod, and other Prairie wildflowers:**

*Legends & Lore of Texas Wildflowers*, by Elizabeth Silverthorne

*And in the evening, everywhere
Along the roadside, up and down,
I see the golden torches flare
Like lighted street-lamps in the town.*

—FRANK DEMPSTER SHERMAN, "GOLDEN-ROD"

Today or tomorrow, the Sun enters the sign of Scorpio.

*The eighth sign of the zodiac, the masculine sign Scorpio (the Scorpion) is ruled by Pluto, formerly by Mars. Although Scorpio is a fixed water sign, its early association with Mars suggests fire, as well. And while Scorpio people may appear calm and unruffled on the surface, they can be as volatile as an undersea volcano. Intense, tenacious, with great willpower, they may also be secretive, compulsive, and easily hurt.*

—RUBY WILCOX, "ASTROLOGICAL SIGNS"

## Scorpio Herbs

Until this century, Scorpio was ruled by Mars. Now, astrologers assign Scorpio to Pluto, which was discovered in 1930. Physiologically, Pluto is said to rule the process of catabolism and anabolism, the continuous death and regeneration of body cells, and is particularly related to cleansing and the elimination of toxins. Pluto's regenerative influence also manifests itself in the sexual union (Mars rules sexual desire). Diseases of Scorpio are said to be involved with the buildup of toxic substances, particularly in the urogenital, intestinal, and reproductive systems. Herbs of Scorpio include:

• Ginseng (*Panax ginseng*). The Chinese value ginseng above most other herbal remedies, using it as a general tonic, restorative, and aphrodisiac. Research suggests that ginseng combats stress and fatigue and may counteract the effects of toxins.

• Southernwood (*Artemisia abrotanum*) and other artemisias have been used to cleanse the body of intestinal parasites.

• Black cohosh (*Actaea racemosa*) and blue cohosh (*Caulophyllum thalictroides*) are traditional remedies for regularizing the menstrual cycles.

• Aloe vera regulates the bowels and has a laxative effect, cleaning the liver and kidneys. Used externally, the gel (which contains allantoin) helps to heal and regenerate tissue.

• Dong Quai root is a general tonic for menstrual cramps, irregular cycles, and menopause. It is also used as a blood purifier.

• Other Scorpio herbs include squawvine, senna, false unicorn, saw palmetto, cascara sagrada, and cramp bark.

*Many thousands and thousands of perils and dangers beset man. He is not fully sure of his health or his life for one moment . . . but the Creator of Nature who has placed us amid such dangers has mercifully provided us with a remedy—that is, with all kinds of herbs, animals, and other created things to which He has given power and might.*

—ANONYMOUS FIFTEENTH-CENTURY GERMAN PHILOSOPHER

# OCTOBER 24

Ramadan takes place about this time.

## Ramadan

Ramadan is the ninth month of the Islamic lunar calendar, when Muslims celebrate the revelation of the Qur'an to the Prophet Muhammad. Time is spent in spiritual reflection, prayer, doing good deeds, and visiting with family and friends. During the month, Muslims fast during the daylight hours. When the new moon signals the end of Ramadan, the community shares a celebratory meal. Traditional foods include this cookie, filled with dates and nuts, which is eaten throughout Ramadan. Another traditional fruit is the pomegranate (see October 9).

### RAMADAN DATE-NUT COOKIES

- 1 cup butter
- 1 cup brown sugar
- 3 eggs
- 2 ½ cups flour
- 1 teaspoon baking soda
- ½ teaspoon powdered anise seed
- ¾ cup of sour milk (add one tablespoon lemon juice or vinegar to ¾ cup milk)
- 2 cups oatmeal

*Filling:*
- 1 8 oz. package dates, finely chopped
- ¼ cup finely chopped almonds
- 1 cup brown sugar
- 1 cup warm water

Preheat oven to 350°. Mix filling ingredients in a medium saucepan and cook, stirring occasionally, until thickened. Set aside to cool. Cream butter and sugar. Add eggs and mix well. Mix flour, baking soda, and anise seed. Add alternately with milk to the butter mixture. Stir in oatmeal and mix to a thick dough. Roll the dough on floured board to ¼-inch thick and cut with a 2-inch round cookie cutter. Place one teaspoon of filling in the center of a round and cover with another round. Use a fork to seal the edges. Bake on a parchment-covered cookie sheet for 15 minutes, or until golden. Dust with confectioners sugar.

# OCTOBER 25

Today is World Pasta Day.

*My idea of a quick and scrumptious dinner is a pot of al dente spaghetti dressed lightly with chopped fresh parsley and a full-bodied olive oil and served with tomato sauce and Parmesan cheese, hot herb bread, and a tossed salad—a meal which takes all of about fifteen minutes to throw together. By the time the pasta pot was boiling, the sauce was bubbling on my old Home Comfort gas range and the air was rich with the summer fragrance of tomatoes and basil.*

—MISTLETOE MAN: A CHINA BAYLES MYSTERY

## Herbs and Pasta

World Pasta Day? Sounds like an invitation to a pot of spaghetti or a steaming dish of any of the wonderful pastas available in the supermarket—or your own homemade pasta. (For a special herbal treat, add 3 tablespoons of your favorite chopped fresh herbs to the pasta dough before you shape it.) And try this fragrant tomato sauce that's a favorite with McQuaid and Brian.

### CHINA'S CHUNKY TOMATO SAUCE

½ cup olive oil

1 medium onion, chopped

3 cloves garlic, minced

4 cups tomatoes (about 4, peeled, seeded, and chopped)

4 ounces chopped fresh mushrooms

1 teaspoon salt or Savory Blend (August 29)

3–4 tablespoons chopped fresh basil

½ teaspoon fresh-ground black pepper

In a large skillet, heat the oil. Add the onion and garlic, and cook until the onions are soft, stirring. Add the tomatoes, cover and cook for about 5 minutes. Add the mushrooms, basil, and salt and cook 5 minutes more. Serve over hot pasta, with grated cheese.

**More Reading:**

*Pasta,* by Anna del Conte

*Discussions about the history and origins of pasta are sometimes acrimonious. Who thought of it first? The Italians—or the Chinese? . . . It is claimed that macaroni in Italy goes back to Etruscan times, which would pre-date the Chinese noodle by about 500 years.*

—REAY TANNAHILL, FOOD IN HISTORY

*Those who forget the pasta are condemned to reheat it.*

—UNKNOWN

*"Hey, China, what's that you're planting?" Ruby Wilcox asked.*

*I patted the dirt firmly around the base of the plant and straightened up. "It's gingko," I said. . . .*

*Ruby bent over to peer doubtfully at the plant. "That dinky little twig is gingko? It's got a heck of a lot of growing to do. The last gingko I saw was a tree. A big tree." She looked up. "Taller than this building."*

*"Give it time," I said with a grin, and picked up my shovel. "Like about 500 years. I started this little guy from a cutting, and it's got some growing to do."*

—"AN UNTHYMELY DEATH," IN *AN UNTHYMELY DEATH AND OTHER GARDEN MYSTERIES*

## Ginkgo: A Very Old Tree

According to scientists, the fossil record tells us that *Ginkgo biloba* is one of the oldest trees on earth: its ancestors were alive some 225 million years ago. This is reason enough to plant one in your yard—but if you need more incentive, listen to this:

• In China, ginkgo has been used for thousands of years to treat coughs, diarrhea, venereal disease, cancer, urinary ailments, and impotence.
• Current ginkgo research in the U.S. and Europe is focussed on ginkgo as a treatment for Alzheimer's disease and stroke. Gingko appears to improve blood circulation to the brain and enhance short-term memory.
• Gingko may be useful in treating macular degeneration, cochlear deafness, and peripheral arterial disease.

If you're thinking of adding a gingko to your landscaping, be sure you have plenty of room: it can reach a height of 100 feet, with a 20-foot girth. Choose a male tree, to avoid the squishy fruit of the female trees. Plant in well-drained soil and stake it until you're sure it's going to grow straight. Water regularly until it's about 20 feet tall. It will grow about two feet a year, and defy insects and disease. In autumn, its ornamental, fan-shaped leaves will turn a beautiful gold.

### GINKGO NUT PORRIDGE

Take one cup of rice and 10–15 ginkgo nuts, cook in 2.5 cups of water over slow heat, until tender. Remove ginkgo nuts, blend rice until creamy, then add ginkgo nuts. Warm and serve. Add honey, butter or olive oil to taste. (Reprinted with permission from Hobbs, *Ginkgo, Elixir of Youth*)

### More Reading:

*Ginkgo, Elixir of Youth: Modern Medicine from an Ancient Tree*, by Christopher Hobbs

*God designed Osage orange especially for the purpose of fencing the prairies.*

—JOHN A. WRIGHT, EDITOR OF *THE PRAIRIE FARMER*, 1850

## Hedge Apples: From Susan's Journal

Here at MeadowKnoll, we have only one hedge apple tree. Growing at the edge of the woodland, it drops its fruits into the grass at the edge of our little marsh. But when I was a child in Illinois, every hedgerow was full of these graceful trees. And at this time of year, the trees were full of hedge apples, which made dandy ammunition for the farm boys in our area. The hedge apple fruits are about the size of a grapefruit and heavy. If you're hit by one, by golly, you'll feel it for a while.

This tree, native to Texas and Oklahoma, was named in 1818: *Macula pomifera*, in honor of the American geologist William Maclure. The common name, Osage orange, reflects the orange color of the bark and wood, which was much used by the Osage Indians who lived between the Arkansas and Missouri rivers. Their Osage orange bows were so widely respected that the tree was called *bois d'arc*, and a well-made bow might bring as much as a horse and blanket in trade. The Comanches made a decoction of the root to treat eye infections, and the Kiowa used the wood to make the staff held by the singer in the sacred peyote ceremony. The Pima used it to tan leather and to make a lovely yellow-orange dye—and so have I.

When the settlers came to the Plains, they used the trees for fencing, planting them close together, so that the thorny branches formed an effective barrier. The trees have a long life, in part because the wood contains an antifungal agent that makes it rot and insect resistant. So when barbed wire began to reshape the prairies, Osage orange was in demand as fence posts—as well as for wheels, mine timbers, and railroad ties.

My grandmother, who grew up on a Missouri farm in the 1870s, gathered hedge apples and stowed them in the cupboard to keep out the cockroaches. If you have roaches and hedge apples, it's worth a try. You might also try growing your own tree. Soak the fruit in water for a couple of days, then break it up. Planted now, the seeds should germinate next spring.

**For another view of the hedge apple, read:**

*The Ghosts of Evolution: Nonsensical Fruit, Missing Partners, and Other Ecological Anachronisms*, by Connie Barlow

*So much do the savages esteem the wood of this tree [the osage orange] for the purpose of making their bows, that they travel many hundreds of miles in quest of it.*

—MERIWETHER LEWIS TO THOMAS JEFFERSON, 1804

# OCTOBER 28

Today is the beginning of the Celtic Month of Reed, according to some sources.

*That worthy Prince of famous memory Henry 8. King of England, was wont to drinke the distilled water of Broome floures, against Surfets and Diseases thereof arising.*

—JOHN GERARD, *HERBAL*, 1597

## The Bonny, Bonny Broom

Scotch Broom (*Cytisus scoparius*) is a perennial shrub, growing six to ten feet tall, that served a variety of important household purposes. In its native England, it was used to make brooms, wattle fencing, and baskets; in Scotland, it was used as a roof thatch. The flowers produced a yellow and green dye.

Broom was also thought to have magical properties, for its golden pea-blossoms were sacred to the sun god Belus. While the plant is toxic, the young petals are somewhat safer and were once used to produce an intoxicating narcotic drink. Roasted, the seeds substituted for coffee. Medicinally, the tops were infused as a treatment for dropsy (congestive heart failure) and kidney and bladder complaints.

In bloom, the plant represented plenty and abundance. According to *The Modern Herbal*, the flowers were used for house decoration at Whitsuntide, but if you used broom for a "menial purpose" at that time, you could find yourself in trouble: "If you sweep the house with blossomed Broom in May, You are sure to sweep the head of the house away."

The wild yellow broom is highly invasive, and you don't want it in your garden. But look for some of the hybrid cultivars in beautiful colors of red, maroon, and orange. You might want to try pickling them, following a recipe from 1736:

### MRS. MCLINTOCK'S PICKLED BROOM BUDS

Gather your Broom-buds about the first of May, pick them clean, sew a Linen Bag, put them in, lay them in a strong pickle of salt and Water, let them lie 5 or 6 Days, change the water every Day, boil them in salt and Water, till they be as green as Grass; then take as much wine Vinegar as you think will cover them, with a little Nutmeg, Cloves, Mace, Ginger; boil all with your Vinegar, and drain the Buds clean from the Water, and put them among the Vinegar, and let them boil awhile; so bottle them up.

**Learn more about the uses of herbs in Scotland:**
*The Scots Herbal: The Plant Lore of Scotland*, by Tess Darwin

*According to tradition, the last herb stalk left in the garden after the harvest is the home of the garden spirit. Ask for its blessing, and hang it in the kitchen.*

## "What Folk Do with Herbs": The Sixteenth Annual Myra Merryweather Lecture

In pursuit of a fully rounded herbal education, the herb guild has established the Myra Merryweather Lecture Series. Each year, they invite a noted herbal expert to speak on an interesting and engaging topic. This year's lecture was even more interesting than usual. Entitled "What Folk Do with Herbs," it was all about herbal folklore. The guest speaker, Mrs. Emmaline Wiggenton, probably could have talked all night (in fact, some people thought she might be going to do just that). But she certainly kept everyone entertained. Here are some of the highlights of her talk.

- Comfrey was not just a medicinal herb, it was a wonder-worker. Comfrey leaves in the bath water could restore your virginity.
- If you take a heliotrope flower into church, it will cause all the unfaithful wives to be frozen in their seats.
- Hide caraway seeds in your husband's pocket, and he will be safe from the lures of the other woman. If that doesn't work and he strays, burn a bay leaf to bring him back again.
- Tie a red onion to the bedpost. It will keep you from catching cold and other unpleasant diseases in bed.

- If you're worried about your moral health, you can get a checkup with a plantain. Pull a leaf and count the number of ribs. This will tell you how many lies you've already told today.
- A young woman who is curious about the identity of her future spouse can find out by setting a dish of flour under a rosemary bush on Midsummer Eve. When she gets up in the morning, she'll find her future husband's initials written in it. Or somebody's.
- Set your cabbage plants out on a Friday new moon, and they'll never be harmed by the frost.
- Fennel is a favorite of snakes. They eat it to restore their youth before shedding their skins.

In token of the Guild's deep appreciation for her erudite lecture, Pansy Pride presented Mrs. Wiggenton with an engraved plaque and a beautiful tumbleweed made of coat hangers, crafted by the Guild's very own Harold Thompson. This brought all the Guild members to their feet in an enthusiastic burst of applause.

The evening ended with a selection of delicious herbal refreshments, although it was remarked that Felicity Firestone's prizewinning fennel pesto, served as an appetizer on toasted crostini, was almost untouched.

**For more on Mrs. Wiggenton's subject:**
*Discovering the Folklore of Plants*, by Margaret Baker

# OCTOBER 30

*Hey-how for Hallow e'en!*
*A' the witches to be seen*
*Some in black, and some in green,*
*Hey-how for Hallow e'en!*

—TRADITIONAL SONG

*And the Great Pumpkin will rise up out of his*
*pumpkin patch with his bag of toys for all the*
*good children.*

—CHARLES SCHULTZ, *IT'S THE GREAT PUMPKIN,*
*CHARLIE BROWN!*

## Pumpkins!

It's time to celebrate that great American ritual, the carving of the pumpkin. It is said that the practice began in Ireland, with lighted coals put into carved turnips. However that may be, the Holloween pumpkin is certainly an American invention, for *Cucurbita pepo* is a native American herb.

An herb? Indeed! The pumpkin in its entirety—the flesh, the blossoms, and the seeds—was a popular, nourishing vegetable, used by many Indian tribes: Apache, Cherokee, Navajo, Ojibwa, Papago, Rappahonnock. But the seeds were also used to treat intestinal parasites and kidney and urinary problems. A decoction of the stems was used to soothe menstrual cramps, and the leaves for upset stomachs. A ground seed paste cleansed and softened the skin.

When you've carved your pumpkin, there's sure to be plenty of pumpkin seeds for the children to roast and eat. Here's the basic how-to: Separate the seeds from the pulp and wash the seeds thoroughly. Spread them on a cookie sheet, sprinkle with salt or Savory Blend (August 29), and bake at 350° for 20 minutes, stirring frequently. And for more eating fun, sprinkle with Mama Mia, Creole Crazy, or Mexi-Corny Popcorn Sprinkle (see January 19)—what's good for popcorn is just as good for pumpkin seeds. Go for it, Charlie Brown!

American Indian tribes had different names for the October full moon:

*Apache: Moon When the Corn Is Taken In*
*Northern Arapaho: Falling Leaves Moon*
*Cheyenne: Moon When the Water Begins to*
*Freeze at the Edge of the Stream*
*Muskogee: Big Chestnut Moon*

# OCTOBER 31

Today is the eve of Samhain. In the Celtic calendar, it marks the beginning of the winter season. In America, today is celebrated as Halloween, a contraction of All Hallows Eve.

*To summon minor devils, burn incense made of parsley root, coriander, nightshade, hemlock, black poppy juice, sandalwood, and henbane.*

—SIXTEENTH-CENTURY FORMULA, CITED IN *ROSEMARY REMEMBERED: A CHINA BAYLES MYSTERY*

## The Witching Herbs

Whether or not Ruby Wilcox is a witch (as some folks in Pecan Springs insist), she is definitely sympathetic to earth religions and pagan traditions. Her studies have taken her into the herbs that were traditionally associated with witches, and she usually teaches a class on them during the last week of October. The following material comes from one of her class handouts. (Please note that Ruby is giving historical information, not teaching people how to use these deadly plants!)

### A TRIO OF BANEFUL HERBS

- Henbane (*Hyoscyamus niger*) was believed to have aphrodisiac properties. The Greek priestesses of the Oracle of Delphi are said to have smoked it to increase their prophetic powers, and it has long been thought to enhance clairvoyance. Ingested, it is fatally toxic.

- Belladonna (*Atropa belladonna*). In legend, belladonna belongs to the devil. The name may refer to the use of the juice by Italian women as an eye-drop, to give brilliancy and beauty to the eye, or to Hecate, goddess of the underworld, who could transform herself into a beautiful woman. A narcotic, pain reliever, and source of atropine, belladonna had important uses in early medicine, although it was known to be fatally toxic. Mixed with fat or oil and rubbed on the skin, the plant was used as an hallucinogen. An ingredient in the infamous "flying ointments."

- Mandrake (*Mandragora officinarum*). A narcotic herb, used in ancient times as an anesthetic during surgery. According to *The Modern Herbal*, "The plant was fabled to grow under the gallows of murderers, and it was believed to be death to dig up the root . . . It was held, therefore, that he who would take up a plant of Mandrake should tie a dog to it for that purpose, who drawing it out would certainly perish." Mandrake was apparently used like henbane and belladonna, as an hallucinogenic ointment.

**More about witching herbs:**
*Magical Herbalism*, by Scott Cunningham
*Murder, Magic, and Medicine*, by John Mann

# NOVEMBER 1

Today is Samhain, the fourth cross-quarter day of the Celtic year. Other cross-quarter days: Imbolc (February 1), Beltane (May 1), and Lughnasadh or Lammas (August 1).

> *The new year of the earth begins. We have reached the midpoint between Autumn Equinox and Winter Solstice. This is the time to think about our own mortality. The veil is the thinnest between the worlds tonight, and dead souls visit their living relatives.*
>
> —ZSUZSANNA E. BUDAPEST, *THE GRANDMOTHER OF TIME*

## Soul Cakes

Samhain was a major celebration in the England of earlier times, for the harvest was complete and the households and farmsteads were stocked with food for the winter. Groups went from house to house, singing or chanting in return for something to eat or drink, as they did at other celebrations. When the pagan festival became All Souls Day, the poor went about chanting prayers for the souls of any who had died that year, in return for "soul cakes," flat oat breads baked with currants. The dead, who were believed to return at this time, were also thought to share the cakes.

There is no record of the herbs that might have been used to flavor the cakes, but rosemary was likely. Begin a tradition in your family by baking these cupcakes and sharing with the neighbors.

**OATMEAL APPLE CUPCAKES WITH NUTS AND ROSEMARY**

1 apple, chopped
½ cup raisins
½ cup chopped pecans
2 teaspoons fresh rosemary, minced fine, or 1 teaspoon dried
1 cup oatmeal
½ cup brown sugar
2 cups flour
1 teaspoon baking powder
½ teaspoon salt
½ teaspoon baking soda
½ teaspoon cinnamon
1 egg
1 cup buttermilk (or 1 cup milk with 1 tablespoon of lemon juice added)
½ cup cooking oil

Preheat oven to 375°. Grease a 24-cup muffin tin, or place paper cups in muffin tin. Mix chopped apple, raisins, nuts, and rosemary. Mix dry ingredients in a large bowl. Mix egg, buttermilk, and oil. Add wet ingredients to dry ingredients in two batches, stirring just to mix. Add fruit-nut mix. Stir just until all ingredients are moistened. Fill muffin cups ⅔ full. Bake for 20–25 minutes or until golden brown. Allow to cool for 5–10 minutes, then remove from the muffin tins. Makes 2 dozen muffins.

# NOVEMBER 2

*Hispanics celebrate their dead throughout the year, but especially on* **El Día de los Muertos,** *the day when families hold reunions at the cemetery, where the spirits of the dead are invited to join the festivities and share in the holiday food, music, flowers, candles, and incense. It's a reflection of Hispanics' respect for death, their belief that death is only a part of life, in the natural progression from this world to the next.*

—BLEEDING HEARTS: A CHINA BAYLES MYSTERY

## El Día de los Muertos

In Mexico, Day of the Dead celebrations usually take place between October 27 and November 2. The rituals differ, depending on family, community, and regional traditions. Families create home altars displaying the *ofrendas*, or offerings, which include flowers and herbs, pictures, candles, and *pan del muerto*, as well as favorite foods. The community celebrates with music, dancing, gay costumes, and quiet visits to family gravesites, where candles and incense are burned. But whatever else the celebration involves, three important herbs are likely to be used.

- Amaranth (*Amaranthus hypochondriacus*) was a staple grain for pre-Columbian Aztecs, who believed it had supernatural powers. Associated with human sacrifice, ground amaranth seed was mixed with honey or human blood and formed into figures that were eaten during rituals. At modern Day of the Dead celebrations, the seeds are mixed with honey and chocolate and made into skulls called *calaveras*, with the name of the dead on the forehead. The skulls symbolize death and rebirth.

- Marigold (*Tagetes sp.*), or *zenpasuchitl* or *cempasuichil*, figured in Aztec beliefs about the seven-year journey to and from the afterworld, which must be completed before the dead could rest. In search of nourishment, souls returned to the land of the living each year. They took strong-smelling marigolds from the *ofrenda* to drop behind them, marking the trail they would take on their return the following year. Often, the living create such trails, from the cemetery (where marigold flowers decorate the grave) to the home.

- Copal, a resin from the copal tree (*Bursera bipinnata*), is an ancient ceremonial incense of the Aztecs, gathered as a resinous sap from their sacred tree. In pre-Columbian times, it was burned, with human sacrifices, on top of the Aztec and Mayan pyramids. It is burned on the *ofrenda* to bless and purify the returning souls of the dead.

**Explore the relationships between people, places, and plants in the American Southwest:**

*Beliefs and Holy Places: A Spiritual Geography of the Pimeria Alta*, by James S. Griffith

*A garden is a thing of beauty and a job forever.*

—RICHARD BRIERS

## Just Say Goodnight

It's sad to watch the garden fading into winter, but at least we don't have to say goodbye. Spring will return, as naturally as the sun will rise tomorrow morning. All we have to do is ready the garden so that it can rest until its renewal a few months hence. Here's a to-do list that will help you prepare your garden for its winter's nap.

• *Clean Out and Cut Back*. Shoals of dead leaves and rotten stalks can harbor disease, even through the winter season. But don't cut plants back to the ground, and don't pick up every dead leaf. Leave seed heads for the winter birds, some plant stalks to protect the crowns, and others for their wintertime beauty.

• *Cover Up*. Mulch is the best winter protection for your plants. Wait until the ground has frozen slightly, to ensure the plants' dormancy. If the snow falls, mulch over the snow. Some woody perennials and shrubs may benefit from soil mounded around the base. Biennials that produce a rosette of leaves on the surface of the ground (foxglove, pansies, mullein, for instance) may benefit from a box covering; other plants will do very well under a blanket of leaves, particularly oak leaves, which mat down less.

Tender shrubs may need to be screened or wrapped (with burlap or something similar, *not* plastic.)

• *Dig In*. A few hardy shrubs and perennials can still be put into the ground, especially corms, bulbs, and roots—saffron crocuses, for instance, and horseradish. Mulch as necessary.

• *Write Down*. You'll find a garden log very helpful next spring, when you're trying to identify those first tentative green shoots and wondering whether you divided that artemisia last fall or should do it now. Draw a diagram of each bed, noting the plants and adding photos where possible. A little extra effort now will pay off next spring.

*The herb garden values its winter's rest:*
*The knot and the border, and the rosemary gay*
*Do crave the like succour, for the dying away. . . .*

—THOMAS TUSSER, *FIVE HUNDRED POINTS OF GOOD HUSBANDRY*

# NOVEMBER 4

In some years, this is Election Day.

## Election Cake

I was browsing through an early nineteenth-century cookbook the other day when I came across a recipe for something called Election Cake. "Old-fashioned election cake," I read, "is made of four pounds of flour . . ."

Election cake? I'd never heard of it! But some on-line research pulled up an answer, from an article written by the well-known food historian Alice Ross. Election cake, Dr. Ross says, was a tradition that began back in England, with the "Great Cake," rich, spicy fruit-filled cakes baked to celebrate important family or community occasions. One such occasion arose during the Revolutionary War, when men flocked to the colonial towns to report for duty in the Revolutionary Army. The inns and taverns served cake: "Mustering Cake." After the War, men came to town again—this time to vote in elections for which they had fought and died. It was time to celebrate again, this time, with "Election Cake."

A recipe for Election Cake appears in the second edition of Amelia Simmons' *American Cookery* (1800)—a truly American cookbook, with recipes for such colonial novelties as Johnny Cake, Indian Slapjacks, "Pompkin pudding" (the first pumpkin pie), cooked squash with whortleberries, even the quintessentially American Spruce Beer. What's more, Mrs. Simmons was the first cookbook author to use the word *cooky*,

from the Dutch "koekje," the treats offered in colonial New York to holiday callers. So it seems altogether appropriate that *American Cookery* should include recipes for three American cakes: Independence Cake, Federal Pan Cake, and Election Cake. Here is Amelia Simmons' recipe for a cake that was obviously intended to be served to a large crowd of enthusiastic voters.

**ELECTION CAKE**

30 quarts flour, 10 pound butter, 14 pound sugar, 12 pound raisins, 3 doz eggs, one pint wine, one quart brandy, 4 ounces cinnamon, 4 ounces fine colander seed, 3 ounces ground allspice; wet the flour with milk to the consistence of bread over night, adding one quart yeast; the next morning work the butter and sugar together for half an hour, which will render the cake much lighter and whiter; when it has rise light work in every other ingredient except the plumbs, which work in when going into the oven.

**Read more about Election Cake (including additional recipes):**
"Election Cake," by Alice Ross, *The Journal of Antiques and Collectibles,* October, 2003.

*Coriander seed was once used extensively in confectionery. They seeds are quite round, like tiny balls, about the size of a Sweet Pea Seed. The longer they are kept the more fragrant they become, with a warm pungent taste.*

—MRS. GRIEVE, *A MODERN HERBAL*, 1931

This week is National Split Pea Soup Week. And tomorrow is National Men Make Dinner Night!

*Pease porridge hot,*
*Pease porridge cold,*
*Pease porridge in the pot*
*Nine days old.*
—TRADITIONAL RHYME

## Pease Porridge Hot

Dried peas were a staple food well into the nineteenth century. They were easy to grow and store, and they made a wholesome, nutritious meal. In many homes, a kettle filled with a thick porridge of peas and other vegetables—with bacon, if the good wife could afford it—hung over the fire. At night, when the fire died down, any leftover porridge got cold. In the morning, when the fire was rekindled, the porridge warmed up, and more peas and vegetables went into the pot. If it wasn't thoroughly stirred, the pease porridge at the bottom of the pot might have been even older than nine days!

At China's house, McQuaid makes dinner at least once a week. And since split pea soup is so easy, it's frequently on the menu. With sausage, hot bread, and a salad, it's a full meal.

**MIKE MCQUAID'S SPLIT PEA SOUP**

2 tablespoons olive oil
2 tablespoons butter
3 slices bacon, chopped
1 medium onion, diced
2 carrots, diced
2 stalks celery, diced
2 cloves garlic, minced
2 cups dried split peas
½ teaspoon dried marjoram
½ teaspoon crushed red pepper flakes
1 bay leaf
fresh ground pepper, salt or Savory Blend to taste
  (August 29)
sour cream, parsley for garnish

Wash and drain the split peas and set aside. In a large, covered pot, heat the olive oil, butter and bacon. Sauté until the bacon is slightly transparent. Add the carrots, onion, celery, and garlic. Sauté over medium heat, stirring occasionally, until the onion is transparent (10–15 minutes). Add the peas, bay leaf, marjoram, and red pepper flakes. Add enough cold water to cover the peas, and bring to a boil. Reduce the heat and cover the pot. Simmer for about 2 hours, stirring every 15 minutes and adding water as necessary. When done, remove the bay leaf and taste for seasoning, adding salt and fresh ground black pepper if you like. If you want a smoother soup, puree about half of it in a blender; return to pot, reheat, and serve. Garnish with sour cream and chopped parsley.

**Find out more about beans:**
*Easy Beans: Fast and Delicious Bean, Pea, and Lentil Recipes*, by Trish Ross

# NOVEMBER 6

## Going Places: Summers Past Farms, Flinn, California

For most of us, summer is only a memory, but at Summers Past Farms, nestled in the foothills 30 minutes east of downtown San Diego, it is summer all year round. With its many gardens of flowers and herbs, this beautiful herb farm is a unique and delightful destination for winter-weary travelers.

Summers Past began in 1987, when Sheryl and Marshall Lozier recognized the potential in the place where Marshall's family had lived for more than half a century. Sheryl, whose love of cooking began in childhood, wanted to plant an herb garden. Marshall, a builder and contractor, wanted to build a barn. The garden blossomed, the post-and-timber barn grew into a showplace, and in 1992 the couple opened the gate to their five-acre dream: Summers Past Farms. Now, the Loziers work in the gardens and in their herbal soap shop, offer classes, and hold such special events as Sweet Pea Day, a Geranium Day, and a fairy festival. "Our lifestyle is our inspiration to keep this small family business growing," Sheryl says.

The holiday season is always a busy one at Summers Past, where the traditions of herbal Christmas are cherished. The season begins with a November Open House, featuring a display of lights, candles, potpourri, and holiday gifts. Hot wassail and fresh-baked cookies are served in the barn loft, and the farm's workshops feature herbal vinegar making (Sheryl has written a book about it, available at the farm) and holiday wreaths. "In my favorite workshop," Sheryl reports, "we make a fresh pine and rosemary centerpiece decorated with cones and cinnamon sticks—a Christmassy fragrance that lasts all through the holiday. We also show people how to craft wreaths of the herbs in their gardens: bay laurel, sages, thyme and sweet Annie."

But behind the scenes, a great deal more is going on, for November is the time when Sheryl and Marshall plant their famous Sweet Pea Maze, which blossoms in April and May. Theresa Loe, a garden writer who often visits Summers Past, told me that she loves to lose herself in the towering maze of fragrant sweet peas, where she gathers her own bouquet as she weaves her way through the labyrinth to the secret garden at the center. "It's magical," Theresa says. "And I love the Soap Shoppe, too—especially the many wonderful bar soaps." Sheryl makes and sells a dozen different vegetable-oil herbal soaps, including peppermint, lavender, rosemary, and cinnamon.

Summers Past Farms is open year-round. You can learn more on-line, at summerspastfarms.com, where you'll find hours and directions, information about workshops, links to photos of the gardens, and that wonderful soap shop, as well.

*Some people like to paint pictures, or do gardening, or build a boat in the basement. Other people get a tremendous pleasure out of the kitchen, because cooking is just as creative and imaginative an activity as drawing, or wood carving, or music.*

—JULIA CHILD

## Bouquet Garni

The idea of a "bouquet"—a gathering of flowers or an aroma—is French (of course), and the "bouquet garni" is a culinary term that combines the two: a bundle of aromatic herbs tied with string. In that way, the herbs leave only their flavor behind. No soggy leaves or twiggy bits mar the clarity or texture—or betray the cook's most closely held herbal secrets! The more we learn about the subtle tastes and aromas of herbs, the more we are likely to rely on this simple culinary technique.

Bouquet garni varies from dish to dish and from cook to cook. The most effective bouquet garni is made with just 2–4 herbs, with a modest amount of each: 2–3 sprigs of parsley, a sprig of thyme, a sprig of dried celery leaves, and a few fennel seeds will season a fish soup. (You can dry the celery tops in your oven, with the pilot on.) The length of time the herbs are left in the cooking pot depends on the taste you want to achieve. Fresh or dry herbs? Fresh have more life, but dry are preferred in stews or soups that involve long cooking.

Here are some suggested combinations, on which you can base your own experiments. You, too, can be a creative French chef!

- Poultry: sage, fennel, rosemary, marjoram, whole clove, juniper berry
- Beef: thyme, parsley, bay, summer or winter savory, dried orange peel, peppercorn
- Vegetable soups, tomato sauces: marjoram, parsley, bay, basil, dried celery
- Steamed fish, clams: oregano, parsley, thyme, chervil, chives

**BUNDLING YOUR BOUQUETS**

- To bundle fresh and dry herbs, tie stems with a string, leaving a 6–8 inch tail that can be tied around the pot handle.
- Bags are useful for bouquets that include seeds, spices, or herbs that are likely to disintegrate. Cut a 4×4-inch cheesecloth square, add herbs, gather and tie. Paper tea bags (heat-sealed) hold up well and can be discarded without guilt. Moisten in hot water before adding to the cook pot. Or use a large (2-inch) stainless steel tea ball.
- You can make up your favorite bouquets in advance. Be sure to label! And do make extras for friends.

**Explore the mysteries of Provencal cookery, rich in herbs:**

*Cooking with Herbs: The Flavor of Provence*, by Michel Biehn

*The juice of marigold [calendula] petals mixed with vinegar to be rubbed on gums and teeth becomes a soveraigne remedy for the assuaging of the grievous pain of the teeth.*

—GARDENERS LABYRINTH, 1577

## Smile!

From the super-whitened teeth evident everywhere today, it's evident that people are paying a lot more attention to their smiles than they have in the past. But it's not necessary to be tooth-obsessed, or spend hours with home bleaching kits and other chemicals, to have a healthy mouth. Here are some herbal options that will combat bacteria, sweeten your breath, help keep you smiling—and even help you out in an emergency.

- Tea tree oil (*Melaleuca alternifolia*). This is a powerful antibiotic infection-fighter. For a mouth rinse, use 3 drops in ½ cup of water. Swish and spit.
- Sage (*Salvia officinalis*). Astringent, antibacterial. Brew a strong tea (2 teaspoons sage per cup of boiling water, steep 10 minutes). Cool and use as a mouth rinse.
- Peppermint (*Mentha x piperita*). The menthol sweetens breath and combats bacteria. Brew a strong tea, or add 2 drops essential oil to a glass of water as a mouth rinse.

- Clove oil (*Syzygium aromaticum*). Got a toothache? Use a cotton swab to dab on a few drops of clove oil until you can see the dentist. The oil will numb the pain enough to tide you over.
- Aloe (*Aloe vera*). The leaf gel has antibacterial and anti-inflammatory properties that help to heal mouth and gum ulcers and canker sores. Apply directly to the infected area.

### MINT TOOTHPASTE

Mix together 3 teaspoons baking soda, ¼ teaspoon salt, 2 teaspoons glycerin, and 10 drops peppermint essential oil. Store in a small lidded container. Refreshing!

*The young branches [of dogwood, Cornus sp.] stripped of their bark, and rubbed with their ends against the teeth, render them extremely white. The Creole . . . who inhabit Norfolk, in Virginia . . . are in constant practice of using dogwood twigs in cleansing their teeth; the striking whiteness of these, which I have frequently observed, is a proof of the efficacy of this practice. The application of the juice of these twigs to the gums, is also useful in preserving them hard and sound.*

—WILLIAM P.C. BARTON, 1817

# NOVEMBER 9

### China Bayles Wins Big in Jelly! by Fannie Couch, special to the Pecan Springs *Enterprise*

The Myra Merryweather Herb Guild put on its herbal holiday exhibition last week, featuring a juried competition in herbal jelly-making. The judges awarded the hotly contested first prize to China Bayles, for her Reasonable Doubt Ginger-Mesquite Jelly. Ms. Bayles is the proprietor of Thyme and Seasons Herbs and an active member of the Guild. She was recently recognized as Pecan Springs' Citizen Crime Fighter of the Year for her help in solving the murder of a well-known high school coach. When asked why she named her jelly "Reasonable Doubt," she countered, "Why not?"

Bertha Rae Biggens won second prize for her Go-Go Garlic Jelly. Third place went to Jimmie Lee Jergens, for Hotsy-Totsy Apple-Chipotle Jelly. All three winners were awarded a ribbon rosette and a tumbleweed made of wire coat hangers, contributed by the Herb Guild's very own Harold Thompson.

**REASONABLE DOUBT GINGER-MESQUITE JELLY**

- 2½ quarts ripe mesquite pods
- ¾ cup chopped ginger
- 1 package powdered pectin
- 4½ cups granulated sugar
- 4 tablespoons lemon juice

Pick the mesquite pods when they are plump and tan-colored, and break them into small pieces without shelling out beans. In a large pan, cover broken pods and chopped ginger with water. Bring to a boil, and simmer until pods are soft. Mash with a potato masher (ginger may not mash well—don't worry about it). Simmer a few more minutes, then strain. Continue to cook until ginger-mesquite juice has been reduced to three cups. Place in a large kettle, add pectin and sugar and bring to a full boil. Stir and boil until the syrup sheets from a metal spoon (about 2 minutes). Remove from heat and skim off foam. Add a drop of red or yellow food coloring to give the jelly more color, if desired. Pour immediately into hot, sterilized jars. Cover with melted paraffin or (if to be used in a short time) a tight-fitting lid. Good as a tasty brush-on for grilled pork chops, chicken. Makes about 3½ cups of Reasonable Doubt.

# NOVEMBER 10

## Sniffle, Sniffle, Sneeze

When I was growing up, Vaporub was my mother's staple cold medicine. When my brother or I began to sniffle and sneeze, out came that little blue bottle, and when bedtime rolled around, we were put to bed with Vicks on our chests. At the time, of course, we had no idea what was in the stuff, only that it smelled good, it cleared our heads, and we could sleep the night through. It wasn't until much later that I learned that it was herbal medicine that did the trick: the magic of eucalyptus and menthol, blended with petroleum jelly. With winter upon us, it's a good time to stock up on these two helpful herbs.

• **Eucalyptus**. In its native Australia, leaves from the eucalyptus tree (*Eucalyptus sp.*) have been an important herbal medicine. Vapor from boiling leaves was used as an inhalant for colds and asthma. The leaves were rolled cigar-style and smoked to treat bronchitis. The plant contains a chemical, eucalyptol, that has a powerful decongestant action, loosening phlegm so it can be more easily coughed up. Eucalyptus oil is used in a variety of commercial cold preparations. Eucalyptol is also antibacterial and antiviral; after minor wounds have been washed, the oil or clean crushed leaves can be applied to help prevent infection. Never ingest the oil; it is highly toxic.

• **Menthol**. Menthol is a constituent of peppermint (*Mentha piperita*) and provides a cooling sensation in the nose, relieves nasal congestion, and relieves sore throat and cough by a local anaesthetic action. Its antimicrobial activity may also help to reduce infection. Never ingest oil of peppermint; it is highly toxic.

### EUCALYPTUS-PEPPERMINT TEA

To brew a pleasant-tasting medicinal tea, use 1–2 teaspoons of dried, crushed eucalyptus leaves and 1 teaspoon dried peppermint per cup of boiling water. Steep 10 minutes. Drink up to 2 cups a day, or use as a gargle.

### EUCALYPTUS-PEPPERMINT INHALANT

Boil a handful of eucalyptus and peppermint leaves in water, put a towel over your head, and inhale the aromatic steam.

### ENERGIZING EUCALYPTUS BATH SOAK

    1 cup Epsom salts
    8–10 drops essential oil of eucalyptus
    8–10 drops essential oil of peppermint
    5 drops essential oil of rosemary

Mix together and store in a lidded jar. Use ⅓ to ½ cup per bath. Energizing and invigorating.

### More Reading:

*The Eucalyptus: A Natural and Commercial History of the Gum Tree*, by Robin W. Doughty

November's theme garden: a Scripture Garden.

*And the earth brought forth grass, and herb yielding seed after his kind, and the tree yielding fruit, whose seed was in itself, after his kind: and God saw that it was good.*

—GENESIS 1:12

## Herbs and Plants of Scripture

People have for centuries been fascinated by the plants of the Bible, and there are many Biblical theme gardens. (For an updated list of gardens to visit, check this website: www.biblicalgardens.org.) As you think ahead to next summer, consider creating a special corner for Biblical plants, so that your garden can enlarge and enrich your understanding of Scripture. Here are a few plants you may want to include.

- Castor bean (*Ricinus communis*). Jonah 4:6–7. The "vine" that sprang up to shelter Jonah was most likely the herb we know as the castor bean, which grows rapidly to 12 feet (40 or more in the tropics). The Hebrews used the oil in their ceremonial rites. Castor oil has been used to treat ringworm and itching, as a treatment for stomach cancer, and as a laxative. Be sure to keep children away from the poisonous seeds.
- Cumin (*Cuminum cyminum*). Matthew 23:23. Cumin is an annual member of the parsley family, used for seasoning An important economic crop in Biblical times, it was heavily taxed.
- Mustard (*Brassica nigra*). Matthew 17:20 and Luke 13:9. The mustard was cultivated in Palestine for its oil. The leaves may have been among the bitter herbs eaten at Passover.
- Myrtle (*Myrtus communis*). Isaiah 41:19 and 55:13. A fragrant myrtle oil was used to celebrate the Feast of the Tabernacles, for the Hebrews used branches of myrtle to shade the huts that were part of the original celebration. It represents peace and joy.
- Rue (*Ruta graveolens*). Luke 11:42. By New Testament times, the plant was subject to taxation under Talmudic law. Rue has a peppery, bitter taste and was used for seasoning and medicinal purposes.
- Wormwood (*Artemisia arborescens, A. judaica, A. absinthium*). Proverbs 5:4 and Lamentations 3:15. Bitter-tasting wormwood appears frequently in Scripture as a symbol of repentance, punishment, and suffering. The plants were used medicinally, as an antiseptic and as a vermifuge.

*For the Lord thy God bringeth thee into a good land. A land of wheat, and barley, and vines, and fig trees, and pomegranates; a land of oil olive, and honey . . .*

—DEUTERONOMY 8:7–9

**Read more about Biblical gardens:**

*Bible Plants for American Gardens*, by Eleanor Anthony King

# NOVEMBER 12

*Where Bayes still grow (by thunder not struck down),*
*The victor's garland and the poet's crown.*
—WILLIAM BROWNE (1590–1645)

## Like a Green Bay Tree

The sweet bay or bay laurel (*Laurus nobilis*) is another of the Scriptural plants, growing wild in the Mediterranean region in Biblical times and so admired for its luxuriant evergreen growth that it became a symbol of prosperity and power. Greek and Roman poets, priests, heroes, and athletes wore wreaths of bay, and it was a mark of distinction for those in political office. It was used as a wedding and a funeral herb, churches were decorated with it, and (like rosemary) it was an herb that people employed throughout their lives: "From the cradle to the grave we have still use of, we have still need of it," Thomas Parkinson wrote in 1640.

But since the bay was so persistently successful, it seemed to have supernatural powers. It was supposed to lend prophetic power to poets and soothsayers. It warded off wizards and witches; it guarded against misfortune and protected people and houses from lightning. "Neyther falling sickness, neyther devyll wyll infest or hurt one in that place where a bay-tree is," Lupton asserted confidently in 1575.

In colder climates, bay makes an attractive tub or container plant for the patio; in warmer regions, it can stay outdoors all year. It is used as a seasoning, garnish, and for pickling. The leaves have the strongest flavor when they are dried slowly, or kept in the refrigerator and used fresh.

### BAY BLEND FOR MEAT & POULTRY
3 parts powdered bay leaf
2 parts rubbed sage
2 parts dried savory
1 part dried marjoram
1 part dried thyme
1 part dried basil
1 part dried rosemary
½ part garlic powder
½ part onion powder

Mix all ingredients. Store in lidded container. Rub into meat or poultry before roasting or broiling.

*Laurel tree, laurel tree*
*Keep house and field lightning free.*
—TRADITIONAL CHARM AGAINST LIGHTNING

*Rosemary wreath to encircle our home,*
*Give us fragrance, protection and light*
*From the mickle march steppers\**
*Who lurk and roam*
*Over hills in the dark of the night.*
—TRADITIONAL

\*The many creatures of the borderland.

### Don't Toss that Peel!

I am not an especially frugal person, but I hate to buy dried orange or lemon peel when I can recall having recently discarded some perfectly good peel in the compost. So to ensure that I always have dried peel on hand for cooking, herbal teas, potpourri, and stove-simmer, I make a practice of drying it regularly—and candying it, too. Makes me feel virtuous, especially with the holidays coming up.

Drying orange, lemon, or ruby grapefruit peel is just about as easy as it sounds. Once the peel and the fruit have parted company, I lay the peels on a cutting board, skin side down, and scrape off the bitter white pith, using a grapefruit spoon with serrated edges. I pop the scraped peels into the oven, with just the pilot light on, and leave them until they are dry but still slightly pliable. I add these to the jar of dried peel I keep on the cupboard shelf.

Candying is almost as easy. When I've scraped the peels, I cut them in narrow strips and drop them into boiling water. I simmer for 10–15 minutes, then drain; if the peels seem bitter, I repeat the process. In another pan, I make a sugar syrup, adding a cup of sugar to a cup of boiling water and stirring until the sugar is dissolved. Then I drop in the peels and simmer until they're translucent and the sugar has been absorbed. (I check frequently, to be sure they don't scorch.) With a fork, I fish them out and drop them, a few at a time, into sugar, shaking to cover, then drop them onto wax paper to dry. If the humidity is high, I pop them into the oven (pilot light only). When dry, they go into a lidded jar.

**Learn more ways to use those peels:**
*Zest: The Very Best Citrus Recipes,* by Coralie Dorman

*Have a bottle full of brandy, with as large a mouth as any bottle you have, into which cut your lemon and orange peel when they are fresh and sweet. This brandy gives a delicious flavor to all sorts of pies, puddings, and cakes. Lemon is the pleasantest spice of the two; therefore they should be kept in separate bottles.*

—MRS. CHILD, *THE AMERICAN FRUGAL HOUSEWIFE,*
*DEDICATED TO THOSE WHO ARE NOT ASHAMED*
*OF ECONOMY,* 1833

Today is National Clean Out Your Refrigerator Day. We must take this as an opportunity to prepare for that looming moment when we have to fit a 20-pound turkey, five vegetables, four sauces, three salads, and two pumpkin pies—all into that same impossibly small refrigerator.

## Curried Leftovers

I know. I shouldn't spoil a conversation about curry by introducing the subject of leftovers. But we need to start practicing so we can handle the flood of leftovers that will soon confront us. And to tell the truth, some leftovers just beg to be curried.

But first, curry. Curry is a spice mixture, the flavor of which depends on the choice and proportion of spices involved. Most commercial curry powders contain some 6–12 spices, and range in flavor from mild to fiery, simple to complex, sweet to slightly bitter. Fresh is always best, though, and it's easy to make your own. Here is a recipe for *garam masala*, one of Bill's favorite curry powders.

**GARAM MASALA**

    2 tablespoons cumin seeds
    2 tablespoons coriander seeds
    2 tablespoons cardamom seeds
    2 tablespoons black peppercorns
    1 tablespoon caraway seed
    1 tablespoon fennel seed

    1 (3-inch) stick cinnamon, broken up
    1 teaspoon whole cloves

Toast all ingredients except for the nutmeg in a heavy skillet (no oil) over medium-high heat. Stir and shake occasionally for about 8–10 minutes, until the spices turn somewhat darker and become fragrant. Cool completely. Divide into three batches. Grind to a powder in a coffee grinder or spice mill. Store in an airtight container in a cool, dry place.

Starting with small amounts and tasting as you go, add this curry powder to those leftover vegetables and chicken, along with some chopped onion, apple, celery, raisins, almonds, and coconut. Serve over hot rice, remembering that you're in training for the Big One, which is coming up in just over a week.

**Read more about coping with leftovers:**

*Leftovers: 200 Recipes, 50 Simple Master Preparations and 150 Delicious Variations for the Second Time Around*, by Kathy Gunst

*To ward off nightmares during the long winter nights, drink a tea of aniseed and garlic before bedtime, or make a pillow of hops and valerian.*

—TRADITIONAL REMEDIES

*To love in the midst of sweets, little children could do that, but to love in the bitterness of Wormwood is a sure sign of our affectionate fidelity.*

—ST. FRANCIS DESALES

## Southernwood

Southernwood (*Artemisia abrotanum*) is one of those herbs that you either like or you don't. Happily for me, I like it. Also happily, it likes my Texas garden, where it is still green and pretty when many other plants are frost-browned. Its feathery foliage (about 24 inches high) creates a soft edging around beds and borders, it's a fast-growing stop-gap filler when something else dies back, and it serves as an ornamental groundcover under the birdbath. I use it in pungent moth-repellant mixes, hang it in the closet, and (in the hot summer) put a few fresh sprigs on the dashboard of the car, for a fresh, clean scent. All in all, a useful herb.

The name southernwood is a contraction for "southern wormwood": getting rid of intestinal parasites was one of the important medicinal uses of this attractive artemisia. It was often planted in graveyards in token of love that endures through the bitterness of loss. Two of the plant's other folk names, lad's love and maiden's ruin, probably came from its inclusion in courting bouquets. (An interesting pair: did a lad's love always mean a maid's ruin?) The French call it *garderobe*, from its use as a closet herb. It was thought to ward off airborne infections, too; in England, branches of southernwood and rue were placed in courtrooms to guard against contagious diseases that might be carried by prisoners in the dock. I've read that it was once popular as a culinary herb—must have been an acquired taste.

*Southernwood tea.—Clip four ounces of the leaves fine and beat them in a mortar with six ounces of loaf sugar till the whole is like a paste. Three times a day take the bignesse of a nutmeg of this. It is pleasant and one thing in it is particular, it is a composer and always disposes persons to sleep.*

—SIR JOHN HILL, *THE BRITISH HERBALIST*, 1772

*Of these worts that we name Artemisia, it is said that Diana did find them and delivered their powers and leechdom to Chiron the Centaur, who first from these Worts set forth a leechdom, and he named these worts from the name of Diana, Artemis, that is Artemisias.*

—*THE HERBARIUM OF APULEIUS*, 1481

(ORIGINALLY WRITTEN IN GREEK, AROUND 400 CE)

*Do not fire the Cellar, There's excellent Wine in't, Captain, and though it be cold weather, I do not love it mull'd.*

—JOHN FLETCHER, *THE LOYAL SUBJECT*, 1618

## Mulling It Over

The Oxford English Dictionary tells us that the word *mull* comes from the Middle English noun "mol," meaning dust or powder. Mulled wine is mentioned in Fletcher's *The Loyal Subject* in 1618, but the first published recipe does not appear until 1769, in *The Experienced English Housekeeper*, by Mrs. Raffald, who began her career as housekeeper in a large country-house. This busy lady went on to operate a confectioner's shop, catering business, and a cooking school for young ladies, as well as writing one of the most popular cookbooks of her day.

Mulling spices are wonderful to have in the pantry for those winter evenings when the clan gathers around the fire. This recipe comes from Fannie Couch, talk-show host on Pecan Springs radio station KPST.

**FANNIE'S FAVORITE MULLING SPICE**

2 cups dried orange peel

2 cups broken cinnamon sticks

1 cup whole allspice berries

1 cup whole cloves

4 broken star anise

Mix all together and store in a closed jar. To use: mix ¼ cup of spices per gallon of wine, cider, or apple juice. Simmer for 30 minutes before serving. Serve in mugs with cinnamon stick stirrers or a punch bowl garnished with orange slices. A spicy bonus: the delightful aroma that will fill your kitchen!

**If you prefer hot stuff, read:**

*Some Like It Hot: 50 Drinks to Warm Your Spirits,* by Holly Burrows

*Ginger beer quickly made. A gallon of boiling water is poured over three quarters of a pound of loaf sugar, one ounce of ginger, and the peel of one lemon; when milk-warm, the juice of the lemon and a spoonful of yeast are added. It should be made in the evening, and bottled next morning, in stone bottles, and the cork tied down with twine. Good brown sugar will answer, and the lemon may be omitted, if cheapness is required.*

—SARAH JOSEPHA HALE, *THE GOOD HOUSEKEEPER*, 1841

# NOVEMBER 17

Today is National Homemade Bread Day.

*Maggie and I shared a light meal of cauliflower soup seasoned with mint marigold (a wonderful substitute for the tarragon that doesn't do well in Texas), jicama and garbanzo salad, and Maggie's famous flowerpot herb bread.*

—HANGMAN'S ROOT: A CHINA BAYLES MYSTERY

## There's Nothing Nicer

. . . than hot herb bread, just out of the oven. To make your bread even more interesting, bake it in clay flowerpots, which produce that lovely crispy crust you never get from a metal baking pan. You can purchase culinary pots, or you can use regular four- to eight-inch flowerpots. Scrub well, or wash them in the dishwasher. Spray with cooking spray and bake at 350° for 30 minutes. Cool and repeat the washing and seasoning process. If your pots have a hole in the bottom, cover it with a wad of aluminum foil. And if you don't have time to make Maggie's start-from-scratch bread, begin with a prepared bread dough and add the herbs. Good both ways!

**MAGGIE GARRETT'S FLOWERPOT HERB BREAD**

    2 packages dry yeast
    ¼ cup warm water
    ¼ cup sugar
    1½ cups scalded milk, cooled
    ½ cup shortening, melted, cooled
    2 large eggs, beaten
    2 teaspoons salt
    6–7 cups whole-wheat pastry flour, sifted
    ½ teaspoon basil
    ¾ teaspoon thyme
    ¾ teaspoon oregano
    1 tablespoon fresh minced parsley

Soften yeast in warm water, with 1 tablespoon of the sugar. Mix milk, shortening, and beaten eggs. Stir in the remaining sugar, salt, eggs, and 2 cups of the flour. Mix well and cover with a damp cloth. Let rise in a warm place until bubbly (about 1 hour). Stir well, and add herbs. Mix in the rest of the flour to make a stiff dough. Knead on floured board until satiny and elastic. Place in greased bowl, cover with a damp cloth, and return to the warm place to rise until doubled in bulk (about 1 hour). Punch dough down, let rest for 10 minutes, and divide into 4–6 pieces (depending on the size of your pots). Place each piece in a pot, filling only half full. Cover with a damp cloth and let rise until the dough has filled the pots (about 45–50 minutes). Bake in 425° oven for 15 minutes, then lower the heat to 350°. Bake small pots an additional 5–10 minutes, larger pots 15–30. Turn out of the pot, return to the oven for a few minutes, then cool on a rack. (Maggie says to tell you that this bread is even better if it's served with an herb butter!)

**Bushels of breads with whole-grain flour:**
*Whole Grain Breads by Machine or Hand: 200 Delicious, Healthful, Simple Recipes*, by Beatrice Ojakangas

# NOVEMBER 18

*Our concern is that we not kill the goose that laid the golden egg. Ancient forests that gave us the yew may give us answers to medical questions we haven't thought to ask.*

—WENDELL WOOD, OREGON NATURAL RESOURCES COUNCIL

## The Secret of the Yew Tree

Until the 1960s, the Pacific yew (*Taxus brevifolia*) was considered just another trash tree. The local Indian tribes knew better: Traditional healers brewed a decoction of the wood and bark to treat gastrointestinal and urinary ailments, made a poultice of the leaves to heal wounds, and used the leaves as a wash to promote health. But it wasn't until the early 1960s that researchers for the National Cancer Institute reported that an extract made from the tree's inner bark inhibited cell division, making it a potential cancer treatment. By the late 70s, they had isolated the anti-cancer compound: taxol. In 1989, clinical trials demonstrated success in the treatment of ovarian cancer; in 1993, it was approved by the FDA.

But the Pacific yew was soon in trouble. Six mature trees must be killed to produce enough of the compound to treat one patient. There are far more patients than there are trees, and the trees are protected under the Endangered Species Act. The choice pitted patients and physicians against those who worried that the tree would soon be extinct and the forest destroyed.

Luckily, scientists have found a viable alternative, which is now being used as the basis for synthetic derivatives. But the real question still confronts us. Ethnobotanists argue that wise gatherers and traditional healers know what plants have the capacity to heal. With their guidance, plants may direct us to new ways of healing that we will never discover in the pharmaceutical laboratory. But these healers, the plants, and even the forests are rapidly disappearing. Unless we act quickly to preserve them, they will be gone, and we will never learn the secrets that they once held—like the secret of the Pacific yew tree, which has now saved so many women's lives.

**More Reading:**

*Green Pharmacy: The History and Evolution of Western Herbal Medicine*, by Barbara Griggs

*The Natural History of Medicinal Plants*, by Judith Sumner

*The Indians' botanical knowledge is disappearing even faster than the plants themselves. What we in the developed world call civilisation is rapidly encroaching on indigenous communities, just as it is encroaching on the plants, and native botanical lore is usually an early casualty. In only one generation, acculturation can lead to the disappearance of botanical knowledge acquired over millennia.*

—RICHARD EVENS SCHULTES, DIRECTOR, HARVARD UNIVERSITY
BOTANICAL MUSEUM, 1994

# NOVEMBER 19

### ❧
## Herbal Remedies to Make You Laugh

Yes, plant medicines (like yew-derived taxol) can be wonderful. But a great many of the herbal remedies that have been proposed over the centuries are pretty silly. Here are some of my favorites, collected over the years. They might not cure you, but maybe they'll make you laugh—and laughter is a fine medicine.

- You need a ribbon for this one. "The dried root [of vervain], peeled, is known to be excellently good against all scrofulous and scorbutic habits of body, by being tied to the pit of the stomach by a piece of white ribband round the neck." If that doesn't work, trying putting the dried leaves into a black silk bag, and tying that around your neck.
- Be careful what you pick. The picking of dandelion flowers leads to bedwetting. The picking of red campion leads to thunder. The picking of the cuckoo flower (also known as lady's smock) will give you a headache. And for heaven's sake, don't bring any cow parsley into the house, because the snakes will follow it, or your mother will die, or both.
- Fumitory was thought to remove freckles, which led to this extravagant promise: "If you wish to be pure and holy, wash your face with fumitory."
- Black hellebore is poisonous, but if your horse has a cough, you should poke a hole through his ear and

put a piece of the root in it. He will be cured in 24 hours.
- To cure your rheumatism, put a potato in your pocket and carry it until it gets hard. It will draw the iron out of the blood, and it's the iron that's causing the stiffness. (This is supposed to work better if you steal the potato from your neighbor's potato bin.)
- Nosebleed? "Houseleek bruised and laid upon the crown or seam of the head, stays bleeding at the nose very quickly."
- And if you really want to get well, use garlic that has been planted on Good Friday, then boiled in sweet milk. "It will cure any disease in people, cattle, or fowl."

**More Reading:**
*The Oxford Dictionary of Plant-Lore*, by Roy Vickery

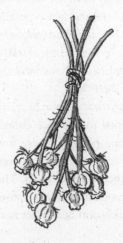

# NOVEMBER 20

Stir-up Sunday occurs about this time.

## Stir Up, We Beseech Thee

The last Sunday before Advent is known in England as Stir-Up Sunday. According to the Oxford English Dictionary (that font of all linguistic wisdom), this name came about because the Collect for this particular Sunday begins with the phrase: "Stir up, we beseech thee, O Lord, the wills of thy faithful people." Stir-Up Sunday, the Oxford English Dictionary remarks, "is jocularly associated with the stirring of the Christmas mincemeat, which it was customary to begin making in that week." Charles Kightly (in *The Perpetual Almanack of Folklore*) reports this popular parody:

> Stir up, we beseech thee
> The pudding in the pot
> And when we do get home
> We'll eat it piping hot.

Kightly adds that Christmas puddings should always be stirred with a wooden spoon, clockwise, and that everyone should take a turn in order of seniority (age before beauty?).

So get out the wooden spoon, gather the family, and start stirring. In England, of course, Christmas puddings are always steamed, a practice that began in the days when few kitchens had ovens and people cooked over open fires. If you prefer to make your favorite American fruitcake (similar ingredients, but baked instead of steamed), be sure to include the traditional Christmas coin, which is supposed to bring wealth to the lucky recipient. (Remind everyone to look for it when they pick up their forks!)

Christmas fruitcakes make sweet presents for friends and family. Bake several (use tin cans in various sizes as baking containers), wrap them in muslin and ribbons, and attach a sprig of rosemary with your gift card.

**More Reading:**

*Favorite Fruitcakes: Recipes, Legends, and Lore from the World's Best Cooks and Eaters*, by Moira Hodgson

*Hallo! A great deal of steam! The pudding was out of the copper [boiler]. A smell like washing-day! That was the cloth [the pudding bag]. A smell like an eating-house and a pastrycook's next door to each other, with a laundress's next door to that! That was the pudding! In half a minute Mrs. Cratchit entered—flushed, but smiling proudly—with the pudding, like a speckled cannon-ball, so hard and firm, blazing in half of half-a-quartern of ignited brandy, and bedight with Christmas holly stuck into the top.*

*Oh, a wonderful pudding! Bob Cratchit said, and calmly too, that he regarded it as the greatest success achieved by Mrs. Cratchit since their marriage.*

—A CHRISTMAS CAROL, CHARLES DICKENS

*There is also a vegetable which has all the properties of true saffron, as well the smell as the color, and yet it is not really saffron.*

—MARCO POLO

## Turmeric

Turmeric comes from the rhizome of *Curcuma longa*, a perennial member of the ginger family that grows in tropical India and South America. Like ginger, the plant is grown from the fleshy rhizome. During the growing season, more rhizomes are produced. These are harvested, cooked, dried, and powdered to produce the yellow spice that gives many curry powders their brilliant yellow color. The taste is distinctive too: warm, peppery, and slightly bitter, with aromatic overtones of orange and ginger.

Turmeric has long been used to color textiles and is one of the traditional skin dyes that have both ornamental and ritual significance. For their wedding ceremony, Indonesian couples stain their arms with turmeric, while Malaysian women use it to color their abdomens after childbirth. Kurdish Jews practiced a circumcision ritual in which the mother was ornamented with turmeric, indigo, and henna, to protect her and her infant son from Lilith, the queen of the demons. (My friend Judith tells me that modern Jewish women view Lilith differently, as the archetype of a woman who refuses to be dominated by a man.)

Medicinally, turmeric has been used for digestive and intestinal ailments, and as a treatment for liver problems. It stimulates the production of bile, thereby lowering serum cholesterol levels. A powerful antioxidant, it may inhibit the formation of blood clots that can lead to heart attack. And more recently, researchers—who report that Indian turmeric users suffer far less Alzheimer's than any other people—speculate that turmeric may play a role in slowing the progression of the disease. Turmeric is a safe yet effective anti-inflammatory drug that has fewer side effects than its chemical counterparts, making it useful in the treatment of rheumatoid arthritis.

Keep turmeric handy for a variety of herbal uses. Add it to egg salad, chicken salad, and salad dressings; mix it with brown rice, raisins, and nuts; include it in poultry stuffings and scrambled eggs; use it as a saffron substitute in dishes like paella; add it to dips, yogurt, and cottage cheese; and brew it with ginger for a healing tea. Once you begin using this good-for-you herb, you'll think of hundreds of other creative ways to include it in your diet.

**Learn more about spices:**
*Spice Lilies: Eastern Secrets to Healing with Ginger, Turmeric, Cardamom, and Galangal*, by Susanne Poth

*Turmeric is used by the Malays and Indians in a curious cosmetic paste which is applied to the body of anyone suffering from demoniacal possession.*

—MRS. C.F. LEYEL, *HERBAL DELIGHT*, 1937

Today or tomorrow, the Sun enters the sign of Sagittarius.

> *The ninth sign of the zodiac, the masculine sign Sagittarius (the Archer) is ruled by Jupiter, the largest planet in our solar system. Sagittarius is a mutable fire sign. While Sagittarians can be jovial and freedom-loving, they are sometimes overly optimistic, careless, and may suffer from accidents.*
>
> —RUBY WILCOX, "ASTROLOGICAL SIGNS"

## Sagittarius Herbs

The planet Jupiter, named for the Roman god of the sky, is said to rule the hips, thighs, lower spine, and the autonomic nervous system, as well as the process of growth and self-preservation. It also governs the body's largest glandular organ, the liver. Herbs related to Jupiter have traditionally been used to treat lower back problems, arthritis, and rheumatism, and to deal with liver ailments. Jupiter is also related to plants with large taproots and trees that produce fruit and nuts. Herbs of Sagittarius include:

- Willow (*Salix sp.*). A tea made of the bark of the willow reduces the pain and inflammation of rheumatism and arthritis. Its chief constituent, methyl salicylate, is the primary ingredient in aspirin.

- Dandelion (*Taraxacum officinale*). A useful herb, dandelion has been shown to stimulate the flow of liver bile. Nicholas Culpeper (who assigned this plant to Jupiter) says it is "very effectual for removing obstructions of the liver, gall bladder, and spleen."
- Sage (*Salvia officinalis*). Sage has been used for centuries as a powerful preservative; research indicates that it contains antioxidants, which slow spoilage. Sage is used to treat wounds, ease gastrointestinal complaints, and heal sore throat and bleeding gums.
- Other Sagittarius herbs include dock (another traditional liver herb); lime blossom, meadowsweet (also contains methyl salicylate and can be used to treat rheumatism); costmary; chicory.

> *O! Mickle is the powerful grace that lies*
> *In herbs, plants, stones and their true qualities;*
> *For nought so vile that on the earth doth live*
> *But to the earth some special good doth give.*
>
> —WILLIAM SHAKESPEARE, *ROMEO AND JULIET*

# NOVEMBER 23

Today is National Eat a Cranberry Day.

## Cranberries for Health

The health benefits of cranberries (*Vaccinium macrocarpon*) have become more widely recognized over the past two decades, as researchers confirm what many have already known: these tart red berries can prevent urinary tract infections and reduce the risk of kidney stones. And recently, a compound in cranberry juice has been found to be effective against plaque-forming bacteria that cause gingivitis and gum disease. The herb has been in long use: Native Americans applied crushed cranberries to wounds and used them to treat scurvy, a disease caused by a lack of vitamin C. If you're using cranberries medicinally, choose pure cranberry juice, not one of the many "cocktails" currently on the supermarket shelf.

**SPICED CRANBERRY ORANGE SAUCE**

1 pound fresh cranberries, rinsed and picked through
¾ cup sugar
juice and zest of 1 large orange (leave the zest in large pieces)
½ teaspoon ground ginger
¼ teaspoon nutmeg
4 cloves, stuck into a section of orange rind for easy removal
1 3-inch cinnamon stick, broken
½ cup light red wine

Combine ingredients in a large saucepan. Bring to a boil; reduce heat and simmer for about 10 minutes, stirring occasionally, until cranberries pop and sauce thickens. Remove from heat and let cool. Remove cinnamon, cloves, and zest. Pour sauce into a bowl and chill. Serves 10. You can make this several days ahead and refrigerate it. A zingy, healthful sauce for that special turkey!

**CAROLEE'S CRANBERRY CORDIAL**

1 pound fresh or frozen cranberries, chopped
3 cups sugar
3 cups light rum
2 sprigs rosemary
2–3 rose geranium leaves

Combine cranberries, sugar, and rum. Place in a clean jar with rosemary and rose-geranium leaves. Cover and place in a cool, dark place, shaking every few days. After 4 weeks, strain the liquid, bottle, and serve. Use the strained cranberries in nut breads, cookies, compotes, chicken salad, or over ice cream. (Thanks, Carolee! For Carolee's Herb Farm, see June 22.)

*Children can very early be taught to take all the care of their own clothes. They can knit garters, suspenders, and stockings; they can make patchwork and braid straw; they can make mats for the table, and mats for the floor; they can weed and garden, and pick cranberries from the meadow, to be carried to market.*

—MRS. CHILD, *THE AMERICAN FRUGAL HOUSEWIFE*

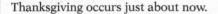
Thanksgiving occurs just about now.

*If the only prayer you said in your whole life was "thank you," that would suffice.*

—MEISTER ECKHART

## A Thanksgiving Potpourri for Sharing

Here's a worthwhile craft that will keep the kids occupied while you're busy with Thanksgiving dinner—unless, of course, they've been assigned to knit garters or pick cranberries.

This recipe for enjoy-it-and-toss-it-out potpourri is only a list of suggestions. Encourage the children to find other things to put into it that will be pretty to look at for a day or two and be beneficial to the birds, squirrels, and other wild creatures when they toss it into the backyard. They'll also enjoy arranging it in pretty bowls or baskets around the house. This potpourri is not scented; if you want fragrance, put scented potpourri into a smaller bowl and nestle it into the center of the larger one, surrounded by this natural mix.

**POTPOURRI FOR SHARING**
sage leaves, fresh or dried
goldenrod flowers
dried strawflowers or chrysanthemums
sunflower seeds
pumpkin seeds
squash or melon seeds
seed pods collected from the garden
shelled or unshelled nuts
popped corn
acorns
pieces of dried orange and lemon peel
dried cranberries or other dried berries
ears of Indian corn
bits of fern, twigs
pretty autumn leaves

*Recipe for Goose Stuffing: Take 4 apples, peeled and cored, 4 onions, 4 leaves of sage, and 4 leaves of lemon thyme not broken, and boil them in a stew pan with sufficient water to cover them; when done, pulp them through a sieve, removing the sage and thyme; then add sufficient pulp of mealy potatoes to cause it to be sufficiently dry without sticking to the hand; add pepper and salt, and stuff the bird.*

—MRS. BEETON'S BOOK OF HOUSEHOLD MANAGEMENT, 1861

Today is the beginning of the Celtic Month of Elder, according to some sources.

*If you chop an elder tree or fell it, or if you want blossoms or fruit, you must say "Please, Mother Elder, may I have . . ."*

—ROY VICKERY, *OXFORD DICTIONARY OF PLANT-LORE*

## Respect Your Elder Mother

Elder (*Sambucus sp.*)—a familiar, common shrub, flourishing in ditches and marshy areas—has for centuries been held sacred throughout England. And while it is a valuable plant, using any part of it without asking permission was courting trouble, for the tree was the dwelling of the "Elder Mother" (Elle or Hyldemoer in Scandinavian and Danish myth), who took offense if any of her trees were harmed.

But the elder must have been generous with her permissions, for everything about this plant, from root to twig-tip, has been put to use. The flowers, roots, leaves, and bark have been brewed, stewed, steeped, pickled, bundled, and minced, serving a wide variety of medicinal purposes. Modern research suggests that elder extract is effective for coughs, colds, and flu. Elder branches (often said to be poisonous) have been used to witch water, and twigs were often hung over the door to keep witches away. A branch buried with a corpse fended off vampires, and a hollowed-out stick could be turned into a Pan pipe.

The flowers were fermented to make ale, wine, and beer, and were battered and fried as fritters. The berries (often called "the Englishman's grape") were turned into sauce, ice cream, jelly, and pie. Here's a traditional jelly recipe. If you pick the elderberries, be sure to say please first and thank-you afterward. The Elder Mother will appreciate it.

### ELDERBERRY JELLY
2 quarts elderberries, washed, stems removed
2 cups water
1 box pectin
5 cups sugar

Bring the berries and water to a boil on a large, nonreactive saucepan. Simmer until berries are soft. Strain through a jelly bag or cheesecloth; for clear jelly, do not squeeze. You should have 3½ cups of juice; if not, pour a little water through the crushed berries. Return 3[h] cups elderberry juice to pan. Add pectin to the juice and bring to a boil. Stir in the sugar and bring to a full rolling boil. Boil for 1 minute. Remove from heat, skim and pour into hot sterilized jars. Seal with hot paraffin immediately.

*Elder Vinegar. Put dryed Elder flowers into Stone or double Glass Bottles, fill them up with good Wine Vinegar, and set them up in the sun or by the Fire till their Virtue is extracted.*

—*THE RECEIPT BOOK OF JOHN NOTT,*
COOK TO THE DUKE OF BOLTON, 1723

*Many of us miss all that is most worth learning in old books through regarding anything in them that is unfamiliar as merely quaint, if not ridiculous. . . . There is only one way of understanding these old writers, and that is to forget ourselves entirely and to try to look at the world of nature as they did. It is not "much learning" that is required, but sympathy and imagination.*

—ELEANOUR SINCLAIR ROHDE, *THE OLD ENGLISH HERBALS*

## Old Herbals

I have always been passionate about books. Among my favorites are books about herbs—not the glossy coffee-table books that have flooded the market since the herb "renaissance" began in the late 1980s, but earlier books, which I've collected in inexpensive reprints and facsimiles.

There's plenty to enjoy in these little volumes. In my facsimile edition of the 1833 *American Frugal Housewife*, for example, Mrs. Child tells us that "a poultice made of ginger or of common chickweed, that grows about one's door in the country, has given great relief to the toothache," and that "plantain leaves laid upon a wound are cooling and healing." A century later, Helen Morgenthau Fox (in *Gardening with Herbs for Flavor and Fragrance*, 1933) prints an "old" recipe for "Marigold Custard" that I've never seen anywhere else. (I'll include it in tomorrow's entry.) Eleanour Sinclair Rohde (*The Old English Herbals*, 1922) offers a careful review of all the important

herbals from the eighth to the seventeenth century, and Rosetta Clarkson's *Green Enchantment* (1940) tells intriguing stories about early garden tools and flowers in herbal medicines. Fascinating, every page.

- *Old Time Gardens*, by Alice Morse Earle, 1901, reprinted 2005
- *The Book of Herbs*, by Lady Rosalind Northcote, 1903, reprinted 1971
- *Old English Herbals*, by Eleanour Sinclair Rohde, 1922, reprinted 1971
- *The Herb Garden*, by Frances Bardswell, 1930, reprinted 1986
- *A Modern Herbal*, by Maud Grieve, 1931, reprinted 1971
- *Gardening with Herbs for Flavor and Fragrance*, by Helen Morgenthau Fox, 1934, reprinted 1970
- *Herbs and the Earth*, by Henry Beston, 1935, reprinted 1973, 1990
- *Rose Recipes from Olden Times*, by Eleanour Sinclair Rohde, 1939
- *Magic Gardens*, by Rosetta E. Clarkson, 1939, reprinted 1992

*The young gardener will have leisure during the long evenings . . . to improve himself by reading. . . . [T]he young man who does not occupy every moment of his spare time in improving himself, has no chance whatever of getting a good situation as head gardener.*

—JOHN CLAUDIUS LOUDON, 1842

*Waxwings are amiable, egalitarian birds with pleasant table manners, never bickering over dessert like aggressive jays and testy titmice. You'll sometimes see ten or fifteen of them sitting shoulder-to-shoulder on a branch, ceremoniously passing a juniper berry from one polite beak to another until one of the birds decides it has his name on it. If the berry makes it to the last bird, back up the row it goes again.*

—BLEEDING HEARTS: A CHINA BAYLES MYSTERY

## Piney, Pungent, Plentiful

Here at Meadow Knoll, the juniper branches are weighed down with ripe berries and feasting birds: the here-for-the-winter cedar waxwings, dapper birds with neat black masks and tails that look as if they've been dipped in yellow paint. They're in cahoots with the blackbirds and robins, and they're gobbling the silvery-blue berries as fast as they can. If I don't hurry, I won't get my share.

Maybe you've never used juniper berries in cooking, but if you've ever had a gin and tonic, you've tasted their clean, pine-flavored pungency. And you've seen the shrub everywhere, for *Juniperus communis,* originally a native of Europe, is now as common as . . . well, weeds. Ours (we have Ashe junipers) grow as tall as 20 feet. The yellow pollen puffing from the male trees in late December is an astonishing sight—and sheer misery for those with allergies.

If juniper is a new herb for you, try the dried culinary berries that come from Macedonia and Albania. (You may have to find a mail order source.) Juniper is often associated with wild game cooking, but it's good with beef, pork, sauerkraut, and other strong-flavored vegetables. The berries are often used in marinades and sauces that feature red wine, garlic, rosemary, thyme, or bay. You'll need only three or four, lightly crushed.

Juniper has long been used for medicinal purposes. The volatile oils aid digestion and reduce gas, although they may be dangerous for pregnant women and people with kidney ailments. Externally, juniper has been used in liniments and poultices to ease pain in the joints or muscles, or in a stimulating bath.

And if you're troubled by witches, juniper is just what the doctor ordered. Witches were said to be offended by the pungent scent, and the plant was burned as an incense in exorcisms. Wear a sprig around your neck to ward off the attacks of wild animals and snakes. And plant a juniper beside your front door. One legend says that a witch cannot pass it until he or she has counted every twig.

Excuse me. If I don't get outside with my basket, the birds will beat me to the last of the juniper berries.

# NOVEMBER 28

Today is National French Toast Day.

## Savory French Toast

French toast isn't just for breakfast, you know. Here is a savory herbal treat that's perfect for a Sunday brunch, especially when the tomatoes are served on an arugula bed, and the plate is accompanied by a bowl of hot soup.

**SAVORY FRENCH TOAST & HAM**
**WITH BROILED TOMATOES**

    4 eggs, beaten
    ¼ cup milk
    1 cup shredded Swiss cheese
    2 tablespoons finely chopped green onion tops
    1 tablespoon minced parsley
    1 teaspoon prepared horseradish sauce or
        grated horseradish
    2 teaspoons prepared mustard
    4 teaspoons butter
    8 slices bread
    4 thin slices ham

In a shallow bowl, whisk together the eggs, milk, Swiss cheese, onions, parsley, horseradish, and mustard. Melt the butter in a large skillet over medium heat. Dip slices of bread into the egg mixture, then place them in the skillet. Cook for 3–5 minutes on each side, or until lightly browned on both sides. Remove bread from skillet. Layer 4 slices with ham; cover with remaining four bread slices. Return sandwiches to skillet; cook until bread has browned. Serve hot, with broiled ripe tomatoes. Makes 4 sandwiches.

*To broil tomatoes*: Slice 4 medium-ripe tomatoes in half. In a pie plate, mix 2 tablespoons olive oil and 2 tablespoons balsamic vinegar. Marinate the tomatoes cut side down for 10 minutes. Place cut side up on foil-lined baking sheet. Sprinkle with 2 teaspoons dried basil and 4 tablespoons grated Parmesan. Broil for 5–7 minutes, until cheese is brown.

*Clear moon, frost soon.*

*A curdly sky*
*Will not leave the earth long dry.*
—TRADITIONAL WEATHER LORE

*He that is merry of heart hath a continual feast.*

—PROVERBS 15:15

## Herbs for a Healthy Heart

Cardiac health—in a broader sense, the health of the entire circulatory system—ought to be at the top of everyone's list of health concerns. You no doubt already understand the importance of a low-fat diet, weight control, exercise, hypertension management, and you don't smoke. But herbs can be an important part of an overall holistic program of cardiovascular health, as well—especially if you grow them yourself and enjoy the beneficial exercise of gardening. Here are just a few of the herbs that have been recommended for circulatory health, along with a list of resources for you to explore. (As with any medication, consult your physician before using herbs therapeutically.)

- Garlic has been demonstrated to lower cholesterol, reduce blood pressure, and help prevent blood clots.
- Hawthorn helps to dilate coronary blood vessels, thereby improving the flow of blood to the heart. The leaves, flowers, and berries contain antioxidants and flavonoids that seem to strengthen the heart muscle, reduce blood levels of cholesterol and triglycerides, and lower high blood pressure.
- Ginger, traditionally used as a digestive aid, helps to control several key risk factors for circulatory disease: cholesterol, blood pressure, plaque build-up, and blood clotting.
- Ginkgo (*Ginkgo biloba*) is widely used in Oriental medicine to treat many heart and circulatory diseases. Plant chemicals improve arterial blood flow, reduce the risk of clotting, and enhance recovery from stroke.
- Turmeric (*Curcuma longa*) stimulates the production of bile, thereby lowering serum cholesterol levels. A powerful antioxidant, it may inhibit the formation of blood clots that can lead to heart attack.

*Hawthorn Berry Syrup. Cover the freshly gathered fruit with water and boil until the fruit is soft. Strain off the juice and return the pulp to the kettle and make a second extraction. For every 2 cups of juice, add 1 cup sugar. Boil until thick and syrupy. Pour into sterilized bottles. Refrigerate and use within two weeks.*

**More Reading:**

*Healthy Heart: Strengthen Your Cardiovascular System Naturally,* by David Hoffman

## Herb Garden Olive Oil

This is the time of year I always make herbed oils for gifts. I'm always careful, because several years ago, herbed oils were incriminated in at least one (and possibly more) cases of deadly botulism. If you follow some commonsense rules as you make these oils for friends or for yourself, you won't stir up any trouble. Be scrupulously clean, sterilize the bottles, and store your oil in the fridge.

This is my favorite recipe. As with vinegar, you can experiment with flavors until you find what suits you.

**HERBED OLIVE OIL**

6 sprigs fresh rosemary, 3 inches long,
   or 1 tablespoon dried
3 sprigs fresh thyme, 1 teaspoon dried
3 fresh sprigs oregano, or 1 teaspoon dried
2 large bay leaves
8 whole black peppercorns
3 cloves garlic, cut in eighths
1 quart extra-virgin olive oil

Wash the herbs and pat dry with a paper towel. Place in a sterilized 1-quart jar. Add olive oil, being sure to cover the herbs, pushing them down, if necessary. Cover and refrigerate for 10 days. (It coagulates when cold.) Taste. If more flavor is desired, continue to taste every 2 days. When you like the flavor, bring to room temperature and strain into a clean bottle. Refrigerate. To give, rebottle in a pretty bottle with a raffia tie. Label with this instruction: *Store in refrigerator. Bring to room temperature before use.*

*If you have parsnips but no sugar, don't lose heart! Make Parsnip-Cakes!*

*Parsnip-Cakes. Scrape some Parsnip-Roots, and slice them thin, dry them in an Oven and beat them to Powder; mix them with an equal quantity of Flour, and make them up with Cream and Spices powder'd; then mould them into Cakes, and bake them in a gentle Oven. —N.B. The Sweetness of the Parsnip Powder answers the want of sugar.*

—R. BRADLEY, THE COUNTRY HOUSEWIFE AND
LADY'S DIRECTOR, 1732

**Read more about olives:**
*Olives: The Life and Lore of a Noble Fruit,* by Mort Rosenblum

# DECEMBER 1

*Come along inside . . . We'll see if tea and buns
can make the world a better place.*

—KENNETH GRAHAME, *WIND IN THE WILLOWS*

## A Cup of Comfort

Got the winter sniffles? A comforting cup of herbal tea
may put you on the road to recovery a little faster.
Here are some herbal remedies for what ails you.

### GINGER AND LEMON TEA FOR COLDS AND FLU

    1½ cups water
    ½ cup lemon juice
    4 slices fresh gingerroot, about ¼-inch thick
    ¼ teaspoon cayenne
    1 tablespoon honey

Bring water to a boil in a nonreactive pan. Bruise
the slices of gingerroot and drop them into the boiling
water. Reduce heat and simmer about five minutes.
Remove from heat, strain into a cup. Add lemon juice,
honey, and cayenne. Stir and sip.

### THYME, SAGE, AND PEPPERMINT TEA FOR COUGHS AND FEVER

    1 teaspoon dried thyme
    1 teaspoon dried sage
    1 teaspoon dried peppermint
    1 cup boiling water

Place the herbs in a tea ball or strainer in a cup.
Pour the boiling water over them, cover and steep
8–10 minutes. Sweeten with honey. Sip while warm,
up to two cups a day, for 3–4 days.

### LAVENDER, ROSEMARY, THYME TEA FOR HEADACHES

    ½ teaspoon dried lavender flowers
    ½ teaspoon rosemary, bruised
    ½ teaspoon thyme
    1 cup boiling water

Place the herbs in a tea ball or strainer in a cup.
Pour the boiling water over them, cover and steep for
8–10 minutes. Sweeten with honey. Sip while warm.

**Learn more about making herbal tea:**
*A Cozy Book of Herbal Teas: Recipes, Remedies, and
Folk Wisdom*, by Mindy Toomay

*There are no flowers that never fade,
yet here are the chrysanthemums
blooming in winter.*

—YUAN HUNG-TAO, 1568–1610

*"I'm afraid we need to talk to you about a rather difficult subject," I said, when Hazel Pennyroyal answered Ruby's knock. "It has to do with your brother's will."*

*Hazel opened the door wider. "The best place for difficult conversations is the kitchen. Anyway, I'm making soap and it needs stirring. Come on."*

*"Making soap?" Ruby asked curiously. "Isn't that a lot of work?"*

*"Not the way I do it," Hazel said. We followed her into the kitchen, where she went to the stove and picked up a spoon to stir something in saucepan. The whole kitchen smelled of roses.*

—"A PENNYROYAL PLOT" IN *AN UNTHYMELY DEATH AND OTHER GARDEN MYSTERIES*

## Herbal Soaps

You can lather up with soapwort or yucca—or you can make your own sweet-smelling herbal soaps, another easy project for children, and perfect for holiday gift-giving.

### HAZEL PENNYROYAL'S EASY HERBAL SOAP

You'll need:

 plastic candy molds or small containers suitable for use as molds

 unscented cooking spray or petroleum jelly

 2 four-ounce bars of castile (olive-oil) soap

 2 tablespoons water

 12 drops rose essential oil

 2 tablespoons red or pink rose petals, chopped

How to do it:

Spray molds with cooking spray or grease with petroleum jelly. Grate castile soap into an enamel saucepan. For rose soap, add water and rose oil and heat slowly, stirring. When the soap has melted and the mixture looks like whipped cream, add rose petals. Quickly fill each mold, then rap the mold sharply on a hard surface to eliminate air bubbles. Allow to harden overnight in the molds. Turn out onto a wire rack and air-dry for a few days before wrapping. If the soap seems rough-edged, wet your hands and smooth it; dry thoroughly.

- Other fragrant floral possibilities: violet oil and violets; lilac oil and lilac florets; orange oil and calendula petals; lemon oil and dried lemongrass with lemon zest; mint oil and chopped mint leaves; lavender oil and lavender buds with chopped rosemary leaves. Be creative!
- To make a gentle scrubbing soap, add 1 tablespoon chopped dried luffa, or ½ cup cornmeal or oatmeal (not flakes). Increase liquid slightly, if necessary.

**Herbal soaps are fun to make:**

*The Natural Soap Book: Making Herbal and Vegetable-Based Soaps,* by Susan Miller Cavitch

# DECEMBER 3

*Deck the halls with boughs of holly,*
*Fa-la-la-la-la, la-la-la-la*
*'Tis the season to be jolly,*
*Fa-la-la-la-la, la-la-la-la!*

## The Hallowed Holly

In ancient cultures, holly was a holy tree, a powerful and protective guardian. The Druids advised people to take it into their dwellings as the dark descended over the land, as a refuge for the spirits of the forest. However, it had to be removed from the house by Imbolc Eve (January 31), for any leaf that was left behind could bring misfortune. It was grown around the home to protect from evil influence, for its evergreen color, its sturdiness, and its slow growth must have made it seem invulnerable. For many, the plant was a symbol of immortality.

Medicinally, holly has been used to reduce fevers and ease coughs and pleurisy. Native Americans burned the leaves and brewed a tea of the ashes for whooping cough. The leaves and bark were used as a poultice to treat sprains. The berries are potentially dangerous—don't eat them!

Holly makes a lovely wreath—easy, too, if you start with a straw form. Cut six-inch holly sprigs and rinse them off. When they're dry, construct small bundles, securing the stems with wire twists or floral wire. Pin the bundles to the straw form with florist pins, covering the stems of one bunch with the leaves of another.

Add pine cones, holiday ornaments, and a ribbon. Cut extra holly to decorate your mantel or tuck behind mirrors and picture frames. Festive! As you work, remember that holly has created Yuletide magic for eons of human history, and that this favorite herbal tree has always been related to the mysteries of rebirth and rejuvenation.

**SOME HOLLY TALES:**
- In Wales, bringing holly into the house before Christmas Eve will cause a family quarrel.
- In England, each leaf of holly that is left in the house past Twelfth Night will cause one misfortune.
- In Ireland, if holly is picked on Christmas Day, it will serve as protection against witches and evil spirits.
- In Germany, it is unlucky to step on the berries.
- In France, a severe winter will occur if holly berries are plentiful.

**Read more about holly's magical history:**
*Tree Wisdom,* by Jacqueline Memory Paterson

*Christmastide*
*Comes in like a bride,*
*With Holly and Ivy clad.*
—TRADITIONAL

Today is National Cookie Day, which seems like a good idea, since lots of us are busy baking holiday cookies.

*"Deck the halls," I said in a celebratory tone, and passed Amy the plate of cookies. "Take two."*

*Amy complied. "Mmm," she said, munching appreciatively. "What kind of cookie is this? It's not like anything I've ever tasted."*

*"It's a Norwegian pepper cookie," I said. "Made with black pepper and cardamom. Designed to wake up your taste buds."*

—A DILLY OF A DEATH: A CHINA BAYLES MYSTERY

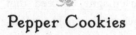

## Pepper Cookies

Pepper cookies, which are baked for the holiday in almost every home in Scandinavia.

### NORWEGIAN PEPPER COOKIES

- 1 cup shortening
- 1 cup sugar
- 1 large egg
- 1 teaspoon vanilla
- 1 teaspoon baking soda
- 2¼ cups flour
- 1 teaspoon freshly ground black pepper
- 1 teaspoon ground cardamom
- ½ teaspoon cloves
- ½ teaspoon ginger

Preheat oven to 350°. Cream together the shortening and the sugar until light and fluffy. Stir in the egg, vanilla, and baking soda. Sift the flour and spices into the butter mixture. Mix well. (You can use a mixer for this.) Roll into ½-inch balls and place on an ungreased cookie sheet. Flatten with a fork in a cross-hatch pattern. Bake at 350° for about 10 minutes, until edges are lightly brown. Cool on wire racks. Makes about 48.

Chocolate Pepper Cookies: substitute 1 cup cocoa powder for 1 cup of flour.

Cinnamon Pepper Cookies: substitute 1½ teaspoons cinnamon for the cardamom, and sprinkle the cookies with cinnamon before they go into the oven.

Orange Pepper Cookies: substitute orange flavoring extract for the vanilla and add 2 teaspoons grated orange zest.

**For more adventures in cookie baking:**

*The Ultimate Cookie Cookbook*, by Barbara Grunes and Virginia Van Vynckt

*I never think that the prospect of the garden in December is much better by making all the flowerbeds too tidy. I feel sure that the dead flower stems . . . must be some protection to the plants; and, when the hoar-frosts come, these dead stems, especially where the dead flowerheads remain, put on a wonderful beauty.*

—HENRY ELLACOMBE, *IN A GLOUCESTERSHIRE GARDEN*, 1895

# DECEMBER 5

Yesterday was the feast day of St. Barbara, who is traditionally invoked for protection against lightning.

*The reason lightning doesn't strike twice in the same place is that the same place isn't there the second time.*

—WILLIE TYLOR

## Lightning Protectors

Since Benjamin Franklin invented the lightning rod, most of us feel pretty safe. But before then, people had a few different ideas for protection against lightning. Please notice that some of the holiday greens that you use for decorations also do double-duty as lightning protectors—how very handy.

- **Mistletoe** (*Viscum album*) was thought to have been planted in trees by bolts of lightning; hence, mistletoe hung over the doors and windows of a house would protect against lightning.
- **Holly** (*Ilex sp.*) and **hazel** (*Corylus avellana*) In Norse mythology, holly and hazel also belonged to Thor the Thunderer, and were thought to protect people from his thunderbolts. Holly trees were planted a little distance from homes to attract lightning strikes away from the house. In Christian times, holly taken into the church for Christmas celebration (or hazel for Easter) was carried home and hung up to ward off lightning the rest of the year.

- **Hawthorn** (*Crataegus oxyacantha*) was said to have been used for Christ's crown of thorns. In Normandy, it was believed that lightning (the work of the devil) could not strike the plant that touched Christ's brow, so people used it to protect their homes. Hawthorn was sometimes employed in house construction specifically as a lightning protector.
- **Houseleeks** (*Sempervivum tectorum*). In Roman mythology, houseleeks (we call this plant hen and chicks) were sacred to Jupiter, and in Norse mythology, to Thor. Both gods were associated with lightning so people reasoned that houseleeks planted on the roof protected the structure against lightning and fire. Charlemagne decreed that these plants should be grown on the roofs of all the structures of his empire. To this day, you'll see houseleeks growing on roofs in England and Europe.

*A natural meanes to preserve your house in safety from thunder and lightening: If the herb housleek or syngreen do grow on the house top, the same house is never stricken with lightening or thunder.*

—DIDYMUS MOUNTAIN, 1572

*Round and green, hen and chick*
*Sting of burns allay*
*Rosy leaves will stick and prick*
*But keep lightning away.*

—TRADITIONAL

# DECEMBER 6

Today is St. Nicholas Day.

*Nose, nose, jolly red nose,*
*And who gave thee this jolly red nose?*
*Nutmeg and ginger, cinnamon and cloves,*
*And they gave me this jolly red nose.*
—FRANCIS BEAUMONT AND JOHN FLETCHER

## Gingerbread Tree Decorations

Christmas is still a few weeks away, which makes this a good time to think about baking some gingerbread decorations for the tree—not as much pressure to get things done, and maybe a little more time to enjoy a project that the kids will love. You'll have to lay down some ground rules about eating their creations, of course, but that's all part of the fun. Since St. Nicholas Day celebrates the person whose legendary generosity inspired our holiday gift-giving, make several batches of these cookie decorations, so the children can share them with their friends.

### GINGERBREAD TREE DECORATIONS
- 1¼ cup margarine, room temperature
- 1¼ cup sugar
- 2 eggs
- 2 teaspoons vanilla
- 4 cups sifted flour
- 1¼ teaspoon salt
- 4 teaspoons cinnamon
- 1 teaspoon ginger
- 1 teaspoon cloves
- 3 teaspoons nutmeg

Combine butter, sugar, eggs, and vanilla extract. Cream well until smooth. Sift together dry ingredients. Stir into butter mixture until smooth, adding more flour if necessary to form a firm, slightly sticky dough. Wrap in plastic and chill until cold. Roll out ⅜-inch thick and cut into shapes. With a chopstick, make a hole through each shape for hanging. Bake at 350° until brown underneath and slightly pale on top. Makes enough for 7–8 large gingerbread figures. If you want to make more, it's easier to make separate batches than to double the recipe. Freeze extra dough. Decorate with frosting and colored candies. (You can also use this recipe to make gingerbread houses. Just roll it out a little thicker.)

The term *gingerbread* originally had nothing to do with bread or cake. The word is an Anglicization of the Old French *gingebras*, which is derived from the Latin name of the spice, *Zingebar*.

**More Reading:**
*Gingerbread: 24 Inspirational Houses and Decorative Gifts to Make*, Joanna Farrow

# DECEMBER 7

*With holly and ivy so green and so gay,*
*We deck up our houses so fresh as the day.*

—POOR ROBIN'S ALMANACK, 1695

## Outside-In: From Susan's Journal

This is the day that I begin bringing the out-of-doors inside, in preparation for our family holiday celebrations. Boughs of juniper and cypress from the trees along our creek make lovely wreaths and a swag for the mantle, and we hang the mistletoe, with great ceremony, over the kitchen door. Rosemary is a green and fragrant addition to the centerpiece on the dining room table, while the lighter, fluffier foliage of southernwood softens the arrangement and the brilliant red berries of pyracanthus and our native yaupon holly perk up the darker greenery. I immerse the clipped greens in a tub of warm water, then drain and stash them in a trash bag and put them where they'll stay cool until I'm ready to use them.

Of course, many of these lovely evergreens have herbal uses, and I remember a few of these as I gather them. Juniper berries are a distinctive ingredient in gin, but they're also diuretic and antimicrobial, while juniper oil is used to treat rheumatism and soothe sore muscles. It's a traditional strewing herb, and Queen Elizabeth I burned it in her bedchamber to scent the air. An infusion of the bark was once thought to restore lost youth, but that's probably wishful thinking. Mistletoe was a sacred as well as a medicinal herb, a protection against sudden calamity (like lightning) and the powers of darkness. Southernwood, in addition to its use as a stimulant, was a folk remedy for baldness. Rosemary's antiseptic, antioxidant leaves help preserve food while adding flavor, and recent research suggests that rosemary really does help to improve the memory.

So I'll sit down and enjoy a cup of rosemary tea while I try to remember where I put all the boxes of holiday ornaments. And perhaps a few drops of juniper oil in a warm bath will take out some of the long day's muscle fatigue and restore a little youth. Baldness won't be a problem until the end of this busy month, when I've torn out all my hair.

*To remedy baldness of the head. Take a quantity of Southernwood and put it on kindled coal to burn; and being made into powder, mix it with the oil of radishes and anoint the bald place, and you shall see great experiences.*

—EDWARD POTTER'S PHYSICKE BOOK, 1610

*This month keep thy body and head from cold: let thy Kitchen be thine Apothecary, warm clothing thy Nurse, merry company thy Keepers, and good hospitality thine Exercise.*

—NEVE'S ALMANACK, 1633

# DECEMBER 8

Buddhists celebrate this day as Bodhi Day.

On this day in 566 BCE, Siddhartha Gautama, meditating under the Bodhi Tree, is said to have attained enlightenment and became the Sakyamuni Buddha. The Dalai Lama says: "At the heart of Buddhism lies the idea that the potential for awakening and for perfection is present in every human being and it is a matter of personal effort to realize that potential."

❧

## Enlightenments

The Bodhi tree, or Bo tree (*Ficus religiosa*), is a large fig tree native to India. It has a great many herbal uses, in addition to being revered as the tree under which the Buddha attained enlightenment. The bark was used to reduce blood pressure, the leaves to soothe earache, and the root to ease toothache. The fruits were thought to prevent cardiac difficulties.

We don't have any Bodhi trees in our neighborhood, but its smaller cousin, *Ficus benjamina*, lives in a corner of my small writing studio, reminding me of the many and various paths the spirit takes on its journey to self-awareness. Buddhism is culturally eclectic, and at this season, some American Buddhists choose to decorate this tree (as Christians decorate the fir tree) with colored lights to symbolize enlightenment, strings of beads to represent the unity of all things, and three decorated balls to signify the three jewels of Buddhism: the Buddha (both the historical Buddha and the Buddha in each of us); the Dharma, or teachings; and the Sangha, or spiritual community shared by all who practice the Dharma. They may celebrate the day with tea, cakes, meditation, and readings.

**THE SYMBOLIC FIG:**

- It has been said that the Tree of Knowledge of Good and Evil described in the book of Genesis may have been a fig tree.
- In the Book of Jeremiah, rotten figs symbolize corruption and destruction.
- In the New Testament, Jesus rebukes an unfruitful fig tree.
- The fig is one of the two sacred trees in Islam.
- Because the fig flower is hidden inside the fruit, the fig was sometimes regarded as a flowerless tree. In Buddhist and Hindu texts, "seeking flowers in a fig tree" indicates a pointless or impossible task.

# DECEMBER 9

"Bocconcini?" I asked, looking at the menu Janet had made up for the Friends of the Library luncheon. "What's that?"

"Mozzarella balls," Janet explained. "Marinated in olive oil and basil vinegar, with red pepper flakes." She looked smug. "One of the gourmet tricks I learned in cooking school."

"Maybe it's a little too gourmet for the Friends of the Library?" I suggested tentatively.

"We have to raise their standards," Janet replied. "Otherwise, I'd be flippin' burgers and fryin' up onion rings, like Lila Jennings, over at the Diner." She frowned. "I hope I don't have any trouble finding those little balls in Pecan Springs."

—"THE KHAT WHO BECAME A HERO," IN
AN UNTHYMELY DEATH

## Cheese and Herb Treats

If you're serving gourmet treats for your holiday get-togethers, be sure to include Janet's basil bocconcini. (Janet? She cooks for China and Ruby at their tearoom.) There are lots of ways to experiment with cheeses marinated in herbed oil. You might want to substitute other flavored vinegars; add sage, savory, rosemary, peppercorns or dill; or add small button mushrooms, cherry tomatoes, and ripe olives.

**JANET'S BASIL BOCCONCINI**

- ½ pound baby bocconcini (substitute cubed mozzarella cheese, if you can't find the balls)
- 3 tablespoons olive oil
- 4 tablespoons basil vinegar
- 2 tablespoons lemon juice
- ½ teaspoon red pepper flakes
- 2 whole garlic cloves
- 3 tablespoons fresh chopped basil, or 1½ tablespoons dried

Mix together the oil, vinegar, lemon juice, pepper flakes, garlic, and basil. Pour over cheese and marinate for at least 24 hours. Serve at room temperature, with toothpicks. Makes about 24. Refrigerate leftovers, if any.

*Garden Basil, if stroked, leaves a grateful smell on the hand, and the author insinuates that it receives fresh life from being touched by a fair lady.*

—MAVOR'S 1812 EDITION OF THOMAS TUSSER'S
*FIVE HUNDRED POINTS OF GOOD HUSBANDRY*

# DECEMBER 10

*Here is a pomander rare*
*A ball of spice to scent the air.*
*Before its fragrance moths do flee*
*Hang it high, then, fortune come to thee.*

—ADELMA GRENIER SIMMONS

## Pomanders

My three children are grown now, but I have pleasant memories of the herbal pomanders we made together during the holidays—a "must" present for each of their grandmothers.

The word *pomander* comes from the Old French *pome d'embre*, or apple of amber, and referred to the aromatic mixture of gums and resins that was enclosed in a bag or perforated metal case and carried or worn as a protection against odor and infection. As time went on, pomanders became decorative and were worn as jewelry; later still, they were made of fruit, scented and preserved with cloves. They were no longer worn, but tucked into clothes presses and drawers to repel moths.

An easy-for-kids-to-make pomander starts with foam balls, oakmoss, a spice potpourri (made of whole allspice, cinnamon chips, sandalwood slivers, star anise, cloves), cinnamon oil, and white glue. Place the oakmoss on a plate. Cover the ball with glue and roll it in the oakmoss until it's completely covered. Let dry, then glue pieces of spice potpourri onto the ball, starting with the largest pieces and filling in with the smaller ones. Dust with powdered cloves and dot with a few drops of cinnamon oil. Hang with a ribbon loop.

To make the real thing, poke holes in an apple, orange, or other citrus fruit with a skewer or a fork, piercing to cover the entire fruit randomly or in a spiral or other pattern. Push whole cloves into the holes. When the fruit is completely studded (the closer the better—the cloves should be no farther than ¼-inch apart), put it in a small paper bag with a mixture of cinnamon, cloves, and nutmeg and shake gently, being careful not to dislodge any cloves. Dry in the oven (pilot light only) overnight, then repeat the paper-bag treatment daily for the next five or six days. Display your pomanders in a basket, or hang in a sling of crisscrossed raffia. When the holidays are over, tuck them into your dresser drawers.

*Scents were more perpetually to be obtained by carrying a pomander, which was originally an orange stuffed with spices, and thought also to be good against infection. Cardinal Wolsey is described as carrying a "very fair orange, whereof the meat or substance was taken out and filled up again with part of a sponge whereon was vinegar, and other confection against the pestilential airs . . ."*

—LADY ROSALIND NORTHCOTE, *THE BOOK OF HERB LORE*

# DECEMBER 11

The theme garden for December: A Windowsill Garden.

## Herbs with a View

Our Texas winters are relatively mild, thank goodness. The winter wind blows hard from the north, and we usually have a string of days with below-freezing temperatures, but snow is a rare thing. Many of my herbs are happy to stay outdoors all winter, but some of the plants like to spend the frosty months inside, where it's warm. If you live in a frostier climate, where the north wind brings plenty of snow, you'll no doubt have quite a few herbs to bring in.

On south-facing windowsills and on shelves and racks in the area I use as a greenhouse, I keep scented geraniums (rose, lemon, lime, cinnamon, Earl Grey), aloe, lemon balm, pineapple sage, and lemongrass. I like to grow annual herbs and some biennials in windowsill pots, too: dill (I'm partial to "Fernleaf," because of its small size), cilantro, basil, chervil, parsley. And I enjoy seeding a few perennial herbs in pots—fennel, borage, catnip—so that they're ready for their great garden escape when the weather warms up. I fill the plant saucers with pebbles so that there's some humidity in the air during these indoor months, mist those that seem to want a shower, and try not to overwater.

None of this is very organized or tidy, of course. There's always a hurly-burly rush on that awful night when the forecast warns of the first hard freeze, and I scurry around, hunting for trays and saucers. But things sort themselves out, and both the herbs and I enjoy the time we spend under the same roof. What's more, when I'm cooking, they're handy for a pinch of this and a leaf of that—and when I'm tired, I don't have to go far for a refreshing sniff.

**For elegant indoor gardening ideas:**

*Tabletop Gardens: Create 40 Intimate Gardens for the Home, No Matter What the Season*, by Rosemary McCreary

*As no Plant can live without Air, a Gardener must now act with Judgment in helping his Green House Plants; for the Air Abroad is now so sharp, that was it to be lett into the House immediately upon the Plants, it would pinch many of them to Death . . .*

—RICHARD BRADLEY, *THE GENTLEMAN AND GARDENER'S KALENDAR*, 1718

# DECEMBER 12

*Ma in her kerchief and I in my cap*
*Had just settled down for a long winter's nap...*
—" 'TWAS THE NIGHT BEFORE CHRISTMAS"

## Winter-Thyme Dreams

Looking at my holiday list (how did it get so long?), I see that I need a few more little gifts. Dream pillows—fun to design, easy to sew, soothing for a long winter's nap—make a unique and interesting present. And I can use up some of those dried herbs I harvested last summer.

For centuries, people believed that herbs placed under the pillow protected against evil, foretold the future, and attracted love. Other herbs simply brought peaceful rest and sweet dreams. The dried material was often stuffed into little pillows and tucked beneath the sleeping pillow.

But instead of ordinary rectangular pillows, I'm being creative. I've raided my fabric stash for pieces of felt, cotton, satin, and silk. With right sides together, I'll cut two layers of different fabrics into various shapes: a crescent moon, a circle, a heart. Then I'll seam the edges, leaving a narrow opening. I can stuff six or seven small pillows with this dreamy mix of calming, relaxing herbs:

- 4 cups rosebuds and petals (for sweet dreams)
- 1 cup dried chamomile flowers (for calm dreams)
- 1 cup dried mugwort (to help you remember your dreams)
- 1 cup dried lavender flowers (in case you have a headache)
- 1 cup dried thyme (to help you dream of faery folk)

Once the pillow is stuffed, I'll turn in the open seam and whip it. And for more fun, I'll add lace, ribbons, and other fine fripperies.

Need more ideas? Try these aromatic herbs:

- Clove, for romantic dreams
- Dill, to go to sleep quickly
- Lemongrass, for dreams of the future
- Mints, for vivid dreams
- Peppermint, for romantic dreams
- Rosemary, for protection from nightmares

**More Reading:**
*Making Herbal Dream Pillows: Secret Blends for Pleasant Dreams*, by Jim Long

# DECEMBER 13

In Scandinavia, today is St. Lucia's Day, celebrated as a Festival of Lights.

*Santa Lucia, thy light is glowing*
*Through darkest winter night, comfort bestowing.*
*Dreams float on dreams tonight,*
*Comes then the morning light,*
*Santa Lucia, Santa Lucia.*

—TRADITIONAL SONG

## Celebrating Light in the Darkness

St. Lucia, whose name means "light," is honored at the darkest time of the year. Throughout northern Europe, this special day marks the beginning of Christmas celebrations, feasting, and merriment. Traditionally, the oldest daughter of the family, wearing a coronet of pine sprigs decorated with five lighted candles, wakened her parents with a breakfast of saffron buns (*Saffronsbrod*) and coffee. The golden saffron was symbolic of sunshine and light.

### SAFFRONSBROD

¼ cup hot water
¼ teaspoon crushed saffron threads
½ cup milk
⅓ cup sugar
2 tablespoons butter or margarine
1 teaspoon salt
1 large egg
1 tablespoon plus 2 teaspoons dry yeast
3 to 3 ¼ cups flour

*Glaze:*
1 egg white, beaten lightly with 1 teaspoon water; sugar

Soften the saffron in the hot water (about 10 minutes). In a mixing bowl, blend the saffron water, milk, sugar, butter, salt, egg, and yeast. Add 2 cups of the flour and mix well, then add enough of the remaining flour to make a soft dough. Knead the dough (15 minutes by hand, 12 minutes in an electric mixer), then set it aside to rise until light and puffy (about 2 hours). Punch the dough down, and let it rest, covered, for 10 minutes. Divide into 16 pieces: divide into fourths, divide each fourth into fourths. Shape each piece into a ball. Place the balls fairly close together (but not touching) in a 9 × 13-inch pan, cover them, and let rise for 1½ hours, or until they're puffy. Glaze the buns with the mixture of beaten egg white and water, then sprinkle them heavily with sugar. Bake them in a preheated 375° oven for 20 minutes, or until golden brown. Yield: 16 buns.

**Learn more about Scandinavian culinary custom:**
*Scandinavian Feasts: Celebrating Traditions throughout the Year,* by Beatrice A. Ojakangas

*Lucy light, Lucy light,*
*The shortest day and the longest night.*

—TRADITIONAL SAYING

# DECEMBER 14

*At Thyme and Seasons, I buy mistletoe from a local supplier and Laurel and I package it in plastic bags tied with festive holiday ribbons. During the Christmas season, we process hundreds of mail and telephone and email orders for the herb, which grows in basketball-sized clumps on the hackberry and pecan trees in the wooded hills to the west of Pecan Springs. Once you've seen those fresh yellow-green leaves and translucent berries, glowing like huge pearls, you can understand why our mistletoe is so popular.*

—*MISTLETOE MAN: A CHINA BAYLES MYSTERY*

## *Mistletoe Man:* About China's Books

As China says, mistletoe is one of her best-selling herbal products, and the mysterious disappearance of her mistletoe supplier in the middle of the holiday season spells serious trouble. And when she and Ruby team up to find out what happened to him—well, it's the usual mix of China's serious detective work and Ruby's high-jinks, made even more poignant when Ruby reveals the painful secret she's been keeping. Everything works out for the best, though, and the book ends with one of my favorite scenes, in which a bare-breasted, body-painted Ruby confronts a cosmetics saleswoman. And throughout, there's plenty of interesting information about mistletoe, everyone's favorite Christmas herb.

North American mistletoe (*Phoradendron tomento-sum*) does not belong to the same genus as the European mistletoe (*Viscum album*), but the legends and lore of the European plant long ago made their way to America. In fact, this evergreen herb that seems to miraculously grow in trees has spread its magic across many different cultures. Here's some fascinating mistletoe information I gathered when I was doing research for the mystery:

- Norwegian peasants hung mistletoe from the rafters of their homes to protect against lightning.
- In Wales, mistletoe gathered on Midsummer Eve was placed under the pillow at Yule-tide to induce prophetic dreams.
- In northern Europe, mistletoe was thought to act as a master key that would open any lock.
- Swedish farmers hung mistletoe in the horse's stall and the cow's crib, to protect against evil trolls. They also used the wood to make divining rods.
- In the south of France, mistletoe was thought to be an antidote to all poisons.
- Everywhere, people enjoy kissing under the mistletoe
- European mistletoe (*Viscum album*) has been used for millennia for a variety of illnesses, including epilepsy, heart disease, rheumatism, anxiety, exhaustion, asthma, diarrhea, and hypertension. Claims for its efficacy as a cancer treatment have not yet been fully evaluated.
- In the Victorian language of flowers, mistletoe symbolized "I overcome everything"; I surmount difficulties"; "I rise above all."

# DECEMBER 15

In some years, today is the beginning of Hanukkah, the Jewish Feast of Lights.

❧

## Celebrating the Return of the Light

The eight-day celebration of Hanukkah opens with the ritual lighting of the Menorah, a candelabrum with eight branches. According to Hebrew historians, a single flask of sanctified olive oil—just enough for one day's lighting—was discovered when the Temple was reclaimed after a period of pagan defilement. Miraculously, this small amount of sacred oil kept the Menorah burning for eight full days. Chanukah, a time of rededication, is celebrated with festive foods fried in oil: fritters, potato pancakes, or latke, and doughnuts. Every family has its favorite traditional foods, the recipes often handed down through the generations.

My favorite potato pancake recipe comes from my mother, who learned to make them during the Depression when she worked for the Schwartzes, a family of Polish Jews in Chicago. My own version leaves the potatoes unpeeled (Mom and Mrs. Schwartz would be horrified!) and adds dried and fresh herbs.

### MOM'S POTATO PANCAKES

1 pound small red potatoes, scrubbed (really well, Mom) and unpeeled tops of four green onions, minced

2 cloves garlic, minced

3 teaspoons fresh or 1 teaspoon dried herbs: oregano, thyme, or savory

2 teaspoons minced fresh parsley

2 tablespoons all-purpose flour

1 egg

1 teaspoon salt or Savory Blend (August 29)

½ teaspoon freshly ground black pepper

oil for frying

Heat ½ inch of oil over medium heat in heavy skillet to approximately 350°. Grate potatoes. In a large glass bowl, mix potatoes and other ingredients and let stand until potatoes soften and become watery (about 10 minutes). Drain most of the liquid. Make small round balls about the size of golf balls. Fry 7–8 at a time, until golden brown (about 5–6 minutes). Turn and press down lightly. Fry 5 minutes longer, until golden brown. Drain on paper towels and serve with sour cream.

**More Jewish foods:**

*The Essential Book of Jewish Festival Cooking,* by Phyllis and Miriyam Glazer

# DECEMBER 16

Today is the birthday of Adelma Grenier Simmons, herbalist, author, and founder of Caprilands Herb Farm.

*Happy is the herb gardener through all the seasons and the years.*

—ADELMA GRENIER SIMMONS (1904–1997)

## Adelma Grenier Simmons: Herbalist Extraordinaire

In 1964, Adelma Simmons' book *Herb Gardening in Five Seasons* broke a long silence. There had been no herb books of any consequence written since 1942, when Rosetta Clarkson's *Herbs: Their Culture and Uses* was published. The war had intervened, of course, and after the war America was captivated by fast foods and modern technology, and the "little green plants" didn't stand much of a chance. But that didn't deter Adelma, who was pursuing her dream. In 1929, her family had bought a farm in Coventry, Connecticut, and over the years until her death in 1997, Adelma made it into an herbal showplace—"America's Herbal Homestead," it is sometimes called. Caprilands became a mecca for herb enthusiasts.

Adelma was not only a creative, inspiring herbalist, however; she was a writer, as well, as her nearly two dozen titles suggest. Some of these are informative pamphlets she published and sold in her shop; a few of these have become collectors' items. Others—*Herb Gardening in Five Seasons*, for instance—are important additions to any herb bookshelf. Everyone who visited Caprilands and saw an "herbal lifestyle" firsthand wanted to taste her food and take away some of her books, as well as the dried herbs, wreaths, and craft items sold in the shop. And everyone took away with them the powerful impression of a woman with tremendous energy and a dedicated commitment to a calling: teaching modern Americans that there is something profoundly worthwhile in the small green plants under our feet.

**BISHOP'S WINE FROM CAPRILANDS**

- 2 quarts sweet cider
- 4 sticks cinnamon
- 6 cloves
- 1 orange, unpeeled, cut in fourths
- ½ teaspoon nutmeg
- 2 quarts port wine

Simmer for 20 minutes. Stir in wine. Heat until steaming and serve in pottery mugs with a stick of cinnamon in each. Makes twelve 8-ounce servings.

Caprilands Herb Farm is located at 534 Silver Street, Coventry, Connecticut 06238 Phone: (860) 742-7244 Web site: http://www.caprilands.com

**Read more:**
*Herb Gardening in Five Seasons*, by Adelma Grenier Simmons

# DECEMBER 17

In Mexico, this is the time of the celebration of "Las Posadas." In Spanish, *posada* means inn or shelter.

> *And it came to pass in those days, that there went out a decree from Caesar Augustus, that all the world should be taxed. . . . And all went to be taxed, every one into his own city. And Joseph also went up from Galilee, out of the city of Nazareth, into Judaea, unto the city of David, which is called Bethlehem . . . there to be taxed with Mary his espoused wife, being great with child*
>
> —LUKE 2:1–5

The posada parties commemorate Mary and Joseph's long and difficult journey from Nazareth to Bethlehem. The parties begin with a solemn candle-lit procession led by a child dressed as an angel and other children carrying figures of Mary and Joseph, followed by adults and musicians, singing and playing traditional songs. When they reach the house where the evening's party is to be held, half of the group goes inside. The other half remains outside, begging for shelter. The door is finally opened, the petitioners are welcomed, and the celebration begins, with plenty of food and drink—and music, of course. The evening ends with the breaking of the piñata, traditionally star-shaped, to symbolize the star that guided the Three Kings to Jesus. The final posada is held on December 24 and followed by midnight Mass.

The biscochito is a traditional cookie served at most posadas.

## BISCOCHITO
6 cups flour
3 teaspoons baking powder
¼ teaspoon salt
2 cups shortening
1 ½ cups white sugar
2 teaspoons anise seed
2 eggs
¼ cup brandy
¼ cup white sugar
1 teaspoon ground cinnamon

Sift flour with baking powder and salt. Cream shortening with sugar and anise seed until fluffy. Beat in eggs one at a time. Mix in flour and brandy until well blended. Turn dough onto a floured board and roll ½" thick. Cut into shapes (the fleur-de-lys is traditional). Mix sugar and cinnamon and dust each cookie. Bake at 350° for 10–12 minutes or until golden brown.

**Use this book to share this holiday ritual with your children:**
*Celebrating Los Posados: An Hispanic Christmas Celebration,* by Diane Hoyt-Goldsmith

# DECEMBER 18

*The onion being eaten, yea though it be boyled, causeth head-ache, hurteth the eyes, and maketh a man dimme sighted, dulleth the senses, ingendreth windinesse, and provoketh overmuch sleepe, especially being eaten raw.*

—JOHN GERARD, *HERBAL*, 1597

## The Magical, Mystical, Magnetic Onion

They've been around all your life. You've avoided them, indulged in them, and maybe even been embarrassed by them. But I'll bet there are things about onions you don't know. You're probably not aware that the ancient Egyptians worshipped the onion, as a gift from the gods. In other cultures, though, onions belonged to the devil. The prophet Mohammed says that when Satan was banished from paradise, onions sprang from the print of his right foot. And the early Greeks believed that the onion, which was ruled by the planet Mars, exercised an attractive force so powerful that it could pull the magnetism right out of the rock magnetite.

It may have been this association with the masculine Mars that gave the Romans the idea that eating an onion would increase the quantity and vitality of seminal fluid. And perhaps the onion's purported ability to attract suggests why some Middle Eastern cultures considered it an aphrodisiac. This magnetic force might also be the reason the eighteenth-century herbalist Nicholas Culpeper thought that an onion could draw poison from the bite of a venomous snake or a rabid dog. It might explain, too, why American colonists hung onions outside their doors. They hoped it would attract, and then deflect, any evil spirits who attempted to come inside.

There are plenty of modern folks who believe that the onion has a magnetic personality. As late as the 1950s, in England, people hung the cut half of an onion in the house to attract infectious germs out of the air. A friend's mother remembers putting a small hot onion in her ear to draw out the pain of a childhood earache. And I recently read in a contemporary magazine that rubbing a bee sting with a raw onion will remove the pain.

Superstition or not, you've got to admit that the onion exerts a powerful force. Think about it the next time you slice into one of these pungent beauties.

*A folk remedy for ringworm: a poultice made of onions or garlic, treacle, rue, wormwood, borage, and soapwort.*

**More Reading:**

*Onions, Onions, Onions: Delicious Recipes for the World's Favorite Secret Ingredient*, by Linda and Fred Griffith

*The shop was beautifully decorated for Christmas, with wooden bowls of clove-studded pomanders and potpourri, a tiny Christmas tree decorated with gingerbread cookies and popcorn-and-cranberry chains, and fresh green branches of rosemary everywhere.*

—MISTLETOE MAN: A CHINA BAYLES MYSTERY

## Holiday Fragrance

In China's shop, the scent of Christmas fills the air. One of her perennial best-sellers at this time of year is her stovetop simmer, which she makes at home in her kitchen and sells in bulk and in smaller packages. Of course, she's always (well, almost always) willing to share her recipes with a few special friends. Here it is, just for you:

**THYME & SEASONS HOLIDAY STOVETOP POTPOURRI**

¼ cup whole cloves

¼ cup cinnamon chips

¼ cup allspice berries

¼ cup whole rose hips

¼ cup dried orange peel

¼ cup dried lemon peel

1 tablespoon cardamom seeds

1 tablespoon aniseed

6–8 bay laurel leaves

Combine all ingredients and store in lidded container. To use, bring 3 cups water to a boil in an old pan. Add 2–3 tablespoons of potpourri and a sliced apple, if you wish. Reduce heat to a simmer, and add water as necessary to keep it from boiling dry. Mixture may be stored in refrigerator between uses (don't drink it!) Makes about 1 ¾ cup potpourri, enough for the rest of the holiday season!

**For more fragrance ideas:**

*Herbal Treasures Inspiring Month-by-Month Projects for Gardening, Cooking, and Crafts*, by Phyllis V. Shaudys

*By this time, the less devoted gardeners have hung up their tools and retired indoors to continue gardening by the fire.*

—MARGERY FISH

# DECEMBER 20

### Pressed Flower Gifts and Cards

"Mom, I'm bored! I don't have anything to do, and it's too cold to go outside!"

If you pressed some of those garden flowers during the summer (see September 11), they'll come in handy for holiday gifts, cards, and stationary. Youngsters enjoy pressed flower crafts, so get out the flowers and herbs you've saved from summer's bounty and let the children go to work.

#### PRESSED FLOWER CHRISTMAS TREE HANGERS
What you'll need:
tiny pressed flowers and leaves
glass microscope slides (available in craft shops)
glue
⅛-inch ribbon

How to do it: Arrange the dried material on a glass microscope slide, securing with a tiny bit of glue dabbed on with a pin. When dry, cover with another slide, securing at the corners with four dabs of glue. Press under a large book until dry. Glue a 1-inch ribbon loop at the center top edge of the slide. When that's dry, glue a ribbon border around all the edges, beginning and ending at the center and leaving 5 inches of ribbon at each end. When the border is dry, tie the ribbon in a bow and trim ends.

#### HOLIDAY CARDS AND GIFT TAGS
Flowers and herbs can be sprayed with gold paint, which will camouflage any imperfections in the flowers. To make the cards, score and fold a 12 × 8-inch piece of red or green card stock or construction paper. Glue the flowers to the cards in a pleasing arrangement. For gift tags, cut out 1 × 2-inch rectangles, decorate, and punch a hole in the corner for a gold tie.

#### CANDLES
Follow the directions for making Brighid's candle (February 1), using a red or green candle and gold-sprayed herbs and flowers. Center the candle in a wreath of rosemary, cones, and holiday ribbon.

#### RIBBON BOOKMARKS
For this project, you will need a wide ribbon (about 1¼ inches) and clear self-laminating film (available in sheets at craft stores). Cut the ribbon into 12-inch lengths. Apply the flowers to the ribbon with a bit of glue (use a toothpick or match). Following the package directions, sandwich the ribbon between two sheets of self-laminating film. Trim. Punch a hole in the top and add a ribbon. (Every grandma needs at least two bookmarks, and probably more!)

*By all those token flowers, that tell,*
*What words can never speak so well.*
—LORD BYRON

Today or tomorrow, the Sun enters the sign of Capricorn.

*The tenth sign of the zodiac, the masculine sign Capricorn (the Goat) is ruled by Capricorn, a cardinal earth sign. Capricorns are practical, prudent and patient, as well as self-disciplined and ambitious; however, they can also be fatalistic, pessimistic, and often grudging.*

—RUBY WILCOX, "ASTROLOGICAL SIGNS"

## Capricorn Herbs

The planet Saturn was said to rule the systems that give the body its structure and form: the skeletal system and the skin, teeth, joints, and knees. Saturn-ruled herbs, useful in treating arthritis and rheumatism, are often high in calcium. The list includes woody plants and shrubs that show annual growth rings, as well as some poisonous plants.

- Comfrey (*Symphytum officinale*). Comfrey leaves boiled in water form a sticky paste that hardens like plaster and was used to set broken bones. (That's how it earned the names "knitbone" and "boneset." Allantoin, a valuable cell-proliferating healing agent, is its principle chemical, making it a reliable wound-healer. In skin preparations, it is used to treat psoriasis, skin ulcers, acne, and impetigo.

- Mullein (*Verbascum thapsus*). Culpeper writes: "The seed bruised and boiled in wine and laid on any member that has been out of joint, and newly set again, takes away all swelling and pain." Mullein has other medicinal uses, chiefly in the treatment of respiratory irritation and as an ingredient in a healing salve.

- Horsetail (*Equisetum arvense*). Rich in silica, horsetail is used in both Eastern and Western medicine as a treatment for arthritis and as a wound healer. In Chinese medicine, the herb is valued for its ability to absorb and dispense the minute amounts of gold that is used to treat rheumatoid arthritis. Recommended by the Roman physician Galen, the herb has been used for kidney and bladder troubles, arthritis, bleeding ulcers, and tuberculosis.

- Other Capricorn herbs. Wintergreen is often a component in liniments for chronic skeletal ailments like sciatica. Goutweed was used in folk medicine to treat gout, rheumatism, and arthritis; it is also known as "goat-herb" because the leaves are shaped like a goat's foot. Slippery elm is made into a poultice to treat boils and abscesses. Black poplar buds have been used in a salve to treat wounds and hemorrhoids.

*The nearer the New Moon to Christmas Day, the harder the winter weather.*

—TRADITIONAL WEATHER LORE

# DECEMBER 22

*Make thee a box of the wood of rosemary and smell to it and it shall preserve thy youth . . . Smell it oft and it shall keep thee youngly.*

—BANCKES' HERBAL, 1525

## Banckes' Herbal: Rosemary

We don't know who the author of *Banckes' Herbal* was, although we know that it was "imprynted by me Rychard Banckes" in London in 1525. It seems to have been based on some medieval manuscript, which is now lost, for (as Eleanour Rohde says in her book *The Old English Herbals*), it gives the impression of "being a compilation from various sources, the author having made his own selection from what pleased him most in the older English manuscript herbals." One of the most charming sections of *Banckes' Herbal* is the chapter on rosemary. These selections from the text will make you "light and merrie"—and perhaps appreciate your rosemary just a little bit more!

- Take the flowers [of rosemary] and make powder thereof and binde it to thy right arme in a linnen cloath and it shall make thee light and merrie.
- Take the flowers and put them in thy chest among thy clothes or among thy Bookes and Mothes shall not destroy them.
- Boyle the leaves in white wine and washe thy face therewith and thy browes, and thou shalt have a faire face.

- Also put the leaves under thy bedde and thou shalt be delivered of all evill dreames.
- Also if thou be feeble boyle the leaves in cleane water and washe thyself and thou shalt wax shiny.
- If thy legges be blowen with gowte, boyle the leaves in water and binde them in a linnen cloath and winde it about thy legges and it shall do thee much good.
- If thou have a cough drink the water of the leaves boyld in white wine and ye shall be whole.
- Make thee a box of the wood of rosemary and smell to it and it shall preserve thy youth.
- Take the Timber thereof and burn it to coales and make powder thereof and rubbe thy teeth thereof and it shall keep thy teeth from all evils. Smell it oft and it shall keep thee youngly.

**Read more about *Banckes' Herbal* and other old texts:** *The Old English Herbals,* by Eleanour Sinclair Rohde

*Evergreen rosemary—the rose of the Virgin Mary—is one of the special plants of Christmas. It was believed to blossom at midnight on Christmas Eve, and to have acquired its scent from the garments of the Infant Jesus, which the Virgin hung out to dry on a rosemary bush.*

—CHARLES KIGHTLY, THE PERPETUAL ALMANACK OF FOLKLORE

# DECEMBER 23

The winter solstice occurs about now: the shortest day and the longest night of the year. The Celtic Tree Month of Birch begins.

> *The north wind doth blow*
> *And we shall have snow.*
> —TRADITIONAL

## The Yule Log

The burning of the Yule log is an ancient tradition that has more to do with the celebration of the solstice than with Christmas. In England and Europe, the logs most often burned were that of the birch, the oak, and the yew, all held to be sacred trees, related to the cycle of birth and death.

Since fire and light were of such great importance at this darkest time of the year, it is easy to see why the burning of a great log was included in the ritual. In England, it was often covered with herbs and lit with one of the candles that had been blessed at Candlemas. The log was burned throughout the twelve days of Christmas, often with the addition of symbolic fuels. In Serbia, for instance, wheat was tossed on the fire to represent the sacrifice of the harvest and ensure a bountiful harvest in the coming year. Even the ashes were disposed of ritually. In France and Germany, they were mixed with the cows' feed to keep the animals safe from harm. In Eastern Europe, they were scattered around the fruit trees to increase their yield.

You can begin a memorable Yule tradition by inviting the children to help with this holiday herbal project. Find a large fireplace log. (Sometimes this can come from a tree that has some special significance for the family.) Using sparing amounts of white glue, cover the log with glued-on oakmoss (available at craft stores) or moss that you have gathered. Decorate with glued-on cinnamon sticks, star anise, whole cloves, juniper berries, holly leaves, pine cones, bits of lichen, and sprigs of rosemary and sage. Drop fragrant herbal oils (balsam, cinnamon, orange, bayberry are ideal) onto the moss-covered log, and add a paper bow.

When it's time to light your Yule log, gather the family for carols, holiday treats, and a ceremonial lighting. If you made Brighid's candle for a Candlemas celebration (see February 1), it would be perfect for the occasion. When the log is almost completely burned, save a last bit to incorporate into next year's log. And don't forget to use the ashes in a way that enriches your garden.

> *Come bring with a noise, my merry, merry boys*
> *The Christmas log to the firing;*
> *With last year's brand light the new log, and*
> *For good success in his spending*
> *On your psalteries play, that sweet Luck may*
> *Come while the log is a-tending.*
> —ROBERT HERRICK, *HESPERIDES*, 1648

# DECEMBER 24

Tonight is Christmas Eve.

❧

## O Christmas Tree,
## O Christmas Tree!

Tonight is a night for friends and family, and—at our house—trimming the tree. We've already chosen a fresh green juniper tree from among the many that grow along the creek, cut it with ceremony, and brought it home, with the help of our dogs, of course, who love to join in the fun. Bill puts the tree up and adds strings of lights, I spread the old quilted skirt beneath it, and—joined by those of the clan that have arrived for the holiday—we decorate it with the herbs and flowers saved from the Lammas gathering (see August 1). When it's finished, our tree is breathtaking, a kaleidoscope of colors and a rich bouquet of fragrances.

   With the decorating, there is music, of course—our favorite carols, old recordings played on an old phonograph. And hot mulled cider and plenty of Christmas treats to munch and share with anyone who happens to drop in. Here are two of our favorite recipes.

### HOLIDAY MINI-FRITATAS
   1 medium zucchini, sliced in ⅛-inch thick rounds
   6 button mushrooms, sliced
   1 red bell pepper, seeded and diced
   1 green bell pepper, seeded and diced
   16 large eggs
   1 tablespoon minced fresh rosemary
   2 tablespoons Savory Blend (August 29) or salt
   ½ cup finely grated Swiss or Gruyère cheese

Heat oven to 400°. Spray two 24-cup mini muffin tins with cooking spray. In a large bowl, thoroughly mix eggs, rosemary, Savory Blend or salt. Distribute the zucchini, mushrooms, and peppers in each muffin cup. Pour egg mixture into each cup, filling to the rim. Sprinkle with cheese. Bake until set, about 8–10 minutes. Serve warm, on platters decorated with rosemary sprigs. (May be refrigerated and reheated for serving at 325°.)

### ROSEMARY WALNUTS
   1 pound shelled walnuts
   2 tablespoons olive oil
   2 tablespoons butter, melted
   3 tablespoons minced fresh rosemary leaves
   2 teaspoons paprika
   ½ to 1 teaspoon salt or Zippy Blend (August 29)

Preheat over to 325°. Place all ingredients in a bowl and toss to mix. Spread on a baking sheet large enough to hold the nuts in a single layer. Bake for 20–25 minutes, stirring once or twice, or until the nuts are golden but not browned and the scent of rosemary fills the room. Remove and cool. May be eaten when warm or stored in an airtight container for up to 2 weeks. Makes 2 cups. (Thanks to Madeline Wajda, of Willow Pond Farm Herbs, for sharing this recipe.)

# DECEMBER 25

Today is Christmas.

*Now Christmas is come*
*Let's beat up the drum,*
*And call all our neighbors together,*
*And when they appear*
*Let us make them such cheer*
*As will keep out the wind and the weather.*

—WASHINGTON IRVING

## A Great Bowl of Stuffing

I don't know which is more important at our house, the turkey or the stuffing. And because none of us can ever agree on exactly which stuffing is best, we usually have at least two kinds: the traditional sage stuffing and Bill's definitely nontraditional favorite South-of-the-Border Stuffing, hot and spicy, with his home-grown chiles. The sage stuffing goes into the turkey and the spicy is baked separately. Your mother probably gave you her sage stuffing recipe, so here is Bill's favorite. Merry Christmas!

**BILL'S SOUTH-OF-THE-BORDER STUFFING**
¼ pound chorizo (spicy Mexican sausage)
1 cup chopped onions
½ cup chopped celery
½ cup chopped roasted poblano chiles
2 ancho chiles, chopped

1–2 habanero chiles, chopped (These are the really hot ones. Use less for less fire-power. Wear gloves or put sandwich bags over your hands when handling.)
4 cloves garlic, chopped
1½ teaspoons powdered cumin
4 cups cubed corn bread, slightly dry
¼ cup minced parsley
½ cup grated cheddar cheese
chicken or turkey stock

Crumble chorizo into a skillet and begin to brown. Add the onions, celery, chiles, garlic, and cumin. Cook, stirring occasionally for about 12 minutes, or until chiles are soft. In a large bowl, combine the corn bread, parsley, and grated cheese with the pepper mixture. Add stock to moisten and mix well. Turn into greased casserole dish. Bake, covered, at 350° for 30 minutes. Uncover and bake 15 minutes longer.

*I am not alone at all, I thought. I was never alone at all. And that, of course, is the message of Christmas. We are never alone. Not when the night is darkest, the wind coldest, the world seemingly most indifferent. For this is still the time God chooses.*

—TAYLOR CALDWELL

# DECEMBER 26

Today is the beginning of the celebration of Kwanzaa.

*The word* Kwanzaa *is derived from the Swahili phrase* Matunda ya Kwanza, *which means "first fruits of the harvest." The additional "a" in distinguishes the African American Kwanzaa from the African Kwanza.*

## Kwanzaa and *Abelmoschus esculentus*

The foods of Kwanzaa reflect the enormous variety of cuisines that are part of the African American culinary heritage. A wide range of herbs are used, many of them hot and spicy, but most cuisines have one important herb in common: *Abelmoschus esculentus*, a native of Ethiopia, now used worldwide. The muscilagenous fruits of this valuable plant are used in soups and stews and as a thickening agent. The leaves, buds, and flowers are cooked as greens, or dried and used as a seasoning. The seeds are ground into flour for bread, roasted and ground as a coffee substitute, and pressed to produce a nutritious oil, low in saturated fat. Medicinally, *Abelmoschus* is used as a poultice to reduce swellings and inflammations. Antioxidant and anti-inflammatory, it helps to lower homocysteine levels, related to higher risk of heart disease. Recent research also demonstrates that it can inhibit the growth of the bacteria that can cause stomach ulcers and cancer.

If the Latin name of this herb doesn't ring a bell with you, you're bound to be familiar with its English name: okra. And if you are looking for a way to commemorate Kwanzaa, consider this simple side dish of golden sautéed okra, accented with turmeric and sesame seeds.

### SAUTÉED OKRA

  1 tablespoon sesame seeds
  1 tablespoon butter
  3 onions, sliced
  2 cloves garlic
  1 pound fresh young okra, sliced in ⅛-inch pieces
  1 ½ teaspoons ground turmeric

In a skillet, toast seeds until golden brown (about 2 minutes) stirring frequently. Transfer to a bowl and set aside. Melt butter in the skillet and sauté onion and garlic until translucent. Stir in okra and turmeric. Reduce heat to low and cook 15 minutes, or until tender. Sprinkle with toasted sesame seeds. Serves 6.

**Learn more about celebrating Kwanzaa:**
*Complete Kwanzaa*, by Dorothy Winbush Riley

# DECEMBER 27

*Why do we like it so much? We only want it for its bite—and we will go to India to get it! Who was the first to try it with food? Who was so anxious to develop an appetite that hunger would not do the trick? Pepper and ginger both grow wild in their native countries, and yet we value them in terms of gold and silver.*

—PLINY, *NATURAL HISTORY*, FIRST CENTURY CE

## Peppercorns

Some people say that if there's only one spice in your kitchen, it should be pepper, for it adds the greatest flavor to the greatest variety of dishes. And they may be right. After all, Rome was ransomed with pepper (Attila demanded 3,000 pounds), people have died for pepper, and oceans were crossed in pursuit of pepper—a highly valued spice.

### PEPPER TIMES THREE
There is only one pepper (*Piper nigrum*), native to India but now grown widely throughout the tropics. Three different peppercorns are produced from this plant.

- Black peppercorns have been valued for centuries as a medicine: a treatment for impotence, an appetite stimulant and digestive, a cure for nausea and flatulence, and an antidote to poison. They are harvested green and left to dry for a week or more, shriveling and hardening. Black peppercorns have the strongest flavor, and are best when freshly ground. Also used whole in pickling spices and soup stocks.
- Green peppercorns are picked green and freeze-dried. They have a fresh, clean flavor, suited to poultry, vegetables, and seafood.
- White peppercorns are allowed to ripen on the vine, producing a large berry with a loose outer shell, which is removed. White pepper is regarded as having a richer, more complex flavor; it is used in light-colored dishes, in sauces, and on grilled poultry.

Here's an easy recipe that will introduce you to the variety of pepper flavors. Super with vegetables, great with fish and poultry.

### PEPPER BUTTER
½ cup butter, softened

3 teaspoons freshly ground peppercorns, black, green, OR white (if mixing, 1 teaspoon of each)

1 clove garlic, minced

3 tablespoons fresh minced parsley

Grind the peppercorns to a medium coarseness (easy in a mortar and pestle). Add to softened butter. Add garlic and parsley and mix. Place in a small dish, cover, and refrigerate at least one hour before using.

*[Pepper] doth assuage the fits that ague make*
*If that you use thereof before you shake.*

—ENGLISH LORE

# DECEMBER 28

*If a man beareth with him one twig of this wort, he will not be terrified with any awe, nor will a wild beast hurt him; or any evil come near.*

—THE HERBARIUM OF APULEIUS PLANTONICUS

## Wortcunning

Wortcunning is an Anglo-Saxon compound: *wort* means plant or herb; *cunning* means knowledgeable or wise. Hence, someone who has wortcunning is wise in the way of worts, which are grown in a *wortyerd*—literally, herb-yard.

And what are the worts? Those who have studied the leechbooks (the healing manuals), tell us that the Anglo-Saxons had names for, and used, at least 500 plants. More than a hundred of these were specifically called worts, although they were all worts, technically speaking. Here are a few, selected, with their descriptions and a few quotations, from that rich bouquet of herbal lore: *The Englishman's Flora*.

- Motherwort, *Leonurus cardiaca*. Also known as "womb plant," used in difficult childbirth.
- Mugwort, *Artemisia vulgaris*. Magical herb, used to keep off the powers of evil. "Whosoever goeth any distance and he bear this herb with him he shall not be weary in his going."—*Agnus Castus*, 1425
- Sneezewort, *Achillea ptarmica*. Tastes hot and sharp, causes a flow of saliva.
- Soapwort, *Saponaria officinalis*. Used as a cleansing herb.
- Figwort or pilewort, *Scrophularia nodosa*. Used to treat "figs" or piles.
- Bairnwort, daisy, *Bellis perennis*. Known to all children, or "bairns."
- Woundwort, yarrow, *Achillea millefolium*. Used to heal wounds made with iron.
- Birthwort, *Aristolochia clematitis*. Resists poison, encourages conception, helps delivery.
- Bishopwort, water mint, *Mentha aquatica*. Strewn where feasts and banquets are made.
- Casewort, Shepherd's purse, *Capsella bursa-pastoris*. Its seed cases are easily broken.
- Lousewort, *Pedicularis sylvatica*. Thought to be the source of intestinal parasites in animals.
- Pennywort or naval wort, *Umbilicus rupestris*. The leaves look like pennies.
- Saint-John's-wort, *Hypericum perforatum*. "If it be putte in a mannes house there shall come no wycked spryte therein."—*Banckes' Herbal*, 1525

**More Reading:**
*The Englishman's Flora*, by Geoffrey Grigson

*St. John's wort, St. John's wort,*
*I envy whosoever has thee,*
*I will pluck thee with my right hand,*
*I will preserve thee with my left hand,*
*Whoso findeth thee in the cattlefold,*
*Shall never be without kine. [cattle]*

—GAELIC WORT CHARM

# DECEMBER 29

### The Popular Poppy-Seed

For millennia, poppies (*Papaver somniferum*) have been cultivated for their black, nutty seeds. (This is the same species that yields opium, but the seeds are non-narcotic.) While it's easier to buy the seeds in the grocery, it's more fun to harvest them yourself, from your garden—and have the flowers to enjoy, as well. A 5-foot row of plants will yield about a half-cup of seeds.* Harvest the seed capsules as they ripen and keep them in a paper box (a shoebox will work). When they've dried, pour the seeds into a shallow pan and pick out the debris. Store the cleaned seeds in a lidded jar in the refrigerator. Wonderful as a sprinkle on baked goods, delightful on fruit salads.

**ORANGE POPPY-SEED FRUIT SALAD DRESSING**
  ½ cup mayonnaise
  ½ cup sour cream or yogurt
  1 tablespoon honey
  2 teaspoons poppy seed
  ½ teaspoon finely grated orange peel
  1–2 tablespoons orange juice
  Fresh fruits, cut up: your choice of pineapple, orange,
    mango, melon, strawberries, grapes

In a small bowl, stir together the mayonnaise, sour cream, honey, poppy seed, and orange peel. Stir in enough orange juice for the consistency you want.

Spoon over fresh fruit in stemmed glasses. Makes 1 cup dressing.

> *Seeds must be gathered in fair weather, at the wane of the Moon, and kept some in Boxes of Wood, some in bags of Leather, and some in Vessels of Earthenware, and well cleansed and dried in shadow. Others, as Onions and Leeks, must be kept in their husks.*
>
> —GERVASE MARKHAM, *THE ENGLISH HOUSEWIFE*, 1615

*In some states, it is legal to possess the seeds, but illegal to possess the plants. Check the laws in your state.

*After the day I'd had, I was ready to pamper my-self. I lit a vanilla-scented candle, added laven-der oil to a tub full of warm water, and climbed in. I leaned back and closed my eyes, letting the thoughts go, letting my body soak in the lavender-scented silence. After a long while I scrubbed with rosemary soap and a luffa, rel-ishing its gentle rasping. When I toweled off, I pulled on a pair of silky pink pajamas—how long had it been since I'd worn anything but a ratty old tee shirt to sleep in?—and climbed into bed with an Agatha Christie mystery. . . .*

—RUEFUL DEATH: A CHINA BAYLES MYSTERY

## Indulge Yourself in an Herbal Bath

What a busy week! It's been just as hectic as the week before Christmas, if that's possible—and the upcom-ing weekend doesn't look a bit relaxing. This evening, pamper yourself in a long, leisurely bath. With music, a scented candle, fresh flowers, and a plush towel, you'll feel like a completely new person when you step out of the bath.

### SKIN-SOFTENING MILK BATH BAGS
You can purchase exotic softening products or you can make your own and have the satisfaction of enjoying something you've crafted yourself. Sunflower seeds provide enriching oil; oatmeal softens; and milk makes your skin feel deliciously smooth. Indulge yourself!

### MILK BATH BAGS
½ cup raw shelled sunflower seeds
½ cup oatmeal
½ cup cornstarch
1 cup dried nonfat milk powder
vitamin E oil capsules

In a food processor or coffee grinder, grind the sun-flower seeds and oatmeal together until you have a smooth powder about the consistency of cornmeal. Stir in the cornstarch and milk powder. Divide into five single-bath portions (½ cup). To each, add your fa-vorite essential oil or oil combinations and mix. When the scent pleases you, put the mixture into a snack-size zipper-top plastic bag, or in a reusable muslin bag. To use, add the milk bath as you fill your tub.

### SOME AROMATIC COMBINATIONS
• For a relaxing bath: lavender and rose
• For a sensual bath: ylang ylang, patchouli, orange
• For a spirit-lifting bath: rosemary, bergamot, euca-lyptus
• For an energizing bath: mint

**Read more about bath pleasures:**
*Rituals for the Bath,* by Kathy Corey and Lynne Black-man

# DECEMBER 31

*A winter evening is the best of times to muse on plans for a garden, for like Bunyan's* Pilgrim's Progress, *gardening is then carried on "under the similitude of a dream." The things we mean to have stand as we mean to have them, thrifty, beautiful, and a pretty tribute to our skill as gardeners; the things we have had, successes and less-than-successes, are something to go on from, are a part of garden history and our lives.*

—HENRY BESTON, *HERBS AND THE EARTH*

## New Year, Next Year

What could be better than planning next year's garden on the last day of the old year? And if you've read all through this Book of Days and you still don't have a garden, it is certainly the right time to begin! Of course, if you've gardened before, you will plan from experience. If you haven't, here are some suggestions.

- Space. You don't need a football field—a plot about 6 × 10 feet will give you room for 18–24 plants. Think small. You can always add on later.
- Outlook. Most garden herbs don't enjoy shade. Give your plants a place in the sun.
- Soil and drainage. Ordinary garden soil is fine; you don't need to add compost or amendments. If the soil is heavy or clayey, sand and small rocks will improve the drainage. Consider creating a raised bed with landscape timbers, bricks, or blocks. Most herbs don't like wet feet.
- Plan to put the taller plants in the back or the center (if yours is a peninsula bed), with the shorter, more compact plants in front and at the edges. Give them plenty of elbow room so they don't crowd their neighbors.
- Come spring, start with nursery-grown plants. Your garden will look like a garden sooner and you'll have an earlier harvest.
- Choose herbs you'll use. Some easy favorites: basil, chives, dill, fennel, lemon balm, mint, oregano, parsley, rosemary, sage, thyme. Spend some time reading about each plant and learning about the way it grows. Read back through this book and make a shopping list.

*Plans should be made on the ground to fit the place, and not the place made to suit some plan out of a book.*

—WILLIAM ROBINSON

**Read more about herb gardening:**

*Your Backyard Herb Garden: A Gardener's Guide to Growing Over 50 Herbs Plus How to Use Them in Cooking, Crafts, Companion Planting and More*, by Miranda Smith

*China, Ruby, and the Pecan Springs gang send their very best wishes for a bright and happy New Year!*

# INDEX OF RECIPES

Apple-Spice Nut Bars, Jan 6, 8

Baked Eggs with Garden Herbs, Feb 17, 50
Banana-Yogurt Frappe, Oct 8, 292
Basil Bocconcini, Dec 9, 354
Basil Pesto Cheesecake, July 31, 221
Basil Pesto, July 31, 221
Bay Blend for Meat & Poultry, Nov 12, 327
Berry-Minty Dessert Frappe, Oct 8, 292
Bill's Incendiary Salsa, July 26, 216
Bishop's Wine, Dec 16, 361
Bisochito, Dec 17, 362
Bouquet Garni, Nov 7, 322
Boursin Basil Rollups, May 16, 142
Boursin, May 16, 142
Braided Herb Loaf, Aug 1, 222
Burgundy with Thyme, Marjoram, and Parsley,
    Jan 22, 24
Burnet Butter, Oct 12, 296
Burnet Vinegar, Oct 12, 296

Candied Angelica, Sept 29, 281
Candied Flowers and Herbs, June 23, 180
Carnation Vinegar, April 13, 109
Chardonnay with Rosemary, Basil, and Garlic,
    Jan 22, 24
Chocolate Pudding with Bay, June 26, 183
Chunky Tomato Sauce, Oct 25, 309
Cilantro-Mint Yogurt Sauce, May 7, 133
Cranberry Cordial, Nov 23, 338
Curry Cookies, July 9, 199

Date-Nut Cookies, Oct 24, 308
Deviled Eggs, July 30, 220
Doggie Biscuits, Feb 23, 56
Dried is Fine Herb Butter, Mar 4, 66

Easy Twelfth Night Cake, Jan 4, 6
Egg Soup with Lemon and Herbs, Oct 7, 291
Elder Vinegar (1723), Nov 25, 340
Elderberry Jelly, Nov 25, 340
Election Cake (1800), Nov 4, 319

Faerie Blossom Cookies, May 1, 127
Fennel and Tomato Pesto, Sept 10, 262
Flowerpot Herb Bread, Nov 17, 332
Frijoles de Olla from the Indigo Café, Jan 24, 26
Fruit Vinegars, Aug 11, 232

Garam Marsala, Nov 14, 329
Garden Punch, Aug 30, 251
Garlic Mashed Potatoes, Aug 20, 241
Ginger Beer (1841), Nov 16, 331
Ginger-Peachy Breakfast Frappe, Oct 8, 292
Gingery Daylily Buds with Rice, July 24, 214
Gingery-Mint Fruit Salsa, May 29, 155
Gingko Nut Porridge, Oct 26, 310
Goose Stuffing (1861), Nov 24, 339
Gourmet Mustard, Aug 7, 228
Green Chile Eggs, April 26, 122
Grilled Tarragon Chicken, July 19, 209

Haroset, April 4, 100
Hawthorn Berry Syrup, Nov 29, 344
Hawthorn Tea, Jan 5, 7
Headache Tea, Feb 21, 54
Herb Biscuits, Jan 12, 14
Herb Bread, Jan 12, 14
Herb Jellies, Aug 8, 229
Herb Marinade for Vegetables, June 17, 174
Herb-Stuffed Mushrooms, Sept 30, 282
Herb Vinegars, Sept 12, 264
Herbal Candies, Jan 31, 33

Herbal Honey, Sept 1, 253
Herbal Syrup, Sept 26, 278
Herbal Tea Blends, Jan 11, 13
Herbed Olive Oil, Nov 30, 345
Herbes de Provence, Aug 15, 237
Holiday Mini-Fritatas, Dec 24, 369
Horseradish Dip, Oct 3, 287
Hot 'N' Spicy Chocolate, Feb 14, 47
Hot Lips Cookie Crisps, April 21, 117
Hungarian Goulash, Aug 21, 242

Iced Herb Teas, June 16, 173

Lemon Butter, June 13, 170
Lemon Dill Butter, Mar 4, 66
Liberty Tea, July 4, 194

Major Grey's Mango Chutney, Oct 13, 297
Maple and Balsamic Vinaigrette, Mar 10, 72
Marigold Custard, July 22, 212
May Wine, May 24, 150
Mexican Garlic Soup, April 19, 115
Mint Butter Cookies, July 9, 199
Mint Julep, May 17, 143
Minted Watermelon and Cucumber Salad, Sept 18, 270
Miss Beecher's Famous Ginger Beer (1857), Jan 13, 15
Mulling Spice, Nov 16, 331

Norwegian Pepper Cookies, Dec 4, 349

Oatmeal Apple Cupcakes with Nuts and Rosemary,
    Nov 1, 316
Oatmeal Gingerbread, Jan 25, 27
Oatmeal and Lemon Peel, Drying and Candying,
    Nov 13, 328
Orange-Mint Fruit Soup, Oct 7, 291
Orange-Mint Mardi Gras Crepes, Feb 4, 37
Orange Poppy-Seed Fruit Salad Dressing, Dec 28, 374
Oven-Poached Pears with Cinnamon Basil Crème Fraîche,
    Oct 14, 298

Parsley Butter, Mar 4, 66
Parsnip Cakes (1732), Nov 30, 345
Peach of a Salsa, May 29, 155
Pedernales Chile, Oct 11, 295
Pepper Butter, Dec 27, 372
Pickled Broom Buds (1756), Oct 28, 312
Pickled Nasturtium Seeds, April 24, 120
Pickled Pink Eggs, April 27, 123
Pickled Rosebuds (1650), Oct 4, 288
Popcorn Sprinkles, Jan 19, 21
Pomegranate Muffins, Oct 9, 293
Potato Leek Soup, Mar 1, 63
Potato Pancakes, Dec 15, 360
Potato Soup with Plenty of Parsley, April 9, 105

Reasonable Doubt Ginger-Mesquite Jelly, Nov 9, 324
Rhubarb Streusel Pie, Mar 26, 88
Rose Geranium Berry Liqueur, Jan 16, 18
Rose Hip Syrup, Sept 2, 254
Rose Sugar, Aug 10, 231
Rosemary Biscuits, Feb 29, 62
Rosemary Friendship Squares, Sept 25, 277
Rosemary Walnuts, Dec 24, 369
Rosemary-Garlic Potatoes, Aug 20, 241

Saffronsbrod, Dec 13, 358
Sage Fritters, Sept 7, 259
Salt-Free Herb Blends, Aug 29, 250
Sautéed Okra, Dec 26, 371
Savory French Toast & Ham with Broiled Tomatoes,
    Nov 28, 343
Slow Cooker Zuchini-Basil Bread, April 25, 121
Smoked Salmon Dip, Mar 23, 85
Southernwood Tea (1772), Nov 15, 330
South-of-the-Border Stuffing, Dec 25, 370
Spiced Cider Wassail, Jan 1, 3
Spiced Cranberry Orange Sauce, Nov 23, 338
Spiced Pear Liqueur, Jan 16, 18
Split Pea Soup, Nov 5, 320
Spring Green Sorrel Soup, Mar 24, 86

Stewed Cucumbers (1769), June 3, 160
Sweet Violet Syrup, Feb 15, 48

Tansy Pudding, April 7, 103
Tulip Cup Salad, May 13, 139

Vanilla Extract, Sept 8, 260
Vanilla Power Frappe, Oct 8, 292

Waffles with Savory Herbs, Mar 25, 87
Wattleseed Chocolate Sauce, Jan 26, 28

# INDEX OF COSMETICS, CRAFTS, AND MEDICINES

Aloe Moisturizer, June 5, 162

Bath Salts, Feb 27, 60
Brighid's Candle, Feb 1, 34
Bug-Bee-Gone, Aug 28, 249

Catnip Mosquito Repellent, May 19, 145
Chamomile Spa Oil, Aug 13, 234
Clay Pots, Feb 25, 58
Cosmetic Herbal Vinegars, Mar 13, 75
Cucumber-Mint After-Bath Spritzer, Oct 20, 304

Dream Pillow Blend, Jan 15, 17
Dream Pillows, Dec 12, 357

Energizing Eucalyptus Bath Soak, Nov 10, 325
Eucalyptus Insect Repellent, Nov 10, 325
Eucalyptus-Peppermint Inhalant, Nov 10, 325
Eucalyptus-Peppermint Tea, Nov 10, 325

Facial Mask, Jan 10, 12
Fairy Garden, April 30, 126
Flea Repellent Oil, July 1, 191
Four Thieves Vinegar (1860), July 29, 219

Ginger and Lemon Tea for Colds and Flu, Dec 1, 346
Gingerbread Tree Decorations, Dec 6, 351

Herb Topiary, Aug 24, 245
Herbal Bath Oils and Milk Bath Bags, Dec 30, 375
Herbal Doggie Shampoo, July 1, 191
Herbal First-Aid Kit, Feb 22, 55
Herbal Mouth Rinse, Feb 9, 42
Herbal Oils and Salves, June 25, 182
Herbal Shampoo, Jan 28, 31

Herbal Soap, Dec 2, 347
Herbal Tinctures, June 4, 161
Herbal Vinegar Housekeeping Tips, July 29, 219
Herbarium Project, May 15, 141
Herbs & Flowers Paper Project,
    May 10–11, 136–137
Holly Wreath, Dec 3, 348
Hydrosol Mists, June 18, 175

Insect-Repellent Tea, May 27, 153

Just-for-Birds Pudding, Jan 17, 19

Lavender Bubble Bath, Jan 8, 10
Lavender Ink, Jan 23, 25
Lavender, Rosemary, Thyme Tea for Headaches,
    Dec 1, 346
Living Ivy Wreath, Sept 28, 280

Mint Soap, July 13, 203
Mint Toothpaste, Nov 8, 323
Moth Foolers, April 28, 124

Nettle Garden Fertilizer and Spray, Mar 3, 65
Nettle Hair Rinse, Mar 3, 65

Oak Gall-Iron Ink (17th century), Jan 23, 25

Pastel Easter Eggs, April 10, 106
Plant Printing, Sept 5, 257
Pomander, Dec 10, 355
Potpourri for Sharing, Nov 24, 339
Potpourri, Sept 9, 261
Pressed Flower Gifts and Cards, Dec 20, 365
Pressed flowers, Sept 11, 263

Red Clover Remedy for Chapped Lips, July 21, 211
Red Clover Tea, July 21, 211
Rose Beads, May 20, 146
Rose Oil, Aug 10, 231
Rose Potpourri, May 2, 128
Rose Rustling, June 24, 181
Rose Water, Aug 10, 231
Rosemary and Egg Conditioner, Feb 16, 49
Rosemary Jojoba Conditioner, Feb 16, 49

Sleepy-time Teas, June 30, 187
Stovetop Potpourri, Dec 19, 364

Strewing Herbs, June 29, 186
Sweet Annie Wreath, Sept 20, 272

Thyme, Sage, and Peppermint Tea for
    Coughs and Fever, Dec 1, 346
Tussie-Mussie, June 6, 163

Walnut Hull Ink, Jan 23, 25
Willow Rooting Stimulant, July 3, 193
Wintertime Treats for Birds, Jan 17, 19

Yule Log, Dec 23, 368

# SPECIAL FEATURES

**ABOUT CHINA'S BOOKS:**

*Thyme of Death* and *Witches' Bane*, Jan 18, 20
*Bleeding Hearts*, Feb 8, 41
*Rosemary Remembered*, Feb 29, 62
*Rueful Death*, Mar 8, 70
*Love Lies Bleeding*, April 21, 117
*Hangman's Root*, May 18, 144
*A Dilly of a Death*, May 28, 154
*Bloodroot*, June 15, 172
*Chile Death*, July 26, 216
*Lavender Lies*, Aug 9, 230
*Indigo Dying*, Aug 17, 238
*Dead Man's Bones*, Sept 19, 271
*Mistletoe Man*, Dec 14, 359

**FROM SUSAN'S JOURNAL:**

Just for the Birds, Jan 17, 19
A Green Life, Feb 26, 59
Mesquite Spring, Mar 22, 84
Mustard Greens Are Sacred, Mar 28, 90
Good Beginnings, April 15, 111
A Desirable Dock, May 25, 151
Prickly Pear, May 26, 152
Spanish Dagger, June 11, 168
Milkweed and Monarchs, July 12, 202
Time Is Still A-Flying, Aug 13, 234
Elderberry-Sumac Rob, Oct 2, 286
Golden, Golden, Goldenrod, Oct 22, 306
Hedge Apples, Oct 27, 311
Outside-In, Dec 7, 352

**THE MYRA MERRYWEATHER HERB GUILD**

All About the Myra Merryweather Herb Guild, Jan 9, 11
An Excerpt from *Happy Thymes: A Calendula of Herbal Dillies*, Feb 27, 60
The Merryweathers Dip Their Chips, Mar 23, 85
The Merryweathers Do Mint, May 7, 133
Herb Guild Holds Big Basil Bash, June 14, 171
The Merryweathers' Passalong Plant Sale, July 27, 217
Lyle Bippert and his Bug-Bee-Gone, Aug 28, 249
The Merryweathers Pick a Peck of Pestos! Sept 10, 262
"What Folk Do with Herbs": The Sixteenth Annual Myra Merryweather Lecture, Oct 29, 313
China Bayles Wins Big in Jelly! Nov 9, 324

**THEME GARDENS**

A Petting Garden, Jan 7, 9
A Garden of the Heart, Feb 10, 43
A Fragrance Garden, Mar 20, 82
A Shakespeare Garden, April 23, 119
A Moon Garden, May 6, 132
An Apothecary Garden, June 27, 184
A Peter Rabbit Garden, July 28, 218
A Tea Garden, Aug 12, 233
A Zodiac Garden, Sept 3, 255
A Garden of Old Roses, Oct 4, 288
A Scripture Garden, Nov 11, 326
A Windowsill Garden, Dec 11, 356

**CELTIC TREE MONTHS**

Rowan, Jan 21, 23
Ash, Feb 18, 51
Alder, Mar 18, 81
Willow, April 17, 113
Hawthorn, May 12, 138
Oak, June 10, 167
Holly, July 8 (See Dec 3), 198
Hazel, Aug 5, 226
Brambles, Sept 2, 254
Ivy, Sept 28, 280
Reed, Oct 28, 312
Elder, Nov 25, 340

## HERBS OF THE ZODIAC

Aquarius, Jan 20, 22
Pisces, Feb 20, 53
Aries, Mar 21, 83
Taurus, April 20, 116
Gemini, May 21, 147
Cancer, June 21, 178
Leo, July 23, 213
Virgo, Aug 22, 243
Libra, Sept 23, 275
Scorpio, Oct 21, 307
Sagittarius, Nov 22, 337
Capricorn, Dec 21, 366

## PLACES TO GO

Fredericksburg Herb Farm (TX), April 18, 114
Buffalo Springs Herb Farm (VA), May 3, 129
National Herb Garden (DC), June 12, 169
Carolee's Herb Farm (IN), June 22, 179
Shady Acres Herb Farm (MN) July 14, 204
The Herb Farm (WA), Aug 19, 240
Long Creek Herbs (MO), Sept 13, 265
Willow Pond Farm (PA), Oct 17, 301
Summers Past Herb Farm (CA), Nov 6, 321

**SUSAN WITTIG ALBERT** grew up on a farm in Illinois and earned her Ph.D. at the University of California at Berkeley. A former professor of English and a university administrator and vice president, she is the author of the China Bayles Mysteries and a family-friendly mystery series set in the early 1900s featuring Beatrix Potter. She and her husband Bill co-author a series of Victorian-Edwardian mysteries under the name of Robin Paige. The Alberts live near Austin, Texas. Visit their website at www.mysterypartners.com.

**PEGGY TURCHETTE** lives and works in Boulder, Colorado, at the foot of the Rocky Mountains, where she draws inspiration from her home and garden. Her work graces a wide range of products, including books, stationery, tabletops, giftware, needlework, packaging, calendars, textiles, wallpaper, and rugs. She enjoys hiking in the mountains with her son, Quentin, and daughter-in-law, Alicia.